# Berkeley at War

Books by W. J. Rorabaugh

The Alcoholic Republic, an American Tradition
The Craft Apprentice, from Franklin to the Machine Age
Berkeley at War, the 1960s

# BERKELEY
# AT
# WAR

## The 1960s

W. J. Rorabaugh

OXFORD UNIVERSITY PRESS
New York   Oxford

Oxford University Press

Oxford    New York    Toronto
Delhi    Bombay    Calcutta    Madras    Karachi
Petaling Jaya    Singapore    Hong Kong    Tokyo
Nairobi    Dar es Salaam    Cape Town
Melbourne    Auckland

and associated companies in
Berlin    Ibadan

First published in 1989 by Oxford University Press, Inc.
200 Madison Avenue, New York, New York 10016

First issued as an Oxford University Press paperback, 1990

Oxford is a registered trademark of Oxford University Press

Library of Congress Cataloging-in-Publication Data
Rorabaugh, W. J.
Berkeley at war: the 1960s/W.J. Rorabaugh.
p.   cm.   Bibliography: p.   Includes index.
1. Berkeley (Calif.) History.
2. Berkeley (Calif.)—Social conditions.
3. University of California, Berkeley History—20th century.
4. Radicalism—California—Berkeley—History—20th century.
5. Vietnamese Conflict, 1962-1975—California—Berkeley.
I. Title.   F869.B5R67    1989    979.4'67053—dc19    88-28575    CIP

ISBN 0-19-505877-1
ISBN 0-19-506667-7 (PBK.)

2   4   6   8   10   9   7   5   3
Printed in the United States of America

For all turtles,
who go forth slowly but surely
by sticking out their necks

We all know that civilization
ends at the Berkeley city limits.
*Berkeley Barb*, 1967

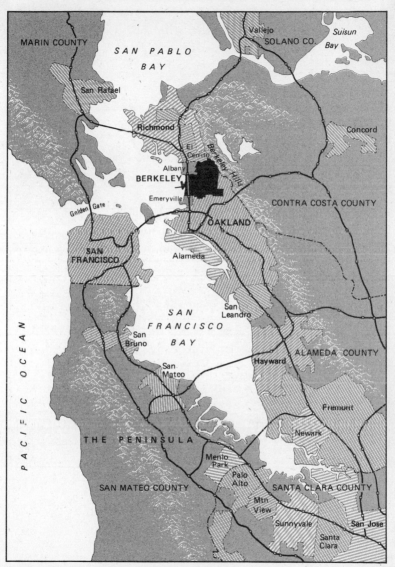

San Francisco Bay Area showing location of Berkeley

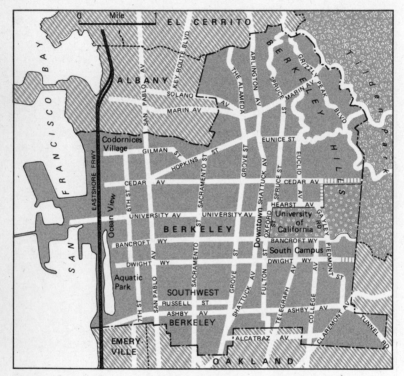

Berkeley city limits with some urban detail

# Preface

This is a book about Berkeley in the 1960s. It is about the city, its university, and its people. It is about some of the organizations and institutions they created, maintained, or let die. Most of all, it is about social change. In the sixties Berkeley was a city at war. Students revolted against the University of California, blacks demanded their rights, radicals surged into prominence, and a counterculture of major proportions blossomed. White, black, red, and green—these movements coincided, fed into one another, and reacted against each other in myriad and sometimes surprising ways. The decade began with President John Fitzgerald Kennedy's Camelot; it ended amid chaos. Berkeley, no less than the country, went through a crisis. On the surface this crisis revolved around turmoil generated by quite specific social issues; it was, at that level, a social crisis.

The underlying issue, however, was one of power. During the sixties *conservatives* hated communism, both abroad and at home, rejected socialism, distrusted all government, disliked labor unions, and abhorred the high level of domestic government spending that was called the welfare state; they admired Barry Goldwater and, later, Ronald Reagan. Berkeley's conservatives, who had long held power in the city, refused to compromise and became paranoid reactionaries. *Liberals* also hated communism and rejected socialism, but they trusted the government, liked labor unions, and favored the welfare state; they admired Franklin Roosevelt, Adlai Stevenson, and, to a lesser extent, John Kennedy. The city's liberals built an unstable, biracial political coalition, used government programs to maintain their power, and ultimately lacked principle. *Radicals* hated anticommunism more than communism, usually accepted some elements of socialism, were ambivalent about government, liked labor unions, and favored either an expanded welfare state or a drastic reconstruction of society; they admired (in varying degrees) Martin Luther King, Jr., Malcolm X, Fidel Castro, Che Guevara, Mao Tse-tung, or themselves. In Berkeley white radicals and black militants angrily tried to seize control and, failing that, were determined to make it impossible for anyone else to hold power.

The social turmoil of the sixties was really a battle over power. College students, young blacks, members of the New Left, and hippies believed that power should flow from the bottom up rather than from the top down. This is an important point, and it suggests that the history of the decade needs to focus on those at the bottom. Historians, however, have written few local studies, and those who have concentrated on the national picture, overly influenced by events at 1600 Pennsylvania Avenue, on CBS News, or in the *New York Times*, have found society to be unraveling. In reality, it was only centralized authority that was in decline. At the local level, those on the bottom saw less a disintegration of society than a rebirth of community spirit and individual liberty in opposition to a corrupt, bureaucratic social order. It is the emergence of this latter vision and its implications for the exercise of power in American society that is the most profound legacy of the sixties.

My book, which follows a narrative format, largely concerns public events covered in the press and in thousands of leaflets. It should stimulate further research both on the sixties and on Berkeley. I hope that scholars will investigate more fully at both the local and national levels the entangled histories of the student movement, race relations, the New Left, and the counterculture. Out of such work, I think, will come a general acceptance of the idea that the sixties did form some sort of watershed in the history of the United States. This work should also encourage further explorations into the history of Berkeley; it only begins to tap the rich materials available for such study. Although I drew upon interviews and spoke with a number of people, more interviewing could produce a very different history. In time, additional materials, now either closed or in private hands, will become available, and a richer, fuller study will be possible.

This is the work of a historian, not the memoir of an eyewitness. Although I learned much about Berkeley when I lived there in the early seventies, my contact with the city in the sixties was limited. As a fourteen-year-old, I first saw Berkeley at a distance in 1960 while stuck with my parents in a traffic jam on the Eastshore Freeway. In the summer of 1963, following my junior year in high school, I accompanied my parents on a two-week vacation to Berkeley, while my father attended an international conference. My recollections from that trip are surprisingly vivid. Decent restaurants were scarce, I was surprised by the large number of black children that I saw bicycling in the flatlands, and Doe Library at the University of California was the first library I had ever visited where it was possible to walk through the building without seeing a book. From 1964 to 1968 I was an undergraduate at Stanford University, and while I made only a handful of trips to Berkeley, I tried to keep abreast of events there. In the fall of 1968 I entered graduate school at Berkeley and witnessed the Moses Hall sit-in, but I left both school and the city at the end of the quarter. In January 1970 I returned to graduate school at Berkeley and remained in the area until 1976, when I moved to Seattle.

Many people helped make this book possible. The idea for the book began one day at lunch at the National Humanities Center in North Carolina, when, it turned out, everyone at the table had been in Berkeley as a student, as a faculty member, or as a summer visitor at some point during the sixties. I was startled at the disparity of these scholars' recollections of Berkeley and quickly noted that the recollections hinged upon whether people had been there early or late in the decade. I decided to write this book, and a paid leave from the University of Washington enabled me to spend the 1985–86 academic year in Berkeley, where I practically lived in the Bancroft Library at the University of California. Director James D. Hart is to be congratulated both for the Bancroft's superb holdings and for a superlative staff. They offered many useful suggestions and much valuable assistance. I owe a special debt to William Roberts, the University's archivist, for making available University files. The Regional Oral History Office is also to be congratulated for a magnificent collection of interviews. At Stanford University the staff of the Hoover Institution was quite helpful. I thank the Bancroft Library, the Hoover Institution, and the State Historical Society of Wisconsin for permission to quote from their holdings.

At the University of Washington the bulk of the manuscript was prepared by Zoe Brennagh, Donna Coke, Margaret Fitzpatrick, Steve Hammer, Margaret Jirucha, and Susanne Young; Kristi Greenfield and Glenda Pearson helped obtain microfilm. Kathy Brown, Peter Hansen, and Marjorie Mortenson served as research assistants. Colleagues in the History Research Group provided useful criticism; so did undergraduates in my seminar on the sixties. I owe a special debt to two department chairs, Wilton Fowler and Jere Bacharach, and to Richard R. Johnson, who shared both his recollections of Berkeley in the sixties and a number of artifacts. He also read the manuscript. Toward the end of the project the Keller Endowment Fund for Research provided a grant for travel to Berkeley to locate photographs. Several people read part or all of the manuscript. I would like to thank Caroline Bynum, Joseph Corn, Lee Drago, William Gienapp, James Gregory, Stephen Maizlish, Phil Roberts, Joseph Ryshpan, Jon Wiener, and Michael Zuckerman. I am particularly grateful to James Rawls, who not only read the manuscript but also provided a film, and to Charles Royster, whose literary sensibility is unsurpassed. Jeremy Popkin and Roger Sharp graciously sent tape recordings, and through the courtesy of Joel Colton, I attended an international conference on youth movements. Research trips to the Bay Area were assisted by Susanna Barrows, William and Beverly Bouwsma, Glenna Matthews, Mary Rorabaugh, Elizabeth Rosenfield, Sheldon Rothblatt, and Charles Sellers. I am also grateful to Tom Debley, Jack Leicester, Guenther Roth, and Charles Sullivan. To the many other people with whom I have had conversations about Berkeley or the sixties, I also give thanks.

Finally, let me express my appreciation to Sheldon Meyer, Scott Lenz, Rachel
Toor, and the staff at Oxford University Press.

Comments and corrections are invited.

*Seattle*                                                                    W. J. R.
*August 1988*

### Note to the Paperbound Edition

Some clarifications are in order. Garfield (later, King) Junior High School is
*at the edge of* rather than *in* the hills. My account of Malcolm Burnstein's
role as counsel in the Free Speech Movement trial understates his
astuteness. He and Charles Garry were joined as co-counsel in the Oakland
7 trial by Dick Hodge. Professor Henry May has supplied some documents
on the Cambodian invasion that support an interpretation different from
mine, and John Thompson has shared materials that confirm the
inadequacy of the press coverage of the street battles in June 1968.

Much work needs to be done. Documents created during the 1960s are
the best sources, but access and ease of use continue to pose problems.
Governor Ronald Reagan's papers at the Hoover Institution remain closed,
while Governor Pat Brown's papers at the Bancroft Library would take ten
years to read. Despite the Freedom of Information Act, FBI files are not
generally available. Faculty voices are muted in my text, partly because the
faculty was bitterly divided but mainly because personal papers, with a few
exceptions, have yet to be donated to archives. Although oral histories are
promising, historians must be cautious when interviewees explain past
events, as evidenced by interview transcripts in the Bancroft Library.
Nevertheless, both Lawrence Crouchett's black oral history project and
Mark Kitchell's filmed interviews and television news outtakes, collected
for the film "Berkeley in the 1960s," should prove valuable, when they
become available to scholars. New books about Berkeley continue to
appear—including those by Howard Bloch, David Horowitz and Peter
Collier, Henry May, and Dale Vree.

# Contents

Preface, ix

Prologue. Gold, 3

Chapter 1. White, 8

Chapter 2. Black, 48

Chapter 3. Red, 87

Chapter 4. Green, 124

Epilogue. Blue, 167

Statistical Tables, 173

A Note on the Use of Language, 187

Notes, 191

Selected Sources, 255

Glossary, 263

Index, 265

*Illustrations follow pages 50 and 126*

# Berkeley at War

# Prologue

# GOLD

*San Francisco! Open your Golden Gate!*
Jeanette MacDonald, "San Francisco"

Berkeley is a city of late afternoons. As the sun sinks beyond the Golden Gate Bridge, it casts long shadows across San Francisco Bay, and a golden twilight settles upon Berkeley with exaggerated shadows falling eastward. The light is magical; it draws people out of buildings to a late afternoon drink or snack on a cafe terrace, into the yard of a home, or even to climb high into the Berkeley hills, which rise just east of the densely populated center of this city of 100,000 people nearly two thousand feet above the bay and the flatlands. To live in the hills is to watch a daily drama. On a rare clear day in the winter, it is possible to see beyond the bridge, some ten miles west across the bay, to the Farallon Islands, which are thirty miles out into the Pacific. On some days in the summer, the drama comes from the afternoon fog that rolls across the bay in as little as forty minutes. A blue sky, the hot California sun, and the vista can disappear in an instant and leave one standing in a soup so thick that one cannot see one's own outstretched hands. In any season one can look down upon the University of California and its Campanile as the winds rustle through the aromatic eucalyptus trees. At the crest of the hills, dusk brings its own rewards. Then the suns sets into the Pacific; lights in the homes and apartments on the flatlands gradually appear; and the enveloping darkness above leaves the lights shimmering like some inverted starry sky beneath one's feet.

Lingering sunsets are matched by the absence of true sunrises. On some mornings in the flatlands the sun appears suddenly at 10 a.m. full-blown above the crest of the hills. On other days the sun does not appear until the fog lifts at noon. Foggy mornings, sunny noons, and foggy late afternoons produce a mild climate. High temperatures range from the 50s in January to the 60s in

3

July, with lows from the 40s to the 50s. There is a rainy season from December through March. This setting dictates Berkeley's rhythm of life. The morning fogs skew life toward the afternoon. Of course, people do get up in the morning and go to work, but the morning rush hour seems leisurely, and only in late morning does the University of California have bustling crowds. Merchants along Telegraph Avenue, at the southern edge of campus, do not open their stores until ten, and few do much business before noon. Only with the lifting of the fog at noon does Berkeley come to life.

The city's roots do not lie deep in history. In the 1840s, when American whalers sailed into San Francisco Bay, they headed for the deeper west or San Francisco side rather than the shallow east or Berkeley-Oakland side. As a consequence, during the Gold Rush, beginning in 1849, Americans poured into San Francisco and ignored the East Bay, which remained a cattle ranch controlled by the Peralta family. José Domingo Peralta lived on a portion of a Mexican land grant that included all of what is now Berkeley, but in the 1850s a number of Americans who had given up their quest for wealth in the gold fields became squatters on the flat portions of the Peralta grant. These enterprising Americans laid out farms and orchards, Peralta lost control of his land, and in 1865 he died a pauper.[1]

In 1860 the private College of California opened in downtown Oakland, but the site was small, and the trustees, who wished to develop an American-style campus with buildings scattered across broad lawns, had already purchased a larger plot of cheap land. They wanted the college to be near enough to San Francisco to be convenient but remote enough to protect students from the city's saloons, gaming tables, and prostitutes. The trustees had picked a site about four miles north of downtown Oakland. This location was agriculturally undesirable, both because of the fogs that rolled in from the west, and because it rose from the edge of the flatlands into hills too steep to be farmed. The tract was close enough to Oakland and its ferry connection to San Francisco for a horse-drawn street railway or steam train line to be built. Standing on the site, one trustee noted the splendid view westward across San Francisco Bay to the Golden Gate and recalled Bishop George Berkeley's poem about the course of empire always moving west. The board of trustees named the place Berkeley. A few years later the state rechartered the college as the University of California, and in 1873 the University moved to its new campus.[2]

The community around the University gradually grew, while three miles to the west, at the edge of the bay, an industrial community called Oceanview developed around a railroad station and ferry dock. Oddly, in 1878 these two settlements as well as the farms and orchards between were incorporated as the city of Berkeley. This new city eventually grew to be about three miles wide and three miles deep. It was bordered by rural Contra Costa County on the north, Oakland on the south, the crest of the hills on the east, and the bay on the west. After 1900, and especially after the San Francisco earthquake and fire of 1906, Berkeley's population soared. It tripled in ten years to 40,000 people by 1910. The area near the University attracted upper-middle-class commuters. Berkeley had fine schools, excellent public transportation, good access to the University's culture, and well-planned suburban subdivisions. The architects Bernard Maybeck and Julia Morgan designed many large, rambling brown-shingled homes. Strong New England influences could be found in the city's architecture, in its Protestant churches, and in streets named Bancroft, Channing, and Dwight. The working-class residents of Oceanview, which was also growing, bitterly resented the fact that the upper-middle-class residents who lived near the University controlled the local government. City officials were elected by citywide voting, and in 1909 the populous eastern portion of Berkeley, where liquor had long been banned within one mile of the University, voted prohibition upon the entire city.[5]

Despite the progressive movement that was so strong at this time throughout California and elsewhere in the United States, conservative Republicans led by the downtown business community, the *Berkeley Daily Gazette*, and real estate developers dominated the Berkeley city government. Conservatives did suffer a loss in 1911, when a socialist, J. Stitt Wilson, was elected mayor, but business interests blocked Wilson's plans for city-owned utilities. After Wilson's one term in office, the city enacted a few reforms. In 1916 Berkeley became one of the first cities in the United States to adopt zoning regulations, and in 1923 the city adopted a council-manager form of government, which divided responsibility between a policy-making council and a professionally trained manager hired to administer the government. Reform appealed to local residents only if it did not increase taxes; between 1924 and 1959 voters rejected all but one school bond issue. During the depression of the thirties, the city stagnated. The population, including Cal students, was nearly 100,000 but had stopped growing. Except for two government buildings, no office space was added downtown from 1935 to 1962, and downtown retail activity gradually dwindled. Throughout this period conservative fraternities and sororities at the University dominated the campus's social and political life. Only during the depression did radicals emerge on campus. Some students became communists, while others joined the nonprofit Co-op retail and grocery movement, which became a distinctive feature of Berkeley community life.[4]

World War II changed Berkeley. During the war the Bay Area grew rapidly in industrial capacity and in population. To the north of Berkeley, the opening of the Kaiser shipyards led to the construction almost overnight of Richmond, a new city with more than 50,000 people. No longer was Berkeley the outermost suburb east of the bay. In Berkeley the federal government had built a huge public housing project, Codornices Village, for thousands of war workers. Many were blacks from the South. Berkeley's black population rose from 4 percent in 1940 to 12 percent in 1950. By the early fifties the overwhelming majority of Codornices Village's 5,000 residents were poor and black. (Among the children who grew up there was the Black Panther party leader Bobby Seale.) In the mid-fifties the city demolished the project; conservatives correctly sensed that the project's residents threatened conservative power. Another threat to that power came from the thousands of veterans who entered the University with the aid of veterans' benefits in the late forties. Enrollment rose from 7,748 in 1944 to 21,909 in 1946 and produced a housing crisis that led local residents to take in lodgers, to build apartments in basements, or to erect cottages in back yards. Much of the city's slummy, make-do housing can be traced to this period.[5]

The late forties brought a few changes. In 1947 a scandal over parking meters led Berkeley voters to elect the Reverend Laurance Cross, a liberal Democrat, to the post of mayor. Cross's one vote on the nine-member council posed no threat to conservatives, but the mayor's frank opinions sometimes provoked controversy. In terms of culture, the city remained barren, although a bond issue did pass in 1948 to build the Berkeley Community Theatre adjacent to the city's high school. While the city lacked distinguished restaurants, Spenger's fish house nightly served thousands of meals. The Co-op thrived, and in 1949 KPFA became the nation's first successful private, noncommercial FM radio station. Supported by listener contributions, the station broadcast classical music and innovative public affairs shows; it even aired communists. Meanwhile, developers demolished the remaining Victorian farmhouses to build apartments, and as blacks left Codornices Village to buy modest homes in the flatlands, affluent whites moved ever higher into the hills, until their modern, glass-walled homes reached the crest at the edge of Tilden Park.[6]

During the fifties conservative control of Berkeley gradually declined. For years the city's conservatives had blocked the University from constructing dormitories, which took property off the tax rolls and competed with landlords' apartments. Conservatives counted as an ally the University's president. Robert Gordon Sproul had even turned down surplus housing offered by the federal government, but in 1959 the new University president, Clark Kerr, built what became the first of a dozen high-rise dormitories. Such living units threatened the conservative fraternities and sororities, which had long dominated the Cal campus. Conservatives also noted the growing black population in the flatlands, and to offset that growth they proposed residential development on San Francisco Bay. Years earlier the city had acquired ownership of a portion of the bay nearly as large as the land area of Berkeley; the baylands stretched halfway to San Francisco. In 1955 planners calculated that the city could dump garbage in the bay for twenty to forty years and then, after allowing the refuse to settle, could build single-story ranch houses on this landfill. The city stood to gain 10,000 homes for 40,000 new, and presumably conservative, suburban residents. This plan failed largely because Bernice Hubbard May, a liberal city council member, and Kay Kerr, wife of the president of the University, questioned the wisdom of any bayfill. Both women's hillside homes had views; they were horrified that someday they might have to look at 10,000 tract homes.[7]

In 1960 Berkeley was a most curious city. Its longtime role as a suburb had come to an end, and conservative control of the city government was about to pass to a liberal coalition. Yet that biracial coalition, which came to power in 1961, was inherently unstable, both along racial lines and along a split inside the liberal white community that became evident during the sixties. At the time the conservative business community remained influential. Although one-fifth of the population was black, blacks had little influence or visibility; the first black councilman was elected in 1961. Schools and housing were segregated in practice, and job discrimination was widespread. The University had risen to international prominence, and its reputation generated both local pride and research grants that brought more people to campus. Bulging enrollments led to housing shortages and parking disputes. At the same time a bohemia began to emerge in the coffeehouses and secondhand bookstores on Telegraph Avenue just south of the University. Telegraph was one of the few places in the United States offering out-of-town newspapers, Turkish cigarettes, or foreign-language films. In 1960, then, Berkeley was poised on the edge of transformation. One school teacher wrote, "Berkeley, we feel, is at last beginning to emerge from the 'Dark Ages' of stand-pattism. . . ." Although Berkeley would not remain what it had been, its future was unclear. The only certainty was that the shadows would be long and golden in late afternoon.[8]

# Chapter 1

# WHITE

*When he says he's white,*
*he means he's boss.*
Malcolm X

On March 25, 1962, President John Fitzgerald Kennedy came to Berkeley to give the annual Charter Day speech. After a luncheon with the University of California Regents and President Clark Kerr at University House on campus, Kennedy made his way to Memorial Stadium, where he spoke to 88,000 people. It was the largest audience Kennedy ever addressed in person. On this happy occasion there were few pickets, and people noted the brisk breezes of a California spring, the sunshine glinting off the president's reddish-brown hair, the good humor and enthusiastic applause of the crowd, and Kennedy's unusual rapport with young people. Alone among his generation of politicians, Kennedy had the capacity to touch the youth of the sixties. While his vigor and energy contrasted with Eisenhower's age and caution, Kennedy's wit and intellect reminded many of Adlai Stevenson. What most captivated students, however, was the president's ability to challenge his audience. Kennedy had first demonstrated this capacity in 1960, when he had unveiled the plan for the Peace Corps and urged students to sacrifice personal comfort and fortunes to serve others. In the early sixties Berkeley furnished a larger number of volunteers for the Peace Corps than any other campus in the country. Kennedy also initiated the space program and endorsed the goals of the civil rights movement, and those policies, too, enjoyed student support. Above all, Kennedy was an optimist, and in early 1962 so were college students. Kennedy's address on Charter Day marked the high tide for liberalism in Berkeley.[1]

Seven months later Kennedy took the country to the brink of nuclear war in the Cuban Missile Crisis. While many Americans held their breaths and trusted the president to guide the United States safely through the crisis, others felt afraid. In Berkeley students turned their fear into questions. After all, what did Kennedy's soaring rhetoric mean if the president practiced the same kind of brinkmanship preached by John Foster Dulles in the Eisenhower administration? Was Kennedy only another in a long line of cold warriors who had pursued a relentless anticommunism since the days when the students of the sixties were small children? The students were not cold warriors, and they were, by and large, prepared to live with Castro, either with or without Russian missiles. A few of them even admired the fiery Cuban for his courage, his feistiness, and his fight on behalf of the peasants against foreign imperialism. None of them thought Castro's presence an issue over which it was worth risking the destruction of the world. Kennedy's behavior troubled students in another way, too. If Kennedy was prepared to risk destroying the world in order to humble Castro and Khrushchev, might not Kennedy be prepared too readily to move militarily on other occasions? To students who carried draft cards in their wallets, this question was not trivial. As the Cuban Missile Crisis had demonstrated, at any moment the government might take the country into war. During the crisis 1,500 students had gathered at Telegraph Avenue and Bancroft Way to debate the issues, and although an overwhelming majority backed Kennedy, the debate suggested that it was possible to question American foreign policy, which from the end of World War II until 1962 had been accepted by almost everyone except communists or pacifists. Liberalism was beginning to fracture.[2]

No man was a better liberal than Clark Kerr, the president of the University. To Kerr, Kennedy's address on Charter Day symbolized the triumph of liberalism both on and off the campus. If Kennedy represented power informed by a restless quest for innovation, then the University of California represented that same quest informed by power. The government and the modern university, in Kerr's view, shared a common responsibility for the good of society and for improving that society. Furthermore, both institutions gained through close cooperation. The prestige of the university and the splendor of its accomplishments bolstered the government, while the authority of the government and its largess assisted the university. Modern society required a large government, and the government depended upon the university both to staff its bureaucracies with properly trained experts and to engage in research that enabled the government to improve its performance. The result was a new kind of large-scale, public university, which Kerr called the multiversity. It had numerous campuses, operated hundreds of research programs, and taught many thousands of students. One consequence, as Kerr noted, was to de-emphasize traditional liberal arts education for undergraduates; another was to turn university administrators into professional managers. Although not entirely pleased with the changes that had occurred in higher education after World War II, Kerr nevertheless embraced the march of progress. For Kerr, accepting the existing world offered the only chance to reform it. His liberalism was rooted in this pragmatic notion. This view was common to Kerr's generation. "You don't make waves, just ride on them," wrote one observer.[3]

By 1964 the world's premier example of a multiversity was the University of California, and the University's crown jewel was its campus at Berkeley. No other campus had such close ties to the government, such a heavy emphasis upon government-sponsored research, or such a neglect of undergraduates. Students were alienated and ripe for revolt. The revolt began in September 1964, when the administration suddenly banned political activists from passing out literature, soliciting funds, or organizing support from card tables set up at the edge of campus. This ban led the activists, largely civil rights workers, to attack the new rules and, following the administration's reprisals, to demand that all sorts of political activity be permitted throughout the campus. The activist students called themselves the Free Speech Movement (FSM). They rallied wide support from alienated students and, after the largest sit-in and mass arrest in California history, gathered overwhelming faculty support. In December 1964 the FSM triumphed. It was to be the greatest success of the student movement during the 1960s.[4]

To understand what had happened, it is necessary to go back to 1930, when California and its university faced bankruptcy, and the University's Regents desperately sought a new president. They appointed Robert Gordon Sproul, an accountant who solved the crisis without dismissing any tenured faculty. By the time he retired in 1958, Sproul had built a great university. The president knew how to spot and recruit talent. In the early thirties, when important scholars fled Germany, some moved to Berkeley. The painter Hans Hofmann stayed only a few years, but this abstract expressionist profoundly influenced art both in the University and in the Bay Area. Another refugee, the sociologist Leo Lowenthal, did not reach Berkeley until 1956, but his use of Marx and Freud revolutionized his discipline. Sproul's greatest success came in helping to develop physics research at the University. In the thirties he had encouraged Ernest O. Lawrence to build the world's foremost nuclear physics laboratory and to staff it with the best young scientists. As a consequence, the University played a major role in the development of the atomic bomb during World War II and, through the Lawrence Radiation Laboratory and its related labs, became the major federal contractor in nuclear weapons research after the war. By the fifties Berkeley boasted the world's largest number of Nobel laureates on a single campus.[5]

Although Sproul spent much of his time raising private funds, he also knew how to coax cash out of the state by a combination of duck hunting with key legislators and of camping at the Bohemian Grove with longtime Governor Earl Warren; their friendship began when both played in the Cal band. Sproul's one failure came in 1950, when he persuaded the Regents to require the faculty to take an anticommunist loyalty oath. After the faculty protested, a badly shaken Sproul, with Governor Warren's support, persuaded the Regents to rescind the oath, which was then replaced by an oath enacted by the state legislature. Some Regents never forgave Sproul for his vacillation; for years John F. Neylan, attorney to the Hearst Corporation, chose to sit at Regents meetings at the opposite end of a long table from Sproul; whenever the president spoke, Neylan glared. Neylan's connections were impressive. Personally close to Ernest Lawrence, he also once hosted a black-tie party for Dr. Loyal Davis (Nancy Reagan's father) at the Pacific Union Club. Years later Governor Ronald Reagan named Ernest Lawrence's brother John to the Regents.[6]

The Regents were the wealthiest and most powerful men and women in California. (The customary capitalization of the word Regents is instructive.) The twenty-four member board was composed of the University president, the governor, certain other public officials, and sixteen gubernatorial appointees, who served sixteen-year terms. The appointees dominated the board, most were large political contributors. During the 1960s the board included John E. Canaday, president of Lockheed; Edwin A. Pauley, a southern California oilman; Catherine Hearst of the publishing clan; Dorothy Chandler of the *Los Angeles Times*; and Edward Carter, the head of a department store chain. The Regents met monthly to buy land, hire architects, let contracts, set policies, and plan the University's future. These bright, aggressive, and impatient men and women were used to getting their own ways, and each found the inability to dominate the huge, diverse board frustrating. Monthly meetings were filled with tension and bitter disputes. For years, it is said, some Regents did not speak to each other. Being a Regent was like being a member of a large, unhappy family.[7]

In 1952, trying to recover from the debacle over the oath, Sproul created the position of chancellor at Berkeley and named Professor Clark Kerr to the post. The two were a study in contrasts. Sproul was large-bodied, loud-mouthed, ebullient, dynamic, forceful, and even physically intimidating; Kerr was quiet, cordial, cerebral, cold, and a master of detail. He could recite statistics and arguments at a Regents meeting for two or more hours without a single note. More to the point, Kerr had been one of the faculty leaders opposing the loyalty oath. Nor was it a disadvantage that Sproul, a lifelong Republican, found in Kerr an active liberal Democrat. But the main reason for Kerr's appointment as chancellor was his standing with the Berkeley faculty. The professor of industrial relations had shown his ability to see all sides and to forge coalitions and comprises. Kerr, however, found the chancellorship frustrating. He saw that Sproul intended to give the post little real power, which remained with Sproul and the president's bureaucracy. Sproul used Kerr and the chancellor's office as a lightning rod.[8]

After Sproul retired in 1958, Kerr became president. Chosen over the objections of Sproul but with support from former Governor Earl Warren, Kerr got the presidency partly because the Regents, still divided from the loyalty oath battle, did not want to offend the prestigious Berkeley faculty, who strongly backed Kerr. The new president had both strengths and weaknesses. One of the most brilliant men in American higher education, he developed California's Master Plan, which divided responsibilities among the University (select undergraduates, most graduates, professional schools), the emerging California State system (most undergraduates, education), and community colleges (many entering students). The Master Plan provided for orderly management of rapid growth just as the baby boom generation reached the colleges and as a higher percentage of high school graduates sought college degrees. The plan both reduced political bickering and enabled the University to maintain quality by shifting much of the burden for undergraduate education elsewhere during a period in which rising enrollments and capital requirements to build new campuses strained the state's capacity to maintain per student expenditures. Despite the Master Plan, Berkeley suffered from physical overcrowding, salaries slipped from fourth nationally in 1959 to twenty-third in 1964, and the ratio of tenured faculty to students declined. In 1964, one-quarter of faculty positions were vacant or filled with temporary appointees. From 1960 to 1964 student enrollment grew from 18,728 to 25,454. By 1964 more than one-third were graduate students, many of whom were in their late twenties or early thirties.[9]

Kerr's weakness was his personality. Like many political figures, he knew that confrontation was counterproductive; to avoid confrontation he preferred to leave the impression of agreement when he encountered opposition. A journalist, George N. Crocker, noted, "At one time or another—and often at the same time—every antagonist in a controversy thinks Kerr is on his side." The difficulty, of course, came when it was necessary to make a decision. Kerr used common bureaucratic techniques to minimize offending people. He avoided meeting those with whom he disagreed, he ordered bureaucratic underlings to make the decisions that would draw the most criticism, and he maintained a low profile—becoming, at times, almost invisible. One administrator said, "There is no Clark Kerr." In 1964 a Berkeley faculty member bitterly noted that while he and Kerr had been on the same campus for sixteen years, he had never seen Kerr. The president's style was unusual. He often worked at home, where he managed massive flows of paper. Every afternoon eight secretaries packed a box of papers to be delivered to Kerr's home high above the campus in the hills of El Cerrito, and the next noon the papers were returned. The president annotated documents in his tiny, crabbed hand in green ink. His comments were cryptic, incisive, pungent, and most of all, masterly. Kerr, however, also had wit. The perfect university, he observed, provided sex for students, sports for alumni, and parking for faculty. His remarks could sting. He once said of Professor T. J. Kent, Jr., a professor of urban planning and longtime Berkeley city councilman who lacked insight into his own limitations, that Kent was the sort of person who believed that urban planning consisted of making one-way streets.[10]

When Kerr became president, the nuclear scientist Glenn Seaborg became chancellor. Seaborg's appointment appeased certain Regents, who had backed Ernest O. Lawrence. Lawrence was unacceptable to the faculty because he had supported the loyalty oath years earlier. While Seaborg dealt with Berkeley's vast nuclear programs, Kerr continued Sproul's practice of running the campus largely through the president's office. In 1961, when Seaborg left to head the Atomic Energy Commission, Edward W. Strong, a professor of philosophy, became the new chancellor. Although Strong was not Kerr's first choice, the new chancellor pleased both conservative Regents and the Berkeley faculty. Strong was a contemplative, intellectual man who had won the respect of the faculty through years of service to its causes. One of his proudest moments came in 1962, when he helped persuade the Regents to abandon mandatory military training. In that battle he made common cause with Kerr, whom he greatly admired. Beyond this devotion, Strong had little to offer. He was a traditionalist who turned brittle at the first sign of crisis, an almost total innocent concerning bureaucratic intrigue, and an idealist devoted to duty in a world run by accommodation and power. He lacked both the bureaucratic experience and the force of personality to be effective. One suspects that Strong's limitations had led Kerr to make the appointment. Strong's true position on the Berkeley campus is indicated by the fact that he did not have his own stationery; the stationery listed Kerr's name above his own.[11]

Strong's limitations became apparent in the chancellor's inept handling of a politically controversial faculty appointment. During 1963–64 Eli Katz had held a temporary position in the Department of German, and that department had recommended Katz for a permanent appointment. Others involved in the hiring process had concurred, and the matter was referred to the chancellor. (Everyone, however, knew that Kerr would have a say in the final decision.) Although Katz had signed the legislatively mandated loyalty oath, rumors had surfaced concerning his involvement in communist politics in earlier years. Kerr's policy as president had been to accept a signed oath at face value. He believed that the proper way to challenge an oath was for the prosecuting attorney to file a perjury charge. Kerr also declined to appoint or retain persons whom government agencies reported in writing to be security risks. In the Katz case, Strong pursued a different policy. Lacking any formal request from a security agency to deny Katz an appointment and unwilling to accept Katz's execution of the oath as evidence of his loyalty, the chancellor decided to resolve his doubts by having a frank talk with Katz. The interview, however, failed to satisfy the chancellor, because Katz declined to discuss his past political associations. This lack of candor led the chancellor to block the appointment. Although Kerr fretted over Strong's handling of the case, the president did not wish to overrule his chancellor. Both the Department of German and the Academic Senate became irritated, and Katz left the University. (He returned in 1966). As ill-will from this controversy swirled around Strong, Kerr contemplated replacing the chancellor. [12]

During Sproul's presidency in the 1930s, a communist-influenced student movement had arisen on the Berkeley campus. Sproul wanted to keep radicalism out of the University; so he banned political activity on campus. No longer could literature be passed out, petitions circulated, funds solicited, buttons sold, or candidates for office presented to students. The harshness of Sproul's ban was offset by geography. In those days the south boundary of the campus ended at Sather Gate, and shops lined both sides of the block of Telegraph Avenue between the gate and Bancroft Way. After the ban, political activists simply moved off campus into the area immediately south of Sather Gate. Since thousands of students had to funnel through Sather Gate and its adjoining footbridge over Strawberry Creek to enter campus, the movement of political activity to the Sather Gate area posed no inconvenience for student activists. Nor was the prohibition against the use of classroom buildings for candidates' speeches much of a handicap. Stiles Hall, operated by the liberal YMCA on Bancroft Way, was available to virtually any group that wished to host a political speaker. Numerous bookstores along Telegraph, including one owned by the Communist party, provided outlets for political materials. [13]

During the 1940s and 1950s campus radicalism declined, and the geography of the Berkeley campus changed. The University bought the land along Telegraph between Sather Gate and Bancroft and expanded the campus southward into the city. An administration building, Sproul Hall, was built on the east side of Telegraph, and in 1961 a new student union building, largely Kerr's project, opened on the west side. The area between was closed to traffic and became Sproul Plaza. These changes took place without substantial changes in Sproul's rules banning political activity on campus. The result placed Sather Gate inside the campus and off-limits, but the issue was more or less moot, since there were few student activists. In 1956, however, presidential candidate Adlai Stevenson found it odd that he could not enter the campus to speak to the students. The liberal candidate, widely popular in Berkeley, talked to thousands of students from an automobile parked at the corner of Bancroft and Telegraph. [14]

McCarthyism had made its mark on Berkeley. The bitterness of the oath fight was matched by the University's quiet condemnation of the communist bookstore. Even the management of Stiles Hall grew nervous when leftists applied to use the hall. The Left seemed to have disappeared in Berkeley, but undercurrents quietly flowed in the growing bohemia of coffeehouses and bookstores along the deteriorated and decaying section of Telegraph in the four blocks between Bancroft Way and Dwight Way. In 1963 Clark Kerr led a fight inside the Regents to repeal one of the last vestiges of McCarthyism: the Regents' ban on communists speaking on any University of California campus. Precisely because the Left was dead Kerr felt comfortable asking the Regents to repeal the ban. But Kerr discovered, much to his annoyance, that the Regents preferred to let the regulation stand; and to get the Regents to act, he had to compromise. The old rule had banned communists but had allowed nonpolitical student groups to invite anyone else, except political candidates, to talk on campus. The new rule allowed communists to speak but required nonpolitical student groups to present balanced programs with opposing sides and a tenured faculty moderator whenever a speaker was "controversial." In practice, Kerr's new regulations left student groups at the mercy of the campus bureaucracy, which inconsistently and arbitrarily judged various speakers as controversial. For students, the greatest irritant was the requirement to find opposing speakers and faculty moderators. If such people could not be found, then the program had to be cancelled—or moved off-campus.[15]

The Kerr rules irritated a growing student movement at Berkeley. It began in 1957 with the creation of a student political party that soon took the name SLATE. (The initials did not stand for anything.) The group advocated the establishment of a co-op bookstore, urged an end to compulsory participation in the Reserve Officers' Training Corps (ROTC), and declared its contempt for the "sandbox" politics practiced by fraternity-oriented student body presidents. SLATE was controversial because it included both leftists and moderates. It was the first post-McCarthy era organization to reject anticommunism and established a working model for later Berkeley umbrella groups. SLATE won few elections, but the victory of a SLATE candidate, David Armor, for the presidency of the Associated Students of the University of California (ASUC) in May 1959 by a margin of thirteen votes over a fraternity-backed candidate alarmed both the Greeks who had controlled the ASUC for years and administrators. The chancellor's office responded by throwing the SLATE oriented graduate students out of the ASUC. To preserve the appearance of democratic decision-making, the administration polled the graduate students and, to obtain the desired outcome, counted abstentions as votes for removal. While the Greeks, who mostly still discriminated against blacks and Jews, rejoiced, the SLATE-backers, who included a large number of Jewish students, fumed at the administration's trick. The most ironic consequence, however, was to destroy any mechanism for communication between the now disenfranchised and unrepresented graduate students and the administration.[16]

Failure at the ballot box perhaps led SLATE leaders to seek success elsewhere. In any event, by 1960 the same students, former students, and hangers-on associated with SLATE and the growing Telegraph area bohemia organized pickets to protest the execution of Caryl Chessman at San Quentin Prison. Just a few days later the House Un-American Activities Committee (HUAC) arrived in San Francisco to hold hearings exposing communist activity in the Bay Area. Locally, HUAC's reputation was poor. On an earlier visit the committee's subpoenaing of a Stanford graduate student had driven that man to suicide, and in 1959 the committee had leaked the names of dozens of Bay Area school teachers to the press and then cancelled its hearings. Many of the teachers, including one in Berkeley, lost their jobs. In 1960 HUAC subpoenaed a Berkeley student, Douglas Wachter, and Berkeley activists then organized a protest against the hearings in San Francisco.[17]

When hundreds of students tried to attend the hearings in San Francisco City Hall, they discovered that HUAC would let in only a handful. All morning on Friday, May 13, 1960, committee supporters, who had been issued white courtesy cards, took most of the seats. The disappointed students were promised admission to the afternoon session, but again the white cardholders got almost all of the seats, and about a hundred demonstrators then sat down in the rotunda to clap, chant, and sing. Without warning the police used the building's fire hoses to wash the students down the marble stairs. As the demonstrators tumbled, slipped, and bumped down the stairs, they rolled into the hands of waiting police, who arrested sixty-four of them. Thirty-one were Berkeley students. This spectacle produced a variety of reactions. The next day five thousand or more protesters, including many Berkeley students, confronted HUAC outside city hall and chanted, "Sieg Heil!" The large turnout showed that the McCarthy era was over, and that student activists could tap mass support if they were able to identify and use popular issues. Eventually, charges were dropped against all except Robert Meisenbach, whom a reporter for the *San Francisco Examiner* had identified as having assaulted a policeman. At the trial the police admitted falsifying reports to make them coincide with the reporter's lurid account, and film footage showed that the reporter had misstated Meisenbach's location. He was acquitted. The protests enraged HUAC, which used subpoenaed television news footage of the events at city hall to produce a film called "Operation Abolition." It was widely shown among those on the political right throughout the country during the early 1960s. The film's dissemination as well as the behavior of the police and the press stimulated resentment among hundreds of Berkeley students.[18]

SLATE leaders were less concerned with HUAC than with a long and growing list of grievances against the University. In the fall of 1960, after activists captured the student newspaper, the Greek-oriented ASUC altered the *Daily Californian*'s structure and seized control of the newspaper. The editorial staff's complaint of interference with freedom of the press made no impression on the administration. In protest, the newspaper's staff (except one) resigned. The administration continued its silence. In 1961, after SLATE drew the wrath of Hugh Burns, a powerful anticommunist state senator, the administration used a technicality to ban SLATE from campus. That same year Malcolm X, a

Black Muslim leader, was barred from speaking on campus on the grounds that he was promoting religion; a year earlier James Pike, the Episcopal Bishop of San Francisco, had been permitted to speak. In March 1964 the Regents turned down a request by Cal students for an FM radio license. In explaining the rejection, Regent Edward Carter said, "You know how we can't control the students' media of communication. How would you like to have the same types running the station that are running the student newspaper?" To this question, Kerr replied that the students seeking the radio license were "engineering types . . . not *Daily Cal* types." A year later the Regents again rejected a radio license for Berkeley while approving a similar request for the more conservative campus at Santa Barbara.[19]

By the early sixties the University's student body had changed. While overall enrollment increased, and a larger proportion of the student body was graduate students, participation in fraternities and sororities declined. Whereas more than 800 young women had rushed sororities in 1958, only 450 did so in 1964, and that fell to 350 the following year. In September 1965 Theta Xi fraternity folded, and three others tottered on the brink of extinction. A female student explained the Greek decline. "They're still living back in the days of the twenties," she said, "You know, lots of booze and very little thinking." To many, Greeks seemed out of step with the liberal sixties; they were steeped in conservatism and ritual, and practiced racial, ethnic, and religious discrimination. One Greek ridiculed the activists and asked, "What about their conformity? Beards and long hair and everybody in pants and sandals?" Part of the reason for Greek decline was conflict inside fraternities and sororities between those who clung to tradition and those anxious to make changes, including an end to discrimination. This split explains why Greeks could be found on both sides during the FSM.[20]

If fewer students lived in fraternities, sororities, boarding houses, or at home with parents, more lived in dormitories or apartments. Apartment dwellers rose from 27 percent of students in 1960 to 39 percent in 1964. Personal choice, economics, and fashion pushed students away from living situations that fostered community and toward those that stressed individual responsibility and independence. This trend may have been related to the greater intellectual maturity of students. One professor claimed that the freshmen of the sixties knew more than the graduate students of the forties. University admissions were more selective; students, brighter and better prepared. Yet another influence toward autonomy was the sense that the hysteria of the McCarthy years had passed; perhaps, now, it was safe to act alone. As a consequence, however, isolation and alienation increased. During the Free Speech Movement, two dormitory residents posted a large sign in the window of their room: "We're lonely 112." Another read: "Girls: For fun call: Ehrman 111." Nor was the sense of independence aided by the bureaucratic nature of the University.

"Welcome to lines, bureaucracy and crowds," noted the *Daily Californian* in 1965, adding, "The incoming freshman has much to learn—perhaps lesson number one is not to fold, spindle or mutilate his IBM card." Despite the bureaucracy and alienation, students liked Berkeley. The congregation of so many kindred spirits, of so many independent souls struggling to rise above mundane life and strive for contact with one another, gave the campus and the city its special quality. "There is no place in the United States more exciting than this campus," boasted the *Daily Californian*. "There is no place or institution offering more varied experiences; there is nothing like Berkeley."[21]

In the early 1960s Berkeley student activists were particularly drawn to the civil rights cause because of the changing racial composition of the city of Berkeley. Due to black migration from the South, by 1960 the city was one-fifth black. Berkeley's blacks lived in a corner of the city remote from the University. One seldom saw a black on campus, black shoppers were not welcome in downtown Berkeley, and both school segregation and discrimination in employment and housing were common. In 1963 Berkeley voters rejected an open housing ordinance, 22,750 to 20,456, and in October 1964 the school board was nearly recalled over desegregation. These votes indicated the city's bitter divisions. The split was ironic, because liberals had long considered Berkeley to be advanced, and they pointed with pride to the black assemblyman elected from a mostly white district as early as 1948. In truth, white Berkeley was schizophrenic—many older residents were native Southerners. Berkeley student activists formed the Berkeley Congress of Racial Equality (CORE) to protest job discrimination. Throughout 1964 CORE and its allies sponsored demonstrations at Lucky's stores in Berkeley, at the Sheraton-Palace Hotel and along auto row in San Francisco, and at the *Oakland Tribune*, organ of William F. Knowland, a former U.S. senator. In the summer of 1964, when the Republican national convention met in San Francisco, activists organized anti-Goldwater pickets on the Cal campus. To some people, it appeared that a handful of agitators systematically used the campus as a staging ground for making trouble.[22]

In keeping with the Sproul and Kerr rules banning political activity on campus, activists for several years had solicited donations and sign-ups for protests from card tables set up on the city sidewalk at the edge of campus at Bancroft and Telegraph. It has been charged that Knowland pressured the University to ban these tables, but the publisher denied the charge, and no evidence supports the allegation. The chancellor's files suggest that a growing concern inside the University's own bureaucracy about the increasing number of activists and their growing visibility led to the crackdown in September 1964. Whether pressured from outside or not, Alex C. Sherriffs, Vice-Chancellor for Student Affairs and a popular psychology professor among students from fraternities and sororities, became upset by the activists' presence. Sherriffs, whose office was in Sproul

Hall, perhaps worried less about political activity itself than about its visibility and the effect that it had upon visitors to campus. In 1964 one of the first sights a visitor saw, at the corner of Bancroft and Telegraph, was a student, possibly blue-jeaned, bearded, and sandaled, manning a card table, jingling a can, and asking for a donation to support civil rights. To Sherriffs, this scene was appalling because it created an image of the University as a haven for eccentrics and malcontents. The vice-chancellor saw himself as a moral guardian bound to protect the purity of the campus and its cleancut fraternity and sorority kids from unkempt beatniks and wild-eyed radicals. In any event, he put the issue on the agenda for discussion among a group of low-level bureaucrats in the spring of 1964, and after several postponements, administrators aired the issue in July and September.[23]

When the University opened that September, activists looked forward to recruitment and fund-raising. Over the summer thirty to sixty students had worked for civil rights in Mississippi, and they returned to campus with renewed dedication and determination. These activists, including Mario Savio and Art Goldberg, were dumbfounded in mid-September when the University suddenly issued new rules that banned tables from the edge of Bancroft and Telegraph, where they had been placed in growing numbers for two or three years. When the activists sought an explanation for the change, they could get no answers. The dean of students, Katherine A. Towle, talked with the activists but declared her own lack of power, while those who held the power refused to talk. Inside the administration Towle, a former colonel in the Women's Marine Corps, had vehemently opposed the ban. The technical reason for the ban was the University's "discovery" that the $26' \times 90'$ area where the tables had been placed was University property and not, as previously thought, city property. (For more than two years the University had sent students to city hall to get permits to put tables in the area the University now claimed.) Later someone dug up Regents' minutes that showed that the Regents had intended to deed the area to the city, but that the administration mysteriously had failed to carry out this order. In a twist of irony, years later it was discovered that the city of Berkeley actually had retained the area when the city had deeded Sproul Plaza to the University; the area subsequently was—and is—covered with city-licensed food vendors. The point, of course, is that one should not make too much of the legal niceties. Neither the administration nor the activists cared about the law. This dispute, at its heart, was about power.[24]

Kerr was in Japan when the administration banned the tables, but he returned to meet with Sherriffs and Towle. Although Kerr did not wholeheartedly embrace the ban, he supported the need to restrict political activity. Towle was apprehensive, Sherriffs looked forward to banning the activists, and Strong began to realize that he might be in for a rough time. Almost immediately the chancellor fell into an attitude of defensive legalism that he retained throughout the crisis. Paralyzed by his own fears and pushed constantly to new action by Kerr operating behind the scenes, Strong's usefulness was at end. In this crisis neither Kerr's analytical brilliance nor his personality helped. Instead of marshaling his administration for war, he vacillated. At times he goaded his underlings to attack the activists but not to quash them; this had the same effect as teasing a bee. At other times he retreated into wondering what had gone wrong, how he had failed, and why his command had proved inept. The administration was already bitterly divided internally over other issues, which ranged from faculty parking to Kerr's proposal to adopt the quarter system, and Kerr was not master of the dual president's and chancellor's staffs through which he directly or indirectly tried to run the campus. These two bureaucracies distrusted each other. Over the years better people had gravitated to the president's staff, where important decisions were made, so that the chancellor's staff, which had primary responsibility in this crisis, suffered from incompetence and a lack of leadership. Neither group was liked. Berkeley faculty members derisively called the president's bureaucracy "All State," because its actions resembled an insurance company's more than a university's. It was a bit like going to war without an army, and while Kerr's instincts were warlike, he handed his enemies victory after victory through self-destructive bold advances alternating with paralysis and retreat.[25]

The activists were better prepared for war than Kerr. First, they knew what they wanted. Although their specific demands changed over time, they demanded an end to the regulation of political activity on campus. This was called free speech. Kerr, on the contrary, could only wave a sheaf of ever-changing regulations, none of which were internally logical and all of which appeared to be shifting responses to pressure. The activists identified the issue as a traditional American right in order to appeal to large numbers of students, who in other circumstances might have sided with Kerr. Second, some of the activist leaders were battle-tested veterans of the civil rights movement. "A student who has been chased by the KKK in Mississippi," observed one student, "is not easily scared by academic bureaucrats. . . ." They knew when to advance, when to retreat, how to use crowds, how to use the media, how to intimidate, and how to negotiate. The activists understood their ultimate weapon, the sit-in, and were prepared to use it. Although the leaders were not close to one another, they spoke a common language gained through a common experience. Kerr, on the other hand, was as unready to do battle as a southern sheriff facing a civil rights march for the first time. Again and again, Kerr showed that he understood nothing about his opponents' tactics. Finally, activist leaders knew how to maintain discipline over their troops. Mass psychology, song, theater, and other techniques long favored among revivalists and street politicians accompanied innovative mass meetings at which people freely spoke and at which collective decisions were made by a kind of consensus that came to be called participatory democracy. Through these techniques and by focusing on the simplicity of the demand for free speech, activists created an environment within which followers were disciplined. They created an army. In contrast, Kerr badgered his beleaguered bureaucracy until it could barely function.[26]

Throughout September 1964 skirmishes continued as defiant activists set up tables and were cited by irritated deans. The angry students escalated the conflict by moving their tables to Sproul Plaza. This protest led to a mill-in inside Sproul Hall and the summary "indefinite suspension" of eight students—Mario Savio, Art Goldberg, Mark Bravo, Sandor Fuchs, David Goines, Donald Hatch, Brian Turner, and Elizabeth Gardner (Mrs. Sydney Stapleton). Finally, on October 1, University police went to the plaza to arrest a former student, Jack Weinberg, who was manning a CORE table. The police drove a car onto the plaza to take Weinberg to be booked, and as Weinberg got into the car, someone shouted, "Sit down." Suddenly, several hundred students surrounded the car. The police did not know what to do, because they had never encountered such massive defiance. Kerr's bureaucracy became paralyzed. This event launched the Free Speech Movement. Participants later recalled the spontaneity of the sit-down, the thrill of power over the police, and the feeling that something important was happening. For thirty-two hours Weinberg sat in the back of the police car. Although students came and went, there were always at least several hundred surrounding the car. Among those who observed the sit-down was Jerry Brown, the governor's son, then living in Berkeley, was hostile to the protest. During the night students who disapproved of the sit-down—many from nearby fraternities—molested the protesters by tossing lighted cigarettes and garbage into the crowd. The activists responded by singing civil rights songs.[27]

During the sit-down the demonstrators used the roof of the police car (with police permission) as a podium to speak to the crowd. People aired all sorts of views, and the discussion moved from the rules banning political activity to analyses of the University's governance. Students expressed their powerlessness, which contrasted with the power that they held over the immobilized police car. So many people stood on the car's roof that it sagged; the FSM later took up a collection and paid the $455.01 damage. Several times a twenty-one year old junior, Mario Savio, removed his shoes to climb atop the car, and when he spoke, his words seemed especially to energize the crowd. He became a celebrity and was identified by the crowd as the leader of the activists. From then on Savio battled Kerr. It was not a fair match.[28]

Savio, the son of devout Italian Catholics, had been educated at the Christian Brothers Manhattan College until he had transferred to Queens College. In the summer of 1963, he had worked for a Catholic relief organization in rural Mexico, and that fall, after his parents had moved to Los Angeles, the former altar boy had entered Berkeley as a junior. During the summer of 1964, he taught a freedom school for black children in McComb, Mississippi; conditions there, he told the press, had made him "very angry." By the fall of 1964, this philosophy major had had unusually broad experiences that stimulated his passionate dedication to the causes he held dear. Savio's father, a machinist, was proud of his son's Catholicism and devotion to social justice. When the son entered Berkeley, he appeared to be searching for new roots; he began to call himself Mario instead of the more prosaic Bob of his childhood.

In 1964 the 6'1", 195-lb. Savio was proud and cocky, angry and defiant. He scowled beneath longish, sandy-red hair. He was not cool. His power came from his ability to articulate a tone that expressed the frustrations and anxieties of his generation. While others were as angry as Savio, they found it impossible to articulate their anger. Savio had the gift, perhaps the result of his Catholic education, to discourse rationally. Even as he did so, there was an undertone of anger. This powerful projection of personality contrasted with his private conversation, which was often marred by stuttering, hesitancy, and coldness. Self-doubts and inhibitions dissolved when Savio spoke to a crowd. His effectiveness came from pushing himself to the brink of losing control.[29]

Much of Savio's appeal came from his ability to blend alienation, sexuality, and politics. In calling the administrators "a bunch of bastards," he declared both their ancestry and their authority illegitimate. At the sit-down he said of the police, "They're *fam*-ily men, you know. They have a job to do!" He added, "Like Adolph Eichmann. He had a job to do. He fit into the machinery." Was it possible that alienated students did not have a job to do, that is, lacked sex partners? Or perhaps they did not fit into the machinery, that is, were impotent? Students, said Savio, were oppressed by "the organized sadism of the power structure." The University forced students to suppress their "creative impulses." What was the result? He declared, "The University is well structured, well tooled, to turn out people with all the sharp edges worn off. . . ." In other words, the University emasculated students. Indeed, taking away the right to place tables at the edge of campus had been an act of "emasculation, or attempted emasculation." By talking about politics in this fashion, Savio guaranteed an attentive audience. Few students cared about political rights, but many felt alienated, and no males wanted to be emasculated. At one rally Savo noted, "The Bible says what knowledge is when it writes that a man knows a woman. Knowledge and action are inseparable." This comment provoked laughter. He then elaborated upon the metaphor. "We want to be able to mount action on this campus," he said. The wording was so powerful that the administration declared that it would never consent to the use of the campus for "mounting" political activity. Yet no student could accept the administration's position without risking a perceived loss of his own sexual potency. After the Free Speech Movement was over, Savio was asked what had been

most important in leading him to oppose the administration. Without hesita-
tion he answered, "Balls."[30]

While the police car was trapped, Kerr's bureaucrats dithered, and the activists came to realize that they could extract concessions from Kerr in exchange
for quietly ending the sit-down. Both sides picked negotiators. Kerr pushed
Strong aside and took on his old role as a labor mediator to deal with the
students. Savio's rage was too deep to allow him to negotiate effectively, and
his personality grated on Kerr, so he had little to do with the bargaining. For
the first time, some faculty members became involved, and they encouraged
both the administration and the activists to accept a compromise. Kerr's terms
appeared to be generous. Jack Weinberg, still in the police car, was to be
booked and then released with the University not pressing charges. The eight
students suspended summarily by the administration for activities prior to the
sit-down were to face discipline before a faculty committee. Another committee, to be composed of administrators, faculty members, and students appointed by the administration, was to negotiate permanent rules for political
activity on campus. Meanwhile, the administration pledged to withdraw the
September regulations, and the activists promised to desist from any illegal
activity. Kerr pressured the activists to accept this agreement by threatening to
order police to remove the protesters from around the trapped car. Hundreds
of officers, called to the campus from throughout the Bay Area, were posi-
tioned nearby. After much internal debate in which Jackie Goldberg and Sandor Fuchs pressured the more passionate activists, the student leaders accepted
Kerr's offer. Savio then returned to the police car to announce the settlement.
He invited everyone to rise up and go home quietly. To many, the crisis appeared to be over.[31]

The activists trusted neither Kerr nor the pact of October 2. On October 4,
eight activists met to plot strategy. They did not know each other very well.
Savio recorded Bettina Aptheker's name as "Patina," and it was not until
late in the meeting that he got her name straight. Aptheker, daughter of the
well-known communist theoretician Herbert Aptheker and herself then an
undeclared party member, proposed that students who were not activists be
encouraged to participate through the creation of an executive committee. Any
campus organization could send one representative; eventually, the Executive
Committee grew to more than fifty members. Day to day decisions were to be
made by a steering committee, whose members were elected from among the
members of the Executive Committee. Although the activists were a minority
on the Executive Committee, their political acumen led them to gain most of
the positions on the Steering Committee, through which they controlled events.
Essentially, the people in the room became the members of the Steering Committee. Aptheker's proposal, which was accepted, was patterned after the Communist party organization of popular front movements during the 1930s. Later,

as the meeting broke up, she noted, "I've got a last name that's dynamite." To Aptheker, the easy identification of her own name with communism made it necessary to bring ordinary students into the movement in order to avoid a smear campaign. At this meeting another participant had stressed building mass support among students to win an ultimate victory; others had emphasized the need to gain faculty support. Savio shrewdly noted the importance of publicity. Therefore, he concluded, "Everything must be completely public." The next evening, at a meeting that ran until 1 a.m., the group picked a name. They rejected the United Free Speech Movement and Students for Free Speech in favor of the Free Speech Movement.[32]

In addition to Savio and Aptheker, the FSM Steering Committee always included Suzanne Goldberg, a philosophy graduate student who married Savio in the spring of 1965; Sydney Stapleton, a leader in the local Trotsky-oriented Young Socialist Alliance; and Jack Weinberg, one of the most effective civil rights organizers, the strategist behind FSM, and author of the statement, "You can't trust anybody over thirty." (This remark was both generational and a sneer at the aging communists.) In its early days the FSM Steering Committee also included several leaders of civil rights groups, such as Brian Turner of the Student Non-Violent Coordinating Committee (SNCC); Dustin Miller, an independent; as well as Art Goldberg, a passionate although not always level-headed devotee of civil rights who planned an autobiography entitled *Commie-jewbeatnik*; and Art's sister Jackie Goldberg, a longtime activist in Women for Peace and delegate to that organization's Moscow conference in 1963. As the crisis continued, the Goldbergs were eased out, the civil rights activists faded, and the remaining leaders broadened their support by adding to the FSM Steering Committee Benson Brown, Steve Weissman, Ron Anastasi, and Martin Roysher. Weissman was a superb tactician; Anastasi and Roysher were level-headed moderates. Later the group regained Art Goldberg and added Mona Hutchins, a libertarian Young Republican, and Michael Rossman, a math graduate student from an old leftist family. Other major figures included Gretchen Kittredge, who served as treasurer; David Goines, who designed FSM art and operated the mimeograph machine; and Barbara Garson, propagandist and later playwright ("MacBird.").[33]

The leftist ties are striking. Aptheker's communist connections were well known, and Rossman considered himself to be a "red-diaper" baby. Like others in similar circumstances, he had been sent by his parents to a Left youth camp. Barbara Garson had belonged to the Young Socialist Alliance. These ties did not go unnoticed by Kerr, who in a press conference indicated that the FSM leaders were red. Although he later said he had been misquoted, Kerr did nothing to remove the public impression that he faced a communist revolt at the University. Kerr's remark and his subsequent refusal to attack the hysterical Right enraged the FSM leaders, who were insulted that the University's president should stoop to the sort of red-baiting once used by Senator Joseph R. McCarthy. Part of the anger came from the fact that while the FSM leaders did not deny their Left orientations, they did not, by and large, think of themselves as leaders of Left political parties. Their radicalism was of a distinctly different type, which during the 1960s became known as the New Left. What was most significant about the Left ties was not ideology but the legacy of McCarthyism. These activists came from families that had been persecuted or knew people who had been persecuted for their political beliefs. It made them hypersensitive about political rights and insecure and suspicious whenever someone in power behaved in such a way that rights appeared to be threatened or clouded. [34]

Except for Savio, the most important FSM leaders were Jewish. Yet they had no particular interest in religion and little understanding of what their Jewishness could or should mean. Their activism was a form of self-identification. The Jewish style, at once playful and aggressive, and harkening back to working-class, immigrant roots that suggested success came only to those who struggled against power and authority, grated against the white, Anglo-Saxon, Protestant administrators who ran the University. Kerr, a practicing Quaker pacifist, disliked the activists' untidiness, their lack of self-restraint, their rudeness and disdain for propriety, their unwillingness to take rules seriously, their defiance of authority—in short, their chutzpah. [35]

While Savio had called for publicity, early press treatment had been frequently inaccurate and almost universally hostile. Photographs of Savio were invariably unflattering. In the early days the local media accepted administration statements uncritically. Only San Francisco Chronicle columnists Art Hoppe and Ralph J. Gleason appeared to understand what was happening. Although local television coverage was less biased, it tended to focus on the theatrical. The best coverage was in the New York Times and the Los Angeles Times. Much later Dean Katherine A. Towle sardonically noted that although she worked in the same building as the reporters for the local newspapers, not one had interviewed her about the FSM. Her first public comments appeared in the New York Times. The FSM held press conferences and issued press releases, but the media, except for a few radical publications and radio station KPFA, largely ignored the FSM's attempts at public relations. Poor press coverage led many students to conclude that the media were wrong about other issues. This result created a market for the Berkeley Barb, which was founded in 1965. [36]

Hostile press coverage generated hate mail. The letters, many anonymous, poured in from all over the country. Most were addressed to Savio, for the same gifts that made him attractive to Cal students frightened many Americans. One taunted Savio, telling him to go to Vietnam. "Savio," read this postcard, "Now are you going to join our services and win complete victory as you call it??? Or will you let others do the *dying?* You get your way—But try even to *over-sleep* in the *army* and see how you come out. They make my boy *toe* the mark. So why shouldn't you serve for *freedom?*" Another message advised, "Go to Hell, all you Rotten Beatnicks!" One letter, signed by a local "red-hot anti-communist" said, "This is so obviously another way the communists are trying to take over, and it should be stopped Now." A Berkeley minister suggested that Savio give up campus politics to lead pro-Vietnam war protests. One wonders if local FBI agents sent any of these letters, for in the 1970s it was revealed that during the 1960s some government officials had used hate mail as a form of harassment. More amusing was the note found on the garbage can at Savio's apartment, which served as the FSM headquarters. "Please don't take *any* garbage," advised the note. "The fire department *needs* an excuse to close down this communist sponsored, pinko-oriented, slack jawed, rabble-rousing, unpatriotic, dribble-spouting, root-gnawing, malodorous, *mafia* of overprivileged, underbrained, bleeding-hearted megalomaniacs." [37]

During October and November the pact of October 2 unraveled. One irritant involved a final resolution of the discipline for the eight students suspended prior to the capture of the police car. The activists, who distrusted the administration, had rejected the normal disciplinary process because it forced them to submit their cases either to the very deans who had cited them or to a faculty committee controlled by the administration. The activists believed that the pact of October 2 required Kerr to send the disciplinary cases to an *independent* faculty committee appointed by the faculty senate. The suspended students planned to use an open hearing to show that the deans had arbitrarily singled out civil rights activists for citation. The activists were convinced that this disclosure combined with proper legal representation would persuade the faculty committee to go easy. Kerr, perhaps, feared the same result. In any event, Kerr insisted on sending the cases to a faculty committee that he controlled. The activists refused to accept this interpretation, and since the wording of the agreement was ambiguous on this point, Kerr finally yielded and let the faculty senate name an ad hoc committee to consider these cases. Professor Ira Michael Heyman chaired this important committee. The administration's unwillingness to move except when pushed only heightened student distrust. Kerr's motives were now as suspect as his policies. It did not help when Kerr insisted that the chancellor had final jurisdiction and the right to alter any penalties the faculty committee recommended. Moreover, despite a plea from the committee, Kerr refused to reinstate the students pending the committee's report. In late November, the ad hoc committee made its recommendations. Heyman infuriated Kerr by reporting to the faculty senate, which publicized recommendations that Kerr preferred to keep secret. Then Chancellor Strong, on Kerr's direct orders and after Kerr had discussed the cases in great detail with the Regents, altered the penalties by increasing them. The consequence was to suggest Kerr's contempt for judicial processes, his disdain for the faculty, and his bad faith concerning the pact of October 2.[38]

Meanwhile, the second committee formed as a result of the October 2 pact also bogged down. Kerr selected this tripartite committee to negotiate permanent rules for political activity on campus by dictating to Strong the names of the four administrators, four faculty members, and four students to be appointed. The administrators and faculty members were Kerr supporters, and Kerr had enraged the activist students by appointing two nonactivist students (one a student body officer) to two of the student positions. After the activists refused to participate in such a committee, Kerr ordered Strong to add six additional members. Since the activists had only four of the six student votes among the eighteen members, at the first meeting of the committee they insisted that a proposal could only be adopted by a majority within each administration, faculty, or student portion of the committee. The administration representatives opposed this scheme, but the faculty members saw that accepting the activist position on organization was crucial to a successful negotiation. Besides, this strategy enhanced the power of the faculty members inside the committee. The administrators grudgingly agreed to this arrangement. The tripartite rules committee, however, never got beyond the organizational issue. The activist students on the committee rejected an administration proposal for limited political rights on campus, while an activist counterproposal that rights be based on the first amendment to the U.S. Constitution got no support from faculty members or administrators. The activists, in the end, rejected a faculty compromise.[39]

In reality, neither side was prepared to settle because each believed that it could get more later. Kerr, convinced that in time support for the activists would decline, calculated that in the end the administration could grant limited political rights that would satisfy the administration, the faculty, and a majority of students. Kerr did not understand the FSM strategy, which was to continue agitation to build wide student support. The agitation, however, had to be controlled so that escalation only took place after a mass student base had been prepared. Always, strategist Jack Weinberg emphasized, the larger purpose for wide student support had to be kept in mind. The leaders knew that students had little real power, and they intended to use large-scale student support to force the faculty to choose between siding with the students or with the administration. They intended, in other words, to bring the faculty into the activist camp on their terms. Several considerations led the activists to envision this outcome. First, Kerr's support from the faculty had declined over the years, and many faculty members were ready to show their independence of the administration. In addition to the Katz case, Kerr's insistence on the University's moving to the quarter system irritated the professors. Second, many faculty members sympathized with civil rights; since the issue of political activity on campus was seen as a question of how much civil rights activity would be permitted, the faculty could be drawn to support the FSM on that basis. But most important to the activists were the twists and turns in Kerr's inconsistent and arbitrary policies, which were neither democratically enacted nor reasonable.[40]

In order to gain student support, the FSM began to hold rallies almost every day at noon on the steps of Sproul Hall. Large numbers of students passed through the plaza, and sunny days brought a large audience. As many as five thousand students sometimes attended. These events both bolstered the confidence of the FSM leaders, whose self-doubts were reduced by mass approval, and ratified and legitimated the FSM demands. Not surprisingly, some administrators proposed eliminating the rallies, but such an act would have driven moderate students into solidarity with the most hotheaded activists. Throughout this period Kerr countered the FSM strategy of building mass support with his own attempt to split the students. On one occasion he met with five moderate members of the FSM Executive Committee. Kerr urged this group, which included the leader of the Young Democrats, to break with the FSM. When the five refused to do so without concessions, Kerr offered a settlement. If the moderates could get the FSM to accept this settlement, fine; if not, the moderates were to pull out. The moderates did not accept this proposal outright, but they did agree to meet with Kerr the next day. At the second meeting, however, the president acted as if he had never agreed to anything. The moderates then concluded that Kerr's only purpose had been to split student support for the FSM.[41]

The Sproul Plaza rallies did have curious aspects. Traditionally, speaking at the plaza, which formed a natural Greek amphitheater backed by the neoclassical front of Sproul Hall, had been prohibited, but early in the crisis Chancellor Strong had granted students the right to use the plaza as a free speech area. To use Sproul Plaza successfully, however, required microphones. University regulations required student groups that signed up to speak in the plaza to use University sound equipment, and so throughout the crisis the FSM leaders requested and obtained microphones with which they denounced the University's regulations. These University-owned microphones were sometimes connected to tape recorders, and both transcriptions of the rallies and eyewitnesses reports circulated throughout the administration. Because administrators rarely talked with the FSM leaders, these transcripts and reports, passed inside the campus bureaucracies, became the main means by which administrators followed the FSM demands. It was a most curious form of student-administration communication.[42]

During rallies the FSM leaders often led mass singing of either civil rights songs or union songs from the 1930s. The FSM also created its own songs, published a songbook, and made recordings, which provided a major source of funds. Most songs expressed alienation. In one song Malvina Reynolds, a professional folk songwriter and longtime Berkeley leftist, called the University a "robot factory." Another song, to the tune of "The Streets of Laredo," depicted the chancellor as unhappy because students did not act like children. Dan Paik's "Womb with a View" suggested that President Kerr wanted to change the students' diapers. Several songs defended the FSM against the charge that it was communist. "Don't know if I'm subversive, just want to say what I please," wrote Richard Kampf. A number of songs satirized Christmas carols; the FSM sold 15,000 carol records. Jolly tunes contrasted with bitter lyrics. One sung to "Jingle Bells" went:

> Oski Dolls, Pompon Girls,
> UC all the way!
> Oh, what fun it is to have
> your mind reduced to clay!
> Civil rights, politics
> just get in the way.
> Questioning authority
> when you should obey.[13]

While students sang, administrators quarreled among themselves. Some urged new disciplinary action; others opposed it. Kerr became irritated when the dean of graduate studies, Sanford Elberg, refused to warn graduate students of disciplinary action if they demonstrated; the president failed to see Elberg's refusal as a sign of faculty hostility and instead contemplated ordering Elberg to issue such a warning. If the faculty did not accept a reasonable compromise on the rules, Kerr warned of arrests, discipline, and a suspension of the tripartite rules committee. After the FSM leaders concluded that the rules committee was hopelessly deadlocked, they decided to resume setting up tables. On most days administrators ignored the tables, but one day assistant deans cited sixty-five students, and more than a hundred students then signed complicity statements. When the University unwisely sent disciplinary letters to those who had signed complicity statements, the FSM responded by sending 835 letters to the dean's office denouncing the administration's violation of constitutional rights. When teaching assistants manned tables, the activists noted that the TAs were not cited. The administration's double standard and obvious fear of a TA strike only disgusted the students. Throughout this period administrators resembled nothing so much as a group of five-year-olds gleefully tossing lighted matches into a jug of gasoline. When the Regents finally met to discuss the issue, the FSM organized a march of several thousand students from Sather Gate across campus to a rally in front of University Hall, where the Regents met. Borrowing an idea from the civil rights movement in the South, Savio insisted that male marchers wear coat and tie. Discipline was maintained by students who

wore yellow signs marked "Monitor," except for one fellow whose sign read
"Merrimac."[44]

Just as matters were quieting down, Kerr intervened maladroitly. In late November 1964, with the disciplinary cases settled amid bitterness and the political rules committee suspended, Kerr decided, perhaps under pressure from certain Regents, to punish the FSM leaders for their role in the events immediately
preceding and surrounding the capture of the police car. Kerr's grant of amnesty in the pact of October 2 had excluded the events that took place during
the actual seizure and holding of the car. Although not widely noticed at that
time, during November the activists became increasingly fearful that Kerr would
seek to impose new penalties. Kerr played a waiting game. Had the tripartite
rules committee succeeded, the president might have ignored the police car
incident. Had the rallies ceased, perhaps that too would have led to a quiet
conclusion. Kerr came to believe, probably incorrectly, that support for the
FSM was waning, and he decided to act. This decision was not Kerr's alone;
Strong concurred, and so did the Regents at a long special meeting on November 20. As customary, Kerr kept a low profile, and Strong announced the ini-
tiation of a new round of punishment by sending out several disciplinary letters. To those outside the administration, Strong's conduct seemed grotesque;
it destroyed the chancellor's remaining support on campus. The administration
had the law on its side, but the decision was mean-spirited. Four activist leaders—Savio, Art Goldberg, Jackie Goldberg, and Brian Turner—were singled
out, and it appears that Kerr intended to suspend Savio and Art Goldberg on
the grounds that on October 1 and 2 they had violated the terms of the retro-
active probation that had been recommended by Heyman's faculty committee
and imposed by the chancellor, on Kerr's orders, in late November. "They are
trying to pick off our leaders one by one," said Steve Weissman, an FSM
spokesman. Kerr's petty act rallied both the faculty and large numbers of otherwise uninvolved students to the FSM cause. The activists, in a spirit of rage,
decided to confront Kerr with their ultimate weapon.[45]

From the beginning the activists had considered a sit-in. The car sit-down
had spontaneously and serendipitously half fulfilled the desire, and now Kerr
had created circumstances that enabled the activists to bring the spirit of the
civil rights movement to the Berkeley campus. Negotiations had failed, and
some activists had concluded that little could be done to gain political rights
on campus. If they could not attain such rights, at least they could embarrass
the man and the university that had thwarted their efforts. Other leaders, long
active in civil rights, believed a sit-in would have other consequences. First, it
would galvanize, mold, and radicalize student opinion. One of the most important functions of sit-ins was to win converts. Friends would join, and then
friends of friends, and the feeling of camaraderie experienced in the sit-in gave
the movement what it needed most: bodies. The fellowship of a sit-in promised

a vast expansion of the activist population on campus and the beginnings of an activist community. Berkeley would have not dozens of activists but hundreds, possibly even thousands. Second, if a sit-in brought police, and the FSM leaders calculated that Kerr was not shrewd enough to avoid this outcome, then the bringing of police onto campus could generate benefits. The presence of police would both demonstrate Kerr's failure to manage the University and generate publicity that would bring sympathizers to Berkeley. Above all, the faculty could not tolerate the University run as a police state. Thus, a large sit-in would demonstrate widespread support for the FSM and push the faculty to act. The activists set a trap to humiliate Kerr and to bring the faculty to the rescue of the FSM.[46]

The sit-in and the administration's response were both carefully planned. Although the administration was closemouthed, leaks occurred, and the activists knew a sit-in would be crushed. The FSM leaders never tried to keep their plans secret, and they freely consulted both with the local clergy, whom they knew to be informants for the administration, and with the ASUC officers, who purposely undercut the FSM. The activists would have been less pleased to have learned that a campus policeman attended their planning meeting on December 1, 1964. At this meeting the FSM leaders declared their intention to create as massive a sit-in as possible, both to show the size and depth of their support and to humiliate Kerr. Steve Weissman estimated that 1,000 to 1,500 students would occupy Sproul Hall. He asked Weinberg how long it would take to arrest that many people, and Weinberg and others agreed that it would take about fifteen hours. About a hundred people had been organized to provide food. After Weissman noted that the FSM was $150 in debt, Weinberg passed around his motorcycle helmet; $147 was collected. Weissman also noted that he would attend the sit-in in order to "get the ball rolling," but that he planned to sneak out to organize a strike planned for Friday, December 4.[47]

At a pre-sit-in noon rally on December 2, Savio spoke his most memorable lines. The machinist's son said:

> There is a time when the operation of the machine becomes so odious, makes you so sick at heart, that you can't take part; you can't even passively take part, and you've got to put your bodies upon the gears and upon the wheels, upon the levers, upon all the apparatus and you've got to make it stop. And you've got to indicate to the people who run it, to the people that own it, that unless you're free, the machines will be prevented from working at all.

In these few words, similar to some thoughts of Thoreau, Savio calmly conveyed the deep anger, the anxiety, the frustration with modern life, and the sense of powerlessness that was the undercurrent of all the turmoil of the sixties. The rally was dirgelike, as if the participants were embarking upon some religious ceremony to bring about their rebirths. Joan Baez sang Bob Dylan's

"The Times They Are A Changin' " and then closed the rally with a funereally slow rendition of the civil rights song, "We Shall Overcome." A large portion of the crowd, more than one thousand, walked into Sproul Hall and settled down for what they hoped would be a long occupation.[48]

Kerr was desperate. Criticized by many people off campus for his handling of the first large-scale demonstrations at any American university in modern times, frustrated by his own bureaucracy, burdened with an ineffective chancellor, and now faced with one of the largest sit-ins in history, Kerr was pushed toward a decision he did not want to make. Painfully aware of the faculty's disdain for the use of police on campus, a disdain enhanced by the large number of European war refugees on the faculty, Kerr did not want to be remembered for using police to make arrests. So he kept his role in the unfolding events secret. Although the president later insisted that he had not authorized any arrests, and he may have been technically correct, Kerr and his administration had spent days preparing for this showdown. Throughout the crisis Kerr had consulted with the chairman of the Regents, Edward Carter, and Carter in turn had frequently talked by phone with Governor Pat Brown. The liberal Democratic governor had long been an admirer and supporter of Kerr's.

The governor, who was in Los Angeles, assumed responsibility for events on the campus. During the sit-in a campus policeman peered into the office of the emeritus president, Robert Gordon Sproul, and, seeing papers strewn about, reported to his superiors that the demonstrators had broken in. This report was false—Sproul was notoriously messy—but it led the assistant county prosecutor sitting in the campus police headquarters in the basement of the building to call the governor and tell him. "They're busting up the place. We have to go in." The governor then issued the order to arrest the protesters. Brown, a former prosecutor and attorney general, did not need to be persuaded of the virtue of law and order. His action, however, and his high visibility were politically unwise. The arrests enraged the protesters, who would have been allies with Brown under other circumstances, and failed to appease those Californians who came to consider Brown as part of the problem of Berkeley's disgrace. Two men played crucial roles in the police action. One was Alex Sherriffs, who had been appalled at Kerr's oscillations all fall and now grimly sought to win his battle against the activists. The other was Edwin Meese III, the prosecutor who had made the crucial call to Brown and who, as liaison between the police and the prosecutor's office, supervised the arrests.[49]

The activists occupied all four floors of Sproul Hall. They held different activities in different areas. In an alcove on the second floor, food was prepared, while elsewhere students watched old Charlie Chaplin films, studied for exams, held a Chanukah service, or sang folk songs. The atmosphere was congenial, relaxed, and partylike. A few smoked pot, and two female students were said to have lost their virginity on the roof. The leaders used walkie-talkies to discipline their followers. The students installed their own public address system to broadcast to passersby and the press. Some brought sleeping bags and prepared to settle down for the night, or perhaps for several nights, while others expected the police to attack with tear gas at any moment. At 3 a.m., after a good many of the demonstrators had gone to sleep, Edward W. Strong appeared with a bullhorn and, carrying out one of Kerr's last directives to the chancellor, read a statement on each floor warning that the police were about to arrest anyone who remained in the building. For several hours entry into Sproul Hall had been blocked, but until this point students had been free to leave the building, and about two hundred had done so.[50]

Then the police came. The FSM leaders had urged students under arrest to refuse to walk in order to force policemen to carry them from the building. The police obliged, although not necessarily in the gentlest manner. While females who refused to walk were taken down the elevator, males were tossed from officer to officer and hurled down the terrazzo stairs. "Take 'em down a little slower," advised one policeman, "they bounce more that way." Although some demonstrators complained about police brutality, few sought medical aid. Bodies were less bruised than egos. The purpose of forcing the police to carry students was to slow down the arrests so that fellow students who walked past Sproul Hall in the morning could see how their classmates were being treated. This tactic was successful for, despite the 367 police officers who took part, the building was not cleared and the last of 773 arrests made until 4 p.m. on the afternoon of December 3. It was the largest mass arrest in California's history. After being booked in the basement of Sproul Hall, the arrestees were put on buses and taken, for the most part, to Santa Rita, a county prison facility about twenty-five miles away. As news of the arrests spread across the campus and throughout Berkeley, faculty sympathizers organized caravans of cars to go to Santa Rita to post bail and retrieve the students from jail after they had been processed.[51]

Who sat in? Survey data show about 85 percent were Cal students; nearly half of the remainder were employees or former students. The overwhelming majority did not resemble the radical activists who led the FSM; in most respects the FSM followers mirrored their fellow students who did not sit in. Largely from middle-class families, the protesters had middle-class aspirations and values, were not particularly active in politics or civil rights, and might be described as liberal Democrats. Although many conservative students, including some Young Republicans, supported the goals of the FSM, few conservatives believed that the issue justified illegal acts. Indeed, it was the willingness to break a law to protest injustice that most clearly set apart those who sat in from those who did not. Perhaps because they were political liberals, many protesters were from Jewish families, but a larger number came from Christian backgrounds (36 percent Protestant, 6 percent Catholic, and 32 percent Jewish). In contrast, among Cal students as a whole, the comparable numbers were 44 percent Protestant, 15 percent Catholic, and 20 percent Jewish. Compared to students who did not sit in, however, those who sat in were less likely to attend church. They had more clearly rejected the religious practices of their parents, or they came from families where religion was nominal. The arrestees did not come from a particular age group or college class; about one-fifth were graduate students, a number only moderately below graduate representation in the University. Those who sat in were concentrated in certain majors, notably speech, anthropology, philosophy, English, and history; not a single student from optometry or business administration sat in. Few belonged to fraternities or sororities, and a large proportion lived in apartments in the South Campus area. One striking trait, which troubled Kerr, was that the protesters' grades were higher than average. It was the more serious and scholarly students who were most committed to the FSM. Psychological data suggested that the arrestees were unusually independent, impulsive, and nonconformist.[52]

As a whole, Berkeley students were split throughout the 1964 crisis. During September most students ignored the controversy, and in October the supporters of civil rights backed the FSM. By November moderates were drawn in, and in December the sit-in led to the FSM's peak influence. After the sit-in, students favored the FSM 55 percent to 38 percent, with 6 percent neutral. Roughly one-third supported both the FSM goals and the FSM's militant tactics. The administration could take little comfort from the fact that as many as 8,000 students might be drawn into future protests. Another third supported the goals but rejected illegal tactics. Only the remaining third upheld the administration's view that politics had no place on campus. The divisions strongly correlated with partisan politics. Democratic students favored the FSM; Republican students did not. In part, this split was due to the Republican party's nomination of Barry Goldwater for president in 1964 in a campaign hostile to civil rights. The outrage of civil rights activists had led to the FSM, and few young people sympathetic to that cause in 1964 called themselves Republicans. But there is evidence that a major change in the composition of the student body was also taking place. Reports of increasing radicalism at Cal had led conservative parents to send their children to college elsewhere. In 1959 freshmen had reported that their fathers favored Republicans over Democrats, 43 to 34 percent; by 1966 fathers favored Democrats over Republicans, 45 to 33 percent. Between 1959 and 1966 the number of students from Protestant families dropped from 55 to 39 percent, while those from Catholic families rose from 11 to 18 percent, those from Jewish families remained at 12 percent, and those from non-religious backgrounds increased from 6 to 27 percent. A different survey suggests that a large proportion of the nonreligious were disaffected Protestants or Jews. By 1965 students were coming from new social groups; 31 percent of Cal students had at least one foreign-born parent.[53]

The sit-in destroyed Strong and ruined Kerr's moral authority. The chancellor, already cold and distant, had retreated into himself as the crisis deepened. Now he felt personally betrayed by Kerr. Strong had thought that he had understood Kerr and had nearly worshipped the president. Now Strong found that the Kerr of bold words and promised tough action was a man of vacillation, of compromise, and of an inappropriate toughness that spawned new crises. The chancellor saw only too clearly that he had been used, and that now Kerr intended to sacrifice him. The chancellor was hurt, and his participation in events drifted toward unreality. On the last memo in which an annotation appears in his hand, he wrote in the margin in a large and shaking hand, "niggardly." Strong was not alone in his gloom. Kerr understood the magnitude of his defeat, that the activists had eroded his moral authority by forcing the use of police, and that bringing police onto campus had pushed the faculty into opposing the administration. If Kerr had paused to reflect, he might have realized that just as the chancellor's disciplinary letters issued in late November to four activists had led to the sit-in, the arrests were almost certain to provoke a counterattack.[54]

Having anticipated the arrests, the FSM leaders were ready to respond to the administration's escalation of the conflict. They called for a student strike. The strategy was to mobilize student support behind the FSM, to paralyze the normal operations of the campus, and to force the faculty, which still seemed to be divided and unwilling to act, to side with the students. While the immediate effect was to humiliate the administration and, they hoped, to shift power from the administration to the faculty, the FSM leaders hoped for long-term gains for students. If students could be organized in a successful strike, a powerful student organization might emerge to represent student interests. The key to the strike's effectiveness was the support of the teaching assistants, who were graduate students responsible for a majority of the small undergraduate classes on the campus. TAs were not always top students; the best graduate students received prestigious fellowships. TAs were poorly paid and shabbily treated, and they tended to identify more with the undergraduates whom they taught than with the faculty. Until the FSM, TAs had been unorganized and, like other graduates, lacked representation in the ASUC. During the FSM the Graduate Coordinating Council (GCC) was established, and TAs tended to dominate the new organization. It was the GCC's leadership that made the strike held on Friday, December 4, surprisingly effective. Administrators publicly called the situation normal but privately expressed near panic. Perhaps half of all students either stayed away from classes or had their classes cancelled. Kerr, understanding the danger of an organized, countervailing center of power, decided to move boldly. The president announced a university-wide convocation at the outdoor Greek Theatre for Monday, December 7.[55]

Over the weekend Kerr consulted with a number of faculty members, especially department chairs, and he intended to endorse a compromise proposal on political rights to be sketched out by the chairs at the Monday meeting. But Kerr's neglect of the faculty had hurt, and a large group of younger and more liberal faculty, the self-styled Committee of 200, many of whom had a concern for civil rights, had already met and prepared a set of campus regulations that essentially granted the FSM demands first articulated in the tripartite rules committee negotiations. Kerr's meeting at the Greek Theatre was strained. He announced an amnesty in the disciplinary cases pending from the four letters mailed in late November and said that students arrested in the sit-in would not face separate University discipline. Then he let Professor Robert Scalapino present the position of the department chairs. As the meeting concluded, it appeared that Kerr had won some support among the sixteen to eighteen thousand students and faculty in attendance. At least it seemed clear that negotiations could proceed with the Scalapino proposals as a basis for discussion and that the activists had been reduced to a small group that posed little harm to the University. All Kerr had to do was to keep things quiet, and the combination of exams and the winter rains would bring the FSM to an end on terms favorable to Kerr. Then, as the meeting ended, Mario Savio jumped onto the stage and headed for the microphone. He later said that he planned to announce a noon rally sponsored by the FSM at Sproul Plaza. He did not make it to the microphone, for campus policemen tackled him and dragged him backstage. A cry rose from the crowd. Kerr's effort had been destroyed. The symbolism was grotesque. A student leader committed to free speech was physically prevented from speaking. Kerr tried to salvage the situation by allowing Savio to make his announcement, but the attack on Savio was all that most people remembered of the tragedy at the Greek Theatre.[56]

Inside the administration some urged Kerr to attend the next day's faculty senate meeting. A personal appearance and strong plea, they argued, might rescue Scalapino's plan. But Kerr chose not to appear. Perhaps he feared humiliation, or maybe he felt that the faculty had to work its own will. The meeting began in Wheeler Auditorium in late afternoon. It was long and raucous. By this time most of the faculty supported the pro-FSM proposals that young, liberal professors had suggested. After the faculty defeated several conservative amendments by wide margins, they approved the liberal resolutions 824 to 115. Many voted to do so knowing that unity was in both the faculty's and the University's best interest. Others, conservatives charged, were influenced by the presence of the 5,000 FSM supporters who listened to the debate on loudspeakers in the dark outside Wheeler. As the faculty exited Wheeler, the FSM supporters opened a corridor through their ranks and broke into applause. Savio spoke with the press, and for the first time during the crisis, he had a grin on his face. It was his twenty-second birthday. When Kerr heard the tally, he was galled. To be attacked by a group of activist students was embarrassing, but to be undercut by one's own faculty, who, in Kerr's eyes, had now played into the hands of his enemies, was quite painful. The faculty did not appear to understand that in attacking the administration, they had not only weakened the administration's power but their own authority as well. Kerr saw only too clearly who had won the war.[57]

Kerr balked at taking the liberal faculty proposals to the Regents, whom he privately described as unreasonable conservatives who would never accept such ideas. But a number of professors had been talking with the Regents on their own and discovered that the Regents were anxious to settle, and if the faculty could arrange a settlement, then the Regents were willing to settle on faculty terms. Professor Arthur Ross played the key role in these discussions. Kerr had a weak case because several other universities, including nearby San Francisco State College, had adopted rules similar to those proposed by the Berkeley faculty. Indeed, by this point the University's attorney, Thomas J. Cunningham, had warned the Regents that if Sproul's old rules or Kerr's September rules were challenged in court, the University would probably lose. Although Cunningham looked like a crusty conservative in public, he worked behind the scenes to persuade the Regents to accept changes. On December 18 the Regents met and enacted new rules that regulated political activity on campus along the lines laid down by the FSM activists during the tripartite rules committee discussions in October. And so it was that a handful of civil rights activists energized a large number of students, persuaded a recalcitrant faculty to accept their position, and went on to gain the support of the wealthiest and most powerful men in the state of California. The result was almost incredible.[58]

The president, as the chancellor had predicted, sacrificed Strong, and few realized how the chancellor had been used. Strong, however, threatened to make a candid report to the Regents about Kerr's constant interference in the chancellor's business. Accordingly, Kerr delayed replacing Strong until January, when the Regents gave the chancellor the choice of resigning, taking a leave of absence, or being dismissed. Strong chose a vacation, and he was irked when Kerr told the press that the chancellor's health had been poor. Strong expressed his anger in a long report circulated among selected Regents and in statements published in March 1965 in the *Oakland Tribune*. By then Mrs. Kerr and Mrs. Strong were not speaking. In September 1965 the former chancellor gave a frank and bitter speech to the San Francisco Commonwealth Club. He said that while he had sought to uphold law, order, and honor, Kerr had pursued a policy of "retreat and capitulation." This contention, however, sounded like self-justification; on campus Strong's reputation remained low.[59]

In January 1965 Kerr named Martin Meyerson, the dean of environmental design, as acting chancellor. Popular with both faculty and students, the ebullient and excitable Meyerson for a time seemed to be just the tonic that the campus needed. His youth and vigor contrasted with Strong's age and caution, and Meyerson listened to all points of view. He was the first Jewish administrator in a top position in a university that had always been run by Protestants. Meyerson had a natural rapport with youths. He noted, "Young people are growing up in an entirely new way, and we really don't understand them at all." They could not be dismissed as troublemakers; their ideas were important. "We are coming upon a generation which, if it follows through," predicted the acting chancellor, "will lead us to a very different world than the one we've known. They have an aversion to the symbols we have built up—the rug on the floor, the name on the door—and they are looking for new values. They are more concerned with product than with 'image.' " Despite his rapport with the younger generation, Meyerson did not gain the confidence of the Regents. He did not aggressively seek the chancellorship on a permanent basis, and the Regents consulted more with the faculty than with Kerr about a permanent chancellor.[60]

In the aftermath of the FSM, the Regents did not close ranks but pointed accusing fingers at each other. One group of conservatives, clustered around Theodore Meyer, produced a report highly critical of both the FSM and the administration. Much to the Meyer Committee's surprise, the majority of Regents, including Governor Brown, as well as the faculty rejected this line of argument. The Meyer report had to compete with a report from a second committee chaired by Regent William Forbes. This committee was dominated by Regents from southern California. To everyone's surprise, they hired an aggressive staff attorney, Jerome C. Byrne, who then hired several young psychologists to interview people throughout the University. Byrne shrewdly ignored the FSM and focused on University governance. He strongly recommended decentralization and that the chancellor at Berkeley be given the responsibility for running the campus. While conservative Regents expressed annoyance at Byrne for ignoring the FSM, Governor Brown enthusiastically endorsed the report. Kerr, hoping to survive, suddenly embraced decentralization, and the Regents sought a strong-willed chancellor for Berkeley.[61]

In early 1965 the campus was quiet, and the FSM seemed to have disappeared, but trouble came in the spring. On March 3, John Thomson, a radical who had been attracted from New York to Berkeley by publicity about the FSM, sat down on the steps of the Student Union and held a piece of paper across his chest that read "Fuck." When University police arrested Thomson for public obscenity, Art Goldberg became angry. He saw a double standard, because Thomson had been arrested while a fraternity had just won the Ugly Man Contest with an entrant named "Miss Pussy Galore." On the following day Goldberg demanded that the administration drop the charge against Thomson, and after the administration refused, Goldberg held a rally at noon on the Student Union steps. For the 150 people who attended, the gathering was boisterous. A conservative student announced that he had ordered one thousand signs reading "Fuck Communism," a freshman was arrested while manning a table marked "Fuck Defense Fund," and a graduate student led a cheer spelling F-U-C-K. As officers led the freshman who had been arrested into the campus police station in the basement of Sproul Hall, a graduate student named Michael Klein followed. Once inside, Klein opened a copy of *Lady Chatterly's Lover*, which the courts had recently declared not to be obscene, and read from a paragraph concerning copulation. After Klein had read the paragraph aloud twice, he, too, was arrested. Klein was about to learn that society distinguished between reading a book in private and reading aloud from that same book in public. Of nine persons arrested during these incidents, only three were registered students.[62]

Art Goldberg had been the major speaker at the March 4 rally, where he had used "the word" liberally. Although some people suspected that the major purpose of the speech was to prop up the sagging popularity of the FSM, Goldberg made three important analytical points. First, an obscene word was not intrinsically offensive, and its offense came only to those trapped in a stuffy, puritanical culture. Goldberg did not want a dwindling, Anglo-Saxon, Protestant minority or an equally insufferable Jewish minority to impose its prudery upon him. Second, Goldberg believed society hypocritical in not allowing public use of a word common in private conversation. (The FSM phone logs show one phone call in which Goldberg asked, "Where the *%&$(%&$& is the truck?") Like others influenced by the beats, he loathed and detested hypocrisy. More importantly, Goldberg dramatized the connection between the attempt to regulate the content of speech through obscenity laws and the Free Speech Movement's protest against restrictions on political speech. The FSM had gained the right of students to speak freely on campus. Could either the administration or the police now abridge this right simply by declaring a statement to be obscene? To Goldberg, free speech meant the right to say anything. If an outside authority could prosecute a person on the basis of the content of a speech, and especially if the grounds for prosecution were that the speech offended the listener, then speech was not free.[63]

Goldberg's point was not trivial, although its exposition at the rally was both ineffective and impolitic. According to one survey, about 80 percent of Cal students opposed filthy speech in public, and most of the remainder were neutral rather than supportive. Titillating an audience with the novel repetition of a word normally not spoken in public failed as a form of argument. Much of Goldberg's point had been uttered with more deftness and humor by the satirist Lenny Bruce, who had performed in San Francisco frequently in the early 1960s. Both Bruce and Goldberg expressed contempt for traditional middle-class values; both were insecure working-class Jews determined to overturn a prudish culture that they hated because they believed that it repressed them.

Goldberg's performance was also impolitic. The FSM leaders, privately furious with Goldberg for jeopardizing the rights won in December, were divided. Some believed that the FSM had no choice but to show solidarity with Goldberg, while others, including Mario Savio, wanted nothing to do with the obscenity issue. Savio believed that the issue badly detracted from the dignity of free speech, and shortly after this incident, he withdrew from the FSM in a public farewell address at a rally.[64]

The Filthy Speech Movement, as it was generally called, nearly toppled the University administration. Certain Regents, including the governor, were personally offended, and Regent Edward Carter demanded that Kerr and Meyerson immediately dismiss the students involved in these incidents. Kerr and Meyerson insisted upon following normal disciplinary processes and provoked Carter's wrath. Tired of the controversy, Kerr persuaded Meyerson on March 10 to hold a joint press conference at which they announced their intention to resign. The press was startled, faculty members were stunned, and even the FSM Steering Committee expressed its shock; among the few who expressed pleasure was Savio, who called Kerr "a two-faced hypocrite." The Regents, as usual, were divided. Although many Regents were angry that Kerr had not informed them of his plan to resign, others saw the ploy for what it was: Kerr's desperate attempt to rally support and rebuild a consensus around himself. The Regents debated whether or not to accept the resignations, but they could hardly have done so without creating even worse problems for themselves. Governor Brown's support was crucial in Kerr's retention. The principal victim was Meyerson, whose participation in Kerr's stunt rankled the board sufficiently to eliminate the already slender possibility that he would be named permanent chancellor.[65]

The activist challenge then shifted to another front. A number of students began to publish a mimeographed magazine called *SPIDER*. The title stood for "Sex, Politics, International Communism, Drugs, Extremism, and Rock and Roll." It had enjoyed modest sales at tables set up at the edge of campus. Now *SPIDER* produced an issue containing "the word." Although Meyerson conceded that the magazine might not be legally obscene, he banned it from public sale on the campus. A student then wrote a play entitled,

*For*
*Unlawful*
*Carnal*
*Knowledge*

This publication was banned on the ground that the arrangement of the title on the cover was obscene. The administration then lifted the ban against *SPIDER* while continuing to ban the play. This action made the administration look foolish. Not only were the decisions banning and then reinstating *SPIDER* arbitrary, but the inconsistency between the treatment of the magazine and the play was glaring. Savio proclaimed "the end of our honeymoon with Marty." The controversy made the administration look clumsy and prudish, and it reinforced Goldberg's point that the principle of free speech required that the University not engage in censorship. From the administration's point of view, the situation was made more difficult by the fact that in 1965 neither the courts nor the culture defined obscenity clearly.[66]

The obscenity cases did have one unforeseen consequence. Four students cited by deans had their cases turned over to a faculty disciplinary committee, as provided in campus rules promulgated in January 1965 by Acting Chancellor Martin Meyerson. The hearing, however, proved to be far from satisfactory. The attorney for the students did not allow them to testify, because the prosecutor might subpoena the testimony in the pending criminal cases that three of the students faced in Berkeley Municipal Court. The refusal of the students to participate fully in the proceedings both irritated the faculty members sitting in judgment and weakened the presentation of a defense case. The five faculty members disliked the judicial nature of the proceedings and could not agree upon penalties. By a split vote, they advised the acting chancellor to suspend three students and dismiss Art Goldberg. Meyerson concurred in those recommendations. This cumbersome hearing led the University to institute a disciplinary system using hearing officers. In the future, a single faculty member, usually trained in the law, heard student disciplinary cases and recommended penalties to the chancellor.[67]

The arrests in Sproul Hall in December 1964 led to a long, involved trial that lasted from May to August 1965; it left a bitter taste. Many liberals assumed that the sit-in participants would follow the Reverend Martin Luther King, Jr 's practice of pleading guilty and accepting a small fine or a short jail term. The students, however, lacked King's patient obedience to legal authority and were outraged at being arrested on their own campus in a protest for student rights that had been won. It did not seem fair that the Free Speech Movement should triumph, while its participants were declared guilty. Besides, the FSM leaders hoped a trial would force the University to reveal how the decision had been made to send police into Sproul Hall. As negotiations opened with the prosecution, the prosecutors, led by Lowell Jensen and Edwin Meese III, indicated that the FSM leaders were to be treated more harshly than the followers. Because the FSM had been born in a spirit of equality that manifested itself as a sense of community, the prosecution's insistence that leaders had to bear heavier responsibility deeply offended the participants. The prosecutors neither understood the movement's sense of solidarity nor its insistence upon a nonhierarchical, nonauthoritarian form of shared, communal leadership. The prosecutors' insistence upon identifying and punishing leaders foreclosed the possibility for guilty pleas and threatened to create a series of individual trials that would overwhelm the legal system. The prosecution insisted that the cases be consolidated. If this was not done, reactionary judges were to be imported from southern California. In the end, the defendants allowed their cases to be consolidated, waived jury trials, and appeared before a local liberal judge.[68]

The lead attorney for the FSM was Malcolm Burnstein. His law partner was Robert Treuhaft, a onetime communist and husband of the author Jessica Mitford. During the sit-in Treuhaft had been inside Sproul Hall with the press, when Meese had suddenly challenged the attorney's credentials and ordered him arrested. Treuhaft's arrest may have spurred on his law partner, but Burnstein, a civil rights expert who had advised CORE, was ill-prepared for this case. Neither Burnstein nor the FSM recognized that this case was not about civil rights. It was, in fact, about politics. Such a case may be handled in two ways. Either one throws oneself upon the mercy of the court and hopes for the best, or else one goes to trial to create a political forum. In the late 1960s the attorney Charles Garry brilliantly pursued this latter strategy in trials involving the Black Panther party. In the FSM case, however, the defendants could not agree on strategy; Burnstein lamented that only 30 percent were willing to plead nolo contendere to a single charge. With lukewarm support from Burnstein for going to trial, the defendants insisted on bargaining with the prosecution. By waiving a jury trial, the FSM precluded staging a political trial and, possibly, winning an acquittal. (One defendant separated his case and got a hung jury.) The refusal to plead guilty, however, meant that the FSM defendants did not cooperate with the judicial system. The outcome was a disaster for them.[69]

The case was heard by Judge Rupert Crittenden, who died, possibly from the stress, after its conclusion. Crittenden's conduct of the trial infuriated the defendants, because the judge neither allowed the questioning of Governor Brown, who took public credit for ordering the arrests, nor required University officials to explain their actions. Kerr was a star witness; his testimony disclosed nothing new, but the court made every effort to accommodate him: When he testified, he sat in an upholstered chair; other witnesses were required to use a hard, wooden chair. As the president was leaving the court, he met Art Goldberg. Trying to be friendly, Kerr smiled, offered a hand, and said, "Hi Jack." "My name's not Jack," replied Goldberg, who kept his hand at his side. The defendants were also angry that the prosecution charged the defendants not only with trespassing but also with resisting arrest. They did not feel that forcing the police to carry the defendants out of Sproul Hall constituted resistance to arrest. The arrest of Treuhaft also produced ill-will, since it prevented Treuhaft from acting as attorney for the defendants, and if convicted, Treuhaft could have lost his license to practice law. As it turned out, that case was eventually dropped. At the prosecution's request and on Kerr's suggestion, Chancellor Strong voluntarily handed over student records, and the University's complicity in the prosecution further enraged the defendants. Nor did the administration allow the defendants to use a University room for a defense planning meeting. A movement by some faculty members to persuade the prosecutor to drop the case was blocked by the administration, which told its staff to oppose amnesty. Later, after the defendants had been convicted, several sought to mitigate punishment by obtaining character references from University officials. A reference written for Jackie Goldberg was leaked to the press, probably by the prosecutor, and Kerr then ordered his staff to provide no further references.[70]

By the time the trial ended, the defendants felt bloodied. To their surprise, the judge had required daily attendance, even though individual defendants were involved in only a small portion of the consolidated trial. Crittenden had systematically denied the defense's line of attack, and rumors circulated that the FSM leaders would draw jail terms. The judge found all the defendants guilty, and sentences did distinguish between leaders and followers. Most participants drew fines of $50 to $150; the usual fine for a first-time trespass was $10. About a dozen leaders, including members of the FSM Steering Committee, were sentenced up to 120 days in jail. As sentences were pronounced in batches throughout the summer of 1965, the court asked defendants to accept up to two years probation. Probation foreclosed the possibility for further sit-ins, since a person who committed a misdemeanor while on probation was immediately jailed. After a number of defendants had accepted probation, Michael Duke refused a $150 fine and one year probation; the angry judge then increased Duke's fine to $250. With protest over civil rights and the Vietnam War in their minds, other defendants also turned down probation. A number of leaders drew lengthened jail terms because they refused probation. After receiving a sentence of 120 days in jail, Savio said, "Revolution is a positive duty when power is in the hands of the morally and intellectually bankrupt." While these cases were appealed, it is doubtful that the defendants believed that the appeals would succeed. By the summer of 1967, the appeals had been denied, and the FSM leaders went to jail. By then, Crittenden was dead, Governor Brown had been defeated, President Kerr had been fired, Meese was an adviser to Governor Ronald Reagan, and political trials were becoming as common as the protest that spawned them.[71]

On July 29, 1965, three days after Judge Crittenden had sentenced Savio to jail, the FSM leader spoke at a rally. "We must construct our own community of protest to take back our self-government," he urged. He now saw himself as an American radical willing to offer voters a choice at the polls to the left of the Democrats. The next speaker was Thomas Parkinson, a professor of English and sometime supporter of radical causes who had been wounded severely and almost killed in 1961 by a deranged rightist. Parkinson accused the judge of bowing to political pressure in imposing varied sentences. The rally concluded with Allen Ginsberg chanting a mantra while beating small silver cymbals. The beat poet said that it was a Tibetan lullaby designed to calm children; he hoped it would calm Judge Crittenden. The previous day Steve Hamilton, one of the last of the Sproul Hall defendants to be sentenced, had told the court that the trial had failed. "This is a conflict between the East Bay power structure and civil rights," he said. "The power structure is on top with its money, cops, and courts." Hamilton refused probation because of his growing concern about Vietnam, but he was not important enough to be sent to jail. Meantime, in Washington the administration announced an increase in draft calls and the expansion of the military by 300,000 men. Savio's willowy radicalism, Parkinson's complaint, Ginsberg's chant, Hamilton's militance, and the thunder of war rolling in from far-off Washington formed a peculiar equipoise. Before the FSM Parkinson and Ginsberg were cultural defiers of the Zeitgeist; with the FSM they had been joined by Savio and Hamilton. After the FSM, which in effect had ended with the trial, Savio and Parkinson faded, but Ginsberg and Hamilton grew in importance while confronting the ever-stronger gales of war. On that day in July the liberalism of Kennedy and Kerr was already finished, and the future could be forecast as easily in Ginsberg's mantra as in the news from Washington.[72]

The FSM had changed the University. One casualty was the concept of *in loco parentis*, an age-old doctrine that a university should maintain parental supervision over the student. "He is urged to be an adult," complained one FSM student, "but he is not allowed to live like one." This student bitterly attacked University housing policies, including regulations for female students that prevented sexual freedom. The demand for independence did not escape Kerr's notice. The Sproul Hall sit-in ended with arrests rather than campus discipline and in effect conceded the FSM demand that students be treated like adults. One reason Meyerson failed was his support of *in loco parentis*. In the obscenity cases, the parentlike Meyerson, bowing to pressure from certain Regents, censored what the childlike students could write, read, publish, or speak. The policy came from Meyerson's deep personal beliefs. "Remember that, when you are a teacher," he told the Alumni Council, "your students are your charges. They are practically your children." The students had a different view. During 1963–64, a tense year in Berkeley, an unprecedented 10 percent of the students sought psychological counseling; the figure had doubled over the previous year. During the FSM the number seeking such help dropped 20 percent. As *in loco parentis* declined, autonomy increased, and psychological health improved.[73]

The teaching assistants continued the Graduate Coordinating Council and went on to organize Local 1570 of the American Federation of Teachers (AFT). The Left, under Robert Kaufman of the Department of History, controlled the GCC; Kaufman was active in the Communist party. Moderates joined the AFT. Part of the pressure for a union came from threats that some TAs had encountered during the short student strike in December 1964. Once TAs began to meet and talk among themselves, they discovered a long list of common grievances. Married TAs struggled financially, office space was inadequate, teaching assignments were often changed at the last minute, and appointments or reappointments sometimes appeared to be arbitrary. By the spring of 1965 about 450 TAs belonged to Local 1570. Some members favored negotiations to gain minor, short-term concessions; others wanted to agitate. During 1965 moderates retained control but rapidly exhausted simple demands that could be easily granted. (One example: history TAs won the right for graduate students to use the lounge previously reserved for faculty members.) By 1966 the local fell under the control of militants and then disintegrated.[74]

The FSM leaders pursued a variety of interests. One faction, including Jack Weinberg, Bettina Aptheker, and Marvin Garson, reconstituted the FSM into the Free Student Union (FSU), which organized students like a labor union. Within a month the FSU had sold 3,200 memberships at twenty-five cents apiece. The organization advocated co-op housing, a co-op bookstore, student parking, a student voice in faculty hiring and tenure decisions, and autonomous student government. The FSU, however, never explained how a union would represent student interests. Some believed that a union might force the University to accept demands by threatening to strike. The industrial analogy seemed farfetched. While a strike was an effective weapon for industrial workers because the lack of production eliminated profit, it was difficult to see how the University would be hurt by students who refused to attend classes or take exams. The FSU's stubborn clinging to the industrial analogy can only be attributed to the temper of the times. FSU supporters were influenced both by the thirties, when organized labor and radicals had moved in tandem, and by the sixties, when militant labor groups such as the teamsters had shown strength.[75]

Another FSM faction became interested in educational reform. Brad Cleaveland declared, "America's most pressing need is an education revolution." To Michael Rossman, the FSM had led to two discoveries. The first was that testing the status quo could bring change. The second discovery was that the FSM itself had been a learning experience. Students who had found learning dull, dreary, and a burden to be endured were jolted by the FSM into hard work that was exhilarating. There was, said the communist organized DuBois clubs, "a new spirit." Rossman concluded that the contrast between the University's joyless learning and the FSM's excited learning could be explained in terms of the culture's outmoded ways of teaching. (Surveys showed that an overwhelming majority of Berkeley students rejected these views.) Learning took place, contended Rossman, when people had new experiences. Teaching, then, should consist of providing an environment favorable to new experiences. In 1965 an optimistic Rossman accepted the University's capacity for change and agreed to teach in the Experimental College organized by Professor Joseph Tussman. A year later, after being fired by Tussman, Rossman considered the University hopeless. More than ever, he believed in learning as an expansion of consciousness, and he began to look for new ways and places for organizing learning.[76]

Rossman and others, including Stew Albert, Brad Cleaveland, and David Goines, created the Free University of Berkeley (FUB). The FUB specialized in innovative courses normally not offered at Cal. In the end, Rossman watched with fascination and then with despair as the counterculture took over the FUB and trivialized it. Although slow to admit that this experiment had failed, he recognized that not everyone at the FUB had his own high ideals. By the late 1960s the Free University was a joke; it was primarily a good place to meet someone to get laid. Rossman recovered from this disappointment and taught in a Montessori school. There he put into practice one of the major lessons learned by participants in the Free Speech Movement. Rossman broadened the horizons of his charges, challenged them, pushed them to grow and develop on their own.[77]

What, then, had the FSM been about? One of the shrewdest insights came from Savio. The world of 1964, he noted, was identical to the world of 1945— a world in which the United States had triumphed, nuclear weapons had been unleashed, Hitler had been vanquished, and the Holocaust disclosed. The general who had done so much to win the war, Eisenhower, had only recently left the presidency, and he had been succeeded by a war hero, John Fitzgerald Kennedy. For twenty years, Savio noted, there had been a continuity of institutions, personalities, and, most important, ideas. Adults, said Savio, believed that they had made the world for all time. Accordingly, in this best-of-all-possible worlds there was no room for change, no room for the further evolution of history. In the sixties young people worried about nuclear war and racial bigotry; they found it difficult to accept that it was the best-of-all-possible worlds. "The reason why liberals don't understand us," said Savio, "is because they don't realize there is evil in the world." Youth was a time for testing and challenge. Young people resented being handed a world delineated, finite, and limited; they expected to make their own world. "I'm tired of reading history. Now I want to make it," Savio had written in early 1964.[78]

The FSM was only the first of many campus revolts in America during the 1960s. The turmoil has often been blamed on the Vietnam War, and the war certainly created tension and provided issues for confrontation. But the revolt at Berkeley preceded large-scale American military involvement in Vietnam, and its roots lay elsewhere. The large size of the baby boom generation, the loss of unskilled jobs, and racial conflict all played a role. But in the sixties student revolts were global. They ranged from the United States to Japan to Germany and France. In Berlin students openly modeled their revolt upon the FSM and actually translated and republished some of the FSM mimeographed handouts. Neither Japan nor Europe suffered racial trouble; nor were they involved in the Vietnam War. What students in all these countries faced, however, was a world created and then frozen into place in 1945. World War II had peculiarly affected the United States, Japan, Germany, and France. In these four countries the political, economic, and social rules had been rewritten in 1945. For students born just before, during, or after the war, the projection of twenty years of stasis indefinitely into the future promised the inheritance of a sterile world without any chance to alter it.[79]

The FSM profoundly changed Berkeley, the University, and Cal students. The movement fostered a questioning attitude that in the mid-sixties led many to challenge the status quo. As Professor Henry F. May observed, Berkeley undergraduates became ruthlessly honest and boldly raised questions. Students neither accepted the wisdom of their elders nor developed a delusionary ideology of their own. The style, as noted by Professor Josephine Miles, was heavily influenced by the beat writers and yet distinctly different. The beats had declared society worthless and withdrew into isolation. Students in the sixties agreed that the society's practices were worthless but saw no reason to withdraw; they became feisty and contentious. To the participants, the FSM had been, in its essence, an epiphany. Michael Rossman noted that the power of the experience transcended the sum of its parts. From the beginning of the spontaneous sit-down around the police car, deep emotion had gripped the students. That emotion did not rise simply either from anxiety about free speech or from the wish to apply civil rights tactics to the University. It expressed deeper feelings, revealed reservoirs of strength, caused the unlocking of hidden talents, and pushed people toward new ventures. The Free Speech Movement unleashed a restless probing of life.[80]

# Chapter 2

# BLACK

*Power to the People
and Black Power
to Black People!*
Black Panther Party

Late in the last century, Oakland became a working terminus for the Southern
Pacific Railroad and a crew change point for the Pullman Company, which
employed large numbers of blacks as porters on its passenger cars. Because
Pullman porters often received large tips, jobs with the Pullman Company were
among the best that a black man could find. Some porters married and settled
down to raise families in a small black community that grew near the railroad
yards. In this community porters remained an elite until the waning of passenger trains in the mid-twentieth century. Among the porters was D. G. Gibson,
who became the black community's political leader. Another porter, C. L.
Dellums, figured prominently in the national porters' union organized by A.
Philip Randolph. In 1967 Dellums's nephew, Ronald V. Dellums, became a
Berkeley city councilman and in 1970 Berkeley's first black congressman.[1]

By the 1920s this still tiny black community had spread from the Oakland
railroad yards into other areas of Oakland and across the city line into Southwest Berkeley. In many of these neighborhoods, blacks lived amid whites and
Asians, and black children attended local schools that were predominantly white.
Blacks, however, faced many difficulties. When Byron Rumford arrived in the
Bay Area from Phoenix in 1926, he was admitted into the University's pharmacy program in San Francisco, but it seemed unlikely that the state pharmacy
board would ever grant him a license to practice. He failed a personal exami-
nation, complained, and was told there was no place for a black in the profession of pharmacy. Rumford finally found a sympathetic state official, who in-

sisted that Rumford be reexamined. This time he passed. However, no white-owned pharmacy would hire him, and the only job Rumford could find was running a venereal disease treatment program at the county hospital. The hospital employed no other blacks, and Rumford could not eat in the employee dining room. His modest but steady salary enabled him to save money, and in 1941 he bought a pharmacy in Southwest Berkeley. Rumford's drugstore offered proof of his success as a black entrepreneur; it also became the political headquarters for Berkeley's black community.[2]

Before World War II Berkeley's blacks were a small, cohesive community of a few thousand people with strong leadership furnished by Pullman car porters and a middle-class elite that had been educated at the University. Despite ties with Oakland's black community, Berkeley's blacks developed a sense of autonomy. Discrimination by whites also forged community ties and pushed blacks into cooperative ventures. Although segregation was never as rigid as in the South, it often crept into the daily lives of black residents. Buses and theaters were not segregated, but certain restaurants refused to serve blacks. In the 1930s county welfare workers kept segregated caseloads, and the county hospital's nursing school only grudgingly admitted blacks. Black nursing students were allowed neither to live in the hospital dorm nor to use the students' day room. As late as 1940, merchants along San Pablo Avenue in Berkeley posted signs near the adjoining black community warning, "No Negro Trade Solicited." The small size and the poverty of the black community forced blacks to cooperate with whites on white terms. Black leaders played on white guilt and politely requested changes. They succeeded in eliminating the most visible indications of racism, such as the signs on San Pablo. Although far from satisfied with conditions in Berkeley, blacks were grateful for the opportunities they did have and gave thanks that they did not live in the South, where blacks were lynched.[3]

During the war 500,000 people migrated to the Bay Area; about 75,000 were black. More than 100,000 jobs were created in the Richmond shipyards, and workers lived in Berkeley as well as Oakland and Richmond. Federal law protected black war workers from discrimination, but some corporations and unions barred the newcomers. White boilermakers, for example, encouraged blacks to set up their own union. Black leaders charged naive blacks from the rural South $7.50 to join a "club" in order to become a member of the black union and get a job. In most cases, poorly educated blacks from the South were assigned to the lowest paid jobs. Even so, black workers found unprecedented opportunities as wartime labor shortages caused the color barrier to crumble. A black state official persuaded both Sears and Safeway to hire their first black employees. Factory work paid better than picking cotton, and few workers returned to the South at the end of the war. Instead, relatives trickled into Berkeley and the Bay Area, although by the late 1940s unskilled laborers struggled

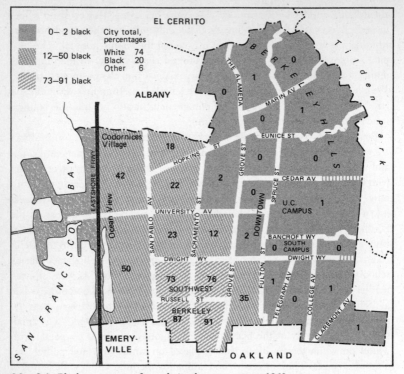

Map 2.1. Black percentage of population by census tract, 1960
(*Source:* U.S., Bureau of the Census, 1960.)

to find steady work. Relations between the better educated and established blacks who had lived in Berkeley before the war and the poorly educated newcomers became strained.[4]

The census records tell the story. Blacks were 4 percent of Berkeley's population in 1940; 12 percent in 1950; 20 percent in 1960; 24 percent in 1970. A city that had been a virtually all-white suburb became, in less than a generation, a racially mixed city with numerous tensions and frustrations. In the late 1940s the larger size of the city's black population produced several effects. First, although leaders of the prewar black community continued to guide the community, these leaders felt less secure about their own leadership, while the newcomers lacked leaders. At the same time, black leaders felt that black contributions to the war effort as well as the community's larger numbers gave blacks a right to more influence in Berkeley. Some whites agreed, but others were uneasy about the city's growing black population. They resented blacks'

In this view of the city of Berkeley, taken from the hills above the University of California in 1963, the Lawrence Radiation Laboratory complex appears in front of the main campus with its Campanile, while the Golden Gate lies across San Francisco Bay in the distance. *(Bancroft Library)*

Governor Pat Brown, Regent Edwin Pauley, and President John Kennedy shared the platform at Memorial Stadium for Kennedy's speech on Charter Day, March 25, 1962. Pauley, a wealthy oilman, was a major Democratic party contributor. *(Lonnie Wilson, Bancroft Library)*

While Kennedy's speech on Charter Day attracted 88,000 people to the stadium, the Left, led by the Trotskyists, staged a small protest rally at the corner of Bancroft Way and Telegraph Avenue. *(Bancroft Library)*

In 1963 Ludwig von Schwaren-
berg, a German shorthair, more
or less permanently guarded this
fountain at the edge of Sproul
Plaza. The Regents named it
Ludwig's Fountain. *(Bancroft
Library)*

During Clark Kerr's presidency of the University, Kerr held formal dinners for the Regents following the monthly business meetings. At this dinner in Santa Barbara in 1959, Kerr is in the center
at the back, Kay Kerr is seated on the left, and Regent Catherine Hearst and her husband Randolph Hearst are standing at the far right. *(Vince Mandese, Bancroft Library)*

In 1961 the London plane trees in the newly constructed Sproul Plaza were staked. A portion of Sproul Hall may be seen at the edge of the plaza. This view looks north through Sather Gate to the heart of the campus. The Campanile towers over Wheeler Hall. (*Bancroft Library*)

This view from the roof of Wheeler Hall looks south through Sather Gate to Sproul Plaza and the new Student Union. A portion of Dwinelle Hall appears on the right. In 1961 thousands of students daily entered the campus through Sproul Plaza and Sather Gate. (*Ed Kirwan, Bancroft Library*)

Edward W. Strong served as chancellor of the Berkeley campus during the
Free Speech Movement. *(ASUC Photography, UC Public Information Office)*

In 1964 many people ate, studied, or talked at the Terrace. This view looks east through Sproul
Plaza to the front of Sproul Hall. The Student Union is at the right edge. *(Bancroft Library)*

Vice-Chancellor Alex C. Sherriffs attacked the Free Speech Movement, lost his job, and joined Governor Ronald Reagan's staff. (*Ed Kirwan, UC Public Information Office*)

Dean of Students Katherine A. Towle had the bearing of a retired colonel—which she was. She quietly, vehemently, and unsuccessfully opposed Sherriffs's policies. (*ASUC Photography, UC Public Information Office*)

During the first, short protest inside Sproul Hall on September 30, 1964, the demonstrators ate heartily. (*Chris Kjobeck, Bancroft Library*)

For thirty-two hours on October 1–2, 1964, protesters surrounded a police car, while arrestee Jack Weinberg sat inside. Activists used the roof of the car as a podium. Note the smile on the policeman's face. *(Howard Harawitz, Bancroft Library)*

On November 9, 1964, Campus Women for Peace defied University regulations by setting up this card table in Sproul Plaza. *(Keith Denison, Bancroft Library)*

In late November 1964 supporters of the Free Speech Movement marched through Sather Gate to a Regents meeting at University Hall. Male marchers wore coats and ties. Note the American flag. *(Bancroft Library)*

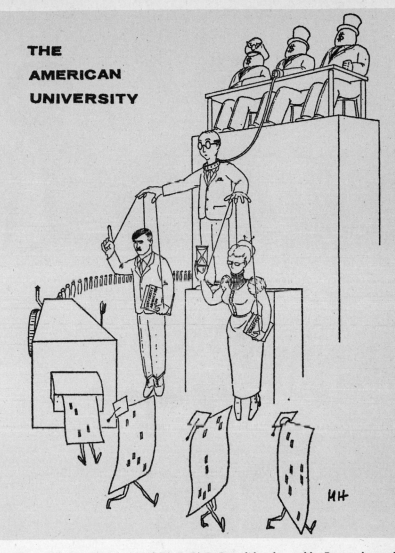

# THE AMERICAN UNIVERSITY

According to the communist-oriented W. E. B. DuBois clubs, the wealthy Regents kept a dog like Kerr on a short leash. Kerr ran the University through his puppets—a fascist (Alex Sherriffs?) and a prude (Dean Towle?). Individuals were, as Mario Savio said, processed by the University and emerged as IBM cards with degrees. The IBM cards, however, were not identical. *(Bancroft Library)*

Just before the Sproul Hall sit-in began on December 2, 1964, Joan Baez sang on the steps.
*(Bancroft Library)*

Following the sit-in, activists
declared a student strike. On
December 4, 1964, pickets
marched at the edge of campus.
*(Bancroft Library)*

Police intelligence officers often photographed public events. This photograph of a rally on the steps of Sproul Hall on December 4, 1964, with radicals and the FSM leaders identified, was one of a large number presented to Governor Pat Brown. *(Bancroft Library)*

At the campuswide meeting in the Greek Theatre on December 7, 1964, the FSM leader Mario Savio listened intently to proposed University rules. *(Bancroft Library)*

During early 1965 Acting Chancellor Martin Meyerson faced the Filthy Speech Movement. Meyerson's inability to master this crisis destroyed his chance to be named chancellor. *(Bancroft Library)*

This view to the south along Telegraph from the corner of Bancroft was taken on March 5, 1965. In the foreground the table at which *SPIDER* magazine was sold displayed a giant floating spidery balloon. *(Hoover Institution)*

Professor Hardin B. Jones bought a copy of *SPIDER* magazine from the editor, Steve DeCanio. *(Hoover Institution)*

The pharmacist Byron Rumford represented Berkeley's flatlands in the state legislature from 1948 to 1966. He was the first black in California ever elected from a mostly white district. *(Bancroft Library)*

In 1963 the city broke ground for a swimming pool at Willard Junior High School. Behind Councilwoman Bernice Hubbard May are Mayor Wallace Johnson, Roy Nichols of the school board, and Superintendent C. H. Wennerberg. Second from the right is longtime City Manager John D. Phillips. *(Bancroft Library)*

...LET'S ELECT HIM!

**WILMONT SWEENEY**
**for the Berkeley City Council**

In 1961 Wilmont Sweeney, an attorney who sought to convey the dignity of his profession, campaigned for a city council seat with this photograph. He became Berkeley's first black councilman. *(Institute of Governmental Studies Library)*

When Eldridge Cleaver ran for president in 1968 as a Black Panther representative on the Peace and Freedom party ticket, he used this photograph.

**HUEY NEWTON**
**FOR U.S. CONGRESS**

**BOBBY SEALE**
**FOR STATE ASSEMBLY**

In 1968 Huey Newton and Bobby Seale, cofounders of the Black Panthers, ran for office as Peace and Freedom candidates. Shown is a portion of a campaign leaflet. *(Bancroft Library)*

demands and would have preferred that the city's blacks go away. This attitude led many whites, especially those who lived in the hills, to pretend that Berkeley did not have any black residents. Sometimes, however, reality intruded. Bernice Hubbard May, a white liberal, invited Frances Albrier, a prominent black leader, to join the League of Women Voters. The league did not object, but the organization met at the all-white Women's City Club. Although the club served Albrier at the league's luncheons, the club chose not to renew its contract with the league.[5]

White liberals looked for ways to reward the black community that did not offend racially sensitive whites. In 1948 liberals joined D. G. Gibson and a number of labor leaders to nominate Byron Rumford for the legislature. The pharmacist's reputation as a solid businessman made him acceptable to whites, while his race made him a visible symbol of success to Berkeley's blacks. Strong backing from black ministers as well as from some conservative unions that wanted to block the influence of Left unions gave Rumford the Democratic nomination in the Berkeley-Oakland flatlands district, and he went on to win the general election. Rumford was the first black elected to the California legislature from a district that was mostly white. A quiet, intelligent man who did not enjoy political razzle-dazzle, Rumford used his post to promote black rights. He also faithfully supported labor issues and slowly gained political influence. During most of his eighteen years in the Assembly, however, his views on black rights were in advance of what the legislature could do. While being in the legislature helped Rumford promote his antidiscriminatory cause, he never became an effective politician. He retained the prewar black community's belief that quiet pleas were the most effective way for blacks to get whites to accede to black demands.[6]

During the 1950s the growing size of the black electorate became increasingly important to Berkeley's white liberals, who were a distinct minority. Conservative Republicans routinely won nearly every race in city elections. The liberal movement had grown significantly among graduate students and younger faculty members at the University when Adlai Stevenson ran for president in 1952. Stevenson's policies were less important than his vision: he advocated a sophisticated, urbane society built upon massive government support for education and the economy. A compassionate and sensitive government would meet people's basic needs, promote economic development, and seek world peace. Stevensonian liberals were never a majority among Berkeley's whites, but by the late 1950s they were well-organized, well-financed, and growing in strength. Conservatives controlled politics through the *Berkeley Daily Gazette* and meetings at the Elks Club; liberals countered with a grassroots politics based on precinct organization and numerous neighborhood political clubs coordinated through the California Democratic Council (CDC), a powerful statewide group for reform-minded Democrats. Berkeley had a peculiar system for electing city council members. All candidates ran on a single, citywide list; the top four vote-getters were elected. By concentrating votes on only one or two candidates, liberals could elect their candidates. Liberal council members such as T. J. Kent, Jr., and Jeffery Cohelan (who became Berkeley's first liberal Democrat in Congress in 1959) advocated better schools, more city services, and higher property taxes to pay for these services.[7]

Until the late fifties white liberals had been unwilling to form a political coalition with blacks because they were afraid of a white reaction against liberals. Racism had continued to lurk just beneath the surface. Despite Berkeley's reputation as an educated, cultured, and in some ways progressive community, many local whites did not accept blacks. Southern roots may have played a part. For example, Claude Hutchison, who served as mayor from 1955 to 1963, was the grandson of slaveholders; his parents had been raised by black women. Sometimes racism was a matter of tone. A community leader displayed a blackamoor hitching post in his front yard; a prominent banker publicly referred to blacks as "these people." At other times racism was overt but subtle. When two black members of the Burbank Junior High YWCA attended a YWCA dance, they were told to check the coats. Sometimes racism was brutal. In 1963 a black male student at the University who had been invited to escort a white girl at a ceremony at a Cal football game was told moments before the event that he could not participate. A junior chamber of commerce official explained, "It was done to protect the mental and physical well-being of the girls."[8]

In 1959 white liberals were willing to overlook these difficulties to form a coalition with Berkeley's black community in order to take control of both the city council and the school board. White liberals, however, found little support inside the black community. Blacks distrusted liberal promises to improve city services and perceived correctly that the underlying racism in Berkeley's white community included some of the liberals who professed friendship. Black leaders were ready to form a coalition with the liberals, but only if the coalition involved biracial support for a biracial slate of candidates. Heretofore, a few blacks had run for office, but they had lost, due both to an inability to attract white votes and to the fact that Berkeley's offices were filled citywide. The liberals let traditional black leaders name a black council candidate. D. G. Gibson, Byron Rumford, Frankie Jones, and the National Association for the Advancement of Colored People (NAACP), a moderate civil rights organization, chose the Reverend Roy Nichols, a widely known minister whose church, Downs Memorial Methodist, had both black and white members. The local NAACP was also integrated; at some meetings more whites than blacks attended. It was closely tied to black churches. The Berkeley Democratic Caucus, composed of representatives from about twenty-five clubs affiliated with the California Democratic Council, named three white candidates, including

Bernice Hubbard May. The caucus's main success had been to elect T. J. Kent, Jr., to the council in 1957.[9]

Because the liberals ran as a slate, May campaigned with Nichols. When compaigning in white homes, they passed around pledge cards; in black homes, they collected folding money. Black hostesses always served homemade cookies. May also spoke at black churches, and when she circulated a sound truck in black neighborhoods, she used a driver who spoke in a black-accented voice. After one joint appearance at the home of a liberal in the hills, Nichols helped May on with her coat, patted her shoulder, and quickly left for another meeting. The hostess then turned to May and said, "Why, Bernice, that man doesn't even know he's a Negro!" A minor radical group had put an open housing initiative on the ballot to embarrass Nichols. The issue attracted little attention and drew condemnation from the NAACP, but it may have contributed to Nichols's defeat. The minister lost because the coalition had blundered and picked him to run for a two-year partial term in which only the leading candidate would win. Nichols might have won one of the four seats on the at-large list with a minority of the vote, but there was no way he or any other black could win a majority of the vote against a single conservative candidate for the two-year position. Of the four liberal candidates, only May and the incumbent Arthur Harris won. Although Nichols lost, he remained an optimist. "Every morning when I get up and look at this kinky hair I get so excited," he said. "I say, 'What other race in the twentieth century is going to have such a great experience?' "[10]

Nichols, however, had received more white votes than any black candidate in city history. Continued in-migration of blacks, a greater black registration effort, an increasing liberalism among younger faculty members at the growing University, and the aging of the conservative white majority predicted a future victory, if the liberal white-black coalition could be kept together. In 1961 the coalition was better organized. For one thing, the liberal minority of Kent, May, and Harris on the council had been strong enough to raise the liberal standard and, in some cases, to win. Berkeley's conservatives seemed worn out and lacked ideas; some of the less imaginative, including Mayor Hutchison, continued to stress anticommunism long after that idea had lost its popularity in Berkeley. In addition, President John Kennedy's election had added to the lustre of liberalism.[11]

In 1961 the coalition recruited able candidates for three council positions and for two seats on the school board. Nichols was elected to the school board; he became the first black board member in city history. T. J. Kent, Jr., was reelected to the council; he was joined by W. T. ("Zack") Brown, who worked for the Co-op. Wilmont Sweeney, an attorney, became the first black councilman. Sweeney was a member of the black political elite; he was Frankie Jones's nephew by marriage. Common sense, political cunning, and a fine sense of humor made Sweeney a superb councilman. In his more than a dozen years on the council, he never lost his sense of proportion. Yet he could be tough. He once said, "When I grew up in Texas, I came to find out early in life, that, when you're dealing with the bad guys, you've always got to remember that it's not enough that you win the game, and win it fairly and squarely, you've still got to win the fight afterwards out in the parking lot." With the incumbents Harris and May, the liberal white-black coalition claimed a five to four majority on the council. For the first time in Berkeley history the Republican business community did not control the council. [12]

Although the liberals had won, they were not a majority of the electorate. They had received support from many moderates who had concluded that the conservatives could not solve the city's problems. In the late fifties the liberals had quietly raised public awareness about the changes that were taking place. The city's excellent social welfare system was increasingly strained with the arrival of large numbers of poor blacks from the South. The situation of some of these families, which could only be described as pathological, came under the close scrutiny of the liberals. Noting connections among racism, low educational achievement, unemployability, slum housing, alcoholism, and crime, they argued that massive government intervention could break this cycle of poverty. Public schools should identify children from deprived families, and special efforts should be made to assist these children to attain normal learning rates. At the same time, welfare programs should be expanded to meet the needs of families where malnutrition, for example, contributed to the poor learning of children. The government should train adults for the skilled jobs that the economy was generating. These proposals were very expensive. They were also beyond the capacity of local government, and in 1961 liberals could not expect the state or federal governments to undertake such programs. [13]

One major, chronic problem for blacks was housing. Ever since the Bay Area's population explosion during World War II, Berkeley had suffered housing shortages. War workers had slept on cots in makeshift rental rooms in sheds or in storerooms. Residents had taken in boarders and had constructed jerry-built cottages on the backs of lots in neighborhoods zoned for single-family housing. The federal government had housed some war workers in huge, shoddily constructed apartment projects that were to be torn down at the end of the war. Codornices Village, which straddled the Berkeley-Albany line near the bay, housed 10,000 people. About half were white; half, black. After the war, few of its residents left the Bay Area, and thousands of ex-servicemen inundated Berkeley to use the G.I. bill to attend the University. Codornices Village remained, the cottages were filled, rents rose, and shortages continued. In this environment blacks suffered in two ways. First, unskilled, low income blacks were simply outbid in the housing market by affluent whites. Second, in a landlord's market, where tenants outnumbered vacancies, landlords could be selective, and many landlords chose not to rent to blacks. Blacks became concentrated in certain neighborhoods, including parts of Southwest Berkeley where Japanese-Americans had lived until they had been forcibly removed during the war. Black areas had high rents and high population densities, and the poorest blacks became trapped in Codornices Village, which turned into a black slum. In 1955–56 the conservative city government condemned and demolished the project. The conservatives, as a matter of philosophy, refused to build public housing.[14]

During the 1950s the housing crisis eased. After the last of the G.I.s had gone to college, the University's enrollment had fallen. At the same time the postwar boom pushed incomes up, and many residents left Berkeley to buy new homes in the suburbs of El Cerrito and Richmond to the north. Affluent whites built in Berkeley on the hills to the east that previously had been considered too steep for building. Many of these houses were on steel piers; the views were breathtaking. Middle-class whites abandoned older homes in the flatlands near the University and relocated in the hills. Some white families who were less well-off moved from the working-class housing that had been constructed in West Berkeley in the twenties into the homes near campus; other older homes became flats rented to students. Blacks moved out of congested Southwest Berkeley and bought small homes in working-class neighborhoods, and some of these areas became integrated. In the early sixties, according to one survey, 70 percent of Berkeley's black families were homeowners; this percentage was far higher than in Oakland or San Francisco. But affluent blacks who sought housing in all-white, upper-middle-class neighborhoods or in the hills discovered that neither sellers nor real estate agents wanted blacks to buy homes in prestigious neighborhoods. In 1960, 98 percent of Berkeley's blacks lived in twelve of twenty-eight census tracts.[15]

In 1961 a group of liberal law students conducted tests that showed widespread discrimination against black home buyers. Some agents flatly refused to show blacks homes in prestigious neighborhoods. Others were more flexible. They would show a black a home in such a neighborhood provided the seller and the seller's neighbors gave prior consent to the possible sale of the house to a black. The agent stressed that as the seller's representative, he had to do the seller's bidding. But the fact that an agent ignored the seller to accommodate the racist sentiments of the seller's neighbors suggested that the agent was less a representative of the seller than an enforcer of community opinion. The real estate industry was rigidly segregated. White companies employed only white agents and did not allow nonwhite companies—including integrated Asian-owned firms—to join the city's realty board; black companies sold to black clients in black neighborhoods. Almost the only blacks who succeeded in buying homes in the hills were those who made purchases through a front. One black judge, married to a white woman, complained that he had to pay for a house without seeing it.[16]

The rental market was also discriminatory. In 1961 CORE undertook a survey. When blacks or interracial couples went to look at vacant apartments, 38 percent were informed that the apartment had just been rented. When a white couple showed up later, however, the vacancy magically reappeared. In 1962 the Japanese-American Citizens' League made the same point using a telephone survey. Of landlords who had advertised rental units in the *Berkeley Daily Gazette*, 71 percent admitted during a telephone interview that they did not rent to blacks. This survey also detected discrimination against Asians, but it was far less common. The liberal council appointed a citizens' committee, chaired by Henry Poppic, that used these surveys as well as much black testimony to paint an unflattering portrait. When the council began to consider an ordinance banning discrimination, one unexpected source of support came from nonwhite foreign students at Cal. The University backed the proposed ordinance because it had adopted a nondiscriminatory policy in its own housing listings. In 1960, when the University had forced landlords to sign nondiscrimination pledges, about one-third had stopped listing property with the University.[17]

Racism in housing genuinely offended liberals on the city council. After two years of study, in 1963 liberals prepared a city ordinance to outlaw discrimination in both real estate sales and rentals. To liberals, the ordinance was morally correct. It also addressed an issue important to the black community, which had complained about discrimination in housing for years. Nor did the measure cost any money. Liberals intended to raise property taxes, but most of the money was to be spent on schools, and the remainder was needed to repair Berkeley's worn-out streets, sewers, and firehouses. (Conservatives, perhaps sensing that they were going to lose control, had virtually abandoned maintenance of the city's physical plant in the fifties.) Housing was one of the few areas involving discrimination where the city council could act. Educational matters had to be left to the school board; job discrimination had been addressed by the state government. Finally, the issue pitted the liberal council against the real estate interests. This delighted the liberals, since none of them had been elected with the support of the real estate lobby, which along with the *Berkeley Daily Gazette* and the city's retail merchants had formed the core of Berkeley's conservative establishment.[18]

In the end this ordinance proved to be very expensive for the liberals. Had it applied only to rental housing, it would have pried open opportunities for the blacks who needed the most help. Opposition would have been restricted to large-scale landlords like Otis Marston, an archconservative who helped organize Berkeley Citizens United (BCU). The BCU was a political organization opposed to desegregation, higher taxes, or increased government spending. The housing measure also applied to home sales. Although blacks naturally applauded the sweeping nature of the ordinance, thoughtful black leaders noted that this aspect of the measure was largely symbolic. Blacks needed good schools and high-paying jobs a lot more than the theoretical right to buy expensive homes in the all-white hills. Black voters could not help but notice the limited way in which the liberal council was prepared to help the black community with its problems. This latter point escaped the more naive liberals, but the shrewder ones recognized that the ordinance would not lead to a massive black migration into the hills. Liberals calculated that symbolic gesture was more important than real change, which was beyond the power of the council to enact anyway. In a sense, they were tragically correct in this analysis. Blacks did praise the liberal coalition for having the courage to take a stand against racism.[19]

What the liberals did not count on was the almost hysterical reaction of hills residents. "We found out," recalled Councilwoman May, " 'It's all right to have a brother of any color, but I don't want him on my block!' " Many conservatives reacted out of an emotion altogether inappropriate to the effect of the ordinance. Symbolic gesture, it turned out, operated on both sides, and an ugly racism bubbled to the surface. Of course, Berkeley's residents were sophisticated, and so the racism seldom took overt forms. Rather, opponents of the ordinance defined the issue as one of private property rights. The government, declared opponents, had no right to dictate to whom a person might sell his house. By phrasing the issue in this way, opponents evaded the racial issue. Rather, conservatives attacked the ordinance as an example of the liberal penchant, evident since the New Deal, for imposing arbitrary and compulsory government upon the individual. The liberal boot, opponents suggested, had just crushed private property rights.[20]

Opponents circulated a petition to put the ordinance on the city ballot. It was the first local referendum since 1929. The measure was voted on at the regular city election in April 1963. The hot and furious campaign was made more so by the perception that the outcome would be close. Conservatives calculated that they could gain enough moderate votes at this election not only to repeal the ordinance but also to defeat the liberal candidates and regain control of the council. On both sides, candidates were forced to take strong stands. Wallace Johnson, the conservative candidate for mayor, tried to waffle but in the end opposed the ordinance; his opponent, Dr. Fred Stripp, embraced the ordinance wholeheartedly. A cross was burned on Stripp's lawn. The culprits, it turned out, were three Berkeley High School students. The *Berkeley Daily Gazette* was flooded with letters from its readers, and an unprecedented 83 percent of the voters went to the polls.[21]

The ordinance was repealed by a vote of 22,750 to 20,456, and Stripp lost to Johnson by an almost identical margin. Oddly, the two incumbent liberal council candidates, Harris and May, won, and so the liberals retained their five to four majority on the council. Apparently, a handful of moderates who could not stomach the ordinance also opposed handing the city back to the conservatives. The result was highly partisan: 70 percent of Democrats favored the ordinance; 84 percent of Republicans opposed it. Partisanship, however, masked rather than revealed the most significant differences. Proponents of the ordinance tended to be black, Jewish Democrats, or Democrats who expressed no religious preference; many were highly educated professionals or civil servants, under age forty, and Berkeley residents for less than five years. Opponents tended to be working-class Catholic Democrats or, especially, Republicans; many were retirees and housewives, over age fifty-five, and Berkeley residents for more than twenty years.[22]

The damage from this election was enormous; the entire history of the city in the sixties might have been different if this issue had never arisen. As it was, the issue and the election returns revealed painful truths that could not be camouflaged. Blacks had long known that they were not entirely welcome in Berkeley, but they had been flattered by the election of Byron Rumford, Roy Nichols, and Wilmont Sweeney and by the personal kindnesses of white liberals. Now, blacks learned that a sizable portion of Berkeley's whites feared or despised them. This humiliating fact, broadcast to the world in the publicity that accompanied the election, upset local blacks. On election night, after the returns came in, Councilwoman Bernice Hubbard May walked along Sacramento Street in Southwest Berkeley. She met a number of black campaign workers; many were in tears—she cried, too. Berkeley's growing racial tension in the sixties, and especially the rise of militancy among young blacks, can be dated to this election. Blacks also learned that white liberals could not deliver on their promises, even when those promises cost no money and had mostly symbolic value. The liberals were shown to be politically naive, foolish, and irresponsible. Never again did blacks entirely trust white liberals, who could neither control nor understand their own white constituents. For their part, white liberals were shaken and demoralized.[23]

Once raised, the housing issue did not die but returned in a different form. For years Byron Rumford had wanted a state law barring discrimination in housing, but Governor Brown had urged the black legislator to wait. After the Berkeley vote, wise politicians, such as Assembly Speaker Jesse Unruh, saw danger in this issue, and Unruh cautioned Brown to move slowly. But the Berkeley vote made Rumford more determined than ever, and Brown's conscience led him to sponsor an antidiscriminatory bill. Brown, Unruh, Rumford, and organized labor used their political muscle to push the bill through the state senate, where conservative Democrats, such as Hugh Burns, opposed it. The law, named the Rumford Act in honor of its initiator, was passed in

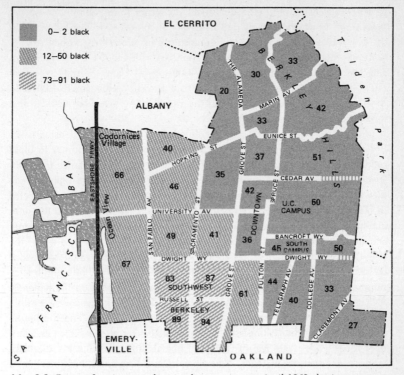

Map 2.2. Percent favoring open housing by census tract, April 1963 election
(Sources: U.S., Bureau of the Census, 1960; Leonard A. Marascuilo, "Attitudes toward De Facto Segregation in a Northern City" (UCB, 1964–65, ERIC research report ED003825, 1967), 44.)

June 1963. As Burns had predicted, the measure set off a firestorm of opposition. Real estate interests, giddy from their victory in Berkeley, launched a statewide initiative, Proposition 14, both to repeal the Rumford Act and to prohibit any state legislation outlawing housing discrimination.[24]

Proposition 14 qualified for the November 1964 ballot, where its presence helped George Murphy, a conservative Republican, win election to the U.S. Senate. All over the state working-class, white Democrats, especially homeowners who lived near black areas, overwhelmingly approved Proposition 14. The statewide vote was nearly two-to-one in favor. Oddly, in Berkeley the measure lost by almost two-to-one. There were several reasons for this local vote. The hysteria of 1963 had dissipated, and voters had come to understand the largely symbolic nature of the issue. In order to heal the community's wounds,

Mayor Wallace Johnson led the council, except for John DeBonis, to oppose Proposition 14. It is also likely that a number of conservatives had left Berkeley; the city was no longer the sort of community in which they wished to live. Some speculated that the passage of Proposition 14 led to the Watts riot in Los Angeles less than a year later; both the housing issue and the riot, as well as the FSM turmoil, contributed to Governor Brown's defeat for reelection in 1966. That same year the author of the Rumford Act was narrowly defeated for a state senate seat.[25]

In the early 1960s liberals on the council dealt with another housing issue. For about ten years speculators had been demolishing older homes to build shoddy apartments. Often called plastics, due to their resemblance to insubstantial, throwaway toys, many of these buildings were near campus, where they housed a considerable number of students. Similar apartments constructed in black Southwest Berkeley pushed that area's population density to two-and-one-half times the city average. For years the hills had had low-density zoning, and none of its residents wanted a higher density. If nothing was done, the long-term effect of the existing zoning was clear: Berkeley would be divided between a small number of affluent white homeowners in the hills and a large number of students and poor blacks jammed into apartments on the flatlands. A black majority was probable. White liberals rallied black homeowners with a promise to ban apartments by rezoning black neighborhoods, and the homeowners responded with enthusiasm. In this battle black real estate interests joined their usual white rivals against the white liberals from the hills and the black homeowners from the flatlands. The liberal council members had the votes to rezone Southwest Berkeley, and in 1965 they did so.[26]

The liberals never dealt with the housing problems of the black poor. Neither rezoning nor the 1963 open housing ordinance had addressed that problem, and although liberals endorsed the idea of public housing, both state law, which required local voters to approve public housing, and lack of funds made it unlikely that any would be built in Berkeley. When the city had undertaken urban renewal on the site of Codornices Village in 1956, the conservative council had rejected any housing. That site was designated for industrial development, despite a lack of interest in it for that purpose. In the early sixties liberals planned to demolish Oceanview, a poor neighborhood in West Berkeley, for another industrial project. Surrounded by factories and warehouses, Oceanview had been zoned for industry. Nevertheless, it was a residential community. Oceanview was naturally integrated, nearly half of its residents were homeowners, and the homeowners had lived in Berkeley an average of twenty years. Many minority residents had bought their homes when they had found it difficult to buy property elsewhere in Berkeley, and there was visible pride of ownership. If Oceanview was condemned, few of its residents could afford to buy or rent elsewhere in Berkeley. Yet the liberal council proposed its demolition. "Apparently we are conducting a *War on Poverty* with one hand and a *War on the Poor* with another," observed one critic. The homeowners in Oceanview fought the council; they were joined by the attorney Stephen Bingham, a young white radical, and the council finally yielded.[27]

Liberals also proposed urban renewal in the South Campus area. Although the University planned to build dormitories, no housing for the poor was included. In 1966, after public hearings produced intense opposition, the council abandoned the South Campus urban renewal project. That same year the council established a city housing authority to take advantage of federal grants, and in the late sixties the city did obtain 900 federally subsidized rental units. In 1967 the city applied for a major federal grant under the Model Cities program to redevelop Southwest Berkeley. Although the prospectus dealt frankly with housing, it proposed rehabilitation of existing units rather than the construction of any new housing. Of course, there was no vacant land on which to build in Southwest Berkeley. By 1967 the liberals had been in power six years, and they had given their black supporters little housing. They had ingratiated themselves with some black homeowners through rezoning, and they had passed a symbolic ordinance that the electorate had repudiated. This record did not win applause in the black community.[28]

Blacks also had a deep interest in education. While a large portion of Berkeley's whites in 1960 were either the elderly or students too young to have families, the city's minorities tended to be young adults and their children. During the 1950s the number of minority children had grown rapidly, and by 1960 public school enrollment was 32 percent black, 8 percent Asian, and 4 percent Chicano. Many black and other minority families had moved to Berkeley because of the excellent reputation of the city's schools. Each year Berkeley High, a citywide school, sent large numbers to the University; in 1959 it was honored as the best comprehensive high school in the United States. One survey found that black parents had high ambitions; they wanted their children to be doctors, lawyers, scientists, and businessmen.[29]

This black enthusiasm for education was not met by local educators' enthusiasm for blacks. During the late 1930s two Berkeley elementary schools had high black enrollments, although both had white majorities. Despite the growing black presence, neither the school board nor administrators hired any blacks. Not only were principals and teachers white, so were gardeners, janitors, and lunchroom personnel. Black leaders who privately pleaded for change were ignored. Finally, in 1939 one black leader, Mrs. Frances Albrier, ran for the city council. She proposed that the school board hire black teachers in elementary schools with large black enrollments. She lost badly, and private pressure resumed. During World War II the school board agreed to hire a black teacher. The board gave the teacher a kindergarten class in Southwest Berkeley. Kindergarten attendance was optional, and the board made it easy for any white parents who objected to their child being assigned to the black teacher's kindergarten to withdraw that child from school.[30]

During the 1950s the school board and the district's all-white central office never came to grips with the changing racial composition of the city's schools. Officials made a few concessions. During the fifties they hired a number of minority teachers, including Asians. All taught in schools with large minority enrollments. The district began to employ blacks in nonteaching positions. Black youths were allowed to swim in the Berkeley High swimming pool, but only on Friday nights. A system of de facto segregation emerged in the elementary schools; in 1960, 92 percent of black students attended six of the city's fourteen elementary schools. Segregation was due to housing patterns and the city's neighborhood schools. However, in one racially mixed neighborhood the district allowed a child to choose one of two elementary schools. One school was overwhelmingly white, the other largely black, and the optional attendance zone subtly drew white students to the white school and black students to the black school. During the fifties the district increasingly ran two separate school systems: one by and for educated, affluent, and academically tough-minded whites in the hills; the other, operated by the same people, for poor blacks in the flatlands. Only in 1957 did the district place its first black teacher in a hills school, and that action was taken at the insistence of a group of white, liberal parents in the hills. Another black teacher assigned to a hills school recalled that on the first day of school a white child mistook the woman for a maid. The child was startled to find that a black person could be a teacher.[31]

In 1960 no one recognized the problems created by de facto segregation in the elementary schools. Black children learned a lot, and by the time these children were eleven or twelve, many of them probably had been taught more than their parents, who had received limited schooling in the South. But few of the black children from the flatlands had learned as much as most of the white children from the hills. Parents, teachers, and peers had all pushed the white children to work much harder. Nationally standardized tests showed a painful division. While one-fourth of Berkeley's children scored in the bottom 10 percent, one-third scored in the top 10 percent.[32]

The crisis came in junior high school, at ages twelve to fifteen, when children left their neighborhood schools to attend one of the city's three junior highs. Although one school drew almost entirely from the hills, the other two contained whites and blacks from a variety of backgrounds. Poor blacks and affluent whites attended the same school, but they had little contact. Like many other cities, Berkeley assigned students to tracks based upon academic ability. There were four tracks—largely two for whites and two for blacks. Students in the two lower tracks, mostly black, had few demands placed upon them. Black peer pressure reinforced academic nonperformance, even as black parents continued to believe that their children were excelling. In fact, most black students fell further and further behind. When black children got to Berkeley High School, they were told to take shop classes and other "practical" subjects. An occasional black student questioned how such courses helped prepare for college, and he was informed that he had missed the route to college when he had not taken algebra in junior high. Some black students dropped out of Berkeley High, others got diplomas and joined the military, and only a few went to college.[33]

Blacks also found discrimination at Berkeley High School. Not only did tracking, which began in junior high, put black and white students into different programs, but school activities separated the races. Many blacks played sports and performed in musical programs, where white admiration of the stereotypical black entertainer overcame (or reinforced) prejudice. But few blacks worked on the school's daily newspaper, except as typesetters. None acted in school plays; in 1960 interracial kissing in a high school play was inconceivable. But what rankled most was that a group of white-only, selective social clubs controlled the school's student politics and social life. Members routinely became Greeks at Cal. In high school this moneyed, cultured, and well-groomed set held exclusive social events on school property, wore distinctive jackets and other clothing, and received permission to reserve their own luncheon areas. Many whites, including some inside the social clubs, deplored the effect that this privileged elite had upon the school.[34]

A diploma from Berkeley High was worth little, because the economy had changed. By 1960 industrial production was being automated, and although production grew spectacularly during the sixties, it did so with only a small increase in the workforce. While Berkeley's postwar black immigrants generally kept their jobs, their children could not easily find industrial work. Nor was the service sector open to blacks. For example, retail merchants in downtown Berkeley refused to hire blacks. Unskilled, unemployable, and unprepared for college, young blacks became embittered and enraged by the trick that they believed the white-dominated school system had played upon them. Unemployed black teenagers joined with their disappointed parents to demand the reform of an educational system that failed to meet the needs of blacks. Blacks demanded change, and white liberals, appalled at the shabby way in which the schools had served blacks, reinforced those demands.[35]

By the 1960s the time had come to dismantle Berkeley's de facto segregated school system. When the Reverend Roy Nichols, representing the local NAACP, first raised the issue in 1958, the school board responded by appointing a committee to investigate. The white chairman, Redmond C. Staats, Jr., began his study as a dispassionate legal fact-finder, but by the time he had finished, he became convinced, largely through articulate black testimony, that the schools needed to make drastic changes in order to meet black needs in a fair way. Nichols had served on this committee, and in 1961 he, along with the white liberal Carol Sibley, was elected to the board. They joined Paul Sanazaro and Spurgeon Avakian, and for the first time the board had a four-to-one liberal majority. Even then, liberals on the board hesitated to ,act. They feared losing control of the board. Furthermore, the highly respected school superintendent, C. H. Wennerberg, instinctively opposed change. Lacking the temperament for controversy, he had devoted his career to improving the schools' academic performance. The superintendent had a like-minded staff. Liberals on the board saw little impetus for desegregation coming from school officials.[36]

On the other hand, a number of parents of both races, some teachers, and liberal community leaders had expressed concern. The board tapped that concern in 1961 and 1962 with two interracial conferences. At these workshops teachers, parents, and community leaders explored the ways in which the schools might deal effectively with race relations and the needs of black students. In no other city in the United States did so much talk precede any action toward desegregation of the public schools. This talk paid off in two ways. First, community leaders and teachers established contacts that were useful in the years ahead, when implementation of desegregation often brought unanticipated crises. Second, the sessions produced a consensus both about the nature of racial problems in Berkeley and about the solutions.[37]

Participants quickly concluded that the problems in the higher grades were impossible to solve, because those children had had such varied experiences both at home and in elementary schools. The school board could not change a child's home life, but it could alter the nature of elementary education. Blacks and whites agreed that their children had different early educational experiences. In mostly black schools teachers had low expectations, peer groups pressured pupils against excelling, and parents were uninvolved. A number of studies suggested that middle-class children, whether black, white, or Asian, did well in school, and that when middle-class children were put into a classroom with poor children, the performance of the middle-class children did not decline. The performance of the poor children, however, improved. Poor children who attended middle-class schools did better because teacher expectations were higher, peer pressure against excelling diminished, and parents became more involved.[38]

In 1962 the board appointed a committee, chaired by John S. Hadsell, to recommend a program for desegregation. While the committee was meeting in 1963, liberals won both the city council and school board elections. The board's four to one liberal majority held. Ignoring pressure both from some blacks who wanted massive desegregation immediately and from some whites who opposed any changes, the board decided to desegregate the schools in a program that would take up to ten years. This committed, cautious approach was in keeping with the sentiments that had developed in the interracial workshops. A black-white liberal consensus had emerged to desegregate the elementary schools. To do so, however, required massive busing, and liberals did not relish such an undertaking. The Hadsell report, issued in November 1963, postponed elementary desegregation and instead recommended redrawing the attendance boundaries for the city's three junior highs. When this proposal was made, a public meeting drew 1,200 angry opponents. However, a second meeting attracted 2,500 residents and included a number of supporters of desegregation. As in the case of the housing ordinance, however, it is not clear that the liberals understood the vehemence of the opposition.[39]

To understand this opposition, one must know something about the schools involved. Willard Junior High, named in honor of the prohibitionist Frances Willard, had been built on the flatlands but near the hills south of the University. It was naturally integrated and had had relatively harmonious race relations. Few of its students were truly poor and few well-to-do. Garfield Junior High was in the hills north of the University. Its students were almost all whites from the affluent hills; Garfield had an excellent academic reputation. Burbank Junior High had been built on the flatlands toward the west of the city. It was rapidly becoming an all-minority school. Many of its black students were from poor families, and its white and Asian students were not affluent. Because of the lower socioeconomic class of its students, Burbank had not offered several of the demanding academic courses found at Garfield and Willard. Liberals proposed ignoring Willard but shifting many white children who lived in the hills from Garfield to Burbank. When this proposal drew the wrath of the parents of those children, the board reexamined the issue. A clever teacher, Marjorie Ramsey, then proposed a solution that was eventually adopted: Burbank became a citywide ninth grade school, while Willard and Garfield were given seventh and eighth grades, with former Burbank students moving to Garfield.[40]

When the newly integrated junior high schools opened in the fall of 1964, matters went smoothly at Willard and Burbank. Willard had few new students, social classes were blurred, and the school had gained some space from the realignment. Burbank had an excellent principal and specially recruited ninth grade teachers. The main difficulty was former Burbank students' resentment against the "invasion" from Garfield and Willard. At Garfield there were difficulties. Many hills parents resented what they considered to be the destruction of an especially fine academic school; their children treated the children from Burbank with sullenness. To the ex-Burbank children, the situation was worse: they had lost their school and had been tossed into an environment which they neither accepted nor understood; they expressed their resentments physically. These problems might have been overcome, but the principal was weak, and the teachers lacked experience in dealing with minorities. Some overreacted; others failed to establish their authority. Although the board regularly issued optimistic reports about Garfield, it remained unstable during the remainder of the decade. In August 1968 it was renamed in honor of Martin Luther King, Jr.[41]

When the board had adopted the Ramsey plan in the spring of 1964, it had decided, over the objections of Nichols and Sibley, to dismiss the incumbent superintendent. The board then conducted a national search for a new superintendent and invited Neil V. Sullivan for an interview. Sullivan had had an outstanding record working with blacks in private schools in Prince Edward County, Virginia, during the period when that county had closed its public schools to avoid integrating them. Treated to a potluck dinner at Sibley's apartment, Sullivan, the board members, and their wives adjourned to Sibley's spacious bedroom for the formal interview. Sullivan later cracked that "he was hired for superintendent of schools in Carol Sibley's bedroom." The new superintendent was an energetic, enthusiastic, and compassionate man of deep moral convictions. Not only did he have empathy for blacks and their problems, but he also had the capacity to motivate subordinates, the ability to speak effectively in public, and the appetite to innovate. Although his experience with desegregation was enormously valuable, his commitment to his cause sometimes slighted education. Among the innovations that he proposed was an appalling plan to put thousands of Berkeley children into an educational park where six-year-olds and eighteen-year-olds would rub shoulders on a single sprawling campus with dozens of buildings. His sincerity exceeded his wisdom, just as his vision exceeded his prudence. Despite his limitations, Sullivan provided excellent leadership for school desegregation.[42]

After the board had adopted the desegregation plan for the fall of 1964, conservatives, heartened by their victory over the housing ordinance in April 1963, decided to challenge the liberals on this issue as well. They did so by creating the Parents Association for Neighborhood Schools (PANS) and by filing a petition to recall the four board members who had voted to desegregate the junior highs. Before the election could be held, two liberals on the board resigned; Nichols left Berkeley to accept a church in the East, while Spurgeon Avakian was appointed to a judgeship. So only two members were involved in the recall. The special election was held on October 6, 1964. Under state law, in a recall election candidates filed against the incumbents. In other words, the recall succeeded if a challenger gathered more votes than an incumbent. In this election a former principal of Garfield Junior High filed for one of the seats. Although PANS began the campaign with optimism, they lost the election by about 23,000 to 15,000. "Berkeley goes down the tube," screamed the headline of the reactionary *BCU Bulletin*, the monthly publication of Berkeley Citizens United, the city's most prominent conservative political organization. Voter turnout had dropped markedly since the 1963 city election.[43]

The conservative rout had several causes. First, conservatives continued to leave the city. Just after the recall's failure, the BCU advised, "If you don't

want to know the Negro mind, then it is time for you to move over the hill."
Second, unlike the housing ordinance, there was no easy way for conservatives
to oppose the board's desegregation plan without appearing to be racist. But
most important in the PANS defeat was the weakness of the two conservative
candidates, who at numerous public meetings revealed their poor grasp both of
the school board's task and of the status of Berkeley's blacks. In contrast, the
incumbent liberals were effective campaigners who won people to their cause.
Carol Sibley, in particular, emerged from this campaign with enhanced prestige and respect. The low turnout also suggested that many residents who did
not like the board's action also resented the recall. To many, the election seemed
mean and petty; three board seats were to be filled at the next regular election,
which was only six months away. Victory did not surprise the liberals, for they
sensed that the hysteria that had accompanied the housing election had dissipated. They were, however, surprised by the margin.[44]

After the recall victory, liberals on the school board proceeded with plans to
desegregate the elementary schools. The board, in other words, came to endorse the position that community leaders had reached in the workshops held
in 1961 and 1962. In order to achieve integration, however, it was necessary
to bus large numbers of small children. Since more white than black parents
opposed busing, the board might have closed schools in black neighborhoods
and sent those children to the remaining white schools. Unlike many other
cities, Berkeley refused to make blacks bear all the hardships. In part, this
policy showed black strength in the liberal coalition that now governed the city.
But the decision was also rooted in certain facts about Berkeley's elementary
schools. The schools in the more densely populated black neighborhoods were
physically larger than those in the lightly populated hills. To have closed only
black schools would have eliminated some of the city's larger, better facilities,
and it would have led to an unreasonable number of school buses trying to
unload children at the physically restricted sites of the hills schools. In the end
the board decided to put grades one through three in the hills schools and
grades four through six in the flatlands schools. Children in kindergarten would
attend neighborhood schools. Each flatlands school was paired with two or
three smaller hills schools.[45]

The Berkeley school district undertook the first non-court-ordered mass busing in the United States. It was a courageous decision; it was also risky. No
one could foresee how the plan would work. If all went well, no student would
have to be bused for more than three years, and each school would be about
half white and half black. (Although no one planned it, Asians came to hold
the balance of power.) The longest bus ride was less than three miles each way.
The new superintendent stressed planning and preparation. First, parents whose
children attended schools that were to be paired visited with each other. Sullivan encouraged parents to speak frankly; he hoped that the uncovering of mu-

tual fears would reduce those fears. He also wanted biracial friendships to develop. The next step was to send classes of students from the paired schools on
exchange visits. Children would gain familiarity with the territory and make
friends. The visits, however, were too short to allow friendships to develop.
Sullivan urged local organizations, such as the Boy Scouts, to undertake similar pairings, and these programs were more successful. Sullivan then called for
a handful of black students to transfer voluntarily from the flatlands schools to
the hills schools. Although this relieved overcrowding in certain schools, the
main purposes were to introduce white children in the hills schools to a small
number of blacks in order to reduce later friction and to give some black children a sense of what attending a hills school with whites would be like. It also
gave teachers in the hills schools their first contact with black students. Finally,
the superintendent required teachers to study race relations.[46]

Numerous community meetings produced painfully frank discussions. At one
meeting a white opponent of integration said of black children, "They're happy
*where they are!*" An annoyed black mother replied, "I see what it is—you're
afraid of Negro kids! Why? We have something to offer you but you've always
turned us down. What if *our* children should slip back in their studies by
coming up here? Did you ever think of that?" Many blacks and some whites
applauded. Another white suggested a gradual approach—waiting another generation. A black mother fumed, "What do you mean—it'll come? By magic?
There ain't gonna be no magic! We've gotta do it ourselves." Another black
mother then faced the audience and said, "We've been waiting ever since the
Civil War. We can't wait any longer!" This black bravado masked great uneas-
iness. Black parents wanted to do what was best for their children. A black
counselor, speaking about her own child, said, "But think of his future: Will
he be happier in a world that is our Negro world, with all the handicaps we
Negroes know, or in a world of Negro and white together as it is meant to be
and can become?" Black hope met white fear. The only difference between
white attitudes in Berkeley and in Virginia, Sullivan once said, was that in
Berkeley people were "more polite."[47]

Only after this long, elaborate minuet lasting four years did the mass busing
of elementary school children take place in the fall of 1968. Sullivan's careful
preparation paid off. Unlike the desegregation of the junior highs, the much
more difficult busing of half the city's elementary students went surprisingly
well. There were few incidents. Of course, one reason for the lack of opposition was the changing nature of the students. Between 1964 and 1968 families
hostile to integration had left the district. Sullivan gave opponents time to change
their minds or leave town. Busing drove some whites out of the schools, but
white enrollment did not fall, because the experiment attracted other whites to
Berkeley. Many white parents wanted their children to go to integrated schools
and learn about other cultures; these parents, however, refused to send their
children to inferior schools. To hold these children, Berkeley stressed quality

education as well as integration. Sullivan did not stay in Berkeley; in the fall of 1968, much to the consternation of community leaders, he suddenly left to become commissioner of education for Massachusetts. Finally, despite the absence of overt incidents, the entire process was unsettling and raised racial tensions in ways that could never be admitted. Integrationists published a book of photographs to show how well white and black children got along; the children appear in the book arm-in-arm. But the eyes of these children suggest confusion, anxiety, and fear.[48]

Neither blacks nor whites were fully ready for the change. Perhaps, given the history of American race relations, neither race ever could have been ready. Most white families who remained in Berkeley and kept their children in public schools had strong convictions about the immorality of segregation. They were prepared to experiment, using their children to combat a racism that they detested. They hoped that if their children and the community's black children went to school together that the next generation of Americans would be less race-conscious, and that in time white racism would diminish. This sacrifice might not have been as noble as Abraham's, but it was a sacrifice. For black parents the issue was quite different. They hoped that integration would enable their children to receive the kind of education necessary to join the mainstream of American society and attain the kinds of jobs that they dreamed about for their children. They had little desire to adopt white cultural values, however, and they feared that their children would lose their black identities. Black children received mixed signals from parents, peers, and whites about how to respond to the experience. While levels of anxiety were raised in both black and white families, it seems likely that the greatest anxiety existed among young blacks.[49]

Although desegregation worked in the elementary schools and at Burbank and Willard, it did not at Garfield, and by the mid-1960s Berkeley High had become a cauldron of racial tension. Black students cursed and spat upon white teachers; students fought along racial lines. Blacks formed the Black Student Union (BSU), which demanded and got more black counselors, black materials for the curriculum, and 'soul food' on the school menu. The BSU also made it difficult for blacks to maintain friendships with whites at school. Blacks dominated the football team, white attendance at games dwindled, and no whites went to the postgame dances. It was an ironic twist to earlier years, when all-white social clubs had held dances on school property. In 1969 the administration established a Community High School for alienated, countercultural white students. When blacks demanded their own alternative program, the administration opened Black House, a racially segregated unit. Meanwhile, Chicanos dropped out in large numbers, and many Asians, who never protested, graduated with honors. By then the liberal dreams of the early sixties seemed remote.[50]

School desegregation did have one curious result in Berkeley. From the 1940s until the mid-1960s, when desegregation began, the percentage of black students in the Berkeley schools had risen steadily. With desegregation, the percentage stopped growing. In part, this was a function of the age structure of the city's black community, which had migrated to Berkeley during the forties and fifties. But the fact that black enrollment in Berkeley stopped growing while it continued to increase in neighboring Oakland suggests another possibility. It may be that some black families preferred to live in Oakland, where their children could attend undemanding, all-black neighborhood schools rather than in Berkeley, where children had to be bused and then had to compete with white children. Oakland's white leaders opposed busing to end school segregation, and they quietly gave blacks control of Oakland's black schools in return for the continuation of de facto segregated schools. For blacks in Oakland who wanted desegregation, a move to Berkeley promised a speedier result than a lawsuit. In fact, no one sued to desegregate the schools in either city.[51]

Despite concerns about housing and education, the main problem for blacks in Berkeley was jobs. During World War II Bay Area federal contractors who had hired skilled labor through union hiring halls received white workers. Although the federal government pressured employers to hire blacks, many American Federation of Labor (AFL) craft unions resisted admitting blacks. Many employers then hired blacks either outside union channels or through newly chartered black craft locals. In other cases, however, the Congress of Industrial Organizations (CIO) organized entire factories that included black workers as members. Blacks battled whites, the CIO fought the AFL, employers maneuvered amid these conflicts, and the federal government kept one eye on labor peace and the other on war production. At the end of the war, these disputes continued. Blacks, however, lost the leverage that they had held during the war's labor shortages, and the integrated CIO gradually lost ground to the more segregated AFL. The federal government left the issue of job discrimination to the states. In the Bay Area some CIO unions were communist-influenced, and with the rise of McCarthyism in the early 1950s, these unions were discredited. Although the campaign against job discrimination waned, black leaders forgave neither employers nor unions that continued discrimination.[52]

When Pat Brown was elected governor in 1958, he promised Byron Rumford that he would ask the legislature to establish the Fair Employment Practices Commission to monitor and punish job discrimination. California was the last major industrial state to establish such a commission. Although the legislature set up the commission in 1959, its effect was limited. In 1960 Berkeley's unemployment rate was 3.7 percent; black unemployment was 10.6 percent. The local labor market had few openings for blacks. Factory jobs did not increase, and, more than in other metropolitan areas, large firms obtained workers through union hiring halls; many unions still did not admit blacks. Attitudes varied.

The machinists' union was 20 to 25 percent nonwhite, while some craft unions were all-white. There were many black plasterers, painters, and plumbers, but they could not always find work. Contractors hired blacks for industrial projects but resisted employing blacks in residential construction on the grounds that nearby white homeowners might object. The local grocery chains were unionized and had nondiscriminatory clauses in their contracts; yet in the late fifties only one of the five chains had any minority employees. Representative Jeffery Cohelan's former union, the dairy drivers, had no black members and claimed that white customers objected to black drivers.[53]

Small businesses offered few opportunities. Many owners hired friends or relatives. One employer summed up the attitude of many when he said, "I'm not prejudiced; I just prefer to have an all-white staff." Another explained, "They wouldn't fit in, and besides we don't have adequate wash-room facilities." In 1959 only two of eighty-eight large firms had any black sales representatives; companies felt that blacks lost customers. Retailing was closed, too. In 1956 a black maid at Hink's department store was the only black employee in all of downtown Berkeley. Downtown merchants worried that black employees would attract black shoppers and that affluent white shoppers from the hills would then abandon downtown for suburban shopping centers. In the whole city there was apparently only one black waitress. A private employment agency stated that it took ten times as long to place a black as a white with the same qualifications. Agencies routinely accepted discriminatory listings and assumed that employers accepted only white workers unless the employer specified otherwise.[54]

Even black influence at the ballot box did not translate into jobs for blacks in the city government. Berkeley's excellent civil service system set educational standards so high that few blacks qualified. In 1961, 79 percent of city workers were white; 18 percent were black. The percentage was close to that of the city's population, but almost all of these black workers collected garbage or swept streets; there was only one black fireman and no black policemen. Over the years the city had hired a few black police officers, but they had resigned to take better paying jobs with the FBI or large corporations. The city had few black clerks, although many worked in state and federal offices. The University staff, too, was virtually all white. After 1961 the liberal council's efforts to hire black administrators were stymied by John D. Phillips, the longtime city manager legally responsible for making the appointments. Only in 1963 did the city begin to recruit minorities aggressively. The following year fifteen of the street and sewer firms that held city contracts remained all-white. Although the council began to require city contractors to hire minorities, the city was unable to extend these requirements to the building trades because of union opposition.[55]

By 1960 black leaders had decided to pressure companies that served black customers to hire more black workers. Informational picketing led a number of businesses to hire black workers, but civil rights leaders found that firms without significant numbers of black customers did not respond to this sort of pressure. Other firms cited labor contracts that forced them to use union hiring halls. Concluding that they needed to use more aggressive tactics, Bay Area black leaders looked closely at black activity in the South.[56]

The Bay Area civil rights movement borrowed heavily from the southern movement organized by black college students who called themselves the Student Non-Violent Coordinating Committee. SNCC's techniques and strategy were applied to the Bay Area. For example, SNCC had made effective use of an elaborate statewide phone network in Mississippi, and Bay Area leaders used phone trees that enabled them to reach large numbers of supporters relatively quickly. SNCC had pioneered the use of ham radio stations and mobile car radios; Bay Area civil rights leaders routinely used walkie-talkies to communicate during large-scale demonstrations. Both in the South and in the Bay Area, leaders engaged in a strategy that simultaneously produced confrontation and negotiation. Confrontations demonstrated commitment and seriousness of purpose, and as time went on, the large size of some protests also showed that the protests had considerable biracial support. But the organizers were always willing to call off demonstrations, with all the bad publicity that they produced, in order to hold private negotiations. Although civil rights leaders were never willing to compromise on basic demands, they were willing to be flexible in terms of implementation and to yield graciously on minor points in order to give their opponents the opportunity to save face.[57]

In the Bay Area, southern-oriented SNCC was far less important than the Congress of Racial Equality. Locally, CORE led the civil rights movment, although actual demonstrations were carried out by ad hoc committees organized for particular occasions. Targets shifted from San Francisco to Oakland to Richmond to Berkeley. Leaders did not want to single out one city, because that would suggest that problems were local rather than regional. Although demonstrators came from throughout the Bay Area, a large number were white college students from Berkeley; many later became activists in the Free Speech Movement. Specific targets were chosen carefully. In late 1963 civil rights groups picketed Mel's drive-ins; the owner was Harold Dobbs, the Republican candidate for mayor of San Francisco. Mel's quickly agreed to hire more blacks. Meanwhile, Berkeley CORE, under Jack Weinberg's leadership, organized up to 150 pickets nightly for three weeks in front of 180 of the 200 businesses on Shattuck Avenue in downtown Berkeley. No settlement, however, was reached, although Hink's, the major local store, signed an agreement in July 1964. This agreement came nearly a year after Montgomery Ward, a national chain, had signed a similar pledge. In early 1964 action shifted to the *Oakland Tribune*, published by William F. Knowland, a prominent conservative Republican. Knowland refused to negotiate.[58]

The most important target was the Sheraton-Palace Hotel in San Francisco. When Professor and Mrs. J. B. Neilands were invited to demonstrate, they replied, "We're saving our trip to jail when you go after PG&E." (Pacific Gas and Electric was Berkeley's public utility.) But many did agree to join the hotel protest. On one occasion leaders organized 1,500 pickets, many of whom were Berkeley students. On another occasion, while pickets circled the hotel, 740 Cal sorority girls held a social function inside. After hundreds of pickets had been arrested, the hotel signed an agreement to hire more blacks. Activists also picketed San Francisco's auto row and won an agreement there, too. These demonstrations radicalized many protesters. "I saw the power structure and understood the hopelessness of trying to be a liberal," said Steve DeCanio, who later went to jail for his role in the FSM. "Man," reported the black CORE leader Chet Duncan, "around here we're up to our ears in walking picket lines, going to jail, going to court." Civil rights leaders knew that they were drawing blood when Assemblyman Don Mulford, generally considered to be Know-land's spokesman, demanded that the University dismiss students arrested at demonstrations.[59]

Of all the Bay Area job protests, the most imaginative—and dubious—were those carried out against Lucky's grocery stores. Lucky's had the smallest percentage of black employees of any Bay Area grocery chain. Berkeley CORE invented the shop-in, in which CORE protesters entered a store and loaded carts with groceries. As the demonstrators reached the checkout stands, they announced that they would not buy groceries where blacks could not work. The carts of groceries were left at the front of the store. It took Lucky's workers several hours of overtime to return the items to the shelves. Not everyone in Berkeley approved. On two occasions students who said that they supported civil rights reshelved groceries to apologize for the conduct of the demonstrators. A Berkeley student, noting that CORE had targeted the Lucky's store on Telegraph near campus, suggested that CORE was too lazy to stage a shop in in another part of Berkeley. Although Lucky's signed a hiring agreement and thus validated the effectiveness of the tactic, the shop-in weakened support for civil rights among Berkeley residents. Conservatives on the city council introduced a resolution condemning the shop-ins, but the liberal majority turned back the resolution four to three on a straight party vote.[60]

Pushing major employers to break the color barrier rapidly put blacks into positions where they had never before been seen, but the campaign failed to solve the problem of black unemployment. Small firms were untouched, and, after large firms had hired the best educated and most talented blacks, a large pool of young blacks remained unemployed. By 1967, in the middle of the Vietnam War boom, 28 percent of the city's blacks under age twenty-five were jobless. About half were high school graduates; indeed, a higher percentage of Berkeley's unemployed blacks than of Oakland's working whites had high school diplomas. Clearly, education did not necessarily lead to a job. The alienation of the jobless rose as they watched some blacks break into affluence, while they remained trapped in poverty and hopelessness. Existing government programs did not solve this problem. For many years the city of Berkeley had employed teenagers in an imaginative summer program called Workreation; youths worked for part of the day and then played sports together. By the mid-sixties the program was so popular that admission was limited to students with B grade averages. Few black youths qualified. Between 1965 and 1967 the city's Youth Opportunity Center registered 1,714 teenage job seekers. Although 69 percent were high school graduates, only 5 percent were placed in jobs. Almost forty percent of the registrants were nonwhite.[61]

By 1965 the federal government recognized the problem, and the Johnson administration created several programs for unemployed blacks. Berkeley used federal money to establish the Neighborhood Youth Corps, which employed 100 youths during the summer of 1965. The following summer the city provided 458 jobs, but in 1967 budget cuts reduced the number of jobs to 210. The Office of Equal Opportunities (OEO) was set up to train unemployed young blacks for work. In Berkeley, as elsewhere, the principal beneficiaries turned out to be the politically connected blacks hired to run the OEO. Participants in the training programs seldom got useful training, or they wasted time playing cards, noted one disillusioned observer. The trainees were not fools. They knew that there were no jobs for which they qualified, and that at the end of the OEO training they would be back on the street fending for themselves. One black youth said, "The poverty program is just a candy coating. What they're saying is, here's some candy, now you be nice and don't make any trouble."[62]

Young blacks were tired of being patronized; they resented attempts by both white liberals and the government to provide for blacks. Nor did they bow and scrape like Pullman car porters. When a University police officer asked Donald Q. Griffin for his student registration card inside the Student Union, the black senior gave his name and address but declined to produce the card; he noted that the officer did not ask any whites for identifications. Griffin argued with the police and wound up in the Berkeley city jail, where he had time to ponder: What did it mean to be black? This issue had been raised by Malcolm X, it had become the basis for the Black Muslim movement in the urban ghettos, and it had entered the mainstream of the civil rights movement through the Student Non-Violent Coordinating Committee. Although SNCC had started as a group of southern black college students devoted to Martin Luther King, Jr., and the Southern Christian Leadership Conference (SCLC), by 1966 SNCC workers had tired of King, of his insistence upon nonviolence, and of white influence inside both the SCLC and SNCC.[63]

Stokely Carmichael moved SNCC from King's slogan of "Freedom Now" to the phrase "Black Power." During 1966 the idea of Black Power swept through the nation's black communities. The word "Negro" began to disappear, and "black" came into common usage. The Negro had been polite and obsequious; the black was angry and proud. Carmichael visited the Bay Area several times. On one occasion he defined Black Power for a mostly white audience at Sproul Plaza. "Power *is*," he said, "You do not create it." He urged whites to work inside the white community, so that blacks could gain a sense of accomplishment inside their own community, which whites had either oppressed or patronized. At a meeting held at a public school in West Berkeley, Carmichael warned his mostly black audience that blacks should not play Jews to whites who played Nazis. On October 29, 1966, he spoke to a mostly white audience of 13,000 at the University's Greek Theatre. The radical Students for a Democratic Society had scheduled the event within days of Governor Brown's reelection bid, in part to embarrass the governor and in part to taunt conservatives. Carmichael's speech was breathtaking and intemperate. Although he defended Black Power, he mainly sought to draw black militants and white radicals together by attacking common enemies—the Vietnam War, the Johnson administration, and the draft. When he told the crowd to say "Hell, no!" to the draft, they approved.[64]

Events in Berkeley moved along a peculiar track. Neither Malcolm X nor King had been local heroes, and both the SCLC and SNCC seemed far away. The black-white liberal coalition that had come to power in Berkeley had given blacks more influence than in any other mostly white city in the country. In 1965 the coalition had won a smashing victory and swept all four council seats for a six to three majority. Councilwoman Margaret S. Gordon attributed the strong showing to the biracial commitment to the housing ordinance of 1963. In 1966, however, the coalition began to disintegrate. The war in Vietnam split white liberals, while the race issue split blacks. Blacks bitterly divided over the successor for Rumford's Assembly seat. The Rumford-Gibson-Sweeney group backed John J. Miller, a young black attorney; the recently organized Afro-American Student Association, composed of young blacks at the University, backed Otho Green, the director of the Berkeley Neighborhood Youth Corps. Miller's supporters empathized with the NAACP and the Urban League; Green's with Malcolm X and Stokely Carmichael. The black leader Ronald V. Dellums urged Green to oppose the war, but Green declined to do so, and he lost the nomination to Miller by 700 votes. (The generation gap among blacks extended to radio. Older blacks preferred black-oriented KDIA; many younger blacks listened to KYA, the white teen station.) Black militants and white radicals then united to back Dellums in his successful bid for a council seat in 1967. Dellums, however, also secured the support of the Cohelan-oriented Berkeley Democratic Caucus.[65]

Politics aside, Berkeley was unusual in its commitment to biracial ventures.

The city YWCA had been integrated for years, and the ad hoc committees to end job discrimination had been biracial. A local biracial theater company had taken a militant black position. In 1965 R. G. Davis's San Francisco Mime Troupe gave numerous performances of a mock minstrel show that attacked both racism and bourgeois social values. During the show performers sang "Old Black Joe." At the words "I'm coming" one of the blackface artists simulated masturbation. The critical point in the show came when a black student picked up a white girl; both roles were played in blackface, and part of the challenge for the audience was to figure out which of the blackface artists were white and which black. The show shocked conservatives, amused liberals, and thrilled countercultural radicals. Blacks could not help but notice that they were the heroes, and yet they could not be certain. Did some of the white audience's amusement come from a racist attachment to minstrelsy? In truth, it was difficult for blacks to be certain of white attitudes.[66]

Here was the paradox: the strength of the liberal coalition and of biracial community ventures in Berkeley made it difficult for blacks to articulate a position of Black Power. Power in Berkeley was destined to be shared through a coalition rather than through any claim to exclusive use of power. Yet the black need to escape the suffocation of white benevolence was just as great in Berkeley as in the rest of black America. Donald Q. Griffin was not the only young black who needed to be proud and independent. The result was that black extremism in Berkeley took a peculiar form. At one and the same time, black militants had to articulate a sense of black autonomy that resonated with the Black Power rhetoric of Stokely Carmichael while acceding to the pattern of biracial cooperation that had become a hallmark of Berkeley politics since 1961. The movement would have to be both autonomous and nonracist.[67]

Such a movement did emerge in the Berkeley-Oakland area. It was called the Black Panther party, and while it achieved national fame, it largely remained a local institution. Its leaders were a group of young blacks who had grown up in the Berkeley-Oakland ghetto. Caught up in Carmichael's demand for autonomy, they retained a faith in cooperation with white people (or at least certain white people) that was never expressed in the SNCC leader's gloomy reverse racism. The Panthers came to this position not from an optimistic assessment of society but from a shallow Marxism that led them to envision themselves as black revolutionaries. Being revolutionaries, they considered it their duty to cooperate with other revolutionaries, regardless of race. Radical ideology enabled the Panthers at one and the same time to call for black self-determination and to urge black-white cooperation. It was an ironic use of revolutionary ideology.[68]

Two students at Merritt College, a largely black junior college then located in North Oakland, founded the Panthers. One was Bobby Seale, who had been born in 1936 in Texas, but who had grown up in Berkeley's Codornices Village. He remembered the project's gangs and fights, as well as its closing and his family's relocation. His father, a carpenter who had to wait a long time to get into the union, was one of only four black union carpenters. Seale attended Berkeley High, where he was placed in the noncollege track usual for poor blacks. He dropped out of school, drifted on the streets, committed a number of petty crimes, realized he had no future, and joined the air force. In another time and place the air force could have been Seale's ticket into the middle class, but in the late fifties it was overwhelmingly white, and the few blacks who had volunteered for it were expected to conform to white standards. There was not, for example, the camaraderie of black sergeants found in the army. Naturally suspicious of whites and especially of whites with power, Seale rebelled against air force authority and eventually was given a bad conduct discharge after a quarrel with a civilian that had racial overtones. Seale returned to the Bay Area and, after a series of jobs, enrolled in a technical program at Merritt.[69]

While at Merritt, Seale met Huey P. Newton. The two were strikingly different and yet shared a surprisingly similar background. Born in 1942 in Louisiana, Newton had grown up in Oakland. For a time he had attended Berkeley High, until school officials discovered that his parents lived in Oakland; he graduated from Oakland Technical High. Just as alienated as Seale, Newton lacked Seale's mechanical aptitude and instead spent much time on the street, where he had a reputation for being tough. (For a time he was close to Richard Thorne, a black founder of the Sexual Freedom League.) Although Newton's formal education was poor, and he lacked the high school grades to attend a regular state university, he had enrolled at Merritt and started to read on his own. Newton was a key person in getting Merritt to offer a course in black history; he subsequently drove the white instructor away. As the two young men drew closer, Seale introduced Newton to the work of the radical black author Frantz Fanon. Fanon's attack upon the French exploitation of the colony of Algeria struck a sympathetic chord with the two young blacks. They noted parallels between French exploitation of the Algerians and white exploitation of American blacks; they began to think of white America as the mother country and the black ghetto as a colony. Fanon's Marxism, unlike that of Marx or Lenin, was addressed specifically to nonwhites. If a black man like Fanon could write such a book, thought Newton and Seale, then surely they could create a black political movement.[70]

The two dabbled in campus politics, and Newton joined the Soul Students Advisory Council (SSAC). Several hundred students attended a rally that the council sponsored. One night in March 1966, Newton and Seale, accompanied by a friend named Weasel, went to Telegraph Avenue in Berkeley to buy phonograph records. As they walked down the crowded street in the bohemian shopping district near the University, Seale began to recite poetry. Seale's friend suggested that he recite the poetry from a chair in front of The Forum, a coffeehouse in the former Lucky's store at the corner of Haste Street. After Seale had spoken a few minutes, a crowd gathered; suddenly a Berkeley policeman appeared. He told Seale he was under arrest for blocking the sidewalk. When Seale protested, Newton began a fight. Both were arrested, and they had to use SSAC money, which the white radical journalist Robert Scheer had given them, to make bail. When the black nationalists inside the SSAC objected to this use of the organization's funds, Newton stacked an SSAC meeting with street fighters to win his point. The SSAC crumbled, Newton fled Merritt for the streets, and the young black leaders decided to arm themselves in self-defense.[71]

In the meantime, Seale had taken a job as foreman at the North Oakland Neighborhood Anti-Poverty Center. He was paid about $660 a month to supervise the youths in the program. Determined to teach his charges some black history, Seale had to drink wine and shoot dice with them in order to be accepted. He taught them to bet rationally. One of the participants was Bobby Hutton. The youths at the center disliked authority, could not read, and had dropped out of school. "They wanted to be slick," recalled Seale, "they wanted to be pimps, they were trying to get them a piece from some of the sisters all the time." By the fall Seale and Newton had organized many of the youths, including Hutton, into a permanent group. A platform in favor of black self-determination had been typed on stencils at the poverty office, and a thousand copies had been produced. Newton read up on the gun laws in the office, and the group obtained its first two weapons, a pistol and an M-1 rifle. Seale took the pistol, and Newton got the rifle, since he was on parole and could not legally carry a pistol. The only thing Newton and Seale lacked was a name for their organization.[72]

Meanwhile, in Lowndes County, Alabama, the long disenfranchised blacks had won the right to vote. They discovered, however, that white Democrats were determined to prevent blacks from participating in that party. Finally, black leaders organized a new party. Alabama authorized political parties to put symbols on the ballot next to their candidates' names. The Democrats were represented by the rooster; the new party chose the black panther. The panther was fierce and fearless, and black leaders wanted to signal both to their own supporters and to local whites that blacks would no longer submit to intimidation. The panther was also aggressive, searching, and roaming, and the party promised, if elected, to pursue black issues with vigor and energy. And finally, the panther was black. The old word "Negro" had given way to the proud word "black." When news of the Black Panther party reached Newton and Seale in California, they decided to borrow the name.[73]

The Panthers knew how to attract attention. They wore black trousers, black leather jackets, and black berets that vaguely suggested a Castro connection, and they carried firearms in the streets. In 1966 California law provided it was legal to carry unloaded weapons openly in public places. At a time when race riots were occurring in almost every black ghetto in the country, the Panthers' arms alarmed not only whites but also the police. One of the Panthers cockily said, "The only way I'm gonna leave the Party will be in a pine box." When the police harassed the Panthers by stopping their cars frequently for traffic violations, the Panthers responded by harassing the police. Whenever a patrol car entered the Oakland-Berkeley ghetto, it was tailed by the Panthers, who had their own communications system. After Don Mulford, the conservative Republican who represented the Berkeley hills in the legislature, introduced a bill regulating guns, the Panthers decided to lobby the legislature. On May 2, 1967, they drove to Sacramento in a caravan, marched with their unloaded weapons into the capitol, and after getting lost inside the building, accidentally walked onto the floor of the Assembly bearing their arms. The legislators were frightened, the media became hysterical, and the Panthers, some of whom were arrested, never again lacked publicity.[74]

Newton and Seale's party grew from a movement in Berkeley and Oakland into a national organization with chapters in several large cities; by the fall of 1968 the Panthers claimed more than 2,000 members. Everywhere, the group provoked hysteria, particularly from white law enforcement officers. Almost all the Panthers were between the ages of fifteen and twenty-five, most had grown up poor, and few saw any opportunities in a society that preached equality while practicing racism. They were very angry. Yet sometimes one gets the impression that the Panthers' real fight was not against the white establishment. Rather, they were determined to overthrow established black politicians, ministers, and community leaders. Traditional black leaders came from families long rooted in northern soil, and they had always worked with the whites who ran the cities. The Panthers, in contrast, came from families without influence who had only recently migrated from the South. They not only felt that black leaders had sold them out, but they had come from the South, where black distrust of whites was far more endemic than it had been in the North. Newton and Seale had little use for blacks like Byron Rumford, who had struggled all his life to build a business and to gain respect inside the white community. The Panthers thought of that sort of behavior as toadying to whites; they would have none of it.[75]

As the Panthers grew in numbers, the leaders became somewhat distant from their followers. Newton and Seale gave speeches, wrote party propaganda, and mediated disputes, but they never succeeded in building a structured organization. A number of Panthers were caught in robberies, and some thought the Panthers nothing more than a crime gang. The Panthers did not remove these suspicions when they made members pledge not to steal from blacks. The absence of a pledge against stealing from whites hinted at Panther approval of such theft. Panther leaders, however, vehemently denied that their party was involved in crime, racially motivated or otherwise. The leaders simply could not control their followers. The Panthers started a highly visible program to give free breakfasts to poor black children, but favorable publicity was offset by the suspicion that the program enabled Panther leaders to extort and skim donations. The Panthers were entrepreneurs. They bought hundreds of copies of Chairman Mao's book of quotations from a Chinese importer in San Francisco at thirty cents apiece and then sold these volumes on the Berkeley campus at one dollar per copy. They used the profits to buy shotguns. Who said that revolution could not be profitable?[76]

The most important recruit was Eldridge Cleaver, who had lived more than half his thirty-one years in California prisons. While in prison the former resident of Los Angeles had become a Black Muslim and, like Malcolm X, had broken with the Muslims. He had also written a startling account of his desire to rape white women. When published in 1968, *Soul on Ice* topped the bestseller list. Cleaver's talent had come to the attention of Beverly Axelrod, a white radical who became Cleaver's attorney. In 1966 Axelrod was able to get Cleaver paroled as a reporter for *Ramparts* magazine, and he was soon writing about the Panthers. He accompanied them on their visit to the capitol in Sacramento. Cleaver's talent as a journalist was too great for Newton and Seale to ignore. In the Panthers' Marxist lexicon, Cleaver was destined to become a part of the party's vanguard. Besides, he was accepted by the New Left intellectuals at the *Ramparts* office.[77]

More than any other Panther leader, Cleaver moved among both black militants and white radicals. For several years he was the main link between the two communities. Axelrod had fallen in love with Cleaver, and after his parole she introduced him to her radical friends. She took him to Stew Albert's, where Cleaver met several white radicals, including the Alberts, Jerry Rubin, Jack Weinberg, and others. They smoked pot and talked about the future, while Cleaver noted the W. C. Fields poster on the ceiling and the Che Guevara poster on the wall. When he was introduced to Albert's wife, Cleaver found Judy Clavir's refusal to use her husband's surname unacceptable. Cleaver was a militant but no feminist. So he called her "Mrs. Stew." When she protested, Cleaver renamed her "Mrs. Gumbo." The name stuck, and for years Mrs. Albert was known among Berkeley radicals as Judy Gumbo.[78]

Throughout 1967 relations between the Panthers and Bay Area police officers deteriorated. The Panthers called the police, almost all of whom were white, "Pigs." The term was thick with meaning. First, it indicated that the Panthers thought the police and the white establishment were smart but greedy. However, it was against nature's hierarchy for pigs to rule men. In 1968 Eldridge Cleaver said that the three major presidential candidates offered a choice of "oink, oink, and oink." Panther literature was filled with drawings of heroic black men and women confronting and overcoming ugly, drooling white pigs. "Pig" had a special meaning in southern black culture: Pig is for pickin'. At a Panther wedding a group of children chanted, "We want a pork chop, off the pig!" A pig, then, was something to be slaughtered, roasted, and eaten. Finally, there was a subtle social element to this imagery. At a southern barbecue a communal group shared a pig. The imagery suggested that the black community should rise up and devour the white police force that operated inside their community. This dimension of the term did not escape the notice of the police.[79]

The Panthers charged police harassment, and there was harassment. For example, Berkeley police patrolled constantly in front of the Panther headquarters, and in Oakland a sixteen-year-old girl was charged with felonious extortion for selling Huey Newton buttons on the street. Harassment was a manifestation of a growing fear among both blacks and whites in America's cities. The Berkeley-Oakland ghetto was one of the few to escape a major riot. The reasons are not difficult to ascertain. On the one hand, the black-white liberal coalition that governed Berkeley acted swiftly to defuse tension by making government responsive to black demands; the city of Oakland used repression. On the other hand, the Panthers absorbed the energies of the angriest young blacks and put that energy into the organization, so that a spontaneous riot was unlikely. Police worried that in place of a riot there would be armed insurrection.[80]

On October 28, 1967, Huey Newton was stopped late at night by a policeman on an Oakland street. Exactly what happened next is unclear, but there was a shootout; one white officer was killed, while Newton went to the hospital with a bullet wound. He soon faced a murder charge, which pushed the Panthers onto the front pages day after day. When the prosecutor asked for the death penalty, some blacks recalled the racist southern justice of their own childhoods. The principal difference between the South and Oakland, it appeared, was that the lynching in Oakland had to follow a legal form. In the black community declarations of support for Newton became a badge of racial honor. Many blacks who had previously ignored the Panthers joined the Newton defense effort. On February 17, 1968, 5,500 blacks celebrated Huey Newton's birthday at the Oakland Auditorium. Among the eight black leaders who quietly sat on the stage was Berkeley Councilman Ron Dellums; Newton's African wicker chair was left empty. The speaker, Stokely Carmichael, not only endorsed the Panthers but accepted a title from the organization.[81]

To most whites, the black community's rallying around Newton was alarming. No white life would be safe if blacks did not respect the authority of white policemen. While white liberals squirmed in silence, white radicals used the trial to build their coalition with black militants. Erica McClain, a Berkeley white radical, organized "Honkies for Huey." When the trial opened in July, 5,000 black and white protesters marched in front of the courthouse chanting,

"Free Huey!" As they did so, the white radical Bob Avakian (son of the liberal judge and former Berkeley school board member Spurgeon Avakian) tore the American flag from its pole; he was then attacked by the Oakland police. The Panthers offended some blacks, including Carmichael, when Newton rejected being defended by a black attorney. The party, it turned out, was less interested in the color of Newton's attorney than in his legal abilities. Charles Garry, a longtime white radical, enhanced his reputation by a superb defense of Newton. On September 8, 1968, the jury rejected the murder charge and convicted Newton of involuntary manslaughter.[82]

The year 1968 proved tumultuous for the Panthers in other ways. Shortly after the Newton birthday celebration, Berkeley police raided Seale's house in the middle of the night. Before the charges were dismissed, an angry Seale took his complaint to the city council; he showed up at a council meeting with 150 or more armed supporters. The council recessed and debated what to do. Councilmen Sweeney and Dellums, both black, argued that the Panthers could be persuaded to leave, and eventually a council majority agreed to let the two make the attempt. Finally, Seale gave a speech and then left with most of his followers. It was 12:30 a.m. After the Panthers left, Dellums turned to Councilwoman Bernice Hubbard May. He said, "Bernice, I do want to compliment you. You sat there just as cool and collected. I kept watching you and thinking, 'Why can't I be that calm?' And then the interesting thought occurred to me: Were you calm really, or perhaps you weren't frightened because you thought nobody would shoot you?"

"Why Ron," May replied, "did you really think they'd shoot?"

"Didn't you see me getting white?" said Dellums.

May had kept cool by believing that they were bluffing.

"Didn't you even think they might shoot?" asked Dellums.

"Yes," confessed May, "I thought, 'If they begin shooting, I'll get under the desk.' " It was made of heavy oak.[83]

On April 3, twelve armed policemen invaded a Panther meeting at St. Augustine Episcopal Church in Oakland. They left when they could find neither Seale nor Cleaver. The next day the Reverend Martin Luther King, Jr., was assassinated in Memphis. Racial tensions rose. Although most whites in Berkeley were horrified, not all were. When told of the assassination, one long-haired hippie on Telegraph said, "Fuck you, nigger lover, fuck you." Black students at Berkeley High went on a rampage breaking store windows in downtown Berkeley and beating up whites in Civic Center Park, across the street from the school. The Panthers urged blacks to be calm; Cleaver visited a black school and begged the teenagers not to burn it. Cleaver was near despair. On the afternoon of April 6, he sat in the *Ramparts* office and dictated his reaction to King's death. "I think that America has already committed suicide," he said, "and we who now thrash within its dead body are also dead in part and parcel of the corpse. America is truly a disgusting burden upon this planet. A burden upon all humanity. And if we here in America—" Cleaver stopped dictating to answer the telephone; after the call, he immediately left the office for Oakland.[84]

That night Cleaver and Bobby Hutton had a shootout with the Oakland police. Cleaver was wounded, and seventeen-year-old 'Li'l Bobby' was killed. One of the first Panther recruits, Hutton was a high school dropout who had once worked for Seale at the federally funded Oakland youth center. Hutton's funeral, held in Berkeley, attracted up to 2,000 mourners; another 5,000 attended a memorial service across from the courthouse. In protest against the shooting, blacks began to boycott stores in downtown Oakland. After the shootout, Cleaver was taken to the hospital, where one of his first visitors was Robert Scheer, his colleague at *Ramparts*. Within hours Cleaver's parole was revoked, and the Panther leader was taken to the state prison hospital at Vacaville. When Cleaver's attorney used his client's testimony to show that the parole board had been under intense political pressure to revoke the parole, a judge ordered Cleaver released. Badly shaken by Hutton's death and his own latest brush with the law, Cleaver became so angry that one Panther began to call him "El-Rage." During much of 1967 Cleaver had kept a low profile, but he now began to speak out politically. His words were always frank and often startling.[85]

During much of 1968 Seale was serving time in jail because of his role in the Panther march on the capitol, and Newton was held without bail pending the conclusion of his murder trial. The Panthers would have been leaderless if Cleaver had not spoken out. Although Cleaver risked being returned to jail as a parole violator, he decided to run for president on the Peace and Freedom party ticket. In late 1967 a coalition of black militants and white radicals had organized the party to run an antiwar candidate for president in 1968. After Lyndon Johnson dropped out of the race, support for Peace and Freedom dwindled, but party leaders, including Robert Scheer, calculated that the party would gain the greatest support by running a well-known black militant like Cleaver. The fact that Cleaver was underage and therefore ineligible for the presidency did not disturb his supporters. Although his name was not on the California ballot, he was a write-in candidate. His campaign manager was Bob Avakian. One Panther said, "If Eldridge is elected president we will paint the White House black and then burn it down." The party nominated Newton for Congress, Mario Savio for the California State Senate, and Seale and Cleaver's wife, Kathleen, for two Assembly seats. Although none of the candidates came close to winning, Newton did draw 12,164 votes or 7 percent of the total cast in the race.[86]

In the fall of 1968, a group of students at the University invited Cleaver to teach a course on racism. They did so under the auspices of the University's Board of Educational Development, which had been established after the Free

Speech Movement to generate innovative and experimental courses. When the appointment was announced, the public, Governor Ronald Reagan, and the Regents fumed. Although Chancellor Heyns privately lamented that Cleaver had been invited to teach, he defended the appointment to the Regents. By one vote the angry Regents allowed Cleaver to give a single lecture in a hastily reconstructed course. An enraged Cleaver then barnstormed the state's campuses. He seemed to get a particular thrill out of cursing the governor. At Sproul Plaza Cleaver led a crowd of five thousand in three cheers: "Fuck Ronnie Reagan." When Cleaver challenged Reagan to a duel, the governor named the weapons: words of more than four letters each.[87]

The controversy over Cleaver came amid rising racial tension on campus. In the spring of 1968, Cal's black basketball players had forced both their coach, a Chicano, and the athletic director to resign. In a racial fight, a white football player was shot just outside the gym. At the time Cal gave few athletic scholarships to blacks, and blacks charged that white athletes got choice summer jobs that were closed to blacks. Chicanos protested the University's refusal to join Cesar Chavez's boycott against nonunion table grapes. Both blacks and Chicanos noticed that the University student body of about 26,000 was almost 90 percent white; most of the rest were Asians. (In 1966–67 there were 236 blacks, 68 Chicanos, and 36 native Americans.) The Cleaver controversy reinforced the perception that Cal was a white institution.[88]

In protest, activists organized a peaceful sit-in in Sproul Hall on October 22, 1968. It swiftly led to 121 arrests (117 students). On the following day radicals seized and barricaded Moses Hall. The demonstrators, borrowing a technique used earlier at Columbia University, piled furniture against the building entrances. The militants renamed the building Cleaver Hall, hoisted red and black flags, and displayed several banners ("Liberated," "Solidarity with Students Forever," "End Regents' Racism"). For several hours into the night leaders spoke from a balcony through megaphones to a crowd of several thousand curious but distinctly nonrevolutionary onlookers. Then police, personally led by Edwin Meese III, entered the building and arrested 77 people (54 students). A number of the protesters, including Tom Hayden, had escaped from the building before the police arrived. As the arrested demonstrators were led to police buses, the women sang "Solidarity Forever." The men, however, did not know the words and sang "Mickey Mouse." Moses Hall had suffered considerable damage; some professors' offices had been entered, and files were tossed about. Radicals blamed the police. Both sit-ins led Chancellor Heyns to suspend dozens of students and place more than a hundred on probation. Three leaders of the Moses Hall sit-in, Paul Glusman, Peter Camejo, and Jack Bloom, were charged with a criminal conspiracy; they were not convicted. Long before their trial and even before the school term ended, Eldridge Cleaver's parole had been revoked, and he jumped bail and fled to Algeria. These incidents bonded radical whites and militant minorities.[89]

In early 1969 that bond was reinforced, after militant black students at San Francisco State College struck over the issue of a black studies program on that campus. Support for the strike spread to the Berkeley campus, where militant black students joined militant Chicanos, Asians, and native Americans to form the Third World Liberation Front (TWLF). The TWLF presented the administration at Berkeley with a list of demands, which included the establishment of student-controlled minority programs. "The real issue," said the TWLF, "is the right of people to determine their own destinies." The administration could not accept the demands, and they were presented in such a way that no acceptance was anticipated. TWLF's black leader, Jim Nabors, declared, "I've been denied so long that anything I take is right."[90]

TWLF leaders then joined white radicals to declare a student strike. As the strike began, one of the University's main lecture halls, Wheeler Auditorium, burned. The fire turned many students against the strike, which drew little support from whites on campus. Even Local 1570, the militant TA union led by Conn ("Ringo") Hallinan, declined to join. TWLF pickets chanted, "Power to the People!" Or they shouted, "Get your asses out of classes—join the masses." When words failed, these multiracial militants blocked entry to campus at Sather Gate with a closely formed picket line, threats, and blows. The University advised students to enter campus elsewhere. Plainclothesmen beat the TWLF pickets with blackjacks. As support for the strike waned, Local 1570 posted informational pickets. Their arrest failed to rally new support. Tactics changed. On one occasion strikers entered the main library to attack the card catalog; it was defended by female librarians, who linked arms with their backs to the catalog. The strikers fought the police in the streets. "It is a war," reported Paul Glusman. When police fired tear gas, the protesters hurled the cannisters back. One day the wife of a high University official was escorting a guest across Sproul Plaza when tear gas suddenly appeared. The two women reacted slowly, and a black man ran past and yelled, "Better run like hell—we're all niggers now!" On February 27, police severely beat Ysidro Macias, a key Chicano leader, and the next day the National Guard arrived. Although this strike, like an earlier one in 1966, failed, the ill-will that it left behind cannot be overestimated. The University administration felt besieged, minority students were frustrated, and everyone was weary.[91]

By the end of the decade both race relations and society were in disarray. Black demands for racial justice had led conservatives to react hysterically and then, in increasing numbers, to flee Berkeley. Their departure deprived the city of the stability, tradition, and sober judgment that is, or should be, the hallmark of conservatism. As experienced conservative leaders vanished, white liberals were unable to fill the void. Liberal leaders understood neither white prejudices nor the practical difficulties in ending discrimination in housing, education, or employment. Berkeley remained one of the few cities in the country where school desegregation was undertaken voluntarily, and the schools did not fall apart, although they disappointed those who thought that desegregation would substantially improve black scholastic performance. Except for school desegregation, the liberal program failed. Its failure disillusioned many blacks, who drew away from white paternalism and toward black autonomy. For blacks the decade had combined hope with frustration. The thrill of the civil rights movement and, indeed, the rise of the Third World enabled many a black to share Roy Nichols's sense of excitement at being alive during this period. But soaring hope invites great disappointment, and the decade ended with Malcolm X and Martin Luther King, Jr., dead, with a number of black leaders exiled or imprisoned, with young blacks trapped in the ghetto, and with white Americans increasingly distracted from black problems by the war in Vietnam.

# Chapter 3

# RED

I'm from Cal—Color Me Red
FSM button

From the late 1940s into the early 1960s, one belief held an otherwise diverse, disparate, and quarrelsome American society together—anticommunism. The American government conducted a bipartisan anticommunist crusade both abroad and at home. Foreign policy was based upon the assumption that communism was a global conspiracy controlled by Moscow, and the American government undertook to contain communism throughout the world. Domestic policy was based upon the assumption that American communists were part of Moscow's conspiracy, and the American government undertook to destroy the American Communist party. Anyone who questioned either of these assumptions or the policies that followed from them risked being called a communist, a communist sympathizer, or a communist dupe. Communists or suspected communists were driven out of labor unions, out of schools and colleges, and out of Hollywood and the media. Anyone who defended constitutional rights for communists risked attack, and anyone who failed to denounce communism fell under suspicion of being a communist sympathizer.[1]

This anticommunist crusade never completely triumphed in Berkeley. The crusade's hysterical tone offended academics, who believed in the rule of reason and judgment. Then, too, academics liked argument. For many, communism had enlivened political debate, and the anticommunist crusade was unappealing because it destroyed diversity and replaced intellectual conflict with a dull, politically enforced conformity. But the crusade failed in Berkeley primarily because the city and especially its university had been home to a number of communists and communist sympathizers in the 1930s. While most of these leftists had become disillusioned with the party and quit, they often re-

87

mained sympathetic to Left principles, including a dislike for industrial capitalism, and were unwilling to denounce communists of former communists. Communists, in other words, had played a sufficiently important role in the community to be somewhat protected from the anticommunist crusade. Leftists who found life in other locales intolerable moved to Berkeley, which became known for its tolerance and congeniality. "There are more Communists per capita in this community," lamented the archconservative Berkeley Citizens United in 1965, "than any outside New York City." The result was that while the Left was being destroyed elsewhere, it remained quietly alive in Berkeley.[2]

Although the Left was alive, it was not thriving. Communists had been thrown out of the Bay Area's CIO unions in the late 1940s, and the *Daily People's World*, the party's unofficial newspaper on the west coast, shrank both in physical size and in circulation. In 1951 editor Al Richmond was arrested on charges that grew out of the Smith Act requirement that Communist party officials had to register with the federal government. In 1957 the nearly bankrupt paper converted from daily to weekly publication. The University had refused to hire members of the Communist party, and state legislators imposed a loyalty oath upon University employees. William Mandel, a Soviet scholar and onetime party member, hovered on the edge of campus; he hinted that he had been deprived of a teaching position at the University because of his pro-Soviet views. Many student leaders in SLATE, the reform-minded campus political party, had been leftists, and in 1961 the University had banned SLATE from the campus. From a distance the federal government kept up the pressure. The radical attorney Vincent Hallinan went to jail for tax evasion, the physicist J. Robert Oppenheimer lost his security clearance, HUAC cited a number of Bay Area school teachers, and in 1963 the U.S. Senate investigated Berkeley radio station KPFA.[3]

The Left, however, continued to occupy a curious and unique place in the Bay Area. During the 1950s, when the national Communist party decided to go underground, party leaders in California remained visible. While national membership dropped by two-thirds, California membership fell only one-third. During the 1960s the national party became stodgy, but California communists, led by Dorothy Healey and Al Richmond of the *People's World*, showed an increasing willingness to make alliances. In most of the country the communist-backed W. E. B. DuBois clubs competed with Students for a Democratic Society, the major national organization for noncommunist liberal or leftist college students. But in the Bay Area, where SDS was weak, the DuBois clubs cooperated with SDS as well as other leftist groups. The Berkeley club even joked, "We are probably represented in the FBI. Our base is getting broader all the time." While the national party attacked the Black Panthers, Bay Area communists expressed sympathy. In 1968 communists in New York defended the Soviet Union's invasion of Czechoslovakia; the party's west coast editor condemned the act. Party leaders sided with Moscow in the Sino-Soviet split, but the *People's World* drew the wrath of the national party by declaring its neutrality. Bay Area communists were, if anything, flexible.[4]

They were also surprisingly visible. Malvina Reynolds, daughter of a founder of the Communist party and a onetime registered party voter, had received a Ph.D. in English at the University. Because of her politics, she could not teach; she became a well-known Berkeley folk singer. Kenneth O. May, the son of Professor Samuel May and stepson of Bernice Hubbard May, the liberal councilwoman, had become a communist while living in Berkeley in the thirties. He had left Berkeley, and while his stepmother was involved in local politics, he tried to spare her any embarrassment. It is possible, however, that Mrs. May gained votes because of her stepson's party ties. Pete Seeger, son of the onetime music professor Charles Seeger, was well known both for his folk music and for his Left politics; while blacklisted, he continued to perform in Berkeley. So did the black communist singer Paul Robeson. When radio station KPFA went on the air in 1949, it followed a policy of broadcasting all points of view. Among its regular commentators was William Mandel. During the fifties leftist parents sent their children to the Berkwood School, a private school with Left ties. Although an effort was made to close the school, it survived. Finally, the Bay Area Chapter of the American Civil Liberties Union was the only ACLU organization in the country that refused to bar communists from membership.[5]

This open atmosphere attracted leftists from all over the country. Max Scherr, the founder of the *Berkeley Barb*, came from Baltimore; Jerry Rubin, a deeply alienated young newspaper reporter, from Cincinnati; and Mario Savio, the Catholic leftist, from New York. The migration had begun in the fifties but grew after 1960, when the HUAC protests drew attention to the Left in the Bay Area. In 1960 Tom Hayden, then a college student and editor of the *Michigan Daily*, read Jack Kerouac's *On the Road*. In imitation, he hitchhiked across the country. Hayden's brief trip to Berkeley brought him into contact with leaders of the student Left, and he returned to Berkeley frequently throughout the sixties. At the end of the decade, he lived in a Berkeley commune with, among others, Anne Weills Scheer. In 1962 Bettina Aptheker arrived from New York to attend the University. As a public institution, the University admitted all qualified applicants and, unlike many private schools, did not bar leftists. About the same time Marvin Garson, who had been expelled both from Brandeis University and from a Trotsky-oriented student organization, arrived to study at the University. (Leon Trotsky, Stalin's deposed rival in the Russian Communist party, advocated worldwide revolution.) After the Free Speech Movement the parade continued. In 1965 Peter Camejo, a second-generation Venezuelan-American and brilliant orator, arrived in town to represent the Trotskyist Socialist Workers party.[6]

In the rest of the country, young radicals reacted to the impotent Old Left and its incessant doctrinal disputes by creating Students for a Democratic Society (SDS). This new organization had its own manifesto, the Port Huron Statement, and its own doctrine, participatory democracy; it stressed pragmatic action on issues. In Berkeley, where old radicals remained a vital force in the community, young radicals found it useful to cooperate with the Old Left. The result was a peculiar local approach to politics reminiscent of the Popular Front of the thirties, when communists had sought power through participation in broad political coalitions. Members of various Left factions had no common manifesto and no common doctrine but joined together in ad hoc committees for specific issues. That approach was used both because the local communists, guided by the *People's World*, were far less sectarian than their eastern counterparts and because the approach offered a means to achieve limited political success. In other words, the Berkeley Left, when united, was not impotent. To leftists, both the large size of the HUAC protests in 1960 and the success of the Free Speech Movement in 1964 offered proof. In this environment SDS had little appeal, and the organization never became dominant in Berkeley.[7]

The price of leftist cooperation in Berkeley was to diminish the role of ideology among local leftists. The result, then, was to free Berkeley radicals from their own pasts. "What do we need the Party for?" asked students, when invited to join the Socialist Workers. On the one hand, this freedom gave Berkeley radicals the chance to develop new ways of thinking about social issues. Throughout the sixties the Berkeley Left was highly innovative and imaginative. Ideology did not restrain action; as a result, Berkeley radicals had greater freedom to maneuver than other American leftists. But the absence of a coherent ideology meant that Berkeley radicals lacked discipline and risked fragmentation. Joe McDonald captured the tone perfectly in his song, "Who Am I." The local leftists tended toward spontaneous action. Their slogan might have been, as Carl Oglesby warned, "I bleed, therefore I am." While it was easy to rally various factions around specific issues, it became difficult to build a cohesive movement. Flexibility created opportunity, but it did so at some cost.[8]

Although Berkeley radicals lacked an ideology, they shared a worldview. Throughout the sixties they were hostile to industrial capitalism, to liberals, and especially to the anticommunist crusade. Many, like Jerry Rubin, became fascinated by the rise of the Third World and, especially, the triumph of Fidel Castro; Rubin visited Cuba in 1964. The leftist Fair Play for Cuba Committee had been active in Berkeley in the early sixties. Its members included Mike Miller, the former chairman of SLATE; Barbara Garson of the Young Socialist Alliance; and Robert Scheer. The group's faculty adviser was Stephen Smale, a professor of mathematics with Left sympathies. In many respects, Rubin was typical of these young radicals. Son of a union official, Rubin had restlessly moved to Israel, returned to the United States, and, inspired by reports of leftist stirrings, moved to Berkeley to study sociology. Dropping out of school shortly after he arrived, Rubin had watched the leaders of the Free Speech Movement create a mass base. Like other young radicals, Rubin understood the contradiction between his own values and the nature of American society better than he could articulate any plan to transform and remake that society.[9]

While radicals were a minority in Berkeley, they planned to seize control; many envisioned a radical Berkeley as the first step toward a radical America. The key was to mobilize support for radical causes and turn moderates, especially students and other young people, into radicals. During the civil rights campaign and particularly during the Free Speech Movement, leftists had enjoyed considerable success. From the radical perspective, the FSM was a success less because of the right to free speech won on the campus than because of the sense of community that had developed among the hundreds of young people under radical leadership who had been arrested in Sproul Hall. That was why radicals emphasized, "The issue is not the issue." The purpose of an issue was to create a confrontation in which moderates were radicalized; in 1969 activists exploited the issue of People's Park in precisely this same fashion. Because of this strategy, leftists usually rejected compromise. "We cannot be coopted because we want everything," said Jerry Rubin. This wry remark was at the heart of Berkeley radicalism.[10]

In the spring of 1965, while the FSM leaders were bogged down in their sit-in trial, President Johnson suddenly escalated American involvement in the Vietnam War. Because the usual radicals were unable to provide leadership, Jerry Rubin moved to fill the breach by organizing a protest against the war. Rubin's prospects were poor. At the time pacifists, leftists, and independent-minded intellectuals who denounced the Vietnam War were ignored. Few Americans objected to the war. In late March the Students for a Democratic Society at the University of Michigan brought opponents together in a marathon debate called a teach-in. Although all points of view were aired, antiwar views prevailed. This teach-in marked the first time since the late 1940s that liberals and leftists had debated in public. Simultaneously, opponents of the war in Berkeley held a public meeting in a large classroom on campus; the room filled and overflowed. The following month SDS sponsored an antiwar march in Washington. Much to the consternation of some of the pacifists, organizers—who included the Berkeley activists Charles Capper and Martin Roysher, recruited through SDS—refused to bar communists, and for the first time in years liberals marched with leftists. To everyone's surprise, the event drew 20,000 people instead of the expected 10,000.[11]

In Berkeley Jerry Rubin and Stephen Smale then organized the Vietnam Day Committee (VDC) to sponsor a teach-in at the University on May 21–22, 1965. Because of lingering tensions from the Free Speech Movement, Acting Chancellor Martin Meyerson tried to be a gracious host. The ASUC Senate unanimously declared its support. The organizers planned a grand event that ran more than thirty hours. Most of the activities took place on the softball field between Harmon Gym and the Student Union. Vietnam Day featured not only speeches on the war but also food vendors, musicians such as Phil Ochs, and entertainers such as The Committee and the San Francisco Mime Troupe. Celebrities included Benjamin Spock, the pediatrician; Norman Thomas, the socialist leader; David Dellinger, the radical pacifist; Dick Gregory, the black comedian; Paul Krassner, editor of *The Realist*; Bob Moses, the black leader of SNCC; and Alan Watts, the student of oriental philosophy. A drunken Norman Mailer laced his antiwar speech with such profanity that KPFA had to terminate its live coverage for fear of losing its radio broadcasting license. I. F. Stone, the independent radical editor, drew the greatest response, a standing ovation.[12]

The State Department declined to send a spokesman to explain Johnson's policy, and both Professor Robert A. Scalapino and Professor Eugene Burdick, who had agreed to defend the administration, withdrew at the last minute; Scalapino called the event "a rigged meeting.'" A nearby food vendor offered a special dish, "Chicken Scalapino." Burdick sat on the grass and glumly watched the proceedings. The administration was represented on the platform by an empty chair. All of the speakers except two opposed the war; Professor Aaron Wildavsky defended the war in a debate with Robert Scheer. Wildavsky was booed, and Scheer proved to be a knowledgable, effective antiwar speaker. After all the talk was over, at midnight on May 22, several hundred participants, led by members of the Young Socialist Alliance, marched to the Berkeley draft board at Bancroft and Fulton; they hanged Lyndon Johnson in effigy, and nineteen draft cards were burned. (Burning a draft card was not yet a federal crime.) These events gave the first indications that the antiwar movement was powered by unusual energy and rooted in deep anger. As many as 30,000 people attended portions of the teach-in. The crowd ranged from ten to fifteen thousand during the afternoon peak to a few hundred in the middle of the night.[13]

Although the teach-in was a success, antiwar leaders had little to cheer in mid-1965. Even in Berkeley an overwhelming majority supported the Johnson administration's war policy. In June the BCU rallied anticommunists around the war with a showing of HUAC's film, "Operation Abolition," at the Berkeley Realty Board. Clearly, more students had been drawn to Vietnam Day to see celebrities and to hear singers than to listen to Left arguments against the war. Yet the audience had been large, and some for the first time had heard attacks not only on the administration's policy in Vietnam but also on the liberal, anticommunist assumptions upon which postwar society had been built. Antiwar leaders knew that they could not stop the war but calculated that they could retard its escalation, expose the flaws in Johnson's policy, and in time force changes in policy. To maintain pressure, it was necessary to generate more publicity. "I shudder to think what these abortions are dreaming up for this fall!" wrote Professor James Basson to Professor William Petersen. Actually, Rubin and the VDC did not plan to wait until fall; they hungered for immediate attention.[14]

An opportunity for the VDC came in August 1965, when the army began to send Vietnam-bound troops on chartered trains through Berkeley to the nearby Oakland Army Base. The Santa Fe Railroad operated the troop trains on a little-used track that cut through residential neighborhoods in the flatlands. For years residents had asked the city to buy the right of way and tear up the track. The VDC decided to picket the trains as they passed through Berkeley. With help from informants who lived up the rail line, the VDC used a phone tree to get dozens of demonstrators to the track before the train appeared. At the first protest 250 demonstrators showed up. They placed a huge banner across the track. It read, "Stop the War Machine." The train smashed through the banner. Plainclothesmen harassed a VDC photographer who took pictures. The following day two more trains came. When the first train passed through Berkeley, it was greeted by 150 or more supporters of the war. The VDC protesters met the train just to the south of Berkeley in Emeryville, but the police pushed them aside. Later in the day about 500 VDC demonstrators met a second train in Berkeley by sitting on the track. About thirty police officers appeared and drove the demonstrators away. As the train rolled past, the crowd chanted, "No! No! No!" Some of the soldiers aboard the train looked bewildered; others grinned.[15]

On August 12, between 500 and 1,000 people showed up for the third VDC demonstration. They carried signs reading "Why Die in Vietnam," "Army Kill, Army Die in Vietnam," and "Why." While waiting for the train, they sang "We Shall Overcome." Police tried to block access to the track, so the protesters ran around the police and north along the track about a mile. The police and television crews followed. When the train came, the engineer sprayed hot steam to get people to leave; some were temporarily blinded. The train slowed down, and several demonstrators boarded the train to talk with the soldiers. They had brought along antiwar leaflets to pass out. One demonstrator aboard the train tried to pull its airbrake. Fifteen to thirty others then leaped aboard, and some climbed atop the train's roof. Police pulled three people off, and the train then stopped. When the police tried to arrest the others who had boarded the train, the protesters fled; two were arrested. Several days later, at another protest, one of the sixty demonstrators was arrested when he tried to throw antiwar leaflets and picket signs through an open train window; he was charged with littering. About half the demonstrators then marched to city hall, where a demonstrator who had received a parking ticket during the protest crumpled the ticket and tossed it across the counter; he, too, was charged with littering.[16]

These protests led one VDC supporter to establish a radical, antiwar newspaper. Max Scherr had been active in the Old Left before moving to the Bay Area. Although trained as a lawyer, he never practiced in California, and for several years Scherr had owned and operated the Steppenwolf bistro, which became a hangout for radicals. In 1960 activists from the Steppenwolf had planned the protests against Chessman's execution and the HUAC hearings. As a bartender, Scherr had grown attuned to the tempo of the local radicals. He sold the bistro and on August 13, 1965, launched the *Berkeley Barb*. Although the first issue, a thin eight pages offset-printed from typescript, was mostly devoted to the VDC protests, a discerning reader could detect elements that predicted broader success. Its layout was ugly, wild, and free. The logo featured Don Quixote astride his trusty steed; the hero, as much an anarchist as a leftist, carried a barbed lance to attack the establishment. The lance was tipped with the University's Campanile. Although Scherr sold only 1,200 copies of the first issue, which he peddled along Telegraph Avenue, he quickly showed business acumen. To cut costs, the publisher used unpaid or poorly paid writers, and to achieve wide circulation, he hired scores of young people, many of them runaways, to sell papers on the streets. Within a few months the *Barb* became a staple in the South Campus area.[17]

The troop train protests shaped events in other ways. The VDC concluded that the soldiers did not favor the war; therefore, from then on, the VDC cultivated soldiers while opposing the war. In the long run, the antiwar movement's sympathy for the draftees being sent to Vietnam had profound consequences. The protests also angered many people. "The manner in which these people protest is tantamount to treason," said conservative Councilman Joseph Bort. The VDC tried to shock people into reassessing the war; the demonstrators, said Rubin, were "psychic terrorists." The movement of troops through Berkeley on their way to Vietnam brought the war home, made it real and immediate, and connected it to the local community. Finally, the trains led the VDC to take its first step into politics. Because of a legal technicality, the trains could continue to operate only if the city passed an ordinance granting permission. When Smale urged the city council to defeat the proposal, he received a lecture from conservative Councilman John DeBonis. "You should not even be teaching at the University!" he declared. "You are out here aggravating a riot! I've been wanting to tell you off for a long time." Then, much to the annoyance of the VDC, liberals joined conservatives on the council to pass the measure permitting the trains to operate; they also refused to condemn the war. Councilwoman Bernice Hubbard May suggested that the members of the VDC complain to their congressmen. "It is an example of the liberals' propensity to ineffectualness," sneered the *Berkeley Barb*, "when courageous, uncompromising action could count the most." Although neither the council

nor the VDC recognized what had happened, this episode marked the beginning of the end of liberal power in Berkeley.[18]

When students returned to Cal in the fall of 1965, the war was a major issue
on campus. Opinions, however, were divided. A number of supporters of the
Johnson administration's policy held meetings and rallies, while opponents increasingly fought among themselves. In the first rallying of opposition to ad
ministration policy in the spring, liberals who doubted the wisdom of American
intervention in the war had joined pacifists and radicals in debate. But the
troop train protests had appalled many antiwar liberals, both because they saw
the protests as childish and ineffective and because, being familiar with the
people who held power, they were scared of a backlash against civil liberties.
In September a number of antiwar professors, led by Professor Carl Landauer,
publicly denounced the VDC. Other antiwar professors then denounced this
attack on the VDC, even as they dissociated themselves from the VDC's tactics. Several professors who favored the administration's policy denounced all
the war's opponents. Eventually, some of the VDC supporters and non-VDC
antiwar professors created an umbrella group, the Faculty Peace Committee.
"Liberals are being flung off in all directions," noted the Berkeley Barb. Many
of the radicals who had organized the VDC disdained all liberals and especially
antiwar liberals. They were perceived not as potential allies but as dinosaurs.[19]

Bursting with a self-confidence that the various liberal groups lacked, the
VDC decided to mount a major offensive by organizing a massive march. It
was planned for Friday, October 15, 1965. Activities were to begin with another teach-in on the Berkeley campus; proponents of the war were not invited
to participate. The mixture of political speeches and entertainment that had
proved popular at the May teach-in was to be repeated. Young people, thought
Jerry Rubin, could "join the revolution and have fun." After thousands of
students had been enticed into this political circus, organizers planned a nighttime torchlight parade down Telegraph Avenue into Oakland, across the black
ghetto of West Oakland, and to the gates of the Oakland Army Base. There a
second large rally was to take place. In some respects, this parade bore a resemblance to the fall Football Festival parades that had been abandoned in 1963.
The entire event was designed as theater in which the participants were both
the performers and the audience. This concept was rooted in an idea inchoate
in the emerging culture of the sixties: doing your own thing. The main points
of the march were to display the antiwar movement's energy, vigor, and courage and to contrast the vitality of radicalism with the anemic dullness of capitalist, anticommunist liberalism. "We sat in Chinese restaurants and coffee
shops," recalled Rubin, "and we knew that we had the power to set off waves
of thought across the country."[20]

Although the University gave the VDC permission to hold the teach-in,

Berkeley officials balked at giving the VDC a parade permit. After the state attorney general's office said that a permit could not be denied, the city decided to allow the parade to take place without a permit. VDC leaders were heartened by Berkeley's capitulation. They received no such satisfaction from Oakland. Mayor John C. Houlihan, who was charged with embezzlement in a major scandal shortly afterward, flatly refused to issue a parade permit. The city argued that a nighttime parade was dangerous, since the Right had threatened to attack the VDC marchers. Oakland officials also declared that it was dangerous for white demonstrators to march through West Oakland; racial tensions were high, and the Watts riot had taken place only a month earlier. The VDC agreed to a daytime march along a different parade route, but negotiations stalled, and it became clear that Oakland officials did not intend to issue a permit. By this time plans for the teach-in and march had proceeded so far that the VDC could not cancel its activities, and the VDC announced that they would test the constitutional right to free speech by holding the march without a permit.[21]

Oakland officials panicked. District Attorney J. Frank Coakley, who publicly stated that the march smacked of "treason," asked Governor Edmund G. ("Pat") Brown, Sr., to alert the National Guard and the highway patrol to prevent a riot; Coakley also wanted Brown to instruct the Regents and Kerr to prohibit the use of the University for staging the march. The governor declined to interfere with the University, but the Guard was placed on alert. The Oakland establishment, led by William Knowland, Don Mulford, and Coakley, never forgave Brown for his lack of total cooperation. "Oakland," wrote the journalist Robert Scheer, "is a terribly primitive place." Coakley then urged Cecil Poole, the federal prosecutor in San Francisco, to investigate the VDC for violation of federal conspiracy laws. Poole, the highest ranking black official in the Bay Area, declined to do so. The prosecutor, too, became the victim of the Oakland establishment's wrath. In 1968, after Poole was nominated for a federal judgeship, conservative Senator George Murphy blocked the appointment. More than the civil rights protests, the VDC touched the nerve centers of the East Bay power structure.[22]

Although organizers had hoped for a large turnout, the crowds at the teach-in were sparser than in the spring. The speeches did not attract students, but entertainers did, and after the teach-in ended near 8 p.m., 10,000 to 15,000 people marched down Telegraph Avenue toward Oakland. Although they included children, grandmothers, and a busload of Ken Kesey's Merry Pranksters (wildly garbed forerunners of the hippies), most of the protesters were college students or other young people. Many linked arms and sang as they marched. A few hostile spectators shouted from the sidelines. Max Scherr personally sold copies of the *Berkeley Barb* by working his way back through the crowd. He shouted, "Read the *Barb*; it's a pleasure not a duty." As the crowd reached the city line, the leaders, who were in front, suddenly faced a solid wall of 400 Oakland policemen. J. Frank Coakley mounted a sound truck and ordered the demonstrators to clear the street. It became clear that Oakland officials would do anything, including provoking a riot, to keep the VDC from marching through their city. The VDC leaders vacillated. Smale favored a sit-down in the street, but Steve Weissman and Jack Weinberg did not want a confrontation that could not be controlled, and after some debate the leaders voted five to four to avoid a confrontation.[23]

The protesters then marched west on Prince Street along the Berkeley-Oakland city limits. When they reached Shattuck Avenue, the leaders considered turning left toward Oakland, but police had blocked the street, and so, despite a chant of "Left, Left," the marchers continued on Prince Street. Eventually, they turned north on Adeline Street and Shattuck Avenue toward downtown Berkeley. The march ended with a rally at Civic Center Park. By that point many demonstrators had gone home, and only a few thousand supporters remained to listen to the speeches. Joe McDonald, a young Berkeley folk singer from an Old Left family, sang his "I-Feel-Like-I'm-Fixin'-To-Die Rag." Although the song was known in Berkeley coffeehouses, this performance enhanced its popularity. Several years passed, however, before this antiwar anthem became generally known; radio stations refused to play it out of fear of losing their licenses. A fight broke out between VDC supporters and opponents, and someone threw a tear gas cannister into the crowd. Robert Scheer urged the crowd to escape the gas by clinging to the ground, but McDonald's band stood silently, as if they were paralyzed. They were high. One hundred demonstrators remained in the park all night.[24]

On Saturday, October 16, the VDC attempted a new march from Civic Center Park into Oakland. When the two to five thousand protesters reached the Oakland city line, they again faced a wall of police. This time the demonstrators seemed less inclined to turn back. The previous day Rubin had noted how turning back had demoralized the participants. In order to prevent trouble, a Berkeley policeman asked the protesters to sit down in the street. They did so, while the leaders debated. At the front of the march Allen Ginsberg played cymbals and chanted, "Hare Krishna." The poet was clearly worried. While the VDC leaders pondered what to do, a number of Hell's Angels, a notoriously tough California motorcycle gang, suddenly rushed through the Oakland police lines, ripped up the VDC banner, and attacked the marchers. One Angel yelled, "Go back to Russia, you fucking Communists!" The Berkeley police then attacked the Angels. One Angel was arrested; a Republican organization provided bail. As an injured Berkeley policeman was carried off on a stretcher, the demonstrators cheered. After this incident, the VDC leaders called off the march and announced plans for a new parade.[25]

A month later the VDC finally marched through Oakland. During its planning some militants wanted an armed march, but the majority insisted upon nonviolence. Ginsberg suggested that the marchers bring flowers and give them to the press, the Angels, and the police. "A demonstration is a theatrical production," he stressed. The VDC hired an attorney to go to federal court to force Oakland officials to issue a parade permit. A federal judge issued a permit, and the march took place on Saturday, November 20. It was anticlimactic. For one thing, the VDC did not secure the permit until the last minute, and that made it difficult to plan a rally prior to the march. Crowd-pleasing stars could not be obtained on short notice. Then, too, the parade route lacked drama. The judge, concerned about a race riot, had barred the demonstrators from the black ghetto. At the army's insistence, he had also kept the march away from the army base. Although the VDC was grateful for the permit, there was little excitement in marching through white Oakland to DeFremery Park. The Hell's Angels, under the influence of Ken Kesey, were bribed to stay away with a generous supply of beer. Between 6,000 and 10,000 people marched.[26]

In August 1965 the VDC had protested to Representative Jeffery Cohelan about the growing war. Elected to Congress as Berkeley's first liberal Democrat in the landslide of 1958, the former milk truck driver and union official was a typical Cold War Democrat. A liberal domestically and a strong anticommunist, Cohelan supported the administration's policy in Vietnam out of belief, out of party loyalty, and out of respect for the AFL-CIO's George Meany, a militant backer of the war. When Dr. Daniel Simon, a Berkeley physician, launched a campaign against the war that resulted in 600 to 1,000 postcards being mailed to Cohelan, the congressman denounced the effort. Later, the VDC met with the congressman to express its concerns, and he dismissed them as a tiny group of extremists. In February 1966 several VDC supporters, including a columnist for the *Berkeley Barb*, held a sit-in in Cohelan's office in downtown Oakland. To the group's surprise, they were arrested.[27]

By early 1966 the VDC was more than an ad hoc committee to protest the war and less than a political movement. There were strains inside the group between those who advocated militant action to radicalize young people and those who advocated political organizing to elect radicals to public office. At an important meeting in January, about 200 VDC supporters debated this issue. Jerry Rubin, Steve Weissman, Barbara Gullahorn, and others supported Robert Scheer's proposal to challenge Cohelan for the Democratic party nomination on a radical, antiwar platform. Jack Weinberg of the Independent Socialist Club, a group with a Trotskyist background, opposed this plan. So did Syd Stapleton of the Young Socialist Alliance, a more orthodox Trotskyist organization. Stapleton drew an ovation when he said, "You shouldn't be burning your draft cards, you should be burning your Democratic Party cards." The Trotskyists refused to support any candidate who did not run as a socialist. A large majority, however, endorsed Scheer's views, and the VDC split in twain.

While Rubin, Weissman, the DuBois clubs, communists, and liberals worked for Scheer's election, the Trotskyists and important independents like Bill Miller and Mike Delacour planned VDC direct action. "It seems," said the former FSM leader Brian Turner, "that we have reached the end of politics." After the communists and liberals left the VDC to work for Scheer, the VDC fell under the control of the Trotskyists and then slowly disintegrated.[28]

Robert Scheer had gradually emerged as one of the most influential leaders inside the VDC. Originally drawn from New York to Berkeley to do graduate work in economics, Scheer's political consciousness had developed while living in the Bay Area. The former campaigner for Adlai Stevenson and full-time worker for the liberal Americans for Democratic Action read widely and drifted to the Left. For a time Scheer worked at City Lights Bookstore in San Francisco, where he not only became acquainted with the San Francisco beats but pushed radical books into the hands of the bohemians who wandered into the store. Among the people he met and became friends with was R. C. Davis, whose San Francisco Mime Troupe became a fixture of Bay Area radicalism. Scheer dropped out of graduate school and drifted into free-lance journalism. In 1962–63 he edited *Root and Branch*, a minor Berkeley radical-beat journal. Scheer had traveled to Cuba and in 1963 published his first book, written with Maurice Zeitlin, about the Cuban revolution. After he returned from Cuba, Scheer grew a beard in the Castro style. The young journalist's infatuation with Castro was matched by a disenchantment with Kennedy; Scheer saw Kennedy as both the architect and the victim of Cold War policies that were about to bring the United States to ruin.[29]

In 1964 Scheer traveled to Vietnam as a free-lance journalist. One of the first American journalists to see Vietnam with independent eyes, he was shaken by what he saw. In Saigon Scheer found a corrupt government totally dependent upon American aid for its existence; in the countryside the communists were in control. His own sympathies for the nonwhite peoples of the world along with his distrust of American foreign policy led him to radical conclusions. He was alarmed that the Americans in Vietnam lacked comprehension of the situation. Either they had deluded themselves or, for the sake of their careers, they chose to believe the optimistic and inaccurate assessments that American officials presented both to Washington and to American newsmen in Vietnam. What separated Scheer from other journalists was both his deeper perception and his willingness to return home and engage in political controversy.[30]

Convinced that the administration was following a disastrous course, Scheer returned to Berkeley and began a quiet campaign against American involvement in Vietnam. He spoke in public meetings, in classrooms, and at a SLATE-sponsored showing of a Viet Cong film on the war in Vietnam. There was some trouble getting the film, however, because the State Department had confiscated it when it was brought into the United States; this incident was Scheer's first exposure to the way in which the government at times conducted foreign policy at the expense of constitutional rights. Scheer then decided to write a pamphlet on Vietnam; after some delay, in which some suspected that the Johnson administration had applied pressure to suppress an unflattering report, the pamphlet was published in July 1965 by the Center for the Study of Democratic Institutions in Santa Barbara. This pamphlet was extremely important; it offered cogent arguments against the administration's policy. Scheer found an audience for his views among Bay Area radicals. The beat culture of San Francisco, the civil rights movement, and the local radicals' lack of ideology pushed Scheer into the VDC.[31]

In 1966 Scheer decided to use the VDC as a base to challenge Cohelan for the congressional nomination in the Democratic primary election in June. The young radical intended to create a broad coalition of leftists and antiwar liberals. In the beginning, Scheer's greatest support came from the VDC; Rubin acted as his campaign manager. Because the VDC's "raucous style" offended liberals, Rubin undertook to subdue the campaign. He nevertheless envisioned street rallies, free rock shows, and teach-ins, as well as more traditional activities, such as door to door canvassing. In Rubin's analysis, these new political tactics had the capacity to change consciousness as the Free Speech Movement had done. "We are building a radical movement that is relevant," he concluded. Radicals felt galled at having to register as Democrats in order to vote for Scheer in the primary. They suspected, correctly, that one of the main results of the contest was going to be an increase in Democratic party registration. As Scheer's support among antiwar liberals grew, his ties to Rubin became embarrassing. After Rubin proposed a fundraising dinner jointly honoring Thomas Jefferson and Karl Marx, he was forced out of the campaign.[32]

Scheer's boldest decision was to accept support from all sources. In other words, for the first time since the mid-forties, a Democratic candidate did not proscribe communists. This strategy had both theoretical and practical dimensions. Scheer was not a communist; but, at twenty-nine years old, he belonged to a generation that did not believe in proscribing communists. Scheer also drew his radical strategy from his analysis of the failure of American liberalism. Liberals could not oppose the war without being accused of giving Vietnam to the communists. So long as liberals accepted the premise of anticommunism, they would support the war. "The war in Vietnam," Scheer noted in a campaign speech, "is a product of American liberalism." Hence, the war logically resulted from this anticommunist belief, and Scheer set out to destroy that belief. The best way to do so was to accept communist support.[33]

Furthermore, communists were numerous and useful within the district. Their support yielded money and volunteers. One of Scheer's most active campaign workers was Carl Bloice, a black reporter for the communist *People's World*.

Communist support also gave the radical campaign a conservative cast; as shown in the Free Speech Movement, communists were the most cautious radicals. Members of the party always dressed formally. "I have been accused of being a Communist," joked Scheer. "I really don't know why, except possibly that I always wear a coat and tie at political meetings." At the same time, communists had been outsiders so long that merely not excluding them won their gratitude. Scheer was free to say whatever he wanted. Nonexclusion also made it impossible for the communists to run their own candidate, which would have divided the Left. Finally, since Cohelan already had the anticommunist vote within the Democratic party, accepting communist help did not alienate potential supporters. Scheer's campaign marked the first step toward the creation of a radical electoral coalition.[34]

Electoral arithmetic dictated another part of Scheer's strategy. Blacks were more than a fifth of the voters in the district—in the Democratic primary, 35 percent. Over the years Cohelan had done little for his black constituents, and he was known as a former official of an all-white labor union. The congressman was not personally prejudiced, and in previous elections he had enjoyed black support, but blacks were restless. The black elite's support for Cohelan gave Scheer the opportunity to appeal to young black militants. Scheer told them that he had met his wife, Anne Weills Scheer, at a civil rights sit-in in San Francisco in 1964. One of the few newspapers to cover Scheer's campaign extensively and to endorse him was the black-owned Sun-Reporter. Published in San Francisco by Dr. Carleton Goodlett, this surprisingly radical newspaper was the most important black paper in the Bay Area. The radical candidate opened his campaign in a black nightclub in West Oakland, and he spent much of his time in black neighborhoods.[35]

Strategy also led to a grassroots campaign. Such a campaign was necessary to offset Cohelan's advantages as an incumbent. Cohelan was endorsed by the San Francisco Chronicle and the Berkeley Daily Gazette, by Senator J. William Fulbright, by five northern California Democratic congressmen, by District Attorney J. Frank Coakley, by all the Democrats on the Berkeley city council, by the Berkeley Chapter of Mexican American Political Action, and by George Meany's unions. The AFL-CIO refused to support any Democratic candidates who did not back Cohelan. Of labor groups, only Harry Bridge's leftist International Longshoremen's and Warehousemen's Union supported Scheer. Cohelan also depended upon testimonials. A television advertisement featuring Senator Robert Kennedy particularly enraged Scheer's supporters; memories of that commercial caused Kennedy problems when he ran for president two years later. Cohelan's advertising portrayed him as a moderate, reasonable peace candidate. In truth, the congressman was not an extreme hawk, even though the Berkeley Barb insisted, "Cohelan has the blood and napalm vote in Berkeley."[36]

Cohelan's strength traditionally had come from the local Democratic clubs.

Scheer, however, knew that the war, by causing bitter divisions within the clubs, was destroying them. The Berkeley-Albany Democratic Study and Action Club, the largest in the county with 260 members, demanded that Cohelan debate Scheer. No debate was held. Although the smaller Albany Democratic Club endorsed Cohelan, the congressman's own club refused to make any endorsement in the congressional race. The head of the statewide California Democratic Council (CDC), Si Casady, had denounced the war. His reward, said to have been dictated by President Johnson, was to be removed from his post. Many clubs revolted against the administration; both Casady and the statewide CDC endorsed Scheer. The final incentive to run a grassroots campaign was the large number of antiwar students on the Berkeley campus. If the energy that had gone into the FSM and the VDC marches could be tapped for precinct work, Scheer could expect to cover all the precincts in Berkeley. More than 1,000 people worked on the campaign; 500 walked from house to house, knocked on doors, and talked with voters. They registered more than 10,000 new voters.[37]

The grassroots campaign meant more than electioneering tactics; it was at the core of the philosophy that underlay both Scheer's campaign and the Berkeley radical movement. Its spiritual ancestor was Benjamin Franklin, who had said, "God helps those who help themselves." Or as R. G. Davis later put it, "If you want something done, do it yourself." Indeed, it became clear that this message, rather than the war, explained why Scheer was running. Scheer saw fundamental flaws in the ways in which liberal America conducted its affairs. The country was misgoverned; the Watts riot, the Vietnam War, and student unrest were symptoms of the rot that liberalism had brought to American society. That rot had to be cut out; to do it, said Scheer, radical means must be used. He called his campaign "unabashedly radical." Scheer lectured to voters in a way that no serious candidate for public office had ever done. "In the campaign," he later recalled, "we were loose, we were free, and we never allowed anybody to be bored. We shunned ideological discussions or arguments. We capitalized on confrontation politics, and we faced the issues."[38]

Scheer's radicalism pursued a profoundly democratic ideal. Power in America, he suggested, was no longer democratic. Whereas power had once flowed from the bottom up, it now flowed from the top down. Cohelan's support for the war illustrated the problem; it was nothing more than a blind obedience to Lyndon Johnson. This conduct, suggested Scheer, was a perversion of democracy. Instead of being the people's representative or exercising conscience, Cohelan acted like a Nazi deputy following Hitler. The cure for this problem entailed more than replacing Cohelan; it required reconceptualizing the relationship between the individual and society. The people on the bottom had to organize politically. Scheer had an absolute faith in the ability of the people, if politically awakened, to regain power over their own destinies. He once lectured a radical audience, "Get out and talk to people. I think a certain amount of alienation is healthy, to approach society in a fresh and vital manner. But one has to be able to talk to the average person in a society. That's one of the nice things about an election campaign: It forces you to do just that."[39]

By election day Scheer had organized almost all the precincts in Berkeley, and he had energized much of the black community. Although he lost to Cohelan, Scheer drew 45 percent of the vote in the district and carried Berkeley with 54 percent. If Scheer had been able to organize outside Berkeley, he might have won the primary. As it was, he carried black neighborhoods where he had workers, and he won overwhelmingly support in the precincts where large numbers of students or other young people lived. His support crossed traditional party lines; in one precinct half the Republicans wrote in Scheer's name. In Berkeley Cohelan carried parts of the hills. Democrats in the hills were older, wealthier, and more cautious; they had known Cohelan a long time, since his days on the Berkeley city council in the 1950s. Nevertheless, Scheer had given Cohelan a bad scare; his long-term prospects looked doubtful. "Poor Jeff is doomed," crowed the *Berkeley Barb*. This contest did not go unnoticed in high places. On election night Lyndon Johnson's assistant, Bill Moyers, incessantly queried the Alameda County courthouse about the contest.[40]

Other Berkeley antiwar radicals attracted attention, too. Jerry Rubin's draft board ordered him to report for a pre-induction physical, although he had recently reached the age beyond which he could not be inducted. Almost simultaneously with this harassment, the House Un-American Activities Committee subpoenaed a number of Bay Area radicals, including Rubin, Stephen Smale, Steve Hamilton, and Steve Cherkoss, to testify in Washington. Stewart Albert was insulted that he had not been important enough to be included. He suffered from what Rubin called "subpoenas envy." Rubin discussed his forthcoming appearance before HUAC with R. G. Davis at the Cafe Med. They agreed that HUAC had given Rubin an excellent opportunity for publicity, but Davis warned that the media invariably distorted radical political statements. To attack HUAC, it was necessary to be visual rather than verbal. "People don't like to read," noted Rubin, "We are an eye and ear culture." Based upon the Mime Troupe's performances, Davis urged that Rubin be theatrical. At Davis's suggestion, Rubin appeared before HUAC wearing a rented American Revolutionary War soldier's uniform. "With that one zap," Rubin later recalled, "I inspired rebellious people everywhere to be outrageous." Rubin's appearance was so startling that when it was his turn to testify, the proceedings were stopped. As marshals carried him out, he screamed, "I want to testify!" He became a media celebrity; HUAC never recovered. Rubin returned to Berkeley a radical hero.[41]

HUAC had difficulty subpoenaing Smale; he was in Moscow attending the International Congress of Mathematics, which had awarded him a major prize.

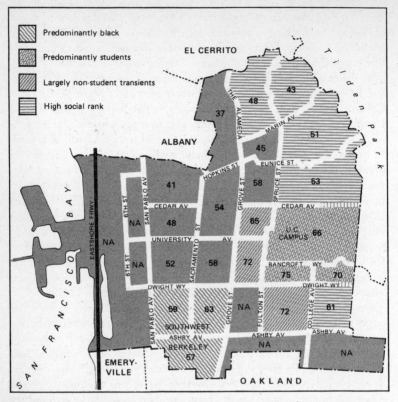

Map 3.1. 1966 Scheer Democratic primary vote, in percentages, by census tract.
(*Sources:* U.S., Bureau of the Census; Richard C. Howell, "A Contextual Perspective on Political Leadership" (M.A. thesis, San Francisco State College, 1972), 82–84.)

Smeared in the press, the brilliant young mathematician had his University summer research grant suspended. A year later Representative Richard Roudebush of Indiana pressured the National Science Foundation (NSF) to deny Smale a major grant that he had been promised. At first the NSF appeared to capitulate, but after a large number of prominent scientists protested vigorously, Smale's grant was partially restored. In a compromise, Smale was given a personal award but was denied the right to administer a grant covering a large research staff. The damage, of course, had been done. Every scientist in the country learned that antiwar activity might lead to embarrassment, harassment, or interference with one's work. This message was precisely the one that the administration wanted to send.[42]

Throughout 1966 many Berkeley radicals increasingly doubted the value of electoral politics. During Scheer's campaign the militants who had taken over the VDC became embittered and disillusioned. Early in the morning of April 9, someone dynamited the VDC headquarters; the building was demolished. A month earlier a similar blast had destroyed the DuBois club in San Francisco. The FBI may have been involved in these bombings. The VDC bombing drove the militants into a rage. "They're escalating," said Stew Albert. "We're going to have to escalate our protests." The VDC planned to hold a rally on Telegraph Avenue without a permit. Scheer was invited to speak but did not show, which caused him to lose face among the militants. At the rally the police moved to disconnect the VDC's illegal sound equipment; a fight broke out. "When your back is to the wall," said Marvin Garson, "you've got to fight." The crowd of 2,000 then left Telegraph and marched to city hall chanting, "Hey, hey, LBJ, How many kids did you kill today?" After a noisy rally, eleven were arrested. None were University students. Arrestees included Stew Albert, Steve Cherkoss, and Mike Smith, who had been expelled from the University some days earlier. Of this protest, conservative Councilman John DeBonis said, "It's disgraceful. Turn the billy clubs on 'em."[43]

Ironically, Scheer's electoral success made militance more likely. Because he had established that the war was unpopular in Berkeley, it ceased to be an issue locally, and even Cohelan made dovelike coos. To many radicals, building an electoral base around other issues seemed unlikely, and they preferred to build radicalism by using militant tactics. Action was crucial to the radical strategy first developed during the Free Speech Movement. According to this strategy, which portions of the SDS espoused in the late sixties, radicalism could best be advanced by actions that created confrontations and repression. Confrontations pushed alienated young people, especially students, into the radical camp, and repression destroyed the possibility for middle ground. This strategy had worked brilliantly during the FSM, and in the fall of 1966 radicals yearned to reproduce their earlier success. Because the need for confrontation precluded compromise, all demands were nonnegotiable. Conservative Councilman Thomas L. McLaren once asked Michael Rossman, "If we give in to your present demand will this satisfy you, or is this only one of a long list of demands?" Rossman replied, "Don't worry, we'll always be one demand ahead of you." Radicals focused on the University, because it had proved vulnerable before, and because it contained a large number of potential recruits.[44]

The man who faced this radical challenge on the Berkeley campus was Roger Heyns, who became the chancellor in the fall of 1965. Kerr said that he had heard that Heyns walked on water and that his capacity to do so was a good sign, since it was the minimum requirement to be chancellor. A Dutch Calvinist by training and a practicing Presbyterian by conviction, Heyns had the stable values of his native Midwest. His cautious reason, staunch integrity, quiet tenacity, and tough-minded sobriety—improbably transplanted to Berkeley—contrasted with the local carnival of mindless ideals. A psychologist by training, the former University of Michigan administrator had a reputation for being able to manage troublesome students. Although Kerr and the Regents promised Heyns autonomy, the new chancellor found that he had little freedom to maneuver. For example, Heyns did not have his own counsel and, unlike other chancellors, was forced to use the Regents' attorney, Thomas J. Cunningham. While Cunningham was an excellent attorney, he knew to whom he owed his loyalty. Whenever he perceived a conflict between the Regents and Heyns, Cunningham sided with Regents. The chancellor sometimes found himself without a legal defense for his administrative action.[45]

Heyns found Berkeley in a state of perpetual war; he privately called the atmosphere "sick." On one side William Knowland, Don Mulford, Frank Coakley, and certain Regents were determined to control Oakland, Berkeley, and the University. Their contact on campus, Professor Hardin B. Jones, described the University as "monolithically Marxist" and its faculty as "demented." Jones, a professor of medical physics and bioradiation at the Donner Laboratory, was one of seven security informants on campus; he and his assistant, retired Colonel Alex Grendon, routinely attended campus political meetings and took notes or made recordings. Jones's voluminous files formed a virtual library of paranoia. These conservatives, if the word fits, seemed obsessed with destroying their enemies. They were, Heyns came to learn, unreasonable men. On the other side, Berkeley radicals were no better. These vain, proud, and cocky young leftists arrogantly sought to seize control of both the city and the University. They, too, were unreasonable; they disdained compromise as hyprocrisy, as selling out, and as undignified conduct to be treated with contempt. Heyns was surprised and appalled by the smallness and the ineffectiveness of the center. In Berkeley most of the middle ground had disappeared. Heyns soon learned by experience that to oppose both the conservatives and the radicals was to be damned by each side. When the chancellor was harassed on his private, unlisted home telephone, he did not know whether the calls came from the Left or the Right.[46]

Heyns set out to build a moderate force on the campus. He stressed cooperation over confrontation, the even-handed application of reasonable rules, and, above all, creating lines of communication to all portions of the University community. When Bettina Aptheker was elected to the campus committee for regulating free speech shortly after she openly declared her membership in the Communist party, Heyns ignored conservative demands to remove her from office. Because radical students felt isolated, Heyns named John Searle, a young professor who had strongly supported the FSM, as his special assistant and liaison with the radicals. The chancellor expected the appointment both to calm the students and to give the administration a listening post inside the radical camp. Conservatives, however, badgered Heyns and Kerr about this appointment, and it became one of the reasons Kerr was fired. By 1966 Searle felt that the radical students had betrayed him, and he quit his administrative post. Never again did the radicals trust a member of the Heyns administration.[47]

Heyns's analysis of student revolt was shrewd and accurate. He believed that the University contained only a handful of radical students. Although the situation in Berkeley was complicated by the Telegraph Avenue bohemia, students and hippies normally did not interact. Campus turmoil occurred when radical leaders created an incident that led the University to bring police onto campus. Radical leaders then rallied normally apolitical students against this display of authority and power to support fellow students under attack. Therefore, Heyns concluded, to manage the campus he should avoid confrontation, even at the cost of tolerating minor violations. Radical leaders understood Heyns's strategy and tried to force confrontations. When such incidents took place, Heyns suggested, it was wise to give students ways to save face and back down. If they did not, then he punished the rule-breakers. It was important to treat the leaders more harshly than the followers. Each incident, he recognized, had the potential for creating new radical leaders from among the followers.[48]

Heyns devised an especially clever way to impose campus discipline upon students who violated rules. When a hearing officer recommended harsh punishment, such as suspension or expulsion, Heyns took the recommendation under advisement and waited a long time before announcing his final decision. During this interval the student under disciplinary sanction tended to restrain his behavior, since he sensed, correctly, that Heyns's penalty was to be based upon the student's behavior during the judicial process as much as upon his behavior during the original incident. Often, Heyns softened the punishment. Such action not only showed the chancellor to be caring, merciful, and generous, but it also subtly reinforced Heyns's desire to coerce good behavior while he pondered his decision. Heyns frequently imposed probation, because, as he explained to the Regents, it had a powerful effect upon behavior. Whereas a suspended student might become an embittered former student who hovered near the campus and made trouble, a student on probation usually tried to avoid further trouble. Statistics confirmed Heyns on this latter point.[49]

Throughout 1966 the University battled radicals over campus rules. Early in the year the VDC held an illegal rally; three students, including Bettina Aptheker, were placed on probation. Then the Trotskyists took over the VDC, and other radicals created the Peace/Rights Organizing Committee (PROC). After University officials discovered that PROC had listed some nonstudents on its registration form, the group was banned. When PROC set up tables in defiance of the ban, three students were cited. Protests ensued, more students were cited, and a number of nonstudents were arrested. Heyns suspended two students, Steve Hamilton and Mike Smith, and placed others on probation. About this time Governor Brown visited campus and stopped at the PROC table, which was being manned by a nonstudent, Stew Albert. They shook hands, and Albert said, "I'm a communist-PLP."

Brown replied, "Oh, yes, I've heard about you. You're the Chinese Communist, aren't you?"

"No," replied Albert, "I'm an American. Would you like a copy of PL Magazine?"

"I don't have any change," said Brown.

Albert handed Brown a copy and said, "If you're short of dough, I'll lend it to you and you can pay me back next time I see you."[50]

On March 25, 1966, Arthur Goldberg, the American ambassador to the United Nations, was the main speaker at the University's Charter Day ceremonies at the Greek Theatre. PROC insisted on distributing antiwar signs to students who attended. Heyns reluctantly agreed to the scheme after PROC had threatened to block the theater entrances. Many of the 12,000 people in the theater carried the signs. Following this event, Goldberg went to Harmon Gym to debate the war with Professor Franz Schurmann. Many of the 7,000 students in the audience were wearing Scheer buttons; Scheer had held an antiwar meeting in the gym only a few hours earlier. At the end of the debate, the moderator polled the audience. A couple of hundred students supported the administration; the remainder silently rose in opposition. That night the VDC held a dance at the gym at which marijuana was alleged to have been smoked. Opponents called it an "orgy." This incident was denounced by gubernatorial candidate Ronald Reagan. In April there was trouble over VDC tables; twenty-one students were cited. At a subsequent disciplinary hearing, most of the students, on the advice of their attorney, walked out. In May the Trotskyists organized a celebration of the VDC's first anniversary, but it drew little attention. In August the administration banned the VDC; it lost the right to place its tables on campus.[51]

By November 1966 the campus was seething. A number of conservatives inside the administration had proposed to ban microphones and noon rallies from the steps of Sproul Hall. Radical opposition was intense, in part because the steps had deep symbolic significance to the students who had participated in the Free Speech Movement. A number of faculty members cautioned Heyns against the proposal, and the chancellor bided his time. On Friday, November 4, an important rally to defend free speech on the steps was held. Mario Savio, who had only recently returned to Berkeley, denounced not only the proposed ban but also the University's existing regulations, which prohibited nonstudents from distributing literature on campus; this most famous of Cal's nonstudents then violated the rules by passing out some VDC literature. Four days later Ronald Reagan defeated Pat Brown's bid for reelection; the new governor had been elected in a landslide partly by campaigning against radicalism at Berkeley. On election day Savio learned that his application for readmission had been denied because of his violation of University rules in the previous week. After the election Republican Regents tried to arrange a meeting between Reagan and Kerr, but Reagan declined to see Kerr, and a number of Regents then concluded that Kerr had to go.[52]

Meanwhile, on campus the ASUC had given the navy permission to recruit at a table inside the Student Union. This table offended radicals, because the navy, which was not a student organization, was allowed to have a table while the VDC and PROC had been banned. On November 30, radicals protested by forming a close picket line and crowding around the navy table. Despite this protest, the table remained. Soon the radicals decided to recreate the spirit of the FSM by holding a sit-in. They expected the administration to order hundreds of students arrested; these students would become converts to the radical cause. Heyns, however, had told subordinates to avoid mass arrests. As it happened, the chancellor was out of town. Had he been in Berkeley, it is possible that no arrests would have been made. If the recruiting table had been removed temporarily, the protesters probably would have drifted away. But Heyns's subordinates lacked the chancellor's craftiness, and they were determined to uphold the law.[53]

Much to the surprise of the fifty to a hundred people who sat in, administrators fingered only a half dozen nonstudents for the police to arrest. They were Mario Savio, the former FSM leader; Jerry Rubin, the former VDC leader; Stewart Albert, a friend of Rubin's and an activist in the Maoist Progressive Labor (PL) party; Steve Hamilton, another PL leader; Bill Miller, an independent radical with anarchist sympathies; and Mike Smith, another independent leftist. Albert had never been a student at Berkeley, although his long, blond hair was a familiar sight to those who passed by the various radical tables, where he often sat. Among those not arrested was Karen Lieberman Wald, who screamed at the police, "You fucking male supremacists, arrest me, too!" She felt insulted that the authorities did not consider her important enough to be arrested. As the administrators had calculated, the crowd began to melt away as soon as the leaders were removed. After a trial in which Melvin Belli defended the six, all except Miller were convicted; they drew jail terms of from forty to eighty days.[54]

The radicals, in a replay of 1964, called for a student strike. The strike, however, drew little support and quickly failed; its main effect was to disclose the weakness of Local 1570, the teaching assistants' union. After this episode, radical leaders came to recognize that Heyns had changed the atmosphere on the campus so much that few students could be recruited. A number of students wrote Heyns to discuss both their opposition to the strike and the larger concerns that troubled them. Although James B. Widess did not strike, he found the University rigid, stultifying, and lacking a sense of direction. "We are frustrated because we have nowhere to go," he lamented. Of the strikers, another student commented, "They criticized the University for presumably failing to save their souls and give meaning to their lives, while they could hardly articulate a coherent sentence. They showed themselves illiterates with an inflamed sense of their own worth, utterly lacking any awareness of their limitations."[55]

Heyns's strategy for building a psychologically healthy campus appeared to be working, but the chancellor suddenly faced trouble from a new direction. In January 1967 several Regents privately urged Kerr to resign, but he refused, and his status was placed on the agenda for the Regents meeting at the end of the month. This meeting was the first one Reagan attended. The board, with the support of Reagan and the other new ex-officio Republican Regents, voted fourteen to eight to dismiss Kerr. This dismissal shocked the public; Kerr's identity was closely tied to that of the University. The inexperienced governor quickly learned that he had made a tactical mistake. Firing Kerr angered the public, made Reagan look petty, turned Kerr into a martyr, and forced the Regents to hire a new president under difficult conditions. After Kerr's dismissal, no distinguished outsider wanted the position. So the board appointed Charles Hitch, a brilliant but colorless University financial analyst with strong ties to the Defense Department. Kerr had arranged matters so that Hitch was the only acceptable person and, in effect, dictated the succession. Kerr's dismissal undid much of Heyns's efforts to build an atmosphere of cooperation, trust, and tranquility, and the sour and nasty mood among the increasingly politicized Regents left many people wondering whether Heyns could survive.[56]

During early 1967 radicals divided over strategy. Militants who saw themselves as victims of Heyns, the Regents, and the business community argued, "We've got to start over and wreck everything before we can save it." They looked increasingly for support not from students but from the ever-growing bohemia of nonstudents who lived in the vicinity of Telegraph Avenue. This nucleus of support led other radicals to fight at the ballot box. Scheer's victory in the Berkeley portion of the district had given the radicals hope; Scheer and others created the Community for New Politics (CNP). At the national level the CNP came to little; black militants took over its national convention, and in 1968, as the Peace and Freedom party, its presidential candidate in California was Eldridge Cleaver. In Berkeley the CNP decided to run candidates in the April 1967 city election. One of its slogans was "Don't Drop Out—Take Over." The CNP became an incubator for radicals into the 1970s. Its newsletter, in keeping with the CNP's belief in grassroots politics and Scheer's vision of power flowing from the bottom up, concentrated on local issues. By shifting the focus from the war, which still divided many liberals from radicals, toward such issues as preserving Berkeley's neighborhoods or building parks, the CNP took a stance that eventually led to local political success. In 1968 the editor of the CNP's newsletter was Ilona Hancock; three years later she was elected to the city council.[57]

During the 1967 campaign the liberal coalition that had governed Berkeley for six years dissolved. Most of the CDC clubs were dead—casualties of the divisions among Berkeley liberals over the Vietnam War. The meeting of the Berkeley Democratic Caucus (BDC) produced a curious result. The BDC endorsed the liberal incumbent Bernice Hubbard May and a new, attractive black candidate, Ronald V. Dellums. Those inside the BDC who detested the antiwar radicals then moved to close the endorsements, and this motion carried 46 to 43. Thus, by a handful of votes, the liberals rejected making an alliance with the radicals. The radicals were enraged at the unwillingness of the liberals to share endorsements. The Community for a New Politics held a caucus to endorse its own candidates: Robert Avakian, Howard Harawitz, Professor J. B. Neilands, and Ronald V. Dellums. Except for Dellums, the CNP candidates were identified with the Left; all had been active in the antiwar movement. Of Avakian, the BCU later said, "When will TREASON be called TREASON and dealt with accordingly."[58]

The campaign was bitter. Radicals considered liberals to be the principal enemy and attempted to destroy the liberal city government. "More and more the left groups concentrated on attempts to discredit the council," recalled Councilwoman Margaret S. Gordon, "for they knew they could take no votes from the Republicans." This radical attack on liberals was partially a matter of calculation. Radicals wanted a whole loaf; liberals always compromised and accepted half a loaf and thereby guaranteed that a whole loaf could never be obtained. Better, thought the radicals, to elect conservatives; they gave nothing, and the reaction might lead to a radical triumph. This sort of reasoning had led Jerry Rubin to vote for Ronald Reagan for governor. Radical attacks were also fueled by anger; radicals keenly felt the liberal disdain for them. Although May won reelection, and Dellums parlayed his double endorsement into a victory, conservative Republicans won the two remaining council seats. Avakian, Harawitz, and Neilands drew nearly a third of the total vote. Trotskyist candidates got few votes. The council continued to have a six to three liberal majority, but it was unstable because Dellums's views were to the left of the other members of the council.[59]

The 1967 mayoral race had its own peculiarities. Wallace Johnson, the moderately conservative Republican incumbent, ran for reelection. As the owner and operator of an important local corporation, Up-Right, Inc., Johnson enjoyed business support. He had joined council liberals to beautify the city with grass plantings, park benches, and underground wiring and had forced the Bay

Area Rapid Transit district to build a subway for its trains in Berkeley. Neither the BDC nor the CNP opposed his reelection. The BDC had agreed not to oppose Johnson in return for Republican support for May. Already, conservatives were showing a willingness to swallow liberals in order to defeat radicals. The CNP calculated that Johnson's combined Republican-BDC support would cause a CNP candidate to lose badly. Since the CNP's main purpose in this election was to demonstrate electoral prowess, such a loss served no purpose. Johnson's only opponents were archconservative Fred Huntley of the John Birch Society, Peter Camejo of the Socialist Workers party, and Jerry Rubin.[60]

Jerry Rubin ran as an independent radical. Without organized support and with a lukewarm endorsement from the Berkeley Barb, Rubin had no chance. Somewhat sleazily, a Rubin accomplice got a job in Johnson's factory and then filed discrimination charges against the firm; this ploy backfired. At a joint campaign appearance Rubin whispered to Johnson, "I hope you realize this isn't anything personal." Rubin's most original contribution was a twenty-six page pamphlet stating his stand on the issues. Thirty thousand copies were printed and distributed to every household in Berkeley. This brochure, co-authored by Stew Albert, capitalized on the bohemian mood that swept Berkeley in 1966 and 1967; it was printed in a rainbow of colors. The clever and slick packaging matched Rubin's bold and innovative political views. The former VDC leader not only urged the city to oppose the war but also proposed an end to the draft, the construction of public housing, strict rent control, a city income tax, community control of the police, legal marijuana and abortions, and child care for working mothers. Rubin's pamphlet set forth the political agenda that dominated local politics for the remainder of the decade and into the seventies. It was a radical, libertarian document that showed the difference between the Old Left and the New Left. Whereas Avakian, Harawitz, and Neilands, as well as Camejo, were tied to the past, Rubin was not. Rubin carried four student precincts. He received 7,385 votes (21 percent) to Johnson's 25,224 and Camejo's 1,019. Huntley drew 2,160 votes. After this election Rubin moved east to organize the antiwar march on the Pentagon.[61]

The radical electoral campaign had again failed. As in the Scheer campaign, radicals had done well, but in the end liberals and conservatives had joined together to defeat the threat to the existing social order. Against Cohelan, Scheer had run surprisingly well; he was an attractive candidate, but his success owed less to his radicalism than to Cohelan's support for a war that was unpopular in Berkeley. When radicals faced other candidates in an election in which Republicans could vote, the radicals still lost, and by larger margins. In part this was due to the weakness of the radical candidates; Avakian, Harawitz, and Neilands were shopworn leftists soft-pedaling worn-out views. Rubin's bold strategy of setting forth a new vision was the correct one, but he lacked the skills for success in electoral politics. (Even his friends couldn't stand him.) "Incidentally," wrote Representative Cohelan to Professor Hardin B. Jones, "I was very pleased that the devout leftists and assorted crack-pots took the election defeat they so thoroughly deserved." Cohelan's arrogance was not justified. Avakian warned the winners not to be complacent; the CNP planned "to take over . . . the whole society," which he called "sick and corrupt." The one leftist winner, Ronald V. Dellums, had used race to obscure the gap between liberalism and radicalism. His victory opened the prospect of building a coalition based upon black militants and white radicals. To build such a coalition required combining the Old Left support that coalesced around the CNP with the black support that had gathered around Dellums, then adding the countercultural support that Rubin had enjoyed. Anyone who could put together that combination could control Berkeley.[62]

Despite these tantalizing long-term prospects, radicals were unhappy. Johnson's war raged on and continued to grow; outside Berkeley, most Americans supported the war. If Berkeley was different, it was because local radicals had presented a far bolder and more accurate analysis of the Vietnam War. Felix Greene, a British subject who lived in Palo Alto, visited North Vietnam, and the slide lectures and book that he produced after his return had a major impact. So did Donald Duncan, a retired sergeant from the Special Forces; he spoke powerfully against the war before local audiences. Also important were reports on KQED, the San Francisco public television station, which had started its own nightly news program in 1966. At a time when few American media outlets carried any views other than those approved by the administration, both KQED and KPFA regularly broadcast radical critiques of the war. By March 1967 the *Berkeley Barb* had a circulation of 16,500, which was about 1,000 more than the increasingly conservative *Berkeley Daily Gazette*. Admittedly, much of the *Barb's* circulation was outside Berkeley, and its radicalism was tempered by countercultural news and sex ads, but the paper remained politically Left.[63]

Local protest often had a zany quality that expressed the Bay Area radicals' lack of ideology and their zest for life. The San Francisco Mime Troupe performed a scathing antiwar skit numerous times in Bay Area public parks, and Joe McDonald, Joan Baez, and other local artists continued to aid the antiwar movement. Barbara Garson wrote "MacBird," a play which made Lyndon Johnson responsible for John Kennedy's assassination. After premiering in San Francisco, the play went to New York in the fall of 1966. The suddenly famous Garsons drove to New York for the opening and along the way stopped at the SDS's national meeting, where they encountered Bettina Aptheker and Carl Bloice. "MacBird" led an alarmed J. Edgar Hoover to order an FBI investigation of the young playwright. In 1967, when Robert Kennedy was featured at a Democratic party fund-raising dinner at the Fairmont Hotel in San Francisco, Rubin, Albert, and several dozen other radicals picketed. They shouted,

"Why pay $100 a plate? FREE BALONEY HERE." While most of the pro-
testers carried signs, Barbara Garson handed out bread and baloney sand-
wiches. Before Kennedy arrived, the police removed all the protesters, except
for Michael P. Lerner, who was dressed in a coat and tie. Lerner joined the
receiving line, and when Kennedy approached, the young radical shouted, "GET
OUT OF VIETNAM." Two officers removed Lerner; Kennedy looked startled.
No one was arrested.[64]

The most important contributions to the radical cause came from *Ramparts*
magazine. Founded in 1962 in Menlo Park as a liberal lay Catholic magazine,
by 1966 it had been transformed. Always a supporter of civil rights, *Ramparts*
followed many of the civil rights activists into the New Left camp. By the time
the publisher Edward M. Keating made Warren Hinckle the executive editor
in 1964, the magazine had already turned in this new direction. The talent
that gathered at the *Ramparts* office, relocated to San Francisco, was almost as
impressive as the scoops. Robert Scheer's in-depth reporting from Vietnam first
suggested the degree to which the administration's war rested on false or faulty
assumptions. Eldridge Cleaver's reporting first enabled many whites to understand racism. In 1966 *Ramparts* disclosed Michigan State University's involvement in the recruitment and training of Saigon's vicious police force, and the
magazine had the fullest account of how the CIA had infiltrated and used the
National Student Association since 1951. (The CIA responded to this disclosure by burglarizing the *Ramparts* office.) An exposé on the city of Oakland
contributed to the resignation of Mayor John Houlihan, and the story of how
Johnson's friends personally profited from the Vietnam War marked one of the
few occasions where an American publication dared to tell the truth about that
corrupt and mendacious administration's practices during its tenure.[65]

Radicals remained a frustrated minority. Teach-ins, peaceful marches, electoral campaigns, and even more militant protests against the navy and the Dow
Chemical Company, which made napalm used in the war, had failed to stop
the war. By 1967 radicals had adopted a new analysis; they concluded that the
war continued because of the flow of draftees. Rather than persuading a majority that the war was wrong, radicals decided to cut off that flow. This decision arose from a hatred of the draft, which was a sore subject for several
reasons. For one thing, it operated outside American tradition; it affronted both
liberty and equality. Radicals objected to the Selective Service System's boast
that it not only supplied manpower to the army but also used deferments to
channel young men into socially approved occupations. Local boards used
"channeling" to coerce men away from civil rights work and into activities that
did not threaten the social order. In addition, many local boards were arbitrary,
incompetent, or corrupt. Then, too, the war had increased draft calls; many
apolitical young men faced conscription. The draft system's temporary deferments and fickle regulations maximized uncertainty and anxiety for these men;

they were potential recruits to the radical movement. Finally, the draft forced radical youths to confront the government individually. Nothing enraged a man who loathed the war like an induction notice.[66]

David Harris, a former student body president at Stanford University, along with the radicals Dennis Sweeney, Steve Hamilton, and Lenny Heller, organized The Resistance. They swore not to cooperate with the Selective Service System; they urged a massive defiance of the draft. (Hamilton soon decided noncooperation was masochistic and dropped out.) On the steps of the federal building in San Francisco, hundreds of supporters tried to hand in their draft cards. U.S. Attorney Cecil Poole declined to accept these cards. In a dignified and solemn ceremony in Sproul Plaza, one member of The Resistance, Lester Fein, burned his draft card. (Congress had made this a felony.) Fein said that he felt like Moses, that he had acted in the tradition of the Jewish prophets, that he was encouraging others to undertake such acts, and that young Americans needed to regain a sense of manhood. A scholar of religion who watched the event whispered, "It's an old-fashioned evangelistic service!" What drove young men to such acts was a sense of moral outrage; many had a sympathy for the Vietnamese and the Third World gained by living either abroad or in a subculture in the United States. Members of The Resistance were bitter. "When you will have watched, and talked, and read the papers, and drunk your coffee and given a quarter," taunted one of The Resistance's leaflets, "but couldn't put your body on the line for what you believed, how will your children judge you? And how will you judge yourself when the pieces of your sons come back in caskets, draped in the flag of a country you allowed to murder him?"[67]

Opposition to the draft also drew support from the Right. One of the most outspoken critics was Dan Rosenthal of Cal Conservatives for Political Action (CCPA). Rosenthal denounced the "Selective Slavery System," accused the government of violating the constitution, and fasted for ten days in front of the Berkeley draft board office. Other libertarians took up the call. "Conscription is the set of fangs wielded by the Vampire State," wrote Tom Jacobsen. In 1966 SDS and the CCPA cosponsored an antidraft rally at Sproul Plaza. Young leftists and young rightists accommodated each other to make bitter and angry attacks against the liberal, anticommunist government they believed oppressed them. The New Left and the New Right were more alike than either was like their older counterparts; the real political division in America was no longer between the Right and the Left but between the young and the old. Nor was it difficult to explain why only the young opposed conscription; they were, after all, the only ones being drafted. "They were fighting for their own existence, not for anything altruistic," noted the community leader Ruth Hart. "It may have *sounded* it, but I mean it was not. It was really for themselves, which would be normal."[68]

Other radicals, including Berkeley SDS, took a different approach; they decided to harass and disrupt the Selective Service System at its most vulnerable point: The Oakland Induction Center, where hundreds of young men were received into the military each day. In early October 1967 an umbrella group drawn from various political viewpoints announced plans for Stop the Draft Week on October 16–20. Responsibility for each day of protest was given to a different faction both to maximize participation and to guarantee a variety of types of protest. On Monday October 16 several dozen pacifists sat in the doorway of the induction center. They included a large number of Quakers; among the group was Joan Baez. One of the demonstrators held a sign that read, "Girls Say Yes to Men Who Say No." After a brief time during which draftees gingerly stepped over the demonstrators, 124 pacifists were quietly arrested and taken to the county jail. While Baez was in jail, the Rev. Martin Luther King, Jr., came to visit. Later, while serving a short jail term that resulted from this protest, Baez was visited by David Harris; soon after, they were married. Then Harris went to federal prison for refusing induction. The Monday demonstration had been quiet and not especially effective; the media gave it little attention.[69]

The leaders of the faction assigned to Tuesday planned a more militant protest. "Our idea was highly influenced by the Black Power people," Frank Bardacke later noted. This demonstration was to begin with a teach-in in Pauley Ballroom inside the Student Union on the University campus on Monday night. After organizers agreed to keep nonstudents out, the University administration agreed to allow the teach-in. Thirty-four antiwar faculty members who opposed the protest at the induction center signed up for most of the speaking time. It began to look as if the radicals had been preempted. But conservatives expressed their anger; Brinton H. Stone of the University's Placement Office warned, "We are at war with the reds wherever they exist." He urged the administration to "beat the living hell out of them." Heyns issued a public statement. "It does not seem to me to be wise to exclude a group which advocates disobedience to the Selective Service Act," he said, "as long as their behavior on campus complies with the law and the University campus rules." This remark did nothing to ease conservative anger. At the last minute the Alameda County Board of Supervisors, controlled by the Knowland-Mulford-Coakley group, persuaded a local judge, over Heyns's objections, to issue an injunction prohibiting both the teach-in and antiwar rallies, and the chancellor locked Pauley Ballroom.[70]

When students who had planned to attend the teach-in found the ballroom locked, they drifted into Sproul Plaza, where they joined a large number of radical nonstudents and held an impromptu, illegal late night rally. A Resistance spokesman told the crowd of several thousand that 300 people had burned their draft cards across the United States earlier in the day; this statement drew hearty applause. Then Professor J. B. Neilands read a telegram of support from North Vietnam. The crowd laughed when a member of the Trotskyist Independent Socialist Club noted that making the rally illegal had caused higher attendance. After midnight many of the participants began to leave. One speaker then noted the spontaneous nature of the meeting and said that it proved that the spirit of the Free Speech Movement lived. At the end of an antiwar skit, the crowd, thinning out, began to clap and sing, "Hell, no, we won't go." Twenty-five faculty supporters, including Eli Katz, Edward Sampson, Thomas Parkinson, and Fred Stripp, appeared before the crowd to a long standing ovation. Two draft cards were then burned. At 2 a.m. the meeting ended with participants assembling in smaller groups led by Mike Smith, Steve Hamilton, Frank Bardacke, and Reese Erlich.[71]

On Tuesday, when 2,000 to 4,000 militants attempted to block the induction center, they were met by several hundred club-swinging Oakland policemen in full riot gear. (Oakland recruited its sometimes vicious and racist officers in the South.) A few protesters were arrested; many were beaten. More were taken to hospitals than to jail. "The street was dotted with blood, broken glass and ripped clothing," noted the Oakland Tribune. After the police attack knots of stunned protesters could be found on street corners muttering, "Hell no, we won't go." The mood was ugly. Scott Newhall, the editor of the San Francisco Chronicle, was outraged that police had roughed up reporters and press photographers. Authorities apparently hoped to drive the press away so that they could attack the demonstrators without being watched. Wednesday was relatively tranquil as thousands of peaceful pickets circled the induction center for five hours; twenty-two Berkeley High School students blocked the center and were arrested. On Thursday, a thousand peaceful demonstrators returned to the induction center to march; they were not allowed near the building, but there was no violence.[72]

Friday was the main event. Up to 10,000 demonstrators showed up at the induction center; they were greeted by 2,000 police officers. Many of the officers were Alameda County deputy sheriffs. Poorly trained, ill-led, and undisciplined, the deputies were patriotic civilians who worked only during emergencies. Some were little better than thugs. When the police blocked the induction center, the demonstrators turned into the business district of downtown Oakland. From 5 a.m. to 10:30 a.m., they went on a rampage. Protesters still angry over the police beatings on Tuesday decided to immobilize the police; they slashed tires, moved cars to block intersections, and let the air out of the tires of city buses. Slogans were painted on walls, and nails were strewn on the streets. For several hours the downtown was gridlocked. Police tactics did not ease the situation. They concentrated on seizing the monitors who wore armbands. Nor did the police have a plan for dispersing this leaderless mob. Police sometimes charged and drove demonstrators down the street and then suddenly retreated. At times the demonstrators discovered more police at their rear. "We finally had ourselves a white riot," Frank Bardacke later commented, adding, "We had the streets." Although no one was killed, the entire episode resembled a military battle. As Dotson Rader once observed, one of the most important functions of violent antiwar protest was to allow the participants to prove that want of courage was not the reason that they refused to participate in the Vietnam War. As the number of police increased, the demonstrators gradually withdrew. Of the 317 arrests during the week, only 15 were Cal students. The radical movement had moved off-campus.[73]

Stop the Draft Week left frustration and anger all around. "If Stop the Draft Week had been a military operation," noted the radical Doug Lummis, "we would all be dead." Radicals were frustrated that the induction center went unscathed, while conservatives fumed that the injunction prohibiting the teach-in or antiwar rallies had proved ineffective. Heyns, as usual, was caught in the middle. The Regents declared that the campus could not be used to plan illegal activity. This policy was unenforcable; its enactment angered the radicals. Heyns believed that he had to discipline students who had violated campus rules by holding rallies during the period in which the constitutionally dubious injunction had prohibited antiwar rallies. Seventy-two students were cited for violating University rules. After a hearing officer recommended suspending eleven students, the chancellor received numerous letters and petitions urging lighter sentences. Professor Thomas Parkinson urged probation. "I think this would affirm the authority of your office," he wrote, "and place us all on an even keel. Without an even keel, we'll be in very bad trouble." One group of graduate students pledged to accept no position made vacant by the suspension of a student; ironically, one of the signers was a designated suspendee. By this time most of the Regents and legislators understood that Heyns was trying to isolate radical leaders from potential followers.[74]

In the end, the chancellor suspended only two radical leaders, Peter Camejo of the Trotskyist Young Socialist Alliance and Reese Erlich of SDS. Erlich noted that, unlike several of the eleven, neither he nor Camejo had ever been cited before. Camejo said, "This whole matter is obviously political." This assessment seems accurate. The *Daily Californian* stated that the suspensions left the campus in "confusion, frustration and moral outrage." The editor added that the suspensions appeared to be arbitrary; they were rooted in the personalities of the two individuals and in the chancellor's desire to split the radical movement. The Academic Senate, however, by a vote of 271 to 97 refused to condemn these suspensions. Although conservatives grumbled, Heyns's greatest problem came from radicals, who continued to make trouble. Several radicals entered a University office through a skylight; one called an administrator a "liberal." In radical parlance this was a curse. Other radicals staged several mill-ins, but there was no violence, although two stand-up ashtrays were destroyed, and Heyns decided to impose campus discipline rather than call the police. In December four of the eleven designated Stop the Draft Week suspendees were elected to the ASUC Senate; Camejo and Erlich drew the greatest number of votes. All in all Stop the Draft Week had taken a heavy toll on everyone concerned.[75]

Conservatives then played their last card. It was a high one, but it involved considerable risk. For years Mulford had urged the prosecution of antiwar radicals, and now Coakley decided to act. The prosecutor charged seven leaders of Stop the Draft Week with a felonious conspiracy to organize followers to commit misdemeanors during the protests. The Oakland Seven, as they styled themselves, were Terry Cannon, Bob Mandel, Reese Erlich, Jeff Segal, Steve Hamilton, Mike Smith, and Frank Bardacke. The seven had numerous radical connections. Cannon was the white editor of *The Movement*, a SNCC newspaper in San Francisco. "The sins of the fathers," he said, "will be punished by the sons." Mandel was a son of the old leftist William Mandel, Erlich and Segal were SDS leaders, and Hamilton and Smith had been arrested together at the navy table protest. Hamilton was a Maoist of the Trotsky variety who had belonged to both Progressive Labor and the militant organization called the May 2nd Movement. Smith, a onetime teacher at the Berkwood School, had been friends with both Hamilton and Stew Albert; he had been active in SDS and PROC but had refused to join PL because its members could not smoke pot. "I was the person who taught Jerry Rubin how to roll a joint," he recalled. Frank Bardacke wrote a sports column for the *San Francisco Express Times* called "From Left Field"; he described himself as a political outlaw. One day he burst in upon R. G. Davis and said, "It's great; we're winning!" A puzzled Davis asked, "Who?" Bardacke replied, "The NLF are kicking the shit out of the Americans."[76]

The 1969 trial of the Oakland Seven was one of many political trials at the end of the sixties. It was in a sense the logical culmination of the conflict between those conservatives and liberals who ran society and the radicals who attacked that power. As it turned out, the trial was a disaster for Coakley. Because of sloppy police work, the prosecution could not establish the whereabouts of the defendants before or during the alleged conspiracy. After the prosecution had presented its case, several reporters agreed that there was insufficient evidence to gain a conviction. Charles Garry and Malcolm Burnstein, the attorneys who represented the defendants, showed that certain people had been prosecuted while others who had acted identically according to the police department's own reports had been ignored. They argued that Coakley had illegally undertaken a selective prosecution. Although the defendants began the trial with a pessimism masked only by bravado for public consumption, by the end they believed that they had won. The jury found them not guilty. Afterward, the judge privately congratulated the jury.[77]

During the early months of 1968 the country underwent near chaos. The Tet offensive in Vietnam destroyed the remainder of the Johnson administration's credibility. Eugene McCarthy and Robert Kennedy pushed Johnson out of the presidential race, and Martin Luther King, Jr., was assassinated. These events formed the backdrop to rising tensions on college campuses. Draft calls remained high, and the draft law had been changed so that many graduate students as well as graduating seniors were scheduled to lose their deferments in June. In February a number of Cal students formed the Campus Draft Opposition (CDO) to protest against both the draft and the war. The CDO planned an antiwar commencement for May 17 at the Greek Theatre. Students were to wear academic gowns, and the roll was to be called of those students who pledged not to be drafted. Antiwar leaders were to come from all over the country to give speeches. Vietnam Commencement had two purposes. One was to demonstrate to the federal government that a large number of serious, responsible young people vehemently opposed the government's policies. The other was to give participants a sense of unity and solidarity in their unprecedented defiance of the government.[78]

As publicity about Vietnam Commencement circulated, conservatives expressed shock and outrage. "This meeting," Professor Hardin B. Jones informed Heyns, "appears to me to be indistinguishable from treason." Although the administration initially approved the plan, it was subsequently blocked by the Regents' counsel. When the administration took the issue to the Regents, that body not only killed the proposal but ordered the chancellor to prohibit any display of academic gowns or use of the word "commencement" on campus without permission of the Regents. The CDO and the administration then reached a compromise. The ceremony, in a somewhat altered form and without gowns, was to take place as a rally at Sproul Plaza. When Governor Ronald Reagan learned about this plan, he called it "obscene." Once again, Heyns was trapped. Outraged conservatives demanded that the event be stopped, while the CDO was determined to hold its commencement. To many of the 866 students—about 30 percent of senior men—who had pledged to refuse induction, the administration's apparent cowardice in the face of conservative wrath offered another proof that the only difference between conservatives and liberals was that conservatives were less hypocritical. In other words, moderate students were being driven into the arms of radicals. No man understood better than Roger Heyns.[79]

The Regents could make pronouncements, and Thomas J. Cunningham could make legal rulings, but neither controlled events on the Berkeley campus. Vietnam Commencement took place in Lower Sproul Plaza. An orchestra provided music, and participants wore armbands to show solidarity. About 200 faculty members stood on the steps and faced an audience of 7,000 to 8,000 people; it was the largest crowd of the academic year. Professor Charles Sellers praised the courage, sacrifice, and patriotism of the students taking the pledge. A citation was presented to the sister of John Wells, a Berkeley student and veteran whom the military had kidnapped and imprisoned for refusing to complete his obligation as a reservist. The actor Sterling Hayden came with his son, Christian, who was a draft resister. The featured speaker, Robert M. Hutchins of the Center for the Study of Democratic Institutions, drew a standing ovation. Phil Ochs sang "I Ain't A-Marchin' Any More," with its memorable lines about the old always leading the young into war. Dan Siegel, a first-year student at the University's Boalt Law School, said, "There's something wrong with a society that labels as criminal Muhammad Ali, Joan Baez, William Sloane Coffin, Benjamin Spock, John Wells, and Stokely Carmichael." He noted that his own deferment was about to expire and declared his refusal to cooperate with the Selective Service System. Those who had taken the pledge then stood and recited it in unison. Finally, Professor Franz Schurmann administered a pledge to hundreds of people supporting those who refused to be drafted.[80]

Vietnam Commencement represented a triumph of pride, integrity, and individualism, but it stopped neither draft calls nor the war in Vietnam. By 1968 both were unpopular among Berkeley students. According to a poll taken by SDS, 81 percent of draft eligible Cal students planned to avoid the draft. In an election on the war sponsored by *Time* magazine, 11,280 Berkeley students cast votes; 49 percent favored withdrawal, while 43 percent favored reducing the American war effort. There was little support for any other policy. Not surprisingly, these attitudes carried over into presidential choices. In the *Time* "election" the overwhelming favorite was Senator Eugene McCarthy, 48 percent; Senator Robert Kennedy placed second, 17 percent; Nelson Rockefeller, 8 percent; Fred Halstead of the Socialist Workers party, 6 percent; and Richard Nixon, 4 percent. McCarthy's strength was derived both from the perception that he was the most vigorously antiwar candidate and from familiarity gained through his frequent trips to Berkeley. It was said that McCarthy had decided to run for president after a hearty welcome on the Berkeley campus in October 1967. McCarthy's grassroots campaign and even his rhetoric echoed Robert Scheer. Although McCarthy lost the California presidential primary on June 4, 1968, he defeated Kennedy in Berkeley. That night Kennedy was assassinated. Antiwar electoral politics had again been defeated, and militants were back in the saddle.[81]

As students left for the summer, militants, hippies, and transients rented the vacated apartments and houses south of campus. The atmosphere in the bohemian ghetto along Telegraph Avenue became tense. After French students had revolted and tried to topple DeGaulle's government, a number of Berkeley militants, led by Peter Camejo of the Young Socialist Alliance, decided to hold a rally to honor the French students in front of Cody's Bookstore on Telegraph at Haste Street. "There has been no action in Berkeley for a long time," said Camejo, "and we have to create something." On the evening of Friday, June

28, 1968, about 2,000 people showed up; the crowd poured from the sidewalk into the street and closed it. Closing the street was intended to provoke a confrontation. Anarchists chanted, "Two-four-six-eight. Organize and smash the state." When the police ordered the crowd to disperse, the crowd shouted, "Fuck you." To clear the street and disperse the crowd, Berkeley police, for the first time, fired tear gas canisters; some protesters responded by hurling rocks. Although most of the protesters left, several hundred regrouped at Bancroft and Telegraph, where they built a barricade in the intersection. Composed of trash cans, bicycle racks, and debris, it was, in the French fashion, set ablaze. Within a few minutes, police discharged more tear gas. On Saturday night the disturbances continued and increased in scale. More fires were set, store windows were smashed, and local police were forced to bring in the Oakland police, sheriff's deputies, and the highway patrol. Sunday brought a third night of violence, a citywide 9 p.m. curfew, and fifty-five arrests. None were Cal students. Mayor Wallace Johnson barely escaped injury from the angry crowd.[82]

On Monday city officials announced that the curfew was to be extended from 8 p.m. to 6 a.m. the following morning. In response, more than a thousand militants held a rally before the curfew in Lower Sproul Plaza. Although some people argued for more violence, most opted to pursue a politically shrewd strategy. "Rather than go into action tonight or Tuesday night," advised Peter Camejo, "it's better that we organize." The militants voted to close Telegraph on July 4 in order to hold a political rally, and they decided to present this nonnegotiable demand to the city council at its regular session on Tuesday morning. This tumultuous council meeting lasted seven hours inside the Community Theatre; a hostile audience of more than a thousand surrounded city officials. Restaurateur Larry Blake, speaking for the Telegraph merchants, begged the council to accede to the militants and close the street on July 4. The council lifted the curfew but, by six to three, declined to close the street. Afterward, an angry teenager told Councilwoman Bernice Hubbard May, who had voted with the majority, "You don't represent us any more." Pressure was brought upon the council to reverse its stand, and the following day the council yielded to the militants by five to four. May and Zack Brown changed their votes to join Dellums, Sweeney, and Gordon. Militancy worked. A handful of radicals had forced the liberals to capitulate, had humiliated them, and from then on enjoyed considerable power in Berkeley.[83]

On July 4, the closure of Telegraph between Channing and Dwight went smoothly. It was a street party more in keeping with the hippie counterculture than with political radicalism. After the city closed the street at noon, people shouted, "The street is ours, the street is ours." Radicals, it turned out, had as strong a desire for possession of property as the capitalist liberals they detested. Between 10,000 and 15,000 people casually strolled along the street. Rock

bands played, actors gave impromptu performances, activists handed out literature, and protest leaders held a political rally. The San Francisco Mime Troupe's
Gorilla Band marched through the street playing "Glory, Glory, Hallelujah."
The band also played a slightly off-key rendition of the national anthem, a
Spanish Civil War song, and "Dixie." At 1 p.m. a gray-bearded man dressed
in a clerical robe mounted a flatbed truck to read the Declaration of Independence. At the end he added, "Let us not forget these people meant what they
said, and we should mean what we say too." In a street theater skit, entertainers
threw bricks at the audience; the bricks were made of foam rubber, and the
audience hurled the bricks back. A hippie spread out his shawl as a rug on the
street, opened a box, and passed out marijuana cigarettes. Someone lit incense.
Many people gave donations to the hippie. No policemen were visible, but
Councilman Ronald Dellums was seen wandering through the crowd.[84]

It was a long way from October 1965, when organizers of the Vietnam Day
Committee politely and obediently followed police orders and stopped their
march at the Oakland city limits, to June 1968, when militants cynically staged
riots in the streets to obtain political demands. The shallow rhetoric of the New
Left, composed of a decaying Marxism that failed to satisfy, had long since
been abandoned; in its place grew an appetite for raw power. Many radicals
had abandoned rhetoric for violence. "The healthy organism," advised an instructor at the Free University, "uses aggression to get what it needs." This
transformation had taken place amid the steady growth of an unpopular war;
the number of alienated young people had increased year by year. In 1968,
however, the street riots foreshadowed the beginnings of a new politics: In the
new political system the voices of the young and the dispossessed were to be
very loud. Since a permanent army of occupation was not practical, the militants who controlled the streets had to be accommodated. Although Heyns had
recognized this point years earlier, it was not understood in high places, including the governor's office in Sacramento. The June troubles, which extended into July and then sporadically recurred in August and September,
revealed a new viciousness on both sides. For the first time people began to
realize the stakes: control of the city of Berkeley.[85]

# Chapter 4

# GREEN

*Get yourself a little green.*
Herman's Hermits,
    "Green Street Green"

In the years after World War II, when the country underwent anticommunist hysteria and turned against the Left, a tide of regimented conformism all but submerged the American tradition of individualism. This trend dominated not only politics but also the arts. Architects turned to the functional, barren Bauhaus school with its cold, hard look. The style echoed, although few Americans knew it, the aesthetics not only of the Weimar Republic but also of Mussolini and Hitler. On the Berkeley campus both Sproul Hall and Dwinelle Hall were built with balconies in the fascist manner. Painters moved from the social realism of the thirties to an unprecedented use of the abstract. At the University both Worth Ryder and Glen Wessels taught abstract expressionism, and local expressionists such as Clyfford Still and Richard Diebenkorn produced canvases that were large-scaled and hysterical. These works could not be condemned politically; their blotches of paint, however, revealed the anger and frustration of their creators, who resented living in a society in which narrow-minded politics all but throttled creativity. For writers, the problem was worse. Words forced authors to run the risk of expressing politically unacceptable ideas. This atmosphere of fear led writers to seek new forms of expression. One form was science fiction, which became popular in Berkeley. Another form was experimental poetry. In the late forties a number of poets congregated as the Berkeley Renaissance. Their work, mostly forgotten now, broke with tradition; it was bold but lacked a philosophical base.[1]

In the early fifties disaffected writers, poets, artists, jazz musicians, and hangers-on began to gather in San Francisco's North Beach, which became the most important bohemia in America outside New York. As North Beach's Ital-

124

ians moved to the suburbs, the beats, as these bohemians called themselves, moved in. The neighborhood was cheap and pleasant, and the city, as the poet Kenneth Rexroth once observed, was easygoing. Many beats were homosexuals, and San Francisco had tolerated homosexuality since the Gold Rush. At the center of the change in North Beach was the poet Lawrence Ferlinghetti, who bought an anarchist bookstore, City Lights, and turned it into a beat headquarters. Beats came from all over the country to visit North Beach, and many stayed to live in the Bay Area. One important colony arose in Berkeley. During part of 1955 Jack Kerouac visited Allen Ginsberg, while Ginsberg and Gary Snyder were living in two of Berkeley's backyard cottages. Snyder introduced the two easterners to the Zen religion, Ginsberg created some of his finest poetry, and Kerouac recorded the events in his novel, The Dharma Bums. All three smoked marijuana and engaged in a number of orgies, although Ginsberg later noted that Kerouac could not bring himself to record homosexual affairs that, at that time, were too shocking to be published.[2]

Although the beats rejected mainstream culture, their values were double-edged. The word "beat," which Kerouac had coined, could be taken different ways. Kerouac said that the beats were beatified, that is, purer than the materialist culture from whence they sprang; but, noted the radical Carl Oglesby, they were also beaten, that is, pounded down by mainstream culture. Hopelessly defensive, the beats, like the French existentialists, could envision nothing beyond enduring in a bleak world. Few beats escaped this sense of doom. Kerouac's great novel, On the Road, rejected the work ethic, the rigid moral standards, and the general narrow-mindedness of the middle class in favor of a life, much like Huck Finn's, that was free-spirited, ribald, and breathtaking in its highs and lows, in its power of discovery, and in its forward, rushing quests. Kerouac's vision, however, proved to be more an illusion than a practical guide for living. Even the author could not sustain the pace; in 1969 he died a broken alcoholic.[3]

Allen Ginsberg, who had a greater capacity for controlling his art, put forth a shrewder and wiser vision. The key to Ginsberg was his overt homosexuality. Long before gay liberation, Ginsberg openly proclaimed his sexual desires, denied that his sexuality was abnormal, and demanded to be accepted on his own terms. In 1955 he expressed these ideas brilliantly in his great poem, "Howl," which he first recited in North Beach. The following year he read a longer version, with a revised ending, in Berkeley. The poem's frank language, complex rhythms, and shrewdly constructed sexual puns caused a sensation. When Ginsberg tried to publish "Howl," publishers declined out of fear of prosecution for obscenity. To many, the real issue was the poem's defiant tone and electric power. Finally, Ginsberg's friend Ferlinghetti published it. Although both Ferlinghetti and "Howl" were prosecuted, by the time the case reached the U.S. Supreme Court so many copies had been sold that a ban would have seemed ludicrous. "Howl" became the best-selling poem in America in the twentieth century.[4]

Whereas Kerouac had sought to redeem America's lost soul, Ginsberg emphasized personal experience. For Ginsberg, the tragedy of postwar America was its refusal to open itself to variety, to experimentation, to a quest for new frontiers of the mind. The poet, imagining himself to be a kind of Jewish prophet, undertook smashing the narrow, Protestant Zeitgeist that had bound the country together since the Civil War. He yearned for a country where the only absolute was freedom, and where the artist could create without social, political, or cultural restraint. Ultimately—and this revealed the limitation of Ginsberg's vision—his vision was escapist. He wanted Americans, as individuals, to be able to escape from the kind of society that they presently lived in. In later years Ginsberg came to see the limitations of this vision, but at the time he felt oppressed, and like all oppressed people, he felt a greater desire to remove the present oppression than a capacity to create an alternative vision of the ideal society. Most of the beats, like Ginsberg, were prisoners of their times rather than harbingers of the future. This limitation gave the beats, like Moses, the power to lead people to the promised land of the sixties.[5]

By 1960, then, the beats were well-known, even notorious; their defiant rejection of mainstream culture had opened the possibility that others, too, might question middle-class values. In Berkeley young intellectuals such as David Horowitz, Robert Scheer, Michael Rossman, and Diane Wakoski expressed a growing restlessness. "Labels mean nothing, the content of ideas everything," wrote Philip MacDougal in launching a serious new journal, *Despite Everything*. Even the governor's son, Jerry Brown, was affected; in 1960 he left a seminary to enter Cal. Many browsed the new and secondhand bookstores along Telegraph Avenue near the campus. In reality, the fare in these stores was not very diverse, but it was more diverse than in other cities, except New York. Young people stumbled across long forgotten political tracts from the Spanish Civil War or, more intelligently, Lorca's poetry. Creed's bookstore or, later, Moe's bookstore contained many battered volumes expressing ideas that did not belong to the middle-class world. Intellectuals delighted in the recent invention of the cheap paperback book; they bought Ginsberg's and Ferlinghetti's poetry, Kerouac's novels, and Robert Heinlein's science fiction. They read the essays of C. Wright Mills, Paul Goodman, and Dwight Macdonald and the existential philosophy of Kierkegaard, Sartre, and Camus. Gary Snyder and Alan Watts recommended Zen, which was explained in numerous paperbacks. Telegraph Avenue became a marketplace for ideas.[6]

Berkeley mixed the cosmopolitan with the provincial. Few residents had traveled abroad, and fewer spoke a foreign language, although a growing number sought to place their country and its culture in a global context. The University, with its teaching of languages and the large number of European war refugees on its faculty, stimulated that interest. Students not only bought an

Throughout the 1960s Don Mulford, a conservative Republican, represented the Berkeley hills in the legislature. In 1960 Mulford mailed this campaign postcard to voters. *(Institute of Governmental Studies Library)*

Max Scherr, a longtime radical and former bistro owner, founded the *Berkeley Barb* in August 1965. Scherr admired Cervantes, and the *Barb's* logo featured Sancho Panza astride his bony steed armed with a lance tipped with the University's Campanile. *(Bancroft Library)*

In April 1965 President Lyndon Johnson sent U.S. marines to the Dominican Republic. Johnson's action led to a large antiwar rally held in the somewhat unusual location of Lower Sproul Plaza.

On September 23, 1965, at 6:35 p.m., Professor Hardin B. Jones removed this leftist poster from one of Sather Gate's pillars. Note the sticker in the upper left corner charging Lyndon B. Johnson with murder. *(Hoover Institution)*

When the American government sent trains carrying Vietnam-bound troops through Berkeley in August 1965, the Vietnam Day Committee organized several antiwar protests. *(Bancroft Library)*

On Charter Day in March 1966 the University honored Arthur Goldberg, the Johnson administration's ambassador to the United Nations. Students protesting the Vietnam War carried neatly made signs into the Greek Theatre. *(C. Ray Moore, Bancroft Library)*

In 1966 Robert Scheer attacked the Vietnam War by challenging the incumbent congressman, Jeffery Cohelan, in the Democratic primary. Bob and Anne Weills Scheer used this photograph on a campaign brochure. Scheer had grown his beard after visiting Cuba. For the campaign, he trimmed it neatly.

Jeffery Cohelan was Berkeley's congressman from 1959 to 1971. A former milk truck drivers' union official, Cohelan was a staunch liberal anticommunist. In 1970 Cohelan lost to the black city councilman, Ronald V. Dellums. *(Bancroft Library)*

In 1966 Robert Scheer used this symbol. The Peace and Freedom party, which Scheer helped organize, adopted a similar theme in 1968.

After six nonstudents were arrested during a protest inside the Student Union, activists called a strike in December 1966. The strike failed. *(William B. Grant, Bancroft Library)*

In May 1968 Governor Ronald Reagan attended the inauguration of Charles J. Hitch as president of the University. *(Norm Schindler, Bancroft Library)*

When Jerry Rubin ran for mayor in April 1967, his campaign poster advocated "Peace in Viet Nam, End Poverty, Stop Police Harassment, The 18-Year Old Vote, Legalize Marijuana, Rent Control, Black Power, Student Power, Fight Racism, Tax the Rich, Plant Trees and Flowers." For years these issues dominated Berkeley politics.

In 1963 yell leaders and pom pom girls represented old fashioned college spirit on the Cal campus. *(Bancroft Library)*

Sam Hinton led a sing-along at the Seventh Annual Berkeley Folk Music Festival at the University's Eucalyptus Grove in July 1964. *(Kelly Hart, Bancroft Library)*

After this 1966 performance of Michael McClure's *The Beard*, Berkeley police arrested the playwright and the actors for obscenity. The courts dismissed the charges. *(Bancroft Library)*

On October 23, 1968, dozens of activists occupied Moses Hall to protest the Regents' refusal to allow Eldridge Cleaver to teach an accredited course. The banners on the left read, "Solidarity Forever," "End Regents Control," and "If not to Learn?" *(Bancroft Library)*

Inside Moses Hall the demonstrators, borrowing a technique used earlier at Columbia University, built barricades by piling furniture against the doors to impede police recapture of the building. *(Bancroft Library)*

Moses Hall suffered considerable damage. In this professor's office, files were thrown on the floor and covered with water from fire hoses. Radicals blamed the police, whose raid was led by Edwin Meese III. Who, the activists or the police, conveniently placed this sign against the waste basket for the police photographer? *(Bancroft Library)*

After Moses Hall was cleared, University employees hunted for important papers. *(Bancroft Library)*

To enter the campus at Sather Gate during the Third World Liberation Front strike in early 1969, one had to cross through a picket line manned by militants. The administration advised people to avoid the area. *(Grover Wickersham, Bancroft Library)*

Authorities used tear gas frequently during the TWLF strike. These National Guardsmen donned gas masks. *(Grover Wickersham, Bancroft Library)*

During the TWLF protest many were clubbed. Here a policeman stands over a victim. The man in the upper right is an officer in plainclothes. *(Grover Wickersham, Bancroft Library)*

On the first, violent day of the People's Park disturbances, May 15, 1969, demonstrators set fire to a city car at the corner of Telegraph and Parker. A policeman barely got out of the car and had to draw his pistol in order to escape from the angry crowd. *(Douglas Hall)*

During the People's Park crisis the National Guard occupied the city. On May 19 Guardsmen blocked Shattuck Avenue downtown. *(Art Frisch, San Francisco Chronicle)*

Long-haired demonstrators gave Guardsmen the "V" peace symbol in front of the Wells Fargo Bank in downtown Berkeley. *(Douglas Hall)*

On May 20, 1969, a National Guard helicopter dropped tear gas on the campus. *(Wide World Photos)*

In late 1970 a weary Chancellor Roger W. Heyns announced that he was resigning at the end of the academic year. *(Dennis Galloway, UC Public Information Office)*

People's Park in August 1972. *(Bancroft Library)*

unprecedented number of foreign-language books but also watched foreign films, which were usually shown with badly edited subtitles. In the early sixties Pauline Kael lived in Berkeley; she wrote a monthly preview guide to these films and aired her views on KPFA radio. She was then married to Edward Landberg, who presented these films at the Studio and Guild theaters on Telegraph Avenue. In another sign of interest in the wider world, the community YWCA sponsored international cooking classes and monthly potluck dinners that featured the food of a particular nationality. "Who knows what exotic meals our members will serve their guests in the future?" asked the YWCA Newsletter. The YWCA's Greek, Italian, or Mexican nights gave many in the city their first introduction to foreign food at a time when few Berkeley restaurants, except for Cantonese and Mexican cafes, served ethnic food.[7]

In the early 1960s outsiders attacked middle-class culture with a new bite. Restless blacks denounced the contradiction between American ideals, which were proclaimed to the world as part of the Cold War, and the harsh realities of racial prejudice. Leftists, driven underground during the McCarthy years, protested the hegemonical nature of mainstream culture. The Berkeley folk singer Malvina Reynolds ridiculed both the suburbs and the standardization of American life in her song, "Little Boxes."[8]

> Little boxes on the hillside,
> Little boxes made of ticky tacky,
> Little boxes on the hillside,
> Little boxes all the same.
> There's a green one and a pink one and a blue one and a yellow one,
> And they're all made out of ticky tacky,
> And they all look just the same.*

A tide of folk music swept the country. Much of this music was political; it had been identified since the thirties with the Communist party. Folk music was better when it was political; its repetitious melodies hungered for biting, sarcastic lyrics. Folk expressed a strong point of view, and to young people in the early sixties, earthy morality made the music appealing. Folk songs were the white civil rights advocate's answer to black spirituals. The music thrived because of new performers like Phil Ochs and the trio of Peter, Paul, and Mary. More important was Bob Dylan, whose raw talent and dazzling performances captivated young America. Dylan's genius was matched by the power of Joan Baez's voice. A Chicana by heritage and a Quaker by conviction, Baez burned with a moral commitment to civil rights and peace. For a star, she had a rare devotion to being arrested. Dylan, she noted, never put his body on the line. Perhaps that failure explained his greater popularity; his nihilism expressed the spirit of the times better than did Baez's commitment. For much of the decade Baez lived near, and influenced, Berkeley.[9]

---

*Copyright © 1962. Schroder Music Co. (ASCAP). Used by permission. All rights reserved.

A more devastating attack upon cultural norms came from a new generation of comedians. Following paths broken by Steve Allen, *Mad* magazine, and Paul Krassner's *The Realist*, comedians such as Mort Sahl and Tom Lehrer, both of whom played the hungry i in North Beach, replaced corny jokes, bad puns, slapstick, and ethnic ridicule with a humor that turned inward. Sahl's jokes in particular were psychological ruminations into the corners of the self that had been largely unexplored until Freud's ideas arrived in America. Lehrer's songs expressed a humor of exaggeration, in which the world appeared to be slightly out of kilter. North Beach was also the home of The Committee, a satirical review headed by Alan Myerson, who had a number of ties to the Old Left. (Myerson's younger brother, Mike, had been a leader in SLATE at Cal.) The Committee mercilessly poked fun at current political issues and figures. Many jokes were ad libbed, the audience suggested topics, and material from the spontaneous part of the show became part of the routine. The emphasis upon audience participation and spontaneity arose from the beat philosophy; political satire diminished political issues by showing politicians to be ignorant and double-dealing. People in the audience were encouraged to develop a skeptical attitude in order to maintain their own sanity. This message, profoundly democratic and hostile to authority, both created and reinforced new levels of skepticism among local residents.[10]

The most shocking—and significant—of the new comedians was Lenny Bruce. He insulted everyone, especially his audience. Instead of playing ethnic slurs against outsiders, he reveled in attacking his audience. Customers frequently walked out. In addition to the insults, Bruce titilated his audience with sexual innuendo, jokes, stories, and gestures. One of his most famous gestures was to masturbate the microphone. His performances assaulted middle-class culture head-on. While his ethnic slurs provoked guilt, his sexual revelry was not unpleasant; prudery was on the wane. Often arrested, harassed, and humiliated, Bruce could not sustain the intensity—in 1966 he committed suicide. Unlike Sahl, Bruce was a true Jewish rebel who had no intention of assimilating middle-class values. He intended to demolish those values, but he was too bitter and angry to articulate any vision of his own. The new comedians, like the folk singers, the young intellectuals, and the beats, lacked a new vision. Yet, ironically, all were dissatisfied with the existing culture. All restlessly attacked it. Still, by 1964 the number of the disenchanted had become a small army.[11]

In Berkeley a bohemian community grew around Telegraph Avenue, which combined the old, the elegant, and the unusual. For more than half a century Whelan's Cigar Store, at the corner of Bancroft Way, purveyed tobacco, magazines, and out-of-town newspapers. Further down Telegraph stood the outstanding Sather Gate Book Shop and Nicole's boutique, where ebony mannequins had elongated birdlike shapes in place of heads. Some of the most unusual shops were between Haste Street and Dwight Way. On the corner at Haste, the Lucky's grocery, closed in the summer of 1964 after numerous civil rights shop-ins, became The Forum, a politically oriented espresso and pastry shop previously located down the block. Next door were Pepe's Pizza Parlor, the bohemian Caffe Mediterraneum coffeehouse, and the slightly unsavory Blue Cue Pool Parlor. On the west side of the street at the corner of Haste, Pat and Fred Cody in 1965 opened a bookstore on the site of a gas station. Their store, set back from the street with trees planted in front, may have been the largest paperback bookstore in the country. Down the street stood the Eclair bakery with some of the best croissants in the United States, Moe Moscowitz's second-hand bookstore, which had moved up from Shattuck Avenue into the building Cody's occupied from 1961 to 1965, and Creed's bookstore, Berkeley's most important secondhand bookstore since 1923.[12]

Telegraph was Berkeley's jewel; it was cosmopolitan, artistically aware, politically diverse, and open to new ideas. The street's ambience subtly drew restless people to the area. Some were like Richard Kampf, a nineteen-year-old Cal dropout who survived on odd jobs, friends' apartments, and small amounts of food; he stretched seventy-nine cents worth of spaghetti to last a week. Others were like a young man identified only as Kevin, whose wealthy family sent him seventy-five dollars a month. It was just enough to keep him from starving. His sparsely furnished apartment, which he shared with three roommates, con-tained one table, a few chairs, mattresses, a record player, and a crate of pa-perbacks. At parties Kevin drank wine, smoked marijuana, and condemned everything. The youth screamed, "The whole scene is so sick, so rotten, so utterly soul-destroying that it has to be smashed!" Less alienated was Susan Druding, a graduate student who lived in the area. She wore blue jeans, mens' shirts, and sandals to avoid being mistaken for a sorority girl and lived with seven Siamese cats in four rooms in a dilapidated building; the rent was sixty dollars a month. Her apartment was filled with arty, handmade objects, cheap reproductions of art were thumbtacked to the walls, and her bed was covered with a handwoven Mexican blanket. Her living room contained an old steamer trunk, mismatched curtains, a mobile made of driftwood and ball bearings, assorted furniture handed down from previous tenants, and her books and rec-ords, which ranged from Bach to Baez.[13]

Druding lived in luxury compared to Lenny Glaser, one of Telegraph Ave-nue's first street people. Virtually every day Glaser stood at the corner of the campus and argued politics from different, sometimes contradictory viewpoints. In 1962 he broke new ground by lecturing on the virtues of marijuana. Al-though the *Daily Californian* covered his talk, it attracted little interest. Late the following year, however, Glaser wandered along Telegraph "very high," and after police found a small quantity of marijuana on his person, he was arrested. In February 1964, during one of the Lucky's shop-ins, Glaser was arrested for throwing food; CORE, the civil rights organization, told police that

Glaser was not part of their protest, and the charges were dropped. A month later, at Glaser's trial on the 1963 marijuana charge, the defendant challenged the government's portrayal of marijuana as a dangerous substance. Although he displayed considerable erudition and unveiled the prosecutor's ignorance, Glaser was found guilty. He received probation. In a letter to the *Daily Californian*, Jerry Rubin angrily attacked the trial. Glaser continued to hang around Telegraph and urge the use of drugs. In October 1964, during the Free Speech Movement, he apparently started the sit-down around the the police car. His role drew notice, and shortly afterward Glaser was stopped, searched, and after marijuana was found on his person, arrested; his parole was revoked.[14]

In early 1964 mainstream culture underwent an unprecedented, frontal attack, when the youthful postwar generation discovered the Beatles. In the fifties Elvis Presley had led the first rock and roll boom; this second, Beatles-led boom was greater. The Liverpool rock group toured the country, performed on television, and for the next two-and-one-half years totally dominated the record charts. Folk music all but disappeared; by 1965 Dylan played folk rock with amplification. The hard-driving, throbbing beat of the new music was overpowering; its attack upon the old culture expressed a zestful self-confidence that contrasted with the muted criticism of the folk singers, the hesitancy of the droll comedians, or the bitterness of Lenny Bruce. Rock succeeded where these earlier attacks against middle-class values had failed because it expressed deep longings inside the American psyche. Bruce had been correct that the culture's most vulnerable point was its repression of sexual desire; he had sensed that the repression was unnatural and had, as Freud might have insisted, caused all sorts of distortions throughout society. Rock liberated young Americans from the repression that gripped their elders, and it did so irrationally, without words or argument, through its psychic appeal. For a long time the culture had successfully repressed sex by keeping the subject taboo. That way the status quo had won all arguments by default. In 1965, during the Filthy Speech Movement, Art Goldberg had tried (and failed) to make this point at a rally. Rock attacked the issue of sex at its psychic core.[15]

Sexual mores were in flux. In the fifties the beats had advocated free and open sex, but they did not so much attack middle-class values as demand the right to be different. In the early sixties bohemians asserted that society's values were antiquated and mistaken; they sought to establish a new norm. In their new view sex was good, and anyone old enough to have sexual relations was capable of deciding when, where, with whom, and under what conditions to have a mutually agreeable relationship. It was none of society's business. The new mores led some couples to an unprecedented display of affection in such public places as the Berkeley Co-op. "The express lane," wrote Oscar London, "is filled with ascetic young couples clutching a loaf of bread, a jug of wine, and each other." People began sleeping around, and the Berkeley Health Department reported that the number of case of gonorrhea increased from 150 in 1960 to 560 in 1965. Young people talked openly and frankly about sex. In a conversation between two young women at The Forum, one said, "And if my parents knew, and my father, God, he'd kill us."

The second asked, "You use the pills, don't you?"

"Yes," the first replied, "but what if they don't work once?"

"If it bugs you that much," advised the second, "maybe you ought to give up sex."

"Give up sex," answered the first, "are you kidding . . ." Both laughed.[16]

In the mid-sixties this casual attitude spread from the South Campus bohemia to growing numbers of University students. They protested dormitory rules that discouraged sexual contact and increasingly moved out of dorms and into apartments in the South Campus area. Perhaps 10 percent of all Cal students were living together. Although Susan Druding lived alone, she approved of the new arrangements; her parents did not. "I suspect," she said, "that they don't object to our politics as much as to our attitude toward love. Mother was always telling me that when a 'nice' boy fell in love with a 'nice' girl he would 'test' her, and if she 'gave in' she was a tramp. I think that's horrible." Student attitudes may have been more liberal than practices. One study of Cal juniors found that 61 percent of males and 72 percent of females reported no sexual contacts.[17]

For centuries one constraint against sex outside of marriage had been pregnancy. In the early sixties, however, reliable and inexpensive birth control pills became available for the first time. In April 1964 the *Berkeley Gate* urged Cowell Hospital, the University's student health service, to provide prescriptions for contraceptives to students. "This is a plain fact of modern life," stated the paper. A year later Brian Turner, an FSM leader and ASUC senator, mailed a letter to fifty colleges stating that the ASUC was considering asking the health service to offer contraceptive advice to students. ASUC President Charles Powell, no friend to the FSM, ordered Turner to mail a letter of retraction for misusing ASUC stationery. Contraceptive pills, however, did not always work, and unwanted pregnancies led to a rising demand for abortions. For almost a century abortions had been illegal and unsanitary. High death rates were tolerated as the price that women had to pay for the "crime" of conceiving out of wedlock; it was thought impossible that a married woman might want an abortion. The new attitude about sex, as well as a quietly rising feminism, pushed both courts and legislatures toward legal abortions, and in 1967 Governor Ronald Reagan signed one of the nation's most liberal laws.[18]

Some people, such as Richard Thorne and Jefferson Poland, embraced a hedonistic philosophy. The black Thorne and the white Poland, who later changed his legal name to Jefferson Fuck Poland, insisted that frequent sexual contact with different partners enriched a person's life. To carry out their ideas, they organized the Sexual Freedom League (SFL). The SFL sponsored nude singles parties in Berkeley homes, urged women to go bare-breasted in public, held nude gatherings at certain beaches, and otherwise reveled in an explosion of sexual display. By 1966 the sexual liberation movement's events were well publicized in the Berkeley Barb, which increasingly shifted from politics to sex. The publisher, Max Scherr, had a keen eye for hippie girls, and the newspaper's descriptive sex advertisements became famous—or notorious. The Barb's advertisers could supply practically any want. The ads appeared to promote prostitution, and a mob ring was rumored to control that industry. On the other hand, sex had become so readily available, lamented one local prostitute, that prostitution might disappear.[19]

The new attitude toward sex brought franker talk, writing, and pictorial display. There were controversies. In late 1965 Ben Jacopetti and his wife Rain experimented by projecting film or slide images on nude bodies before select audiences of sixty or seventy people in a private home. When the Jacopettis made the mistake of asking police for permission to stage a public performance of their Open Theater, they were turned down. Some months later they left Berkeley to live in a rural commune. Meanwhile, North Beach's entertainers began to offer topless female dancers (or in one case, topless female impersonators). Arrests were made, but juries did not convict, and the clubs thrived. In December 1965 Michael McClure's play, "The Beard," opened in San Francisco. In this play the characters Billy the Kid and Jean Harlow, a film star from the forties, engaged in a sexually charged conversation that ended with the Kid simulating cunilingus upon Harlow. Police closed the show, and in 1966 it reopened in Berkeley, where authorities arrested McClure and the actors; the audience included Lawrence Ferlinghetti, Alan Watts, and the American Civil Liberties Union attorney Malcolm Burnstein. The courts declared McClure's play a work of art. It was scarcely art, but it captured the spirit of the era.[20]

In the long run, as Margaret Sanger had foreseen, sexual liberation led to women's liberation. Yet there was scarcely a women's movement in the midsixties. During the FSM, women, except for the fearless Bettina Aptheker and a few others, routinely cooked, cleaned, typed, and filed, while men held meetings and made crucial decisions. Neither the VDC nor other major antiwar groups, with the important exception of Women for Peace, had significant numbers of female leaders, although the Vietnam War was especially loathsome to women, as evidenced by the large number of women who marched. Since the early sixties Women for Peace had been an important organization in Berkeley, but only in 1968 did significant numbers of women begin to discover their own oppression. Among the first to state the problem were female supporters of The Resistance. Another was Helen Heick, who offered a course on male-female relationships at the Free University in the summer of 1968.

"Because this traditional relationship has infected everything else in the world," she noted, "the problem's dimensions are without limit." That same year Laura Shaw Murra (also called Laura X) organized liberated women into a group that eventually took the name SPAZM (a contrived acronym). Not everyone approved of the women's movement. When a feminist group that included Anne Weills Scheer, wife of Robert Scheer, held a meeting, they were interrupted by a messenger, who arrived at the door with a package. It contained a vibrator and a scroll that read,

> Free at last! Free at last!
> Great God Almighty
> I'm free at last.[21]

In the fifties black jazz musicians had called white jazz lovers "hipsters," and the beats had called jazz lovers from outside their community "hip," because they shared some beat values. In the mid sixties the beats, most of whom were past thirty, noticed a large number of teenagers who affected beat taste, and yet distanced themselves from the beats. Herb Caen called these young bohemians "hippies," and *Ramparts* magazine popularized the term. Hippies were distinct from beats in several respects. Whereas the beats had been born during the depression, had lived through World War II, had been gnarled and toughened by McCarthyism, and had dropped out of the postwar consumer society in defiant nonconformity, the hippies had been born after the war, had grown up in affluence, and had become satiated by a consumer culture. Although both beats and hippies despised materialism, their attitudes varied. "The hippies," declared Gregory Corso, "are acting out what the beats wrote." The beats as self-defined eccentrics had little ambition to change society; the hippies expected, through mass conversions, to reshape the country's values. These grandiose expectations were rooted in numbers. The postwar generation was gargantuan, and a far higher percentage of young people in the sixties adopted bohemian values than had ever been true for the beats. Finally, almost all hippies were white. The beats had been drawn to jazz, which linked them to blacks. Jazz met the emotional needs of people, both white and black, who lived in an oppressed subculture. Hippies from affluent, middle-class families felt no such oppression and embraced rock.[22]

Hippies dressed outrageously. In the fifties middle-class men wore white shirts, ties, and suits and kept their hair short; women wore dresses or skirts. Beat men wore dumpy or second-hand work clothes and had beards, longish hair, and sandals; beat women were similarly attired. In the early sixties, when white college students worked for civil rights in the South, they were embarrassed at being better dressed than poor blacks. Civil rights workers, male and female, began to wear Levi's jeans and jackets, blue-gray cambray shirts, and sneakers. When the civil rights workers returned to campus, their style gradually displaced neatly tailored casual wear and Brooks Brothers suits. While some hippies dressed in cast-offs, and others followed the civil rights workers (and the New Left) and wore blue jeans, many hippies developed a new style. Males donned brightly colored jeans, shirts, and bandannas; many had beards. Females wore men's clothes, especially jeans, or long, old-fashioned granny dresses made out of printed fabrics or, in some cases, from a grandmother's trunk in the attic. Some males and females had hair so long that it reached the knees. They put on elaborately decorated boots and wore beads, amulets, or other trinkets designed to ward off evil or improve sexual performance; some neck ornaments had secret compartments for drugs. Hippies countered the reality of their poverty with extravagant display.[23]

For hippies, the key concepts were spontaneity and theatricality. Like the beats, hippies respected the expression of feeling, and they believed the significance of any act lay almost entirely in the degree of its spontaneity. Spontaneity denied repression and celebrated emotion. (For years graffiti on a wall on Shattuck Avenue read, "Feeling is good for you.") If an act became important by being spontaneous, rather than by intrinsic merit, then hippies could not prove to others that any particular act was purely motivated, unless it was outrageously nonconventional. That is, all conventional acts were suspect products of rote, tradition, or habit. In this way, spontaneity was linked to theatricality. A startling, dramatic, or outrageous act, by its very boldness, and by the attention that it drew, transcended the routine and proved spontaneity. Hippies were accused of being exhibitionists, and they were, but their loud, even raucous, display of themselves and their feelings expressed their philosophy. Theatricality served one other purpose. It was possible to dislike hippies, but it was almost impossible to ignore them.[24]

Berkeley's first hippie may have been Charlie Brown Artman. A minister's son, he had originally come to study at the University and, like many others, had dropped out to examine in detail the cultural richness found along Telegraph Avenue. Like Leonard Glaser, Artman was attracted to marijuana, which the beats had adopted from jazz musicians. Artman's use of the forbidden drug did not make him a social deviant; he expressed a strong desire to find a philosophy of life that incorporated drugs. He participated in the FSM and spoke at the filthy speech rally in March 1965; he was arrested. At the trial in April Artman argued that the regulation of the content of speech was a form of cultural hegemony not in keeping with the spirit of a free society. His argument was long, and he lacked style and grace, so that no one, least of all the court, paid his words much heed, and he went to jail for his trouble. To Artman, his sentence was proof not of his own guilt but of society's sickness. At the later free speech trial in the summer of 1965 he told the court, "Your days are numbered, because this rotten-to-the-core society is tumbling." And the young man began to think about the nature of society, its limits, and its prospects.[25]

For Artman, as for so many bohemians, the crucial point was always per-sonal experience. He cared little about either the law or social norms but sought to create a system of values that enabled him to incorporate his practices into an overarching philosophy. He smoked grass, and he believed that it was good. Therefore, any system of values had to be congruent with the use of marijuana. Americans labeled marijuana use as either deviance or defiance. After Artman learned that American Indians used peyote, a powerful hallucinogen, he began to study Indian philosophy. Swept up in the white guilt for colored peoples, Artman came to believe that he was a reincarnated Indian. To prove the point, he took peyote, wore Indian garb, and lived in a teepee. He defended his use of peyote as Christian. Artman explained, "Christ appeared and said, 'Here—eat this.'" He saw "the dawn of a new age." Astrologically speaking, it was the Age of Aquarius. "But many of us," he said, "are being born into the Christ consciousness. Soon it will happen to everyone." He predicted, "This is the true second coming." Meanwhile, he lived on unemployment benefits.[26]

When Artman set up his teepee in the backyard of a friend, neighbors com-plained, and the police made him remove it, since it was an illegal dwelling unit. He then tried to erect the teepee on a vacant lot, but the police ordered Artman to move from there, too. For a time he pitched his teepee high in the hills on University land. One day the police came and tore down his teepee. Finally, the unwanted Artman moved his teepee to the woods at Canyon, where he lived quietly for a time. He began to call himself "Little Eagle." Artman, however, was incapable of being quiet, and after he boasted publicly that he carried drugs for religious ceremonies in a cross that hung around his neck, the police moved in, arrested him, and confiscated what turned out to be Art-man's supply of the drug LSD. Artman was not so much outside the law as beyond it. "There is no power on Earth that can stop us from winning now," he said. In 1967 he offered a course at the Free University entitled, "The New Age Consciousness and Various Paths to Enlightenment." Under the influence of LSD, Artman conceived of levitating the Pentagon. (Thousands of people were to meditate to raise the Pentagon off the ground.) This idea reached Jerry Rubin, who organized the levitation at the march on the Pentagon in October 1967. Artman's quest for meaning and a system of values ended in a closed system of drug use that caused him to lose whatever charm and innocence he had once possessed. A victim of his times, he gained weight and became Berke-ley's first burned-out hippie. He was not the last.[27]

Rock music made possible the creation of a new culture; in time it was called the counterculture. Rock was about inner drives and how society organized, controlled, and shaped those drives. At the crudest level this music encouraged the passions and brought sex from a repressed to an overtly expressed state. At a deeper level, as conservative critics charged, rock music subverted all author-ity; the music's defiance came through both in its loud beat and in lyrics that threatened traditional values. When Jim Morrison of The Doors sang, "We want the world, and we want it NOW," older people shuddered. The younger generation, having thrown off the repressed ways of its elders, held the oldsters in contempt. "Well," Tom Hayden told HUAC, "I think we will at least out-live you." Young people increasingly disdained parental, institutional, or gov-ernmental authority as the rule of the ignorant over the enlightened. At a still deeper level, this music was about power. Performances enabled rock stars to generate a sense of power, and the youthful, powerless audiences worshipped the stars because of their powermaking capacity. The purpose of a public per-formance was for the stars to empower the audience. The stars who understood and did this best, like Morrison, Jimi Hendrix, and Janis Joplin, paid the high-est price.[28]

At the deepest level rock expressed emotions scarcely ever admitted to exist in rational, bourgeois society. The critic Greil Marcus observed that under-standing rock was like penetrating folk wisdom, that is, one had to look under the surface. He gave an example. The meaning of 'don't tread on me,' said Marcus, was a warning to be careful about what you say or do, lest your neigh-bors string you up. In other words, the slogan's celebration of autonomy masked a subliminal recognition of everyman's violence. If all were violent, then a potential mob was inherent in every social situation. Rock expressed those fears, but its exuberance also gave comfort. The critic Ed Denson described rock concerts as religious experiences. The ecstasy, he noted, was similar to that traditionally found in camp meetings. The music captured the aura but lacked moral substance. The social critic Paul Goodman thought youths were in a religious crisis.[29]

San Francisco rock developed along a peculiar path. The Bay Area had a relatively small black population, and, oddly enough, North Beach lacked the strong jazz tradition of New Orleans, Memphis, Chicago, or New York. Jazz and black rhythm and blues contributed only modestly to San Francisco rock. At the same time local rock artists developed a freer style, because they were also unencumbered by the country western influences so crucial for southern rock. Nor was the tin-pan alley tradition strong. The local musical tradition harkened back to the union songs of the thirties, the prominence of the Left in the Bay Area, the rhythms of beat poetry readings, the spontaneity of the beats, and the popularity of folk and protest songs in the early sixties. "We Shall Overcome" may have been the most popular song in Berkeley. Local circumstances pushed Bay Area rock groups either toward folk rock, as in the cases of Country Joe McDonald and Creedence Clearwater Revival, or toward a radical, experimental style in which powerful lyrics rode above a light me-lodic line that in turn was drowned out by a horrendously loud, thumping beat. The predominance of the beat, which in 1965 and 1966 shocked visitors from other parts of the country, was the Bay Area's most imaginative and original contribution to the development of rock music.[30]

Bay Area rock was more attuned to drugs, and especially to LSD. Acid, as it was popularly called, became known in the Bay Area long before it reached the rest of the country. In the late fifties the Veteran's Administration Hospital in Palo Alto conducted experiments with LSD. Among those who learned about these experiments was the novelist Ken Kesey, who was then in residence at Stanford University. Kesey tried LSD. Like many others, he found his whole frame of reference shattered. The drug transformed reality, and traditional categories of analysis seemed trite. In the hands (or minds) of less perceptive individuals, LSD usually provoked only a broad grin and a loud "wow," but Kesey was one of a handful of people who immediately understood the drug's significance. LSD unlocked repressed feelings and enabled its user to lose his identity and become at one with the world. That is, the ego dissolved. Kesey tried other psychedelic drugs, including morning-glory seeds, mescaline, and psilocybin; all altered consciousness. Kesey, who lived in the Perry Lane bohemia near Stanford, shared these drugs with his friends and neighbors, and, partially under the influence of peyote and acid, he wrote One Flew over the Cuckoo's Nest, which was published in 1962.[31]

The restless, questing Kesey decided to perform LSD experiments, which he called "acid tests," upon himself and his friends. In 1964 at a rented estate in the woods near Stanford, the group explored how LSD distorted perceptions. While drugged, they made movies, played music, and used loudspeakers to blast sounds in the woods around the estate. The experimenters became the Merry Pranksters, and they bought an old bus which they painted in weird colors, wired for sound, and drove across the country. After the Pranksters partied with Kerouac and Ginsberg in New York, they drove to the Millbrook estate to meet Dr. Timothy Leary. Leary had been a psychology professor at Harvard, until he was dismissed for experimenting on his students by giving them LSD. Leary moved to Millbrook, where he surrounded himself with acid users, but the self-proclaimed guru of acid refused to meet Kesey; their views about LSD were very different. Leary lacked Kesey's manic probing and imagination, and most of Leary's drug experiments had been carefully controlled. To Kesey, Leary's work missed the whole point. LSD so changed perception that no controlled experiment could measure the drug's effect. In the midsixties Leary came to share Kesey's conclusion, but the tardiness of the psychologist's realization put the eastern experimenters about two years behind Kesey's Pranksters.[32]

In California LSD was legal until October 6, 1966. By the summer of 1964, it was widely used in some circles. The activist Michael Rossman dropped his first acid that summer; he claimed that the transformation of reality created by acid played a crucial role in the formation of the Free Speech Movement. That is, people who were naturally suspicious of the people who held power and had good reasons to resent the status quo found, through their acid experiences, that the logic and mystique by which power was exercised no longer made sense. It is doubtful, however, that many of the FSM activists had taken acid in 1964. Some, perhaps half of the FSM Steering Committee, had used marijuana. Leary believed that LSD was a radical drug, because it so altered consciousness that existing worldviews could not be maintained. At the time the finest, purest acid in the country was being made in the Berkeley laboratory of Augustus Owsley Stanley III. It was not a minor business; at one point in 1965 Owsley, as he was called in hippie circles, ordered raw materials to make one and a half million doses. Owsley was a Kentucky aristocrat who had originally migrated to Berkeley to study chemistry at the University. Since he had a private fortune, he cared little about profits and often gave away his high-quality acid. [33]

By late 1965 Kesey decided to share LSD with the world. In order to get acid to the masses, he needed a gimmick. Kesey had discovered that LSD went well with rock music's strong rhythmic beat, sense of vitality, and strident tones, so he held a series of Acid Test concerts. Using Owsley's money, Jerry Garcia of the Pranksters put together a band, which became the Grateful Dead. In publicity for these events, Kesey taunted, "Can YOU pass the Acid Test?" LSD was provided at each performance. Chet Helms of the Family Dog had already staged several rock concerts; the first, at the Longshoremen's Hall, had followed the October 16, 1965, VDC march and attracted many Berkeley radicals. The Jefferson Airplane played. Meanwhile, Bill Graham, then the manager of the San Francisco Mime Troupe, decided to hold a benefit in the Troupe's loft. Although poorly advertised, the event's promise of free acid had spread by word of mouth, and as many as a thousand people came. The police forced Graham to turn away hundreds from the overcrowded loft. The Jefferson Airplane, which had ties to the Pranksters, played; most of the crowd stayed all night; and in the morning Allen Ginsberg ended the benefit by chanting a mantra. At the suggestion of the *San Francisco Chronicle* columnist Ralph Gleason, Graham then rented the larger Fillmore Auditorium for another benefit. Gleason promoted this concert during an interview with Bob Dylan shown on public television station KQED, and on December 10 about 3,500 people paid $1.50 each to attend Graham's first Fillmore concert. [34]

In January 1966 Graham and Helms continued their rock concerts; Kesey, his Acid Tests. At the end of the month Stewart Brand, a friend of Kesey's— later the compiler of the *Whole Earth Catalog*—asked Graham to stage a three-day Trips Festival at the San Francisco Longshoremen's Hall. Music, lights, and pictures were to simulate the acid experience. After the festival grossed $12,500 in three nights, Graham saw a gold vein to be tapped and left the

Mime Troupe to produce weekly rock concerts at the Fillmore. Rock and acid exploded together throughout the Bay Area. Concerts were held in Berkeley at the Finnish Brotherhood Hall, at a small club on Alcatraz near the Berkeley–Oakland line, and at the Pauley Ballroom on campus. Graham and other promoters decided not to furnish acid; some patrons arrived stoned. Throughout the spring and summer rock musicians performed in San Francisco at both the Fillmore and Avalon ballrooms each Friday and Saturday night. Each dance attracted 500 to 600 concertgoers, who came costumed with painted faces. People shared food and body paint. Trips festivals took place throughout the area; one in Berkeley was called Trips A Go Go. Graham had to hustle to find bands. Many of the groups took drug-related names. Jefferson Airplane was a code for "free trip," because acid had been available at their first concert. Big Brother and the Holding Company, which featured the blues singer Janis Joplin, was a play on the idea that dealers "held" dope.[35]

The local groups had difficulty gaining national recognition. Poorly managed and organized, they played music that was meaningless to most Americans, who had never dropped acid. Their hard-driving, bitter music was an acquired taste. It was often spontaneous, involved audience interaction, and had the jazz performer's delight for the moment at the expense of anything permanent. These attributes did not record well in a studio, and the groups' early records were flat compared to the live performances. The most popular local group, the Jefferson Airplane, quickly landed a major recording contract, but their first album, released in 1966, failed. In 1967 the Airplane's Grace Slick scored a number five hit single, "Somebody to Love." It expressed, perhaps better than any song of its time, the plea for the right to personal happiness in a world gone mad. "White Rabbit," another Slick song, reached number eight; it dealt overtly with drugs. Acid, suggested this song, could help a person grow, change, and become something new. White Rabbit was Owsley's nickname. It was late 1968 before a Bay Area group had a number one album; Big Brother and the Holding Company's *Cheap Thrills* rose to the top on Janis Joplin's pain.[36]

Several groups enjoyed local popularity. They included Steve Miller, Moby Grape, Redwing, Sopwith Camel, the Tower of Power, and the Quicksilver Messenger Service. One group that played mainly in Berkeley was the Joy of Cooking. Founded in 1967, it was unusual because its two songwriters and lead singers were women; it was lionized locally for its feminist message. National recognition eventually came to Country Joe and the Fish, the group which dominated Berkeley. For years Joe McDonald's band was a fixture in local coffeehouses and night clubs. The most overtly political rock star in the country, McDonald even gave his group a leftist name; Mao had said that a revolutionary must move among the people like a fish in the water. The group's music gradually shifted to the hip; one piece, "Bass Strings," was called "The

Dope Song." In 1965 locally cut singles were sold in Berkeley, but the Fish did not produce a nationally distributed album until 1967. Another important group was Sly and the Family Stone, which, under the genius of the black musician Sylvester Stewart, blended soul and rock into acid soul. In 1969 their "Everyday People" became the first number one single by a Bay Area group. Other later successes were Santana, which mixed San Francisco and Latin sounds, and Creedence Clearwater Revival, which played folk rock.[37]

Bay Area rock concerts left other legacies. Conceived as multimedia events attacking the senses from all directions, the early concerts had included film projected on the walls and light displays. While the film disappeared, later concerts continued to use pulsing strobe lights, rotating colored filters, and lights projected on colored oils to produce weird effects. Another legacy was posters and postcards used to advertise the concerts. In the early days these items were freely distributed either on street corners such as at Bancroft and Telegraph or wherever concert tickets were sold. The designs, influenced by LSD, featured exaggerated letters that swirled in patterns to represent objects. Wes Wilson innovated the lettering style, which he patterned after the dust jacket for *Rubber Soul*, a Beatles album released in December 1965. "The letters are used as art objects, not communications devices," explained Wilson. "It's as if words were going to become obsolete if we don't make them attractive." Wilson's comment revealed the relative importance of sight and sound and the unimportance of language and thought to the hippie culture. Berkeley artists John Thompson and Tom Weller, who designed ads for Country Joe and the Fish, portrayed female nudes with small heads and voluptuous hair; these women were militant and entranced. The posters, especially those by Wilson, Victor Moscoso, and Stanley Miller (who signed his work Mouse), were among the lasting tributes to the energy of Bay Area rock.[38]

Bay Area radio stations refused to play the new music, partly because the managers were of an older generation and did not like the sound and partly because the government-regulated broadcasting industry shied away from music that promoted drugs. In April 1967 Tom Donahue, a longtime rock disc jockey, started a free-form rock show on a nearly bankrupt FM station, KMPX. The station had neither listeners nor advertising, and Donahue used the opportunity to play long, uninterrupted sections of the new music; it marked the beginning of album rock. Word about Donahue's radically unstructured program traveled by word of mouth and through the underground press, and when the next radio station ratings appeared, advertisers were amazed. KMPX had become the leading FM station in the Bay Area among males aged eighteen to thirty-four. The station innovated in other ways as well. During a newspaper strike, local columnists and *Ramparts* magazine reporters read news summaries on the air. In 1968 Donahue and the disc jockeys at KMPX went on strike in a dispute with the owner, and album rock quickly moved to KSAN, where it remained a powerful force for years.[39]

From the beginning the new music had attracted the attention of a few critics. The most important were Ralph Gleason, the *San Francisco Chronicle*'s jazz columnist, and Jann Wenner, who wrote for the *Daily Californian*. Wenner grappled with rock's social significance; he wrote with knowledge and insight about connections between the new music and psychedelic drugs. For a time he reported for *Ramparts* magazine, but he did not share the New Left's overbearing earnestness, and after the editors caught Wenner smoking marijuana in the office, he was fired. The *Ramparts* editors, paranoid about a drug raid, could not afford to have illicit drugs on the premises. Wenner then decided, with Gleason's financial backing, to launch a magazine devoted to rock music. In the fall of 1967 the first issue of *Rolling Stone* came off the press; it sold only 5,000 copies. By May 1970 the magazine's circulation had reached 250,000; this was higher than *Ramparts* at its peak distribution, which must have given Wenner satisfaction. Wenner's disdain for radical politics did not bother his countercultural readers, and when the FBI put pressure on Columbia Records and other recording companies to quit advertising in the politically radical underground press, *Rolling Stone* became the only vehicle for the rock music industry to reach its audience. In 1977 Wenner moved his magazine from San Francisco to New York.[40]

In January 1967 a number of hippies celebrated the first anniversary of the Trips Festival with a Human Be-In in San Francisco's Golden Gate Park. Although radicals wanted a political rally, the more numerous hippies wanted music, and radical leaders had to accept lesser billing. Some of the 20,000 to 50,000 participants arrived stoned; many openly smoked marijuana. The poet Gary Snyder launched the Be-In by blowing on a conch shell, Allen Ginsberg chanted, "Om . . . ," and, among others, the Jefferson Airplane and the Grateful Dead played. Timothy Leary advised, "Tune in, turn on, and drop out." His line was appropriate for the event. Late in the day the radicals took the microphone and harangued the crowd, which drifted away, until the radicals were talking only to themselves. "I think," wrote Jerry Rubin, "the New Left can learn a great deal from the people in the Haight–Ashbury." The radicals learned that rock music and LSD were more popular than the New Left. Yet both radicals and hippies were rebelling against social norms, and so the radicals took heart and began to work with the hippies. A shared joint went a long way toward a hippie–radical fusion.[41]

Berkeley was in ferment. In March 1967 rumors surfaced that scrapings from the inside of a banana peel produced a legal, marijuana-like high; Berkeley's markets sold out of bananas, and a Banana Turn-On was held on Sproul Hall steps before the mania was revealed to be a hoax. Meanwhile, at the corner of

Bancroft and Telegraph Bob Weinzeimer, the publisher and editor of the mimeographed *Berkeley Gate*, sold buttons. He stocked more than 500 buttons; the leading sellers included "Impeach Ronald Reagan," "Curse You Red Baron," "Freedom Under Clark Kerr," "LSD Did This To Me," and "Relax." Many were bought by out-of-town high school students visiting the campus. The same month Dan Burnstein became the first pushcart food vendor at the same corner; his snow cones were soon joined by Jonathan Gontar's hot pretzels. That summer the city manager recommended a ban against pushcarts, but the council declined to act.[42]

Another sign of change involved experimentation at radio station KPFA. In the summer of 1965, the station had broadcast a special series featuring Gustav Mahler's classical music; at the time Mahler was rarely heard. A year later, the University orchestra performed one of Mahler's symphonies. Professor Carl Schorske noted Mahler's sudden popularity; the composer had captured and even satirized the mood of crisis amid decay in Vienna at the turn of the century. To many, Berkeley, too, seemed about to go the way of the Hapsburgs' Vienna. In October 1966 KPFA's *Program Folio* introduced a monthly arts calendar; it was arty and featured calligraphy. Three months later the station announced that its morning concert programs, hosted by Charles Shere and Scott Beach, would stress "spontaneity." That same month the *Folio* began to be filled with countercultural art symbols, and a year later the program guide ran its first silk-screened psychedelic cover.[43]

Also important was the emergence of Robert Crumb's Comix. Inspired by S. Clay Wilson, Crumb combined a highly elaborated drawing style with a rapier wit and a dirty mind. "There's a lot of weird shit in everybody's head," he said, adding, "It takes courage to let it all out." Crumb was not afraid to let go. "People are hot about sex," he noted. More disturbing to the establishment was Crumb's contempt for authority. His Comix sold well. In 1968 police raided Moe's bookstore for selling Crumb's "Zap No. 2," but a local judge dismissed the case; the easing of censorship by the courts gave Crumb freedom of expression. Crumb drew the cover for Big Brother's *Cheap Thrills* album. A year later the Free University catalog appeared as a Comix book. In July 1967 the tenth annual Berkeley Folk Music Festival included rock performers—Joe McDonald and Steve Miller. Rock swamped folk music; that same month the Jabberwock, Berkeley's last coffeehouse that presented live performers and long the principal place for folksingers and hootenannies, closed.[44]

It is difficult to convey the frenzy. Within the space of a few years came the invention of the waterbed; the founding of a hippie taxicab co-op; the proliferation of exotic, imported foods at the Co-op; the emergence of the *Berkeley Barb*; the collapse of censorship; Herbert Marcuse's Freudian Marxism; R. D. Laing's insistence that society was clinically schizophrenic; Carlos Castaneda's exploration of alternative realities; the discovery of transcendental meditation, mysticism, astrology, scientology, and satanism; and widespread use of drugs. By 1966 it was estimated that 20 to 40 percent of Cal students had tried marijuana. "Drugs, drugs, it is all about drugs," wrote Michael Rossman. Marijuana and LSD dissolved traditional culture and its rational values. Emotion, not reason, predominated. In the prevailing atmosphere, people asked, "Does this feel right to me?" Rossman wrote, "The whole fabric and most intimate textures of our lives kept changing." Later he noted that the man who had best understood his feelings was the Reverend T. Walter Herbert, who insisted that Rossman and others were undergoing the sense of crisis commonly found among persons anxious to have Christian conversion experiences.[45]

This sense of crisis was so frightening that the hippies turned to visual display as a substitute for stating their beliefs. "To brand yourself as beat," stated the Barb, "you have to be as bushy as possible." Long hair was more political than sartorial. Jerry Rubin asserted, "Through long hair we're engaged in a sexual assault that's going to destroy the political-economic structure of Amerikan society." (Alienated young people used the spelling "Amerika" to suggest that the country was fascist.) A columnist for the Daily Californian wrote, "The 'hippies' have it over the radicals. They're living in their ideal society NOW." Perhaps. But much had been lost in the process. As Rubin observed, "Grass destroyed the Left as a minority movement and created in its place a youth culture." The Left had failed because it was rooted in ideas. "Our generation," he continued, "is in rebellion against abstract intellectualism and critical thinking." Rubin concluded, "The intellect is but a speck on the ocean of emotion." Or, as Rossman once said, "We no longer believe that the way to bring about change is by words or persuasion . . . , it is by example." In the new order people were to be as free as the thousands of dogs that roamed Berkeley's streets. "We have no precedent for the depth of the cultural transformation we are entering," concluded Rossman.[46]

In the fifties the beats had dominated San Francisco's North Beach, but by the early sixties police stalked that area looking for homosexuals and drugs. Some beats moved to the Haight-Ashbury, a decaying and inexpensive white, working-class neighborhood on the edge of a tense black ghetto, the Fillmore district, and adjacent to Golden Gate Park. By 1965 North Beach was quiet, except for the bawdy strip along Broadway where tourists gawked at topless dancers. Much of San Francisco's bohemian life had moved to the Haight-Ashbury (or the Hashbury, as the columnist Herb Caen called it). Throughout 1966 young people, including many college dropouts from Berkeley and San Francisco State, quietly moved into the area; they were soon identified as hippies. As the Haight evolved, it continued to have strong ties to local college communities. Among those who visited the area was Jerry Rubin, who smoked his first joint and dropped his first acid there. By the end of 1966 the Haight was becoming known throughout the country as America's first hippie bohemia.[47]

In 1967 the district continued to attract young people seeking drugs, sex, and thrills. In May, Scott MacKenzie sang a hit single that advised young people to come to San Francisco wearing flowers in their hair; as many as 75,000 youths did, although few stayed for long. The media proclaimed "The Summer of Love." Gray Line rerouted its buses through the Haight to enable its middle-class, elderly passengers to stare at the hippies. In reality, the situation in the Haight became desperate, as thousands of nomadic youths, along with rip-off artists, descended upon the neighborhood. Work, food, and shelter were scarce; sex, drugs, and trouble plentiful. Dealing marijuana was the backbone of the community's economy. By the end of the summer, blacks from the Fillmore made prowls through the Haight to roll spaced-out hippies. The district's hip businessmen sponsored a ceremony declaring The Death of Hippie. This ceremony warned young people to stay away; it also celebrated the birth of a new consciousness, which was expressed in 1969 with the hit song, "The Age of Aquarius." Ironically, the Haight truly was dying. Within a year the area had been abandoned by all except derelicts and heroin addicts. Junkies survived by capturing and eating the neighborhood cats.[48]

The Haight established a sense of community for hippies. The large numbers and abundant energy of the new arrivals led to a self-confident assertion about the nature of the emerging hippie subculture. A hippie philosophy began to be worked out by a group of Haight residents called the Diggers. They took their name from a group of seventeenth-century English religious radicals who had denounced the concept of private property, insisted upon users' rights, and embraced a kind of philosophical anarchism rooted in individualism. The Diggers opened a store, where every item was given away; each day they provided a free hot meal in Golden Gate Park. Local grocery stores donated most of the ingredients, although the Diggers had trouble getting meat, which they sometimes stole. The Diggers expanded the concept of free sex to free food, free rent, and free expression. Through their propaganda division, the communications company, or comm/co, they published wall posters. They became the high priests of the counterculture.[49]

As the Haight began to choke on the influx of young people in the summer of 1967, many of the original hippies fled. Some moved to the country; Mendocino County was popular, because it produced excellent marijuana. Those who favored a close-in rural setting sometimes chose the mysterious and odd settlement at Canyon, tucked away in a rainy spot in the Berkeley Hills behind Oakland. The East Bay Municipal Utility District owned most of this onetime logging settlement, but hippies moved into abandoned houses, and some found private land and put up tents. In 1965 Canyon had forty houses and about 130 people. The community was closely tied to Berkeley, and hitchhiking to and from Berkeley was common. Canyon became Berkeley's only suburb. In 1967 Canyon's hippies held a benefit concert to raise money to rebuild their general store. Country Joe McDonald, the Grateful Dead, and others came to play; the narrow, winding road into Canyon was clogged with flower-painted VW vans. During this same period antiwar protests at Port Chicago near the north end of San Francisco Bay were regularly organized in Canyon. The benefit concert and the antiwar protests brought the community to the attention of county authorities, and building inspectors harassed the hippies. Canyon's residents, like other Americans in the sixties, resisted these officials' orders; they discovered that stubbornness and resourcefulness could overcome bureaucratic power and could allow one to bend the law to one's will. The Canyon community survived.[50]

Other residents of the Haight moved to the South Campus area of Berkeley. For one thing, it was a good place to panhandle. Many young people discovered a living could be made by begging on the streets. The hippie ethic of sharing made panhandling an honorable calling. More important were the close ties between Berkeley and the Haight; Cal students found the Haight a good source for drugs. At the same time, attitudes along Telegraph Avenue made the hippies feel welcome. Most important to the hippie invasion of Berkeley, however, was cheap housing. A number of white families had fled the city during the controversy over school integration and thereby abandoned a large number of decaying older homes in the South Campus area. Many students left Berkeley each summer, and so as hordes of outsiders invaded the Haight during the Summer of Love, many longtime Haight residents moved across the bay. In the fall Telegraph Avenue replaced Haight Street as the center of hippie life in the Bay Area. By 1970 the city contained about 20,000 white nonstudents in their twenties; in five South Campus census tracts they were a majority of the residents.[51]

For years conservatives had resented the emerging bohemia in the South Campus area. They complained bitterly and loudly, and in 1966 the city adopted a policy of intense law enforcement along Telegraph in order to drive away the growing number of hippies. Pairs of uniformed policemen patrolled each block on foot. Officers ignored people in middle-class garb and stopped longhaired bohemians for parking cars too far from the curb, for jaywalking, or for loitering. Many people were stopped for a check of identifications—sometimes three or four times in one evening—and older males without draft cards on their persons ran the risk of prosecution. Police told juveniles that they were violating a nonexistent city curfew and ordered them to leave the area or risk being locked up. Because both hippies and students had long hair and wore jeans,

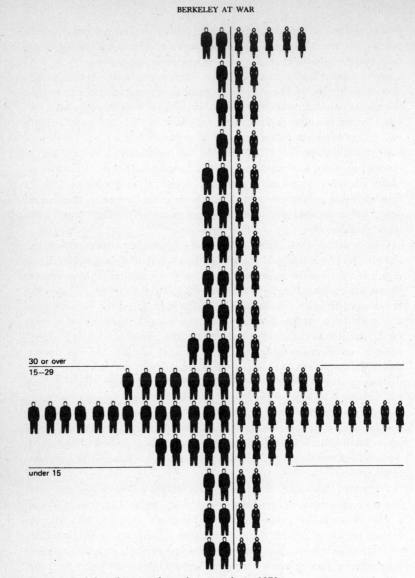

30 or over
15—29

under 15

Fig. 4.1. Berkeley white population by age and sex, 1970
Each figure represents 1 percent of the population.

police frequently stopped Cal students, who came to resent the officers. Street people heckled patrolmen, and on one occasion an anonymous telephone caller told the wife of a policeman that her husband was dying.[52]

After a time a number of students, activists, and Telegraph merchants, including Fred Cody, decided to challenge the foot patrols. They organized the Better Berkeley Committee (BBC), which undertook its own foot patrols along Telegraph. Equipped only with armbands and walkie-talkies, BBC monitors discouraged both drug deals and police harassment of passersby. The monitors carried affidavit forms for those who had witnessed police harassment; in a month of patrolling they collected twenty statements of police misconduct. Unlike the police, the monitors greeted people in a friendly way and offered advice about shopping. Finally, the BBC, after negotiations with the city government in which Michael Rossman played an important role, persuaded the city to withdraw the uniformed foot patrols. Plainclothesmen continued to watch for drug deals, and uniformed officers hovered on the side streets in case of trouble. In return, the BBC monitors circulated to discourage mobs and street crimes. Among the monitors was David Goines, who had designed and made posters for the FSM.[53]

Tensions between police and hippies did not ease. By 1967 the BBC patrols had ended, and many of the youths on Telegraph were teenaged runaways from all over the country; they considered Berkeley to be a "liberated city." These young people were penniless, hungry, and unemployed. From 1960 to 1967 white unemployment in Berkeley rose from 3.9 to 9.4 percent, at a time when the national rate fell. The young bore the brunt of the increase. In April 1967, 1,500 youthful residents of the South Campus area defiantly closed down Telegraph for an illegal block party. The I Ching was thrown, a band, the Loading Zone, played in front of Cody's, and several children laid down in the street in the shape of a peace symbol. The police watched but did not move. One night in June, however, the police cracked down. The Forum, the Blue Cue, the Med, and Pepe's, which normally stayed open until 1 or 2 a.m., suddenly closed at 11 p.m. As juveniles poured into the street, they were arrested. This kind of police harassment drove timid, law-abiding people out of the area. It also produced ill will. The hippies did not disappear, and the police were discouraged and embittered both by the hostility they encountered and by their own ineffectiveness; Berkeley policemen and bohemians grew to hate each other.[54]

During 1968 both sides engaged in guerilla war. When Sergeant Darryl Bothwell chased a drug suspect into a closed restaurant, a crowd gathered at the window and shouted, "Down with the pigs." Six policemen who tried to arrest a group of people smoking marijuana on the sidewalk at Bowditch and Haste were attacked by three hundred people. The Red Mountain Tribe, a communal living group, controlled half a block on Parker Street. When a police car stopped on the block, members of the Tribe blew whistles, rushed to meet the officers, and surrounded the patrol car. If a policeman chased a suspect, Tribe members tripped him or splashed red paint on the patrol car's windshield. On the other side, the police regularly harassed well-known activists, such as Bill Miller, owner of The Store, which sold drug paraphernalia. They drove away his customers, arrested him for jaywalking, and once publicly thanked him on the street to create the impression that he was a police spy.[55]

In July 1968 the *Berkeley Barb* ran a cover featuring a coiled snake with the words, "Berkeley Commune—Don't Tread on Me." Communes (the hippie term) and collectives (the radical term) sprang up all over the neighborhood. Group living fostered solidarity and suppressed individualism. All summer Haj Razavi, one of the street people who called themselves the Persian Fuckers, sold tea from a samovar and harangued passersby from a box in front of Cody's; once he was assaulted by two plainclothesmen. One used a blackjack, the other brass knuckles. On a happier occasion Razavi and Charlie Brown Artman officiated at a wedding ceremony in front of Cody's. Afterward, the crowd surged into the street. One person challenged cars with a bullfighting cape, black and red flags were flown, and someone painted "liberate Berkeley" on the pavement. At the end of the summer, amid rumors of deportation, Razavi disappeared. At his last appearance he said, "Well, capitalist Cody, this is a summer you will not forget, eh?"[56]

Over the summer of 1968 some activists, a few Telegraph merchants, and a handful of city officials met occasionally in the backroom of The Forum. These meetings led to a reinstitution of the BBC foot patrols, but the patrols did not impress the police. Although crime was rising throughout the city, police found crime, and especially drug-related crime, to be concentrated in the South Campus area. A longhaired youth could not walk along Telegraph without being offered marijuana, acid, or speed at least once per block. Apprehended juvenile runaways rose from 424 in 1966 to 846 in 1968. Conservatives were outraged. As early as 1960, Don Mulford, the conservative Republican who represented the South Campus area and the hills in the state legislature, had proposed the death penalty for marijuana dealers. Drug deals did lead to violent crimes. In July 1968 a man was murdered a block off Telegraph; three months later another victim was killed only fifty feet away. South Campus residents, however, argued that the crime wave was mainly due to intensive police activity. The police presence, they argued, had driven away normal people, while arrests were made in order to demonstrate the existence of a crime wave and thereby prove that the community was so unstable and dangerous as to require massive intervention from outside. Some even charged that high officials in state government were responsible for this policy. This analysis was not entirely inaccurate.[57]

In 1956 the University had begun to buy property both above and below

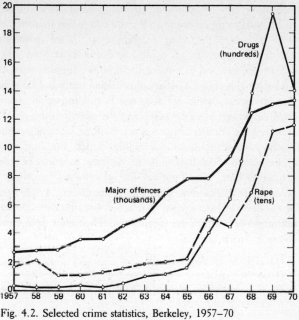

Fig. 4.2. Selected crime statistics, Berkeley, 1957–70
(*Sources:* Berkeley Police Department, *Annual Reports, 1961, 1966, 1970.*)

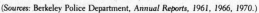

Telegraph between Bancroft and Dwight to construct student dormitories. The University built three of a projected six high-rise complexes. Although federal funding ran out, land continued to be acquired. Meanwhile, in 1960 the city had designated a South Campus urban renewal project covering sixteen blocks. The city planned to use the University's expenditures on the dormitories to obtain federal matching funds to rebuild the commercial area along Telegraph. The original plan was to turn Telegraph, which was quite narrow, into a pedestrian mall and to construct two parallel one-way streets at the rear of the stores. Although merchants were positive, students protested the destruction of cheap housing, and the city reexamined the issue. At a public meeting in 1964 property owners and merchants complained about the uncertainty of the proposed renewal project. Old buildings were not being repaired, and no new ones were being constructed. In 1966 new hearings were held. A local artist, Patricia Oberhaus, denounced "rows of ticky-tacky boxes with Barbie Dolls and Ken Dolls living in them." Opponents presented a petition with 651 signatures. Although some merchants and area residents supported a mall, the city found that federal money could be used to build a mall only if commercial structures were brought up to current earthquake standards. To do so would have ruined the merchants, and so the council voted six to two to abandon the project.[58]

Despite the collapse of the urban renewal project, the city government acted aggressively. It was determined, according to the *BCU Bulletin*, "to clean up the South Campus area and to run out the beatniks, hippies, and other undesirables." The Neighborhood Youth Corps hauled trash and demolished outbuildings at no charge, while building and health inspectors intensively inspected the area. In one block 85 percent of the structures did not meet code. Officials checked the number of persons per dwelling unit and watched for the unlawful conversion of homes into boarding houses. Buildings were demolished; the elimination of dwelling units was designed to reduce population densities and to raise rents. "Since most of the undesirables have little or no income," noted the *BCU Bulletin*, "they will be forced out." While conservatives applauded the demolitions as proof of progress, area residents became uneasy about what might be built on the vacant land. Their fears were expressed in a nursery rhyme in the *Berkeley Barb*:

> This is the house that Jack built.
> This is the bulldozer that leveled the house that Jack built.
> The is the crackerbox apartment that Nakamura built in place of
> 　the house that Jack built.[59]

The university continued with its plans. "I wouldn't be too surprised," predicted John Leggett, "if the political elites tried to eliminate non-students by using Urban Renewal strategy and taking over the area." The radical assistant professor of sociology, who had been denied tenure, made a shrewd prediction. Although conservative Councilman Joseph Bort accused the University of stalling on its land purchases, the institution moved as fast as its limited resources permitted. Assemblyman Mulford urged the University to demolish buildings it already owned to eliminate a "human cesspool." He explained, "I want the University to tear these houses down to the ground and build parking lots, tennis courts, anything." Mulford was furious that the University rented many of its dwellings to beats and runaways. He promised to get special funding to buy and demolish old houses. "We must get rid of the rat's nest that is acting as a magnet for the hippie set and the criminal element," he insisted. Mulford delivered the promised funds, and in July 1967 the University used $1.3 million to buy the remaining property that it did not own in the block above Telegraph between Haste and Dwight and prepared to demolish the entire block. In late September police raided one house on Haste three times in four days. The police claimed it was University property, but records showed that the property was in escrow; the residents were squatters. They were arrested on drug charges.[60]

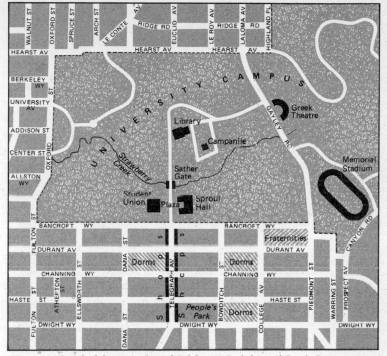

Map. 4.1. Detail of the University of California, Berkeley and South Campus

Although the University had targeted the block between Haste and Dwight for quick action, the bureaucracy moved slowly, and the first demolitions did not take place until November 1967. While the buildings remained, the University continued to rent rooms and apartments. In return for unusually cheap rent, tenants had to agree to vacate the premises on short notice. The low rents attracted impoverished students, and when the University ordered the premises vacated, tenants had trouble finding places at equally low rates. As far as the tenants were concerned, the plan to destroy low cost housing was proceeding only too well; some saw themselves as the victims of a conspiracy by the city's real estate interests. The University's bureaucrats showed no sensitivity; on one occasion they ordered property vacated the week before final exams. After protests, the University relented and delayed further demolitions until the end of the school year. It was December 1968 when the last building fell. Thus, for more than a year residents, former residents, and neighbors watched and reflected upon the transformation of a block of old but habitable dwellings into a vast urban wasteland. "We have to destroy the village in order to save it," someone had said in Vietnam. To many, the same principle appeared to be at work in Berkeley.[61]

Much as the Diggers had become the theoreticians of the Haight, the Provos, led by Bill Miller, became Berkeley's hippie leaders. Their name was borrowed from a group of Dutch anarchists; provo was short for provocateur. The Provos began by giving away soup in Civic Center Park, which the hippies renamed Provo Park. To get served, one had to bring a bowl and a spoon. Although distribution was erratic, thirty to fifty people consistently showed up for the handouts. On Saturdays or Sundays free rock concerts were held in the park. It was later disclosed that the city had provided the money for the food and concerts in order to lure hippies away from Telegraph Avenue. The Provos also operated the Free Store on San Pablo Avenue, where donated clothes, toys, and kitchen utensils could be obtained. At night seven Provos slept on the store's floor, and during the day they baked bread for distribution at the park. For a time the Provos dyed their bread in psychedelic colors. A benefit at the Steppenwolf, at which the Loading Zone, Country Joe McDonald, and MAD River played, raised $650, and the Provos bought an old bus. They offered free trips around Berkeley and between Berkeley and the Haight, until someone put sugar in the bus's gas tank. On one occasion two workers from the Free Store married two couples in a hippie ceremony in Provo Park.[62]

Two young ministers, Richard L. York and John Pairman ("Jock") Brown, organized the Berkeley Free Church. Its symbol was a cross inside a Greek omega, which was the symbol for The Resistance's antidraft activities. Much of the preaching at the Free Church was directed against the war. The church motto was "Celebrate life—off the world pig!" When York started the church in the summer of 1967, up to two hundred teenagers a day came to his house; about ninety were allowed to sleep inside, but the door was never locked, and in the morning up to thirty more kids were to be found sleeping on the living room floor. York and Brown opened a successful free dining room but their main concern was to adapt Episcopalian practices to hippie needs. Thus, they held large outdoor communions using elaborate costumes, body paint, chalk, candles, incense, incantations, and rock music. The BCU called these ceremonies a "depraved mockery of a Christian celebration." Although scarcely a fair characterization, the Free Church did seem more devoted to form than to the substance of Christianity; it was highly ritualized and seemed to lack moral toughness despite its devotion to liberation theology.[63]

In contrast, the Reverend Hubert Lindsey brought evangelical convictions to Berkeley. Arriving in December 1965, Holy Hubert, as he was called, began to preach daily on the edge of campus at Telegraph and Bancroft. Among Lindsey's faithful listeners was the dog Ludwig, who became so identified with

a fountain in front of the Student Union that it was named Ludwig's Fountain.
In his attempt to bring born-again Christian salvation to the University, the
street preacher faced an uphill battle. When he arrived, he found no organized
evangelical groups on campus and estimated that only 4 percent of Cal students
from Christian backgrounds had any interest in religion. Lindsey could preach
for hours without losing his voice, had the saving grace of humor, and, like all
street preachers, loved to argue with his enemies in order to build an audience.
He did not win all the disputes. Lindsey told one student, as he often did,
"You've got a dirty heart."

The student replied, "What do you mean—I took a shower this morning."
Lindsey insisted, "You've still got a dirty heart."

The student answered, "Next time I'll take an open heart shower." Holy
Hubert developed a rapport with many radicals. Once the police harassed the
street preacher, and the story got into the *Barb*. Rubin then told Lindsey that
if the police arrested him, the radicals would send 25,000 people to sit in at
the police station. When two high school students visited the campus, one
wanted to stay and listen to Lindsey, but the other said, "Look, if we come
back in five years, the man will still be here and you can listen to him then!"
Lindsey made few converts.[64]

The beats had found Christianity wanting. Gary Snyder, among others, had
gone to Japan and studied Zen Buddhism. By the early sixties knowledge of
Zen, with its emphasis upon ritual, self-discipline, and controlled breathing,
was widespread in the Bay Area's bohemian community. Although the hippies
never embraced Zen, they did become acquainted with some of its practices.
Hippies admired and respected disciples from the East. Of more consequence
in Berkeley by 1968 were the Hare Krishnas, who dressed in flowing saffron
robes, shaved their heads, lived communally in a house on Channing Way,
and chanted their "Hare Krishna" mantra as they danced up and down Telegraph seeking alms. The Krishna religion emphasized the spirit of the group,
the search for holiness through devotion to the mantra, and a certain distancing
of the purified self from the contaminated world. Krishnas cared little about
intellect; their religion was more instinctive than moral, although, of course,
it did contain a code of ethics. While outsiders often believed that the Krishnas
had gone mad, the Krishnas believed that their religion offered solace and
protection in a world gone mad.[65]

For many young people all organized religion was archaic; it was neither
scientific nor modern. As social change, particularly in race relations, eroded
tradition, a tide of solipsism became, as the poetry critic Yvor Winters had
warned, a route to a situational ethics in which moral principle no longer
existed. Poetry turned stark, bleak, and nihilistic, and at some readings the
most significant act was when the poet and the audience undressed. Sculpture,
too, lacked moral content and degenerated into a despairing primitivism known

as junk sculpture. For a time, giant iron and wood sculptures could be seen on the mudflats adjacent to the Eastshore Freeway; the highway department finally demolished these sculptures as traffic hazards. Age-old verities no longer mattered. Professor Hardin Jones once had a conversation with a student, who stated, "I intend to live my life without any restraint over me."

Jones then asked, "Won't you at least accept the Ten Commandments as being for 3,400 years a minimal guide to law in most countries?"

"No," replied the student, "I don't accept the Ten Commandments."

"Don't you have any concept of right and wrong?" inquired Jones.

"Now we have come to the point," said the student. "My generation has learned that what people do is simply what people do. There is no right or wrong."[66]

By early 1969 the South Campus community was in a sour mood. When militant minority students organized the Third World Liberation Front and struck the University, the strike enjoyed support among area residents. The strike turned violent, and because Berkeley's police force was too small to curb the disturbances, the city called for outside assistance. Under state law, these outside forces came under the county sheriff's control. Frank Madigan, part of the hardline Knowland-Mulford-Coakley regime, turned the police loose against militant strikers, longhaired hippies, and innocent students. "When I witness four or five officers literally pummel a student into submission," one outraged student wrote the chancellor, "I must ask if this is the answer to anything." City and University officials were particularly exasperated at the unprofessional conduct of the amateur sheriff's deputies. Militants called the deputies the Blue Meanies, because they wore blue, were vicious, and resembled the evil characters in the Beatles' move, *Yellow Submarine*. In early February Governor Reagan proclaimed a state of emergency in order to send in the California Highway Patrol. The patrolmen, however, were not effective in ending the turmoil, and on February 21, the National Guard was called. Violence quickly subsided, the Guard was withdrawn, and conservatives concluded that they had finally found a way to control Berkeley. The state of emergency remained in effect.[67]

In April 1969 the city held its regular election for members of the council. The Berkeley Democratic Caucus backed two incumbents, Zack Brown and Wilmont Sweeney, and two newcomers, Joseph Grodin and Warren Widener for regular four-year terms; they supported the appointed incumbent John Swingle for a special two-year term. The *Berkeley Daily Gazette* endorsed Sweeney, Swingle, and two Republicans, Thomas McLaren and Borden Price. The Community for New Politics, renamed the Berkeley Coalition, joined the newly organized Black Caucus to nominate Sweeney, Widener, and Ilona Hancock. The candidates ignored the South Campus issue, except for Hancock's *Coalition News*, which denounced the University's condemnation and demolition of old houses. Hancock, a South Campus community activist previously involved in Women for Peace, had gotten into politics when the city decided to demolish her daughter's day-care center. The activist Bill Miller ran as an independent. He, along with Hancock, was endorsed by the *San Francisco Express Times*. Miller's sound truck advised, "To get a head, you have to vote for a head."

The Left seemed weaker; it had, in a sense, been swept away by the counterculture. Turnout was low, and votes split among twenty-one candidates. On election day Swingle won the short term, and Sweeney, Widener, McLaren, and Price won regular seats, although Zack Brown and Hancock ran a close fifth and sixth. In precincts near campus Hancock ran second. Everyone noted Hancock's strength, the splintering of the electorate, and the hopeless fragmentation of the new council: John DeBonis, a maverick conservative who preferred theatrics to compromise; Mayor Johnson, McLaren, and Price, moderate conservatives; Swingle, in the middle, although he usually voted with the liberals who had originally appointed him; May, Sweeney, and Widener, liberals; and Dellums, on the left.[68]

Even before the city election, residents of the South Campus area had talked about the need for a park in their neighborhood. In June 1968 the city demolished a boarding house that had long stood on the southwest corner of Dwight Way and Telegraph Avenue in order to rebuild the intersection so cars could easily turn from Dwight onto Telegraph. For a time the site stood vacant, and Cliff Humphrey memorialized a friend who had been killed in an automobile accident by building what he called a "People's Park." Few noticed the park, and it was soon demolished. In October a citizens' committee chaired by Paul H. Williamson reported to the city manager that the densely populated South Campus neighborhood needed a park. They urged the University to lease its vacant land near Telegraph for a city-sponsored tot-lot and crafts area. Two months later a University employee made a similar proposal to the University administration. This proposal creatively suggested that students design the park and that the local community participate in its development. The administration, immersed in the controversy over Cleaver's appointment as a University lecturer, did not respond.[69]

All winter Michael Delacour, the owner of a dress shop called the Red Square on Dwight near Telegraph, mused upon the numerous cars that were parked above Telegraph in the muddy University-owned block that had once housed students and hippies. The University's stewardship of the property had been neglectful. The area had not even been properly cleared; foundations and weeds remained. It had become a convenient parking lot, but the mudholes had deepened with the winter rains. The University ignored this mess until early April 1969, when an article in Marvin Garson's *Good Times*, the successor to his *San Francisco Express Times*, expressed disgust with the University's neglect of the site. Within days the administration responded by placing a proposal to build a playing field on the agenda for the June meeting of the Board of Regents. The activists, however, did not intend to wait until June.[70]

On April 13 Delacour met with Bill Miller, Stew Albert, Paul Glusman, Art Goldberg (of the FSM), Wendy Schlessinger, and others to discuss the site. Delacour suggested that the local activists could rally both the hippie and radical communities to build a park. To the hippies, the park could symbolize the community's hope for the future, could be a place for rock concerts and other community gatherings, and could offer a bit of the greenery and flowers that seemed missing from a generally bleak urban setting. The discovery of an issue with ecological dimensions was significant; the environment was becoming an issue, and a year later a global Earth Day was celebrated. To the radicals, the park offered several opportunities. In addition to forging a radical-hippie alliance, the issue promised confrontation, repression, and new recruits. Abbie Hoffman, visiting from the East, stood on the site with Frank Bardacke and Stew Albert as the latter explained how the issue would "suck Reagan into a fight."[71]

Other radicals thought the park could lead to a community willing and able to defend its turf. Tom Hayden's Berkeley Liberation Program, a specific platform articulated in leaflets, wall posters, and the underground press, conceived of Berkeley as an island, like Stalin's Russia, that would serve as a model for a future revolutionary America. Not all radicals, however, approved of People's Park; Progressive Labor called the park "bourgeois reformist." The communists were baffled; they found it difficult to embrace the park as a crucial issue in the Marxist-Leninist class struggle. This confusion led the anarchistic leaders of the park movement both to discredit the communists and to persuade them, through a tactical demonstration, that the park was a crucial issue. Of more importance to the leaders, however, was the park's capacity to rally hippies to a political cause. Militants planned a civics lesson for the politically naive hippies; the leaders cynically calculated that the park, which appealed to hippie idealism, would be crushed, and the dirty truth about power would then bring the hippies into a radical-hippie political union.[72]

Five days later the *Berkeley Barb* carried an anonymous story, written by Albert, under the name "Robin Hood's Park Commissioner," rallying support for the park. "The University," wrote Albert, "has no right to create ugliness as a way of life." The article called for a public gathering on Sunday, April 20, 1969. Hippies, radicals, activists, and other park enthusiasts were invited to come to the site with shovels, picks, and hoes to engage in the creative act of building a park out of the University's muddy ruins. "Nobody supervises," promised this libertarian and anarchist manifesto, "and the trip belongs to whoever dreams." The importance of this appeal cannot be overestimated; at the time the *Barb* had a circulation of about 95,000.[73]

When Delacour and his friends showed up at the park site on Sunday, they were astonished to find several hundred people already there. They were as motley a crew as ever gathered in one place for a single purpose. Hippies and radicals were joined by straight-looking professors, students concerned about the environment, curious neighborhood residents, and grandmothers. Someone had brought a tractor, which was used to demolish the remains of the old foundation and gently grade the land. Many people worked hard with shovels and picks. "For the first time in my life," wrote Stew Albert, "I enjoyed working." Others just stood idly and watched; progress was slow. It became clear that the site was too large to be developed by dozens of people using handtools on a single afternoon. That night the workers built a fire, and the leaders gave food to the workers. Many in the group agreed to return the following Sunday and take up work again.[74]

During the following week the project snowballed. Building People's Park became the main topic of conversation along Telegraph, and the *Berkeley Barb* put a photograph of a handmade "People's Park" sign on its cover. Among those who visited the site and came away impressed was Bobby Seale of the Black Panthers. "You mean you just took that land without asking anyone?" inquired Seale, who never achieved the white middle-class's assumption that it owned everything. For once, young people's energies seemed to be directed toward creative activity rather than destructive riots. As attention increased, Delacour and his friends lost control. For one thing, their libertarian anarchism hampered the project. Each new participant envisioned a somewhat different park, and these differences threatened to degenerate into chaos. For example, one man began to dig a hole for a barbecue pit, while another man started to fill it in. This particular battle became a contest of wills. Because the users had designed the park, the conflict could not be resolved. The mightiest pick won. Worse, the founders had no political theory to justify their park-building, which seemed to be nothing more than personal whimsy confronting power, law, and private property rights. The park could not survive without some sort of theory to support it against its enemies.[75]

One day Delacour met Frank Bardacke at the Cafe Med. Bardacke understood the philosophical limitations in Delacour's position, and the onetime political science graduate student introduced Delacour to the concept of users' rights. The doctrine of users' rights had enabled European explorers to claim North America and take land away from the American Indians. According to this theory, land could be claimed if the claimant could show that he could use the land more productively and more wisely than the prior owner. Bardacke suggested that the University had abused its ownership of the site of People's Park by leaving it vacant and unkempt, and that the developers of the park could claim the land under the doctrine of users' rights. A manifesto stating this claim, reproduced over a shadowy figure of an Indian, was published in the *Barb* and widely distributed throughout Berkeley.[76]

Even more people showed up to work on the park on the second Sunday, neighbors complained to police about noisy rallies, bongo drums, and bonfires, and University officials grew nervous. Although University administrators did not want to concede the use of the land to outsiders, they lacked the power to stop the hippies and radicals from building the park. The Regents, however, were furious; they were determined to regain control over their property. Chancellor Heyns preferred a low profile. The odds were that the next winter's rains would ..ipe out an ill-drained park, and the University might then quietly reclaim the site. More embarrassing to University officials was the fact that they had no money to develop the property. At the last moment, the University obtained funds for an unwanted soccer field, but it was clear that this proposal was merely a device to assert University control. "They could as well have said," park supporters derisively noted, "they needed it to stage debutante balls for the children of the Regents." While the University bureaucracy debated what to do, park builders brought in sod, laid it, planted trees, and started a vegetable garden.[77]

In early May 1969, Heyns stalled. As usual, the chancellor was trapped. "Commie illegal takeover of the property is the first step in planned confrontation," warned the conservative *BCU Bulletin*. "We need the park to live and grow, and eventually we need all of Berkeley," claimed the militant park builders. Heyns had to take into account that Edwin Meese III, who had prosecuted the Free Speech Movement protesters, and Alex Sherriffs, who had opposed the FSM while on the chancellor's staff, served in high positions in Governor Reagan's administration. Just before arriving in 1965, Heyns had decided to remove Sherriffs from his administrative post at Cal, and now he was Reagan's chief aide for higher education. Sherriffs went to Regents meetings, appeared to instruct Reagan how to vote, and insisted on attending the executive sessions as the governor's representative. When some Regents protested, Reagan got angry, and the Regents decided to protect their budget by allowing Sherriffs to continue to attend the closed sessions. For years Sherriffs had wanted to clean up the South Campus area, and People's Park certainly did not cause a change of heart.[78]

While conservatives pushed Heyns to crush the militants, the chancellor knew that park supporters outnumbered the Berkeley police force. And the militants knew it. If police were called from outside the city, Heyns and city officials would lose control. Events during the Third World Liberation Front strike in early 1969 had shown the danger that came from outside authorities. Heyns sensed, correctly, that the issue might die down over the summer; at least, if school were out, the dispute between the University and the hippies need not involve students. The chancellor tried to lease the site to the city, so the city and hippies could negotiate terms for the construction of a park. The city, however, showed little interest in acquiring this political nuisance. Then

Heyns asked the Regents to lease the park to the hippies. Although a few Regents approved, most opposed the University being blackmailed by the occupation of its land. The chancellor came to realize that he could get the Regents to act only if he could find a respectable group to take legal control of the park.[79]

Heyns negotiated with the park builders to create such a responsible organization, but the chancellor found that no one was willing or able to accept responsibility for the park. The originators of the scheme denied that they were leaders, in the traditional sense of the word, and even those who were willing to be bound by negotiation were not willing to bind others. Heyns's last hope came from Professor Sim Van der Ryn of the College of Environmental Design. Van der Ryn was willing to work directly with the park builders to create a user-designed park. All he asked in return was that the University declare the site an experimental field station under his control. Heyns, however, disliked the University taking so great a responsibility for the park; there were, among other issues, concerns about legal liability. And Van der Ryn never convinced either the hippies or the Regents that he could work successfully with both sides. In the end negotiations, much to Heyns's sorrow, collapsed.[80]

On Sunday, May 11, the Reverend Richard York of the Free Church consecrated People's Park in an elaborate ceremony. On the following day Heyns stated that he had been unable to find a responsible group for conducting negotiations, and on Tuesday the chancellor announced that the site was to be fenced. Heyns was trapped between the park builders, who saw no reason to negotiate, and the Regents and high state officials, who insisted that the site had to be used for University purposes. Construction of the fence was imperative because of an upcoming Regents meeting; the chancellor expected to be grilled about the park, and he knew that he had to act before the meeting. Before dawn on Wednesday a crew arrived to post no trespassing signs around People's Park. As fast as the signs went up, dozens of park supporters, who were keeping vigil, ripped them down. They were burned in the park's communal fire pit. At noon the Liberated Women of Berkeley held a press conference on the site; Ilona Hancock defended People's Park. In late afternoon 400 students met and voted to defend the park; they appointed an eleven member negotiating team that included Michael Delacour.[81]

At 4:30 a.m. on Thursday, May 15, 1969, 250 California highway patrolmen arrived at the park; a helicopter circled overhead. Fifteen minutes later the several dozen people keeping vigil were told to leave or face arrest; all except three who were heavily drugged left. About an hour later a bulldozer began to clear the perimeter in order to build a fence; the police sealed off eight blocks. Onlookers were generally quiet, but some shouted taunts at the workmen. At 10 a.m. faculty members of the College of Environmental Design made one last appeal to Heyns to declare the site an experimental field station. In late morning, as the construction workers were finishing the fence, the police prepared to withdraw. University officials were hopeful but apprehensive; a number of inflammatory leaflets had been distributed along Telegraph. One stressed, "Let's tell the University that we want the South Campus area to remain a beautiful place of homes and parks, and not become a place of ugly dormitories and parking lots."[82]

At noon a large rally, attracting several thousand people, took place at Sproul Hall steps. The atmosphere was tense. The hippies were angry, the radicals ready for revenge, and even many students spoiled for a fight. Students still smarted over the administration's capitulation to the Regents in the controversy over Cleaver's lectures, and now the administration was moving against the hippies to destroy a park that even students could enjoy. The administration seemed arrogant and ignorant of student concerns. After several speakers denounced the fence at the park, Dan Siegel, a law student, a draft resister, and the president-elect of the ASUC, took the microphone. He laid out the history of the site, noted how the University had evicted students and hippies from the old houses and then destroyed the buildings, and charged that now the University had destroyed the park. The University's thoughtless and wanton destruction in Berkeley was compared to the United States government's in Vietnam. Then, said Siegel, "Let's go down and take over the park." He may have spoken metaphorically, and there is evidence that he planned to continue the speech. Other speakers were on the program. But Siegel's remark marked the end of the rally. The crowd began to chant, "Take the park! We want the park!" Thousands spontaneously surged away from Sproul Plaza, whooped like the revolutionaries in the movie *The Battle of Algiers*, and marched down Telegraph Avenue.[83]

The two to six thousand protesters never got to the park, which was heavily guarded. Blocked from access at Haste Street, the crowd suddenly halted in the middle of Telegraph Avenue. When it became clear that the protesters' will was being stopped, the mob split into small groups and carried out petty violence of the type that had been employed the previous summer. Among the first windows broken were those in the Bank of America branch at the corner of Telegraph and Durant. A block away someone opened a fire hydrant, many protesters hurled rocks, and the police fired tear gas into the crowd. The *Berkeley Daily Gazette* described two intersections as "open door gas chambers." A large portion of the mob retreated toward campus. As the afternoon's protest continued, demonstrators noticed that some of the Blue Meanies had stopped firing tear gas. Instead, one squad began to load and fire birdshot. Some shots were fired directly into clumps of people. The demonstrators fled the shots, which ricocheted off buildings, trees, and telephone poles in all directions. Pellets struck innocent passersby blocks away. In the remote center of the campus, members of the San Francisco Tactical Squad fired bullets that nicked the granite of the University's main library and then, much to the alarm of Professor Henry F. May, bounced into a classroom. No Berkeley policemen fired.[84]

The Tac Squad's bullets produced less damage to the campus's tranquility than had protesters' assaults that had gone on continually for years. By 1969 most members of the University community were angry and exhausted, almost shell-shocked. Radical graffiti, spilled garbage cans, false fire alarms, and stink bombs formed a tedious routine punctuated only by an occasional noisy sit-in, disrupted class, or sound of a rock breaking a window. Wise administrators got unlisted home telephone numbers, while cautious professors put masking tape over the glass in the windows of their office doors and thereby revealed their anxiety. Prudent faculty members removed valuable possessions, including research notes, and took them home for safekeeping. It was difficult to work on campus, and the University's overall efficiency in its research and teaching dropped considerably. The senseless, random nature of the violent attacks pained and puzzled the faculty, who increasingly came to see the protesters in pathological terms. Students, too, resented the turmoil, even when they agreed with the protesters' political goals.

In the midst of the turmoil over People's Park, an announcer from radio station KPFA talked on the telephone with John Lennon in Montreal. Lennon, who had been barred from the United States by the Nixon administration, was in the middle of an antiwar protest; he and Yoko Ono, whom he had recently married, protested by conducting a bed-in; i.e., they refused to get out of bed. Lennon told KPFA he supported People's Park but rejected confrontation. "I don't believe there's any park worth getting shot for," he said. Lennon advised the park protesters to stage a festival and sing "Hare Krishna." In a later call Lennon explained, "The students are being conned! It's like the school bully: he aggravates you and aggravates you until you hit him. And then they kill you, like in Berkeley . . . . The monster doesn't care—the Blue Meanie is insane. We really care about life. Destruction is good for the Establishment. The only thing they can't control is the mind, and we have to fight for sanity and peace on that level. But the students have gotten conned into thinking they can change it with violence and they can't, you know, they can only make it uglier and worse."[85]

All afternoon the battle raged. At the corner of Telegraph and Parker Street protesters burned a city car. An officer yanked from the burning vehicle was nearly killed by an angry crowd; he pulled his pistol and escaped. Nearby, one youth was shot, while another escaped by ducking under a car; its windows were destroyed by birdshot fired from 120 feet away. The *San Francisco Chronicle* published a photograph of one demonstrator being shot in the back while fleeing down a side street. The officer was more than thirty feet away when he fired. A painting contractor making repairs at a house more than a block from Telegraph was intentionally shot in the leg from a distance. A highway patrol car cruised Telegraph and gave chase to demonstrators, who responded by breaking the car's windows with rocks. KPFA reported that a deputy sheriff was seen randomly shooting from the rear of a jeep that drove through the area. It was later revealed that one squad of Blue Meanies had fired all the shots near Telegraph. Late in the afternoon, the police finally prepared to escort the trapped fence builders out of the area. Meanwhile, a group of officers inexplicably launched tear gas on the campus. Hundreds of students who had been eating peacefully outdoors at the Terrace adjacent to the Student Union suddenly fled.[86]

In any battle it is wise to hold the high ground. The police had been unprepared for the afternoon's events. During previous disturbances the police had occupied the rooftops of the one- and two-story buildings along Telegraph, but in this protest demonstrators controlled the roofs. They hurled chunks of concrete and metal onto the police in the street below. Judging from the mounds of debris that remained on the roofs at the end of the afternoon, militants had been stockpiling materiel for a considerable time. Also on the rooftops were a number of innocent onlookers. From the ground, enveloped in clouds of tear gas, it was impossible to tell who was hurling debris and who was merely watching. In midafternoon a small number of sheriff's deputies replaced the birdshot that they had been firing with more lethal buckshot. Who gave the order to do so, or whether it was done without an order, has never been determined, although some have implicated Edwin Meese III, who was in Berkeley that day; he carried a custom-fitted gasmask. The buckshot was nasty. On one rooftop on Telegraph between Dwight and Parker, Alan Blanchard, an artist who worked as the assistant manager at the Telegraph Repertory Theater, was blinded. Nearby, James Rector, apparently an innocent bystander, received several buckshot pellets; he died four days later from a pellet lodged in his heart. All in all, 110 people were shot. No one fired at the police.[87]

That night, at the urging of the sheriff and the mayor, but without a request from the chancellor, Governor Reagan called upon the National Guard to restore order. They, along with the highway patrol, sheriff's deputies, and the police, occupied Berkeley for seventeen days. Guardsmen bivouacked on the site of People's Park. Although the occupation had its amusing side, such as the fact that some guardsmen were Berkeley students who encountered friends and roommates as people to be pacified, the occupation left much bitterness due to the occupying forces' erratic behavior. During the emergency it was illegal for more than three people to congregate in one place. Given the population density of the South Campus area and the natural tendency for young people to knot together, especially paired as two couples, there were many inadvertent violations. Usually, the Guard and the police looked the other way, but many people were stopped and frisked, and while arrest was not likely, some were manhandled or beaten, and a few had their property stolen. It was unwise to carry a camera on the street. Officers even rushed into apartment buildings and seized cameras that had been pointed out of windows. On one occasion police threw tear gas cannisters inside Tolman Hall on campus and then held the doors closed to prevent people from escaping the gas. Guardsmen smashed the windows or the radio antennas of parked cars that belonged to people they disliked. Residents found main entrances to the city sealed, and arriving by car after dark was risky.[88]

During the occupation rallies and marches were illegal, but they took place anyway. On Friday, May 16, a peaceful vigil supporting People's Park attracted 3,000 people to the Campanile on campus. When police appeared, the meeting disintegrated. That afternoon 4,000 people met at Provo Park; they, too, were peacefully dispersed. Later, however, police broke up a crowd at Lower Sproul Plaza only by using tear gas. On Saturday demonstrators gathered on Shattuck Avenue in downtown Berkeley; stores were closed for the day, and police pushed the protesters back toward campus. On Sunday more than a thousand people held a vigil at Herrick Hospital, where victims of the shootings were recovering. That afternoon a number of protesters built the People's Park Annex on Bay Area Rapid Transit district land at Hearst and Grove. After police and the Guard told the group to disperse, they did. The crowd then marched into the hills and planted flowers along their route. For a time police officers followed along and pulled up the flowers. Late in the afternoon the police returned to the People's Park Annex and pulled up the flowers there. After the police left, more flowers were planted. A National Guard helicopter landed, and its crew complained about kites interfering with the helicopter's flying. Suddenly, kites were flown everywhere.[89]

The most bizarre episode occurred on Tuesday, May 20. In early afternoon the Guard formed a long line along Bancroft and blocked access to or from the campus; other guardsmen sealed Sather Gate, while the highway patrol cleared and locked the Student Union. Thousands of students, shoppers, onlookers, and University employees found themselves trapped inside this box. The only escape route was a narrow passage between Zellerbach Hall and the ASUC office building; this exit was not visible to most of the crowd. Suddenly, the police announced that chemicals were to be used. People looked around and saw nowhere to go. No one moved. Many did not even hear this announcement. Then a National Guard helicopter appeared overhead and sprayed the crowd with the most potent type of tear gas. "There is nothing like standing under a helicopter as it swoops down to begin its gassing run to inspire one with new vision," observed Michael Rossman. People panicked. Some fled through the narrow escape route, others pushed their way through police lines, and many made their way into the ASUC stores in the lower levels of the Student Union. Soon the gas was everywhere, and people vomited. The cloud of gas drifted up the hill to Cowell Hospital, where it tortured polio victims hooked to iron lungs, and it caused skin burns to swimmers at the Strawberry Canyon pool, more than half a mile from Sproul Plaza.[90]

Two days later several hundred people tried to construct yet another park—this one called People's Park #5—on vacant land at Henry and Berryman. When the highway patrol expelled the group and tore up the flowers, the demonstrators marched downtown. The Guard blocked Shattuck Avenue, and the protesters turned up a side street and found themselves trapped in a parking lot. Innocent passersby who were shopping in the stores in the block came out and were forced by the police into the lot. Within an hour hundreds of people stood in the parking lot under police guard. Soon police buses arrived, and the group was placed under arrest. The 482 arrestees included Robert Scheer of *Ramparts* and Tim Findley of the *San Francisco Chronicle*. Taken to Santa Rita, the arrestees were forced to lie face down on gravel in sun and fog for five hours, while the sheriff's office decided what to do. While on the ground, the victims were not allowed to go to the bathroom, had guns thrust in their ribs, and were sometimes savagely beaten for no reason at all. Some people were detained, even after bail had been posted. In the end, the prisoners were released and charges dropped. Findley's front-page account on Saturday did much to discredit Madigan.[91]

By then the residents of Berkeley were angry. The occupation had produced a kind of anarchy, and on the whole, Berkeley's citizens preferred local radicals to foreign invaders. Everyone knew that the Guard could not stay, and after they departed, city and University officials would have to deal with the militants. On Friday, May 23, the mayor and the sheriff traded insults, and the next day a special council meeting voted 8 to 1, with John DeBonis dissenting, to ask the governor to remove the Guard. Although Reagan declined to send the troops home, he did pull the guardsmen off the streets, and tension immediately eased. On Sunday park builders constructed yet another People's Park Annex, and this time police did not interfere. The militants, therefore, had won a kind of political legitimacy. Far from being crushed by the Guard, the militants had gained numerous recruits through the Guard's arbitrary and clumsy tactics. The radical strategy remained the same as it had been at the time of the Free Speech Movement. Confrontation brought repression, and repression created converts. Only now the stakes were higher: control of the city.[92]

Local residents, whether militant or not, needed to show that they could control their city. After militants planned to organize a Memorial Day march to seize the park from the guardsmen who camped there, moderates, who feared a bloodbath in which an ill-trained and panicky guardsman might shoot civilians, decided to take over the march and tame it. Pat and Fred Cody asked Peter Bergel and Rick Eckels to plan a peaceful march. On a perfect, balmy Memorial Day 25,000 to 50,000 people marched; they included Richard Fos-

ter, the new school superintendent, as well as the Mime Troupe's Gorilla Band.
A banner on one Cal sorority house proclaimed "Power to the People's Park."
The Quakers distributed 30,000 daisies, which marchers passed out to guardsmen, who put the flowers on their bayonets and in their rifle barrels. By this
point the guardsmen had begun to talk with the local residents, especially the
women, and many citizen soldiers sympathized with the desire of the local
people to control their city. The marchers carried green banners and flags made
from old girl scout uniforms; they had created a new symbol beyond revolutionary red and black. "The green flag," predicted Philip MacDougal, "was
symbol only of new indelible connections in the mind which will re-color
popular protest in every country in the world, from this time on." The demonstrators approached the park, but no one moved to enter the site, and it
remained guarded and fenced.[93]

The Guard was quietly removed, and in June 1969 the Regents met in
Berkeley. Chancellor Roger Heyns had continued his negotiations with the city
government concerning the site of People's Park, and the city council had at
last voted 5 to 4 to accept the lease of the land from the University. When the
chancellor put the proposal to the Regents, Ed Reinecke, the lieutenant governor and a Reagan supporter, erupted in anger. He and Heyns exchanged
words. Heyns looked professorial, but his eyes were tired and sad. "They spoke
of things no professor had ever seen," noted William J. McGill. Although
Heyns made a brilliant presentation to the board, the Regents did not yield.
Some Regents smelled capitulation in Heyns's plea, but a larger number were
pragmatists who, with one eye on the budget, voted down the proposal because
they did not wish to antagonize Reagan. The governor had made it clear that
he opposed a park. As the 18 to 6 vote was announced, the chancellor left the
room. McGill assumed that Heyns was leaving to give President Charles Hitch
his resignation. Although the chancellor was depressed, he did not resign. "No
one who lived through those times," later recalled McGill, "is ever likely to be
entirely at peace again."[94]

Conservatives never recovered from the fact that they had advocated the occupation. Mayor Johnson was discredited, and Don Mulford, thanks in part to
the new eighteen-year-old vote, was defeated by Ken Meade at the next election. Liberals were tainted by their ineffectiveness, and they, too, began to pass
from the scene. In 1970 Jeffery Cohelan lost his reelection bid to Ronald Dellums in the Democratic party primary. Dellums won because of the Vietnam
War, lingering bitterness from Robert Scheer's campaign, and enthusiastic black
support. Dan Siegel, charged with a felonious intent to provoke the riot of May
15, 1969, was acquitted. His bitter trial revealed that the police had been recording speeches made at Sproul Plaza, although the scale of this monitoring
was scarcely guessed at the time. During the crisis the ASUC had sponsored a
referendum on the park, and students had favored the park by 12,719 to 2,175.

It was the highest percentage of student participation in ASUC electoral history. In 1971 radicals won the mayor's office and three other seats on the city council. Among the victors was Ilona Hancock, who had watched policemen armed with shotguns on the street of her South Campus neighborhood during the crisis; her daughter's nursery school had been gassed. Ronald Reagan remained an object of local scorn; in 1984 Walter Mondale received 83 percent of the vote in Berkeley. In 1986 Hancock was elected mayor. All in all it was hard to escape the conclusion that Delacour, Bardacke, Albert, and the *Barb* had won.[95]

The Regents turned a portion of the park into a parking lot, but no one parked there. Considering the shortage of parking in Berkeley, this result was noteworthy. This boycott showed solidarity with the hippies; it also avoided slashed tires. A militant was caught painting "Reserved for James Rector" signs on the parking spaces. The University abandoned the parking lot, and the block became overgrown with weeds, overrun with dogs, and a haven to only a handful of hippies and drug dealers. For years many residents believed that Rector's blood cursed the site. In the long run, both neighbors and the city forced the University to mow the weeds, and the area became green, although devoid of landscaping. Several times the University tried to build dormitories, but the city government and the neighbors opposed any construction. On the other hand, the increasingly radical city government refused to pay any money to purchase the property from the University. Roger Heyns barely escaped from the incident, and in 1971 he quietly left office. The next year a mob spontaneously tore down the hated fence. Liberals continued to control the University, but the city fell to the radicals, and the governor also prospered. In the final analysis, the changes that took place during the sixties had produced three winners: Ronald Reagan, whose contempt for liberals and opposition to Berkeley radicals helped him, with the support of Edwin Meese III, into the White House; Ronald Dellums, whose coalition of hippies, white radicals, and black militants put him into Congress; and Alice Waters, whose recognition that Berkeley was no longer a provincial suburb led her in 1971 to open Chez Panisse, Berkeley's first gourmet restaurant.[96]

# Epilogue

# BLUE

*I'm just like a turtle,*
*it's hidin' underneath its horned shell.*
Janis Joplin, "Turtle Blues"

One morning in Berkeley in the spring of 1970, just a few months after I had moved to the city, my clock radio clicked and on came the CBS News. Lying in bed, I heard the newscaster report on President Richard Nixon's announcement, the evening before, of the American military invasion of Cambodia. "What!" I shouted, as I bounded out of bed. Adrenalin flowed. It took some time for me to realize that Nixon's secret invasion, by the very nature of its secrecy, could not be major, since no great event can be a secret in modern America. Still, the invasion shattered Nixon's carefully cultivated illusion that the administration was rapidly moving to extricate the United States from the war in Vietnam. And I knew what the reaction to the invasion would be both on campus and throughout the South Campus area of Berkeley. One only had to live in Berkeley a few months to understand the depths of alienation, bitterness, and anger that gripped both students and other young people. Yet Nixon's act did not provoke a riot. Rather, it confirmed the assertion of the hippies that politics was beyond redemption. "Lies," Jann Wenner had said, "We get lies . . . ."[1]

On the Cal campus there were urgent meetings of students and faculty members. At a meeting of history graduate students in Dwinelle Hall, dozens of normally reasonable but suddenly hysterical young people shouted. As far as I could determine, the procedural and tactical issues that divided the students in that room were trivial; no one approved of Nixon or his policy. At the substantive level antiwar students agreed, after suffering too many defeats over too many years, that the war had a life of its own and that energetic opposition to the war was futile. Since everyone in the room agreed on that point, it was just as useful to argue about procedures and tactics as it was to propose the organization of anything concrete. Amid this despair, the meeting predictably ended in chaos. At another meeting held in the Newman Center, students and faculty members hotly debated whether the History Department, as a unit, ought to condemn the war and the invasion. Professor Henry F. May passionately defended the position that the department must always be politically neutral, and after it became clear that he was on the losing side, he rapidly strode from the hall with eyes blazing and face scarlet. In contrast to the pandemonium among the historians, the University's geneticists, both students and faculty members, stopped their research, planned a canvassing campaign, and collected several thousand signatures on antiwar petitions from the distant Republican suburbs.

The historians' shouting and anger as well as the geneticists' disciplined campaign were the surface manifestations of enormous tension that gripped Berkeley's residents in the spring of 1970. Although the war was a main source of that tension, it was not the sole source. The memory of the bitter Third World Liberation Front strike was still fresh, the full integration of Berkeley's public schools was only in its second year, and the large number of angry young blacks troubled many older black residents even as it terrified large numbers of whites. Because of Berkeley's reputation as a liberal city, and even more because of the hypocrisy that had long governed race relations in Berkeley, racial fears lurked below the surface and had to be suppressed, even on those occasions when racial incidents did take place. In 1970 I saw few, if any, blacks near campus, and I did not expect to see any, but even whites who had been the most devoted supporters of the civil rights movement frequently whispered their fears of nighttime muggings by blacks or of the Oakland-Berkeley ghetto exploding in an insurrection that would engulf Berkeley. "You be good little Panthers now," advised one restaurateur, as the angry, cocky young blacks swaggered into his establishment.[2]

The darkest shadow that hung over Berkeley was cast by the Lawrence Radiation Laboratory and its cyclotron, the giant atom smasher that had long stood behind a fence in the hills above campus. In 1962, when President John Fitzgerald Kennedy had come to Berkeley to give his Charter Day address, he had also inspected the newest addition to the Rad Lab complex. By far the most expensive public works project in the city's history, the addition was a tribute both to Representative Jeffery Cohelan's power and to Berkeley's unique role in Cold War science. It is worth noting that few blacks who lived in the flatlands worked at the Rad Lab. There were, however, places in the flatlands from which one could see the cyclotron. At night the security lights glowed eerily yellow-green, and the complex looked like some medieval cathedral; it was hard to forget Berkeley's special role in ushering in the nuclear age. Without Berkeley's physicists, there would have been no bomb. In the fifties and sixties nuclear research, much of it classified, continued; the element berkelium had been synthesized on campus. No other city could boast an atomic element. No other university conducted so much government-sponsored nuclear research, required its regents to deal with so many matters requiring security clearances, or found it necessary to seal permanently a room in a campus building after it was contaminated with radioactive material.³

Once a person stepped outside the frame of reference that had governed the Cold War, or broke through to a new vision, as the hippies who used LSD put it, Berkeley's special role in nuclear research took on a new and horrifying meaning. If, as the poet and critic Tuli Kupferberg suggested, Auschwitz-Hiroshima came to be a single word in the future, then Berkeley's residents, and especially its Jewish residents, faced the difficulty of explaining the difference between Hitler's extermination of the Jews and the nuclear extermination of Hiroshima's citizens. These feelings were seldom expressed openly in the sixties, but they appeared with surprising frequency just below the surface in remarks that are too pointed to be ignored. The hippie rebellion, in particular, was an affirmation of life that rejected death in holocausts, whether conventional or nuclear. Furthermore, it was easy to make connections between Berkeley and Hiroshima. These two cities were about the same size in population and in land area, and one tiny bomb had wiped out Berkeley's Japanese counterpart. Guilt and fear of a similar fate produced much of the frenzy of the decade. During the Cuban Missile Crisis one Cal student called her boyfriend and said, "Listen, I'm ready to get laid." Michael Rossman referred to this syndrome as "the Freedom of the Children of the Bomb." Perhaps. By 1970 many people knew that Berkeley's only possible sister city was Hiroshima-in-the-ashes.⁴

In 1970, after four students who had been present during a protest against the invasion of Cambodia were killed at Kent State University in Ohio, Governor Ronald Reagan, showing more wisdom than during the People's Park dispute, ordered California's universities closed. It was a quiet, almost ghostly time in Berkeley. One beautiful morning I came down to the sidewalk and half consciously made my usual turn north toward campus, remembered the closure, and decided instead to walk south away from the University along College Avenue. I walked through Elmwood and across Claremont Avenue into Oakland. Passing boarded-up stores in the Rockridge neighborhood, I walked under the Bay Area Rapid Transit station and Grove-Shafter Freeway, both under construction, and reached the end of College Avenue at Broadway. Once a Peralta family home had stood at that spot. I stopped suddenly. Across Broadway, at the California College of Arts and Crafts, the art students had decided to honor the slain Ohio students. Four white crosses were imbedded in the green lawn that rose up to the college building. Each cross was inscribed with the name of a victim. I stared, and it was a long time before I turned around and retraced my steps to Berkeley. The sixties, I then knew, were over.

What, then, had the sixties been about? The decade was primarily one of testing, when all social, political, and economic assumptions came under attack. During the fifties established institutions had become complacent and flabby, and in the sixties those institutions did not respond very well to a rising demand for change. College students, spurred on by the success of the black-led civil rights movement, borrowed black strategy and tactics; activists demanded immediate, drastic changes in campus rules, in community mores, and in foreign policy. Unresponsive institutions drove impatient students to a frenzy, while the frenzy itself produced exasperation on all sides. At Berkeley, the Free Speech Movement proved to be the key event. The FSM established that activist students could, under certain conditions, win victories against large, powerful bureaucracies. You could fight the university. Or city hall. Or the draft system. While much of the frenzy in Berkeley in the late sixties revolved around attempts to recreate the atmosphere of the FSM, radicals also came to understand the full potential for protests in the streets. Radicals had the capacity to exhaust the establishment's bureaucracies, to discredit government, and upon occasion to win victories. People's Park became a monument to the power of protest.

Few liberals in Berkeley ever grasped radical needs. Although liberals on the city council and in the University begged radicals to compromise, the liberals' pleas were as ignored as Lyndon Johnson's pleas to Ho Chi Minh, and for much the same reason. The liberals failed to recognize that the radicals could not negotiate, because the radicals lacked any institutionalized bases of power, all of which the liberals controlled. For radicals, negotiation brought an inevitable capitulation to the tradition-bound bastions of the establishment. Only in the streets could radicals gain power. Conservatives, having been ousted from power by the liberals, understood better the radicals' frustration with liberals. Both conservatives and radicals especially hated the liberal University. At the heart of the contempt for liberalism on the part of both the New Right and the New Left was a seldom acknowledged but growing libertarianism. Jefferson and Thoreau were the secret heroes of the sixties.

One should not dwell too much upon politics: There were fewer Marxist-Leninists than John Lennonists. The music of the Beatles transcended politics; it gave shape to and was shaped by the coming of the hippies. Unlike the civil rights movement or the New Left, the counterculture did not fade away in the seventies but blossomed, became co-opted, and eventually was accepted as a vital strand of mainstream, middle-class culture. The hippies brought a more casual, permissive attitude toward sex and drugs, an open expression of personality through clothes and hair, the sanctification of leisure in lieu of the work ethic, the adoption of born-again Christianity or eastern religions, and the acceptance of rock music. To understand the sixties fully, rock must be analyzed more completely than it has been to date. Country Joe McDonald's music may be the most important cultural artifact from Berkeley in the sixties. The new culture, blended from the old culture and the counterculture, generated its own peculiar politics. By the end of the seventies, Berkeley residents bitterly debated rent control, street barriers, and the merits of the city's growing number of gourmet restaurants and food vendors along North Shattuck Avenue.

The sixties, like a tidal wave that had crashed onto a beach, drastically changed Berkeley. Gone was the University's traditional power over its students as well as the idea of *in loco parentis*. Also gone was the cruel, institutional racism that had existed since Berkeley's earliest days. Although prejudice remained, racial tolerance increased. Gone, too, amid assassination and the war in Vietnam was self-confident, triumphant liberalism. Never again did liberals hold a firm, comfortable majority on the Berkeley city council. Most significant was the counterculture's effect upon traditional values. As the University official James Corley once told an interviewer, "This is a kind of social revolution. . . . I am talking about the standards on which you and I were born and raised being quite different." In place of the old verities, survivors gathered bits and pieces of the old culture, fragments from the civil rights movement, chips from the New Left, and larger chunks from the counterculture to erect a new building in which to live. That edifice is still under construction. It marks the beginning of postmodern America.[5]

# Statistical Tables

**Table 1.** Berkeley Population by Race, with Percentages

|      | White  | %  | Black  | %  | Asian  | %  | Other | %  | TOTAL      |
|------|--------|----|--------|----|--------|----|-------|----|------------|
| 1940 | 80,267 | 94 | 3,395  | 4  | NA     |    | 1,885 | 2  | 85,547[a]  |
| 1950 | 96,100 | 84 | 13,650 | 12 | 3,836  | 3  | 269   |    | 113,855[b] |
| 1960 | 82,081 | 74 | 21,850 | 20 | 6,825  | 6  | 512   |    | 111,268[c] |
| 1970 | 79,041 | 68 | 27,421 | 24 | 8,578  | 7  | 1,676 | 1  | 116,716[d] |
| 1980 | 69,159 | 67 | 20,671 | 20 | 10,311 | 10 | 3,187 | 3  | 103,328[e] |

Sources: U.S., Bureau of the Census, 1940–80; Berkeley Planning Department, *The People of Berkeley: Who They Are? Demographic Profile* (Berk., 1973), 40.

[a]excludes University of California, Berkeley (UCB) students
[b]includes an undetermined number of UCB students
[c]includes 14,706 UCB students
[d]includes 20,419 UCB students and 6,464 Hispanics
[e]includes an undetermined number of UCB students and 5,177 Hispanics

**Table 2.** Berkeley Public School Enrollment by Race, in Percentages

|      | White | Black | Other | TOTAL  |
|------|-------|-------|-------|--------|
| 1958 | 63    | 29    | 8     | 15,375 |
| 1960 | 60    | 32    | 8     | 15,761 |
| 1963 | 54    | 37    | 9     | NA     |
| 1965 | 50    | 40    | 9     | NA     |
| 1968 | 50[a] | 43    | 7     | 16,204 |
| 1970 | 45    | 45    | 10    | 15,908 |

Sources: Staats report, 8, 32; Berkeley Unified School District, "Co-Sponsored Workshop on Interracial Gains and Goals" (Berk., 1961), 5; Hadsell report, 4; Carol Sibley, *Never a Dull Moment* (Berk., 1972), 95–96, 204; Sally E. James, "School Desegregation in Berkeley, California" (1977), 2.

[a]includes 3 percent Hispanic

174

**Table 3.**   Berkeley Criminal Offenses

|      | Major Offenses | Murder | Rape | Drugs | Drunkenness | TOTAL (includes traffic) |
|------|----------------|--------|------|-------|-------------|--------------------------|
| 1957 | 2,606 | 3 | 16 | 23 | 670 | 33,650 |
| 1958 | 2,820 | 1 | 20 | 12 | 634 | 32,390 |
| 1959 | 2,798 | 4 | 9 | 17 | 766 | 32,194 |
| 1960 | 3,572 | 4 | 10 | 36 | 724 | 32,197 |
| 1961 | 3,644 | 5 | 12 | 21 | 578 | 31,541 |
| 1962 | 4,510 | 2 | 14 | 48 | 589 | 35,314 |
| 1963 | 5,037 | 6 | 19 | 102 | 595 | 40,518 |
| 1964 | 6,892 | 6 | 20 | 104 | 686 | 41,102 |
| 1965 | 7,681 | 4 | 21 | 148 | 606 | 45,430 |
| 1966 | 7,899 | 4 | 52 | 392 | 574 | 59,792 |
| 1967 | 9,258 | 3 | 44 | 639 | 612 | 64,803 |
| 1968 | 12,252 | 8 | 69 | 1,383 | 547 | 58,952 |
| 1969 | 13,017 | 10 | 111 | 1,948 | 470 | 78,460 |
| 1970 | 13,220 | 12 | 116 | 1,393 | 536 | 86,716 |

*Sources:* Berkeley Police Department, *Annual Reports*, 1961, p. 15; 1966, p. 16; 1970, p. 52.

**Table 4.**   Property Tax Rates in Dollars per Thousand of Assessed Value

|      | City | School | County | Special District | TOTAL |
|------|------|--------|--------|------------------|-------|
| 1952 | 1.70 | 2.66 | 2.13 | .45 | 6.94 |
| 1954 | 1.80 | 2.70 | 2.52 | .43 | 7.45 |
| 1956 | 1.87 | 3.24 | 1.84 | .36 | 7.31 |
| 1958 | 2.02 | 3.24 | 1.98 | .39 | 7.63 |
| 1960 | 2.41 | 3.53 | 2.30 | .41 | 8.65 |
| 1962 | 2.67 | 4.61 | 2.27 | .39 | 9.94 |
| 1964 | 2.67 | 5.22 | 2.23 | .69 | 10.81 |
| 1966 | 2.78 | 7.32 | 2.30 | .98 | 13.38 |
| 1968 | 2.83 | 7.61 | 2.40 | 1.56 | 14.40 |

*Sources:* Berkeley Planning Department, *Berkeley Facts* (Berk., 1971), 50.

**Table 5.** Employment in the Berkeley-Albany Labor Market

|  | July 1960 | July 1966 | July 1968 | July 1970 |
|---|---|---|---|---|
| Construction | 2,400 | 2,500 | 2,500 | 2,500 |
| Manufactures | 8,800 | 8,600 | 8,800 | 9,100 |
| Transportation, Communi- | | | | |
| cations, Utilities | 1,600 | 1,700 | 2,100 | 2,100 |
| Trade | 8,800 | 9,200 | 8,900 | 9,200 |
| Finance, Insurance, Real | | | | |
| Estate | 3,100 | 3,100 | 3,100 | 3,000 |
| Service | 7,700 | 12,700 | 13,300 | 14,400 |
| Government | 13,900 | 29,000 | 30,400 | 31,800 |
| City of Berkeley | 954 | 1,087 | 1,177 | 1,288 |
| Police | 148 | 176 | 222 | 272 |
| Other | 100 | 200 | 200 | 300 |
| TOTAL | 46,400 | 67,000 | 69,300 | 72,400 |

Source: Berkeley Planning Department, *Berkeley Facts* (Berk., 1971), 21–22.

**Table 6.** Berkeley Female Regular Newspaper Readers, 1964, in Percentages

|  | UCB Students | UCB Employees | Berkeley Residents |
|---|---|---|---|
| Daily Californian | 64 | 46 | 7 |
| Berkeley Daily Gazette | 2 | 19 | 55 |
| Oakland Tribune | 4 | 27 | 14 |
| San Francisco Chronicle | 38 | 42 | 60 |
| San Francisco Examiner | 1 | 6 | 9 |
| San Francisco Call Bulletin | 0 | 0 | 2 |

Source: Mail sample by John S. Harrison and Terry G. Walker, "Media, Merchandising, and Potential Market Analyses: A Report Prepared for Joseph Magnin's New Store in Berkeley" (M.B.A. report, Univ. of Calif., 1964), 37.

**Table 7.** Berkeley Voter Registration

|  | Democratic | Republican | Prohibition | Peace and Freedom | American Independent | Decline to State | Other | TOTAL |
|---|---|---|---|---|---|---|---|---|
| 1958[a] | 32,851 | 28,223 | NA | — | — | NA | 2,564 | 63,638 |
| Jan. 6, 1960 | 20,329 | 21,333 | 36 | — | — | 1,452 | 119 | 43,269 |
| 1960[a] | 32,799 | 25,982 | NA | — | — | NA | 2,338 | 61,119 |
| Jan. 1, 1961 | 21,409 | 21,765 | 15 | — | — | 2,020 | 354 | 45,563 |
| Jan. 19, 1962 | 31,561 | 25,068 | 17 | — | — | 2,549 | 442 | 59,637 |
| Jan. 17, 1963 | 25,578 | 20,871 | 4 | — | — | 1,786 | 416 | 48,655 |
| Dec. 31, 1963 | 29,644 | 21,694 | 17 | — | — | 2,172 | 363 | 53,890 |
| 1964[b] | 41,708 | 25,169 | NA | — | — | NA | 3,764 | 70,641 |
| Dec. 31, 1964 | 34,717 | 20,731 | 13 | — | — | 2,676 | 141 | 58,265 |
| Jan. 14, 1966 | 35,911 | 20,983 | 12 | — | — | 2,893 | 132 | 59,931 |
| Apr. 1966[c] | 42,571 | 22,331 | NA | — | — | NA | 3,082 | 67,984 |
| 1966[b] | 44,727 | 22,441 | NA | — | — | NA | 3,589 | 70,757 |
| Jan. 1, 1967 | 32,243 | 16,941 | — | — | — | 1,509 | 553 | 51,246 |
| Mar. 1967[c] | 34,626 | 17,717 | NA | — | — | 2,122 | 2,626 | 57,091 |
| Jan. 13, 1968 | 30,769 | 17,566 | NA | NA | NA | 2,374 | 13,646 | 64,355 |
| June 1968[b] | 41,440 | 17,662 | NA | 8,164 | 89 | NA | 2,133 | 69,488 |
| Oct. 1968[b] | 42,470 | 17,553 | NA | 7,089 | 88 | 2,855 | 120 | 70,175 |
| Dec. 28, 1968 | 33,622 | 14,398 | — | 3,826 | 75 | 2,003 | 72 | 53,996 |
| Jan. 16, 1970 | 38,833 | 14,787 | — | 4,308 | 77 | 2,984 | 109 | 61,098 |
| Jan. 3, 1971 | 37,956 | 11,966 | — | 1,405 | 45 | 2,766 | 74 | 54,212 |

Sources: Berkeley Planning Department, *Berkeley Facts* (Berk., 1971), 64, except
[a] *Berkeley Review*, May 12, 1960, p. 4; [b] *Berkeley Daily Gazette*, Oct. 1, 1968, p. 2; [c] *Berkeley Daily Gazette*, March 10, 1967, p. 1.

**Table 8.** Berkeley City Council

| 1959 | 1961 | 1963 | 1965 | 1967 | 1969 | 1971 |
|---|---|---|---|---|---|---|
| Hutchison[e] | Hutchison | Johnson[e] | Johnson | Johnson[e] | Johnson | WIDENER[e] |
| DeBonis[e] | DeBonis | DeBonis[e] | DeBonis | DeBonis[e] | DeBonis | BAILEY[e] |
| Harris[e] | Harris | Harris[e] | Harris | DELLUMS[e] | DELLUMS | HANCOCK[e] |
| May[e] | May | May[e] | May | May[e] | May | Kallgren[e] |
| Thomas[e] | Thomas | Bort[e] | Bort | Bort[e] | Swingle[e] | SIMMONS[e] |
| Beckley | Beckley[e] | Beckley | Dewey[e] | Dewey | McLaren[e] | McLaren |
| Kent | Kent[e] | Kent | Gordon[e] | Gordon | Price[e] | Price |
| Richards | Brown[e] | Brown | Brown[e] | Brown | Widener[e] | vacant |
| Stone[e] | Sweeney[e] | Sweeney | Sweeney[e] | Sweeney | Sweeney[e] | Sweeney |

Sources: Harriet Nathan and Stanley Scott, eds., *Experiment and Change in Berkeley* (Berk., 1978), 488–96; press endorsements and election coverage.
Mayor listed first
conservatives in Roman
liberals in *Italics*
radicals in CAPITALS
[e] = elected in that year

**Table 9.**  City Election, April 1961

| Council | Vote | Affiliation |
|---------|------|-------------|
| Kent[e] | 24,100 | L, G |
| Sweeney[e] | 20,301 | L |
| Z. Brown[e] | 18,563 | L |
| Beckley[e] | 18,419 | G |
| Stone | 16,103 | |
| Wittich | 14,679 | |
| B. Brown | 11,227 | L |

Sources: *Berkeley Daily Gazette*, Apr. 5, 1961, p. 1; *Berkeley Review*, Mar. 30, 1961, p. 1; Apr. 6, 1961, p. 1.

L = liberal slate, endorsed by *Berkeley Review*

G = endorsed by *Berkeley Daily Gazette*

[e] = elected


**Table 10.**  City Election, April 1963

| | Vote | Affiliation | Position on Ordinance |
|---|------|-------------|-----------------------|
| **Housing Ordinance** | | | |
| Yes | 20,456 | | |
| No | 22,750 | | |
| **Mayor** | | | |
| Johnson[e] | 22,450 | C | N |
| Stripp | 20,440 | L | Y |
| Jersawitz | 532 | Socialist | Y |
| **Council** | | | |
| Bort[e] | 22,955 | C | N |
| DeBonis[e] | 22,598 | | N |
| Harris[e] | 21,147 | L | Y |
| May[e] | 21,080 | L | Y |
| Dewey | 19,647 | L | Y |
| Linford | 19,075 | C | N |
| Lem-mon | 10,016 | | N |
| Clarke | 8,328 | Ind. Black | Y |
| Huntley | 6,476 | Ind. Right | N |
| White | 2,986 | Socialist | Y |

Source: Thomas W. Casstevens, *Politics, Housing and Race Relations: The Defeat of Berkeley's Fair Housing Ordinance* (Berk., 1965), 63, 81.

C = conservative slate

L = liberal slate

N = opposed ordinance

Y = endorsed ordinance

[e] = elected

**Table 11.** School Board Recall Election, October 1964

| Candidate | Vote |
|-----------|--------|
| Sibley | 23,118 |
| Haas | 14,846 |
| | |
| Maisel | 23,126 |
| Baxter | 15,022 |

*Source: Berkeley Daily Gazette,*
Oct. 7, 1964, p. 1.

**Table 12.** Berkeley Vote, November 1964

Proposition 14, a statewide Initiative. Should the Rumford Act, the state antidiscriminatory housing law, be retained?

| | |
|-----|--------|
| Yes | 34,285 |
| No | 18,563 |

*Source:* Kathryne T. Favors, "A Study of the Intergroup Education Project of the Berkeley Unified School District" (Ed.D. diss., Univ. of Calif., Berk., 1969), 55.

**Table 13.** City Election, April 1965

| Council | Vote | Affiliation |
|---------|--------|-------------|
| Sweeney[e] | 22,094 | L, G |
| Brown[e] | 19,766 | L |
| Gordon[e] | 18,616 | L |
| Dewey[e] | 18,164 | L |
| Corlett | 15,713 | G |
| Takahashi | 15,684 | G |
| Harberts | 14,196 | G |
| Huntley | 4,643 | Ind. Right |
| White | 2,051 | Socialist |

*Source: Berkeley Daily Gazette,* Apr. 2, 1965, pp. 1, 10; Apr. 3, 1965, p. 2; Apr. 7, 1965, p. 1; Apr. 9, 1965, p. 10.

L = liberal slate, endorsed by AFL-CIO Committee on Political Education

G = endorsed by *Berkeley Daily Gazette*

[e] = elected

**Table 14.**  City Election, April 1967

|                | Vote   | Affiliation       |
|----------------|--------|-------------------|
| Mayor          |        |                   |
| Johnson[c]     | 25,224 | G                 |
| Rubin          | 7,385  | Ind. Left         |
| Huntley        | 2,160  | Ind. Right        |
| Camejo         | 1,019  | Socialist Workers |
| Council        |        |                   |
| Bort[c]        | 21,494 | G                 |
| May[c]         | 20,522 | L, G              |
| DeBonis[c]     | 18,817 | G                 |
| Dellums[c]     | 17,171 | L, R              |
| Price          | 15,312 | G                 |
| Neilands       | 10,876 | R                 |
| Avakian        | 10,490 | R                 |
| Harawitz       | 8,025  | R                 |
| (8 others)     |        |                   |

Source: *Berkeley Daily Gazette*, Apr. 3, 1967, p. 1; Apr. 6, 1967, pp. 1–2.
L = Berkeley Democratic Caucus (liberal)
R = Community for New Politics (radical)
G = endorsed by *Berkeley Daily Gazette*
[c] = elected

**Table 15.**  City Election, April 1969

|                    | Vote   | Affiliation |
|--------------------|--------|-------------|
| Council            |        |             |
| Sweeney[c]         | 19,493 | B, L, G     |
| McLaren[c]         | 13,527 | G           |
| Price[c]           | 12,627 | G           |
| Widener[c]         | 11,962 | B, L        |
| Brown              | 10,634 | L           |
| Hancock            | 9,963  | B, R        |
| Grodin             | 8,775  | L           |
| (11 others)        |        |             |
| Council Short-Term |        |             |
| Swingle[c]         | 17,299 | L, G        |
| Wilson             | 8,908  |             |
| Bursey             | 1,651  |             |

Sources: *Berkeley Daily Gazette*, Apr. 1, 1969, p. 1; Apr. 3, 1969, p. 1; *Coalition News*, Mar. 27, 1969, pp. 2, 4.
B = Black Caucus
L = Berkeley Democratic Caucus (liberal)
R = Berkeley Coalition (radical)
G = endorsed by *Berkeley Daily Gazette*
[c] = elected

180                                    STATISTICAL TABLES

**Table 16.** Vote for Selected Neighborhoods, City Election, April 1969, in Percentages

|  | Thousand Oaks | Southwest Berkeley | Campus |
|---|---|---|---|
| Sweeney | 59 | 76 | 55 |
| McLaren | 69 | 14 | 38 |
| Price | 64 | 14 | 37 |
| Widener | 20 | 60 | 31 |
| Brown | 30 | 46 | 26 |
| Hancock | 18 | 29 | 47 |
| Grodin | 22 | 23 | 36 |
| Weekes | 21 | 6 | 15 |
| Hurtley | 27 | 7 | 13 |
| Pecot | 5 | 36 | 14 |
| Miller | 2 | 8 | 13 |
| Coe | 2 | 6 | 8 |
| Turnout | 68 | 51 | 41 |

*Source: Berkeley Monitor, May 3, 1969, p. 4.*

**Table 17.** Berkeley Vote for President, 1932

| Candidate | Vote |
|---|---|
| Hoover | 21,750 |
| Roosevelt | 14,713 |

*Source: Kyle Benham, Alcohol Control in Berkeley: An Historical Overview (Berk., 1981), 35.*

**Table 18.** Berkeley Vote for Governor, 1966

| Candidate | Vote |
|---|---|
| Brown | 32,073 |
| Reagan | 14,567 |
| blank | 861 |
| write-in | NA |

*Source: Berkeley Gate, Nov. 29, 1966, p. 7.*

**Table 19.** Berkeley Vote for President, 1968

| Candidate | Vote |
|---|---|
| Humphrey | 33,143 |
| Nixon | 12,072 |
| Peace and Freedom | 1,665 |
| Wallace | 895 |

*Source: Berkeley Daily Gazette, Mar. 10, 1969, p. 1.*

**Table 20.**   UCB Employment, Full-Time Equivalent

|      | Academic | Non-Acad. | Lawrence Radiation Laboratory | TOTAL |
|------|----------|-----------|-------------------------------|-------|
| 1964 | 5,309    | 6,853     | 3,184                         | 15,346 |
| 1966 | 6,529    | 9,056     | 3,272                         | 18,857 |
| 1970 | 10,205   | 6,184     | 2,448                         | 18,837 |

Source: Berkeley Planning Department, *Berkeley Facts* (Berk., 1971), 21.

**Table 21.**   UCB Enrollment

|      | Male Undergrad | Male Grad | Female Undergrad | Female Grad | TOTAL |
|------|----------------|-----------|------------------|-------------|-------|
| 1960 | 7,992          | 4,422     | 5,102            | 1,212       | 18,728 |
| 1962 | 8,758          | 5,871     | 6,051            | 1,669       | 22,299 |
| 1964 | 9,681          | 6,595     | 6,982            | 2,196       | 25,151 |
| 1966 | 9,419          | 7,344     | 6,543            | 2,615       | 25,921 |
| 1968 | 10,350         | 7,422     | 7,641            | 2,719       | 28,132 |
| 1970 | 10,474         | 6,904     | 7,688            | 2,635       | 27,701 |

Source: Berkeley Planning Department, *Berkeley Facts* (Berk., 1971), 45.

**Table 22.**   UCB Student Residence, in Percentages

|      | Within 10 Blocks UCB | Rental Housing |
|------|----------------------|----------------|
| 1960 | 67                   | 32             |
| 1965 | 62                   | 51             |
| 1970 | 52                   | 57             |

Source: Leland G. Neuberg, "Rents, Changes in Rents, and Rent Control in Berkeley" (Master of City Planning thesis, Univ. of Calif., Berk., 1974), 36–37.

**Table 23.** Religious Affiliation and the FSM, in Percentages

|  | UCB Students | Father's Religion | FSM Sit-In | Father's Religion |
|---|---|---|---|---|
| Protestant | 45 | 44 | 20 | 36 |
| Catholic | 14 | 15 | 5 | 6 |
| Jewish | 16 | 20 | 26 | 32 |
| None | 24 | 21 | 49 | 26 |
| Number = | 146 | | 172 | |

Source: William A. Watts and David Whittaker, "Free Speech Advocates at Berkeley," *Journal of Applied Behavioral Science*, 2 #1 (Jan.–Mar. 1966), 54.

**Table 24.** UCB Graduate Student Values, in Percentages

| Ideology | | Party | | Religioin | |
|---|---|---|---|---|---|
| Liberal | 43 | Democrat | 34 | Protestant | 31 |
| Moderate | 28 | Republican | 19 | Catholic | 9 |
| Conservative | 8 | Independent | 26 | Jewish | 7 |
| | | Socialist | 5 | Other | 11 |
| | | Other | 2 | None | 27 |
| | | No Answer | 10 | No Answer | 15 |

Number = 2,173

Source: Ann M. Heiss, "Berkeley Doctoral Students Appraise Their Academic Programs" (Center for the Study of Higher Education, Univ. of Calif., Berk., 1964), Appendix pp. 6–7.

**Table 25.** UCB Lower Division Grade Distributions, in Percentages

|  | A | B | C | Pass | D | Fail | Not Pass | Incomplete |
|---|---|---|---|---|---|---|---|---|
| 1961 | 14 | 31 | 40 | — | 8 | 5 | — | 2 |
| 1963 | 15 | 31 | 38 | 1 | 8 | 5 | — | 1 |
| 1965 | 18 | 34 | 35 | 1 | 6 | 4 | — | 1 |
| 1967 | 19 | 29 | 24 | 18 | 4 | 3 | 1 | 2 |
| 1969 | 22 | 29 | 20 | 18 | 4 | 3 | 1 | 2 |

Source: University of California, Berkeley, Office of Institutional Research, "A Report on Scholarship Grades— University of California, Berkeley" (Berk., 1970), 18.

**Table 26.**  Turmoil at UCB, 1964–69

| Event | Dates | Character | Arrests | Student Discipline |
|---|---|---|---|---|
| Free Speech Movement | Sept. 14–Dec. 9, 1964 | 5 disruptive days | 773 | — |
| Obscenity Rally | Mar. 4, 1965 | nonviolent | 7 | 4 |
| VDC Rally | Feb. 2, 1966 | violation UCB regulations | — | 3 |
| PROC Protest | Mar. 24, 1966 | 2 hours, nonviolent | — | 17 |
| AFT 1570 Incident | Oct. 21, 1966 | violation UCB regulations | — | 2 |
| Navy Table and Strike | Nov. 30–Dec. 6, 1966 | half day disruption | 3 + 6 nonstudents | 89 |
| Stop the Draft Week | Oct. 16–18, 1967 | violation UCB regulations | — | 81 |
|  |  | violence, Oakland | 300 | — |
| Dow-CIA Protest | Nov. 6, 1967 | disruptive | — | 34 |
| Sproul Hall Mill-Ins | Nov. 29–Dec. 1, 1967 | disruptive | — | 41 |
| Sproul Hall Sit-In | Oct. 22, 1968 | disruptive | 126 | 124 |
| Moses Hall Takeover | Oct. 23, 1968 | violent, disruptive | 76 | 52 |
| Attempted Strike | Oct. 28–30, 1968 |  | — | — |
| TWLF Strike | Jan. 20–Mar. 7, 1969 | sporadic violence | 99 + 52 nonstudents | 99 |
| People's Park | May 14–June 3, 1969 | violent | 285 + 574 nonstudents | pending |

Source: Jim Lemmon to Jay Michael, Aug. 7, 1969, 9:99, Univ. of Calif., Berk. Chancellor's Files.

**Table 27.**  ASUC Election, November 1966

Should birth control pills be distributed at Cowell Hospital?

| | |
|---|---|
| Yes | 1,580 |
| No | 398 |
| No Vote | 372 |

Source: Daily Californian, Nov. 30, 1966, p. 1.

**Table 28.**  ASUC Election, November 1967, in Percentages

| Vietnam War Policy | % |
|---|---|
| Withdrawal | 55 |
| End bombing, negotiate | 20 |
| Defensive enclaves | 10 |
| Present policy | 6 |
| Escalate | 7 |
| Number = | 4,550 |

Source: Daily Californian, Nov. 9, 1967, p. 3.

**Table 29.**   ASUC Election, April 1968

Should the new auditorium be named for Martin Luther King, Jr., instead of Zellerbach?
Yes      7,705
No       2,011

*Source: Daily Californian,* Apr. 25, 1968, p. 1.

**Table 30.**   College Mock Presidential Election, 1968, in Percentages

|  | UCB | Stanford | National |
|---|---|---|---|
| Eugene McCarthy, Dem. | 48 | 56 | 28 |
| Robert F. Kennedy, Dem. | 17 | 13 | 21 |
| Richard M. Nixon, Rep. | 4 | 7 | 19 |
| Nelson Rockefeller, Rep. | 8 | 11 | 11 |
| Lyndon B. Johnson, Dem. | 1 | 1 | 6 |
| Ronald Reagan, Rep. | nil | 1 | 3 |
| George C. Wallace, Am. Ind. | nil | nil | 3 |
| Charles Percy, Rep. | 1 | 1 | 2 |
| Hubert H. Humphrey, Dem. (write-in) | — | 1 | 2 |
| Mark Hatfield, Rep. | 4 | 2 | |
| John Lindsey, Rep. | 2 | 2 | |
| Fred V. Halstead, Soc. Workers | 6 | 2 | |
| Dick Gregory, Peace and Freedom | — | 1 | |
| Martin L. King, Jr. | 2 | nil | |
| Harold Stassen, Rep. | nil | nil | |
| Number = | 11,280 | 4,326 | 1.1 million |

*Source: Daily Californian,* May 1, 1968, p. 2; May 6, 1968, p. 1; May 9, 1968, p. 1. Sponsored by *Time.*

**Table 31.**   College Referendum on Vietnam
War Policy, 1968, in Percentages

|  | UCB | National |
|---|---|---|
| Withdrawal | 49 | 17 |
| Reduce | 43 | 45 |
| Maintain | 3 | 9 |
| Increase | 2 | 8 |
| "All out" | 3 | 21 |
| Number = | 11,280 | 1.1 million |

*Source: Daily Californian,* May 9, 1968, p. 1. Sponsored by
*Time.*

**Table 32.**   ASUC Election, May 1969

---

Should People's Park be restored as an unfenced park?
   Yes            12,719
   No              2,175
   No Vote           75

---

*Source: San Francisco Chronicle,* May 23, 1969, p. 1.

# A Note on the Use of Language

During the sixties, as during other times of social change, it was necessary to invent new words, to redefine old ones, and to use language in new ways. In part, this use of new language was a reaction against the existing social order with its coded words, but it was also a search for self-definition by people who envisioned themselves as harbingers of a new social order. The most significant change was the substitution of *black* for *Negro*. For proponents of this change, *Negroes* had been enslaved and subservient; their organizations, such as the NAACP, had plaintively begged for justice. *Negroes* were, in the minds of these advocates of change, as well as in the minds of many whites, an inferior underclass with only those rights that whites chose to bestow. Malcolm X understood this problem, and he was among the first to advocate the use of *black* as a badge of racial pride and honor. From 1965 to 1967, a growing number of Afro-Americans, especially younger people, declared themselves to be *black*. Stokely Carmichael of the Student Non-Violent Coordinating Committee popularized the concept of racial liberation from white domination through his slogan of Black Power. In the Berkeley-Oakland ghetto the Black Panther party insisted upon *black*. Unlike SNCC, the Panthers had never been tainted by the word *Negro*. *Blacks* saw themselves as fully equal to whites and demanded either full equality inside American society or *black* autonomy. Throughout this volume I have used *black*.

The New Left was also attuned to the nuances of language. Young radicals noted that the Old Left had rather laboriously defined itself through linguistic subtleties. Thus, communists had long reverenced their political organization by calling it the *Party*, with a capital P. The world had many political parties, but from the Marxist-Leninist perspective, only one true *Party*. Communists told friends that they were *CP*, an elegant combination of initials that meant nothing to the apolitical masses, who were more likely to refer to communists as *reds*. I have avoided both *CP* and *reds* as pejoratives, and I have not capitalized *party*.

The most bitter dispute inside the Old Left was between the followers of Stalin and the followers of Trotsky. Those loyal to Stalin referred to themselves rather grudgingly as *Stalinists* and denounced the *Trotskyites*. Those loyal to Trotsky called themselves *Trotskyists* and denounced their rivals as *Stalinoid*.

The use of any of these four terms identified the user with one faction or the other. An advantage of a Berkeley education, a professor once observed to me, was that one learned the difference between a *Trotskyist* and a *Trotskyite*. As soon as one uttered either word at a social event, one had informed those present how one stood on this issue. For the historian, *Trotskyist* v. *Trotskyite* poses a dilemma. Although archconservatives, in an attempt to humiliate the followers of Trotsky, followed orthodox communists and used *Trotskyite*, it has seemed fairer to employ the term used by the *Trotskyists* themselves.

In the forties newspaper headline writers had abbreviated the House Un-American Activities Committee as *HUAC*. When leftists attacked the committee by calling it "hew-ack," the committee responded by changing its name to the House Committee on Un-American Activities and calling itself, in committee publications, *HCUA*. The press and the public, however, continued to use *HUAC*, and only the most slavish followers of the committee, such as Berkeley's anticommunist periodical, *Tocsin*, adopted the cumbersome *HCUA* designation. I have followed popular usage. In the sixties radicals referred to themselves as the *Movement*, a term that in the East was synonymous with membership in Students for a Democratic Society. Because of the vague sentimentality that surrounded this word, it has seemed wiser to avoid the term.

Most communist language had little relevance to the sixties, but one word that did survive was *progressive*, which communists had adopted during the Henry Wallace presidential campaign in 1948. It is significant that when Robert Scheer ran for congress in 1966, he did not run as a *progressive*. Scheer needed to build a political coalition that included both *progressives* and left-liberals, i.e., domestic supporters of leftist ideals who abhorred communism. Thus, Scheer called himself a *radical* democrat. The New Left adopted the word *radical* both to distinguish itself from the Old Left and to build a new political coalition. One communist term that did linger into the sixties was *folksinger*. The party had long used folk songs to recruit members. Of course, communists were not the only ones who sang folk songs, and the folk music boom of the early sixties was not a *folksinger* boom. In 1965 a British journalist, unaware of the political meaning of the term, asked Bob Dylan if he were a *folksinger*. Much to the journalist's consternation, Dylan denied that he was a *folksinger*, although he did admit to singing folk songs.

At the University of California, leaders of the student movement also invented language. To the older generation, the University was *Cal*, but young radicals called the University *Berkeley*. I have used both terms in this study. Californians generally capitalized University and always capitalized Regents; so have I. Supporters of the Free Speech Movement referred to the *FSM*, whereas opponents called it the *F.S.M.* Radical students belonged to *SLATE*; opponents denounced *Slate*. In both cases I have followed the practice of the proponents. One of the most confusing problems is *Viet Nam* v. *Viet-Nam* v.

*Vietnam.* In the early sixties many officials in the United States government used *Viet Nam;* later, *Viet-Nam.* One of the first groups to use *Vietnam* was the Berkeley Vietnam Day Committee in 1965. It is likely the committee chose *Vietnam* to promote the abbreviation VDC over the less euphonious and more awkward VNDC. Midway through the war, the Associated Press changed to *Vietnam,* and by the end of the war that spelling predominated. It may have been the antiwar movement's greatest triumph.

In the late sixties young people who rejected middle-class values and life-styles called themselves *flower children* or *street people;* if they used drugs heavily, they were *heads.* Radicals (and sociologists) said these youths belonged to a *counterculture.* The media and the middle class labeled such youths *hippies.* I have used the latter two terms. Young radicals who banded together in cooperative living groups belonged to *collectives.* In contrast, hippies lived in *communes.* These are important distinctions; the self-described term often is the single most important clue as to the relative militance of a particular group. Finally, in the hippie subculture those who sold drugs were *dealers.* To opponents, they were *pushers.* A *pusher* insidiously corrupted community morals, whereas a *dealer* was an entrepreneur supplying a product to a market.

# Notes

Unless otherwise indicated, all unpublished sources are in the Bancroft Library, University of California, Berkeley. For manuscript collections, box:folder have been indicated prior to the name of the collection. It has not always been possible to give pagination for citations to newspaper clippings. Frequently cited items have been identified by the following abbreviations:

| | |
|---|---|
| BP | Berkeley Police Department |
| BPC | Berkeley Planning Commission |
| BPD | Berkeley Planning Department |
| BPP | Black Panther Party, 1966–72, folder, SPP |
| BUSD | Berkeley Unified School District |
| CRF | California Research Foundation |
| CORE/WRO | Congress of Racial Equality, Western Regional Office Papers, State Historical Society of Wisconsin (film). |
| FM | Faculty Memoranda, Reports, Handbills, etc., 1964–65. Bound vol. |
| FMS | Faculty Memoranda . . . , 1964–65. Supplement. Bound vol. |
| FSM Arch. | Free Speech Movement Archives and Papers, 1964–65. |
| FSM/CSHE | Free Speech Movement, Center for the Study of Higher Education Collection |
| FSM EC | Free Speech Movement Executive Committee |
| FSM/H | Free Speech Movement, 1964–65, handout supplement. Bound vol. |
| FSM SC | Free Speech Movement Steering Committee |
| HI | Hoover Institution, Stanford University |
| IGSL | Institute of Governmental Studies Library, UCB |
| PPS | People's Park Strike of May 1969 Collection. Loose items. |
| SC | Scheer Campaign folder, SPP |
| SPP | Social Protest Project |
| UCB | University of California, Berkeley |
| UCBCF | University of California, Berkeley Chancellor's Files |
| UC/H | University of California, Free Speech Movement, 1964–65, handbills. Bound vol. |
| UCPF | University of California, President's Files |
| VDC | Vietnam Day Committee folder, SPP |

## Prologue

(epigraph) "San Francisco," the title song to the 1936 film, is available on *Jeanette MacDonald Sings "San Francisco" and Other Silver Screen Favorites* (RCA Vic-1515).

1. On the Peraltas see BPD, *Berkeley Facts* (Berk., 1971), 1–2; *Berk. Gazette*, Oct. 26, 1977, pp. 37, 39; Edward Staniford, "Domingo Peralta," in *Exactly Opposite the Golden Gate*, ed. Phil McArdle (Berk., 1983), 33–36; George A. Pettitt, *Berkeley, the Town and Gown of It* (Berk., 1973), 14, 18, 25.

2. BPD, *Berkeley Facts* (1971), 2–3; Pettitt, 43–44, 46, 54. Dates are in BPC, *Berkeley Master Plan—1955* (Berk., 1955), 8. The naming of Berkeley is recounted in *Berk. Gazette*, Oct. 26, 1977, p. 3.

3. Incorporation is in BPD, *Berkeley Facts* (1971), 3. On development see BPC, *Berkeley Master Plan—1955*, 10–11; Mason-McDuffie Co., *75th Anniversary, 1887–1962* (Berk.?, 1962), 2–3; Harriet Nathan and Stanley Scott, eds., *Experiment and Change in Berkeley* (Berk., 1978), 50; Pettitt, 27–41. For a list of Maybeck and Morgan homes see Urban Care, *Concerns*, Mar. 1972. On Oceanview and prohibition see Kyle Benham, *Alcohol Control in Berkeley: An Historical Overview* (Berk., 1981), esp. 16. I have also profited from reading Randolph A. Roth's unpublished senior thesis.

4. *Berk. Gazette*, Oct. 26, 1977, pp. 11, 17; BPC, *Berkeley Master Plan—1955*, 11–12; Pettitt, 85. The bond issue record is in Berk., Citizens Advisory Comm., *Construction Needs in the Public Schools of Berkeley, California* (Berk., 1960), 19. Absence of debt is noted in BPD, *Berkeley Facts* (Berk., 1964), 17. Decayed infrastructure is in Bernice H. May, "A Native Daughter's Leadership in Public Affairs" (1976), interview, 210. Downtown office space is covered by Richard M. Betts and G. Michael Yovino-Young, "The Berkeley Downtown in Depth" (M.B.A. report, UCB, 1963), 18. On retail see ibid., 22–23; May interview, 212. On fraternities see James H. Corley, "Serving the University in Sacramento" (1969), interview, x, 75. On radicals see Joseph Conlin, *The Troubles* (N.Y., 1982), 114; Thomas J. Kent, Jr., "Professor and Political Activist: A Career in City and Regional Planning in California, 1950–1980" (1983), interview, 2:15; Josephine Miles, "Poetry, Teaching, and Scholarship" (1980), interview, 320. *Co-op News*, Apr. 1962, 25th Anniversary Issue, in Pamphlet Boxes of Materials on Berkeley Business and Commerce.

5. *Berk. Gazette*, July 27, 1961, pp. 21–40. On Codornices see Berk., "The First Fifty Years of the Community Welfare Commission" (1959), 40–44; William B. Rumford, "Legislator for Fair Employment, Fair Housing, and Public Health" (1973), interview, 54–55; Rumford press release, Mar. 22, 1954, 9:2, Rumford Papers; Jerry S. Mandel, "A Residential Alternative to Special Industrial Zoning" (1965), frontispiece and passim. Enrollment is in BPC, *Master Plan—1955*, 12.

6. On Cross see T. J. Kent, Jr., in Nathan and Scott, 77; Claude B. Hutchison, "The College of Agriculture, University of California, 1922–1952" (1961), interview, 479–82. The bonds are noted in Berk., Citizens Advisory Comm., *Construction Needs*, 3. On Spenger's see *Berk. Gazette*, Oct. 31, 1967, p. 11. *KPFA Program Folio*, Apr. 12, 1959, commemorated the founder Lewis Hill and celebrated the station's tenth anniversary. See also U.S. Senate Subcommittee on Internal Security of the Comm. on the Judiciary, *Pacifica Foundation Hearings*, 88th Cong., 1st Sess. (Wash., 1963), Pt. 1, Senate Library vol. 1581. On development see Frederick G. Dutton, "Democratic Campaigns and Controversies, 1954–1966" (1981), interview, 17; Arthur Harris et al., *Bernice Hubbard May* (Berk., 1971), 34–35; May interview, 333; Nathan and Scott, 41, 74–75, 79.

7. On opposition to dormitories see Ruth N. Donnelly, "The University's Role in Housing Services" (1970), interview, 49–53, 58–60, 67–71, 81–82; Joseph R. Mixer, "Student Housing, Welfare, and the ASUC—with a Look at the University's Future" (1973), interview, 17, 53; Alex C. Sherriffs, "The University of California and the Free Speech Movement: Perspectives from a Faculty Member and Administrator," in "Education Issues and Planning, 1953–1966" (1980), interview, 14; Elinor R. Heller, "A Volunteer Career in Politics, in Higher Education, and on Governing Boards" (1984), interview, 480. On Sproul see Robert M. Underhill, "University of California Lands, Finances, and Investments" (1967), interview, 341, 345; Agnes R. Robb, "Robert Gordon Sproul and the University of California" (1976), interview, 45–46. On the new dormitories see Berk. Gate, Nov. 19, 1963, p. 1; Berk. Review, Jan. 7, 1960, p. 1; Feb. 4, 1960, p. 1; Donnelly interview, 85–87, 101, 107; Lee A. Duffus, "The Administration of Residence Halls at the UCB" (M.B.A. report, UCB, 1960), ii, iv, 2, 8, 9; Underhill interview, 328; Architectural Forum, July–Aug. 1967, pp. 91–97. On bayfill see BPC, "Berkeley Waterfront Development" (1961), 1; BPC, Master Plan—1955, 97–100; BPC, Berkeley Master Plan Amended to October 1964 (Berk., 1964), new pp. 97–98, 101. On May see May interview, 322–24, 335–36; Harris, May, 32–33. On Kerr see ibid., 71–78; Ruth A. Hart, "Concern for the Individual: The Community YWCA and Other Berkeley Organizations" (1978), interview, 174.

8. The teacher is quoted in AFT Local 1078, The Classroom Teacher, Sept. 17, 1960. For business influence see, in addition to the Hutchison interview, Cutter Laboratories, "Cutter Laboratories, 1897–1972: A Dual Trust" (1975), interviews.

## Chapter 1.

(epigraph) Malcolm X in Malcolm X Speaks, ed. George Breitman (N.Y., 1966; orig. 1965), 163.

1. Daily Cal., Mar. 26, 1962; Garff B. Wilson, "The Invisible Man" (1981), interview, 252. On the small protest see Tim Wohlforth to Geoffrey White, Apr. 10, 1962, 1:18, White Papers, HI. On the Peace Corps see Daily Cal., Mar. 2, 1961; Mar. 7, 1966, p. 5; Berk. Gazette, Sept. 21, 1962; N.Y. Times, Nov. 6, 1965, p. 6; unidentified clipping, Apr. 2, 1965, 10:110, UCBCF. Berkeley as the leading source is in America, June 3, 1967, p. 817; Stanford Observer, Jan. 1988, p. 16.

2. Daily Cal., Oct. 24–25, 1962; Despite Everything, Feb. 1963, pp. 3–8; James P. O'Brien, "The Development of a New Left in the United States, 1960–1965" (Ph.D. diss., Univ. of Wisconsin, 1971), 196, 198; Henry Nash Smith to Leo Marx, Nov. 14, 1962, 3:3, Smith Papers.

3. The quote is from Ralph J. Gleason column, S.F. Chronicle, Dec. 9, 1964. Clark Kerr, The Uses of the University (Cambridge, Mass., 1963). For an early, astute critique by three members of SLATE see the 1962 essay by Bruce Payne, David Walls, and Jerry Berman in The New Student Left, ed. Mitchell Cohen and Dennis Hale, rev. ed. (Boston, 1967), 226–36. See also Abbie Hoffman, Soon To Be a Major Motion Picture (N.Y., 1980), 36.

4. Two useful short accounts of the FSM are Eugene Bardach, ed., "The Berkeley Free Speech Controversy" (1964), typescript, and a special issue of Calif. Monthly, Feb. 1965. The only full study is Max A. Heirich, The Spiral of Conflict (N.Y., 1971). This book, by a Berkeley graduate student in sociology, is insightful, but the author lacked access to many sources.

5. On Hofmann see Thomas Albright, Art in the San Francisco Bay Area, 1945–

*1980* (Berk., 1985). On Lowenthal see Leo Lowenthal, *An Unmastered Past*, ed. Martin Jay (Berk., 1987). See also Reinhard Bendix, *From Berlin to Berkeley* (New Brunswick, N.J., 1986). On Lawrence see Herbert Childs, *An American Genius* (N.Y., 1968); J. L. Heilbron, *Lawrence and His Laboratory* (Berk., 1981). On Nobel laureates see Joseph Conlin, *The Troubles* (N.Y., 1982), 114.

6. On Sproul see G. Edward White, *Earl Warren* (N.Y., 1982), 67; James H. Corley, "Serving the University in Sacramento" (1969), interview, xii–xvi; Clark Kerr, "University of California Crises," in "Earl Warren: Views and Episodes" (1976), interview, 19; Donald H. McLaughlin, "Careers in Mining Geology and Management" (1975), interview, 40, 57, 68–69; Josephine Miles, "Poetry, Teaching, and Scholarship" (1980), interview, 141; Joseph R. Mixer, "Student Housing, Welfare, and the ASUC" (1973), interview, 43; Garff B. Wilson, "The Invisible Man" (1981), interview, 213, 382–83. Standard accounts for the oath are George R. Stewart, *The Year of the Oath* (Garden City, N.Y., 1950); and David P. Gardner, *The California Oath Controversy* (Berk., 1967). See also John E. Canaday, "Alumni Officer and University Regent" (1975), interview, 77–78, 81, 156; Kerr interview, 2–3; McLaughlin interview, 83–84; Harry R. Wellman, "Teaching, Research, and Administration" (1976), interview, 73, 158. On Neylan see Kerr interview, 2; John Gofman, "Medical Research and Radiation Politics" (1985), interview, 69–70; Elinor R. Heller, "A Volunteer Career in Politics" (1984), interview, 493, 504.

7. Heller interview, esp. 402–3, 411, 475, 478, 499, 501, 504, 536, 543–44, 548–72, 585–91, 609–13, 617–20, 627–36, 653–57; Kerr interview, esp. 2–3; Canaday interview, esp. 75–78, 81, 156–64; Wellman interview, esp. 73, 184–85, 199–200, 221; Robert M. Underhill, "University of California Lands, Finances, and Investments" (1967), interview, esp. 220–21, 312–21.

8. *Berk. Gazette*, Mar. 10, 1965; *S.F. Examiner*, Mar. 10, 1965; Kerr to Roger Kent, Aug. 10, 1962, Kent Papers.

9. On Kerr's appointment see Kerr interview, 12; Ida A. Sproul, "The President's Wife" (1981), interview, 163–64; Transcript of Portions of Notes Taken at Regents Only Session of the Board, Feb. 19, 1965, p. 3; Ralph E. Shaffer to Savio, Dec. 5, 1964, 2:13, FSM Arch. On the Master Plan see Heirich, 51–52; Albert S. Rodda, "Sacramento Senator," in "Assembly, State Senate, and Governor's Office" (1982), interview, 85–86; Keith Sexton, "Legislating Higher Education," in "Education Issues and Planning, 1953–1966" (1980), interview, 9–16. See also Kerr, *Uses of the University*. Statistics from *Daily Cal.*, Mar. 1, 1961, p. 1; Heller interview, 581; Mixer interview, 50–51; Rodda interview, 159; AFT Berk. Faculty Branch statement, 3:20, FSM Arch.; Lawrence H. Davis, "Report on Berkeley to the National Supervisory Board and the 18th National Student Congress" (1965), 5–7; Heirich, 57–58; Alex C. Sherriffs, "The University of California and the Free Speech Movement" in "Education Issues and Planning, 1953–1966" (1980), interview, 86–88; *L.A. Times*, June 7, 1965, p. 3; BPD, *Berkeley Facts* (Berk., 1971), 45. See also Henry Nash Smith to Henry May, July 11, 1963, 4:1, Smith Papers.

10. Crocker quoted in *S.F. Examiner*, Mar. 21, 1965; unidentified administrator quoted by William Trombley in *Sat. Eve. Post*, May 16, 1964, p. 24. Charles M. Otten, *University Authority and the Student* (Berk., 1970), 159–62; H. Meyers to friends, Dec. 25, 1964, quoted in *Despite Everything*, Jan. 1965, pp. 9–11; Robert Beloof in Colin Miller, "The Student Revolt at Berkeley," *Frontier*, Apr. 1965, pp. 11–20; Michael Nelken in *Grad. Student J.*, Spring 1965, p. 32; Clark Kerr in *N.Y. Review of Books*, Apr. 8, 1965, pp. 35–36; Trombley, 22–29; Heller interview, 483, 530, 548–

49; Sherriffs interview, 39; Wellman interview, 109–10, 159; Wilson interview, 206–7, 213, 220–22. For an acute assessment see Henry Nash Smith to Walter Blair, Aug. 4, 1960, 1:8, Smith Papers. On Kerr's wit see Peter Tauber, *The Last Best Hope* (N.Y., 1977), 569. On Kent see Thomas J. Kent, Jr., "Professor and Political Activist," in "Statewide and Regional Land-Use Planning in California, 1950–1980" (1983), interview, 2:118–20; Catherine B. Wurster to Margie and Martin Meyerson, June 30, 1963, 8:3, Wurster Papers.

11. On Seaborg see Lincoln Constance, "Versatile Berkeley Botanist" (1987), interview, 223; Wellman interview, 107–8. The first choice was Kenneth S. Pitzer. Pitzer to Hardin B. Jones, May 3, 1965; reply, May 7, 1965, both in Box 2, Jones Papers, HI; Pitzer to Kerr, Mar. 8, 1966; reply, Mar. 22, 1966; Don McLaughlin to Pitzer, Mar. 11, 1966, all in 1303:6, UCPF. On Kerr see Heller interview, 483, 532–33, 544, 553, 594. On ROTC see *Daily Cal.*, June 29, 1962, p. 1; David Horowitz, *Student* (N.Y., 1962), 23–29, 115–20. On Strong see Meyers in *Despite Everything*, Jan. 1965, p. 11; Constance interview, 238, 253, 256; Sherriffs interview, 39, 55, 78; George R. Stewart, "A Little of Myself" (1972), interview, 65–66; Wilson interview, 222–23; *L.A. Times*, April 17, 1965. Strong's lack of power is noted in Kerr interview, 17, 21–22; McLaughlin interview, 67–68; David W. Reed to John H. Reynolds, Dec. 6, 1964, FM.

12. On Kerr's policy see Kerr to Carlos Bee, May 9, 1961, and related correspondence, 1302:4, UCPF; Alex C. Sherriffs memo of a meeting with Kerr, Oct. 8, 1964, 2:10–2:40 p.m., 3:40, UCBCF. The fullest account of the Katz case is in Calif. Senate Fact-Finding Comm. on Un-American Activities, *Thirteenth Report Supplement* (Sacramento, 1966), 136–53. See also *Berk. Gate*, Mar. 8, 1966, p. 7; *Daily Cal.*, Sept. 27, 1965, p. 1; Sept. 30, 1965, p. 3; Oct. 22, 1965, p. 1; Heirich, 220; Robert Kaufman and Michael Folsom, "FSM: An Interpretive Essay," in a W. E. B. DuBois Club publication, *FSM, the Free Speech Movement at Berkeley* (S.F., 1965), 33; Constance interview, 250–53; Prof. Joseph Garbarino, chairman, Comm. on Academic Freedoom, to Strong, Nov. 19, 1964, FM; Kerr to Dick Jennings, Nov. 25, 1964 (not sent), 1294:1, UCPF; Lincoln Constance memo of phone call from Garbarino, Nov. 20, 1964, 8:90, UCBCF; Kitty Malloy memo, Mar. 21, 1962, Box 45, and materials in Box 15, Jones Papers, HI.

13. Conlin, 114; Lewis S. Feuer, *The Conflict of Generations* (N.Y., 1969), 439–40; Heirich, 61, 68–70; Max Heirich and Sam Kaplan in *Calif. Monthly*, Feb. 1965, pp. 20–23; Henry F. May, "The Student Movement," *American Scholar*, 34 (1965), 388–89; Dorothy Deane to Kerr, May 31, 1961, 1302:5, UCPF. On Stiles Hall see Mixer interview, 2.

14. Heirich, 71; Heirich and Kaplan, 24–26; Sherriffs interview, 19. On the new union see *Daily Cal.*, Mar. 14, 1961, p. 1; Catherine B. Wurster to Paul Ylvisaker, Mar. 19, 1960, 7:1, Wurster Papers. The restrictions are discussed in Katherine A. Towle, "Administration and Leadership" (1970), interview, 200; *Daily Cal.*, Sept. 18; Dec. 5, 8, 1958.

15. The bookstore is in *Tocsin*, Oct. 16, 1963, p. 3. On Stiles Hall see *Berk. Review*, Jan. 25, 1962, pp. 5, 9; *Tocsin*, May 22, 1963, p. 4; Mixer interview, 71; Ward Tabler in *Humanist*, Mar.-Apr. 1965, p. 53. The Telegraph bohemia is noted in Miles interview, esp. 164–65; Horowitz; see Chapter Four, notes 12–13. On deterioration see De Mars & Reay, *Design Program for the South Campus Urban Renewal Project* (Berk., 1964); Riches Research, Inc., *Economic Analysis, South Campus Area* (Palo Alto, 1964). Repeal of the communist ban may be followed in Heirich and Kaplan, 29; *Daily Cal.*,

June 29, 1962, p. 1; June 20; Oct. 30, 1963, p. 1; Heller interview, 536; Don Mulford to Kerr, May 7, 1963; reply, same date; Alex C. Sherriffs to file, July 1, 1963, all in 1293:1, UCPF. The effect of the new rules is shown in Michael Rossman et al., "Administrative Pressures and Student Political Activity at the University of California" (1964), Introduction, 3–6; Appendix D, 1–2.

16. Fullest accounts of SLATE are in Horowitz, 18–21; Michael Myerson, *These Are the Good Old Days* (N.Y., 1970), 38–48. See also Feuer, 397; Nathan Glazer, "What Happened at Berkeley," in *Student Activism*, ed. Irving Howe (n.p., n.d.), 16; Heirich, 71–75, 79, 88–89; Kaufman and Folsom in *FSM*, 27–28; *Daily Cal.*, Oct. 25, 1960, p. 1; Mar. 1, 1961, p. 1; Oct. 30, 1963, p. 1. Also useful is the film, "The Torch Is Passed" (Sharon Genasci and Bill Goetz, 1985). On David Armor's election in 1959 see Heirich, 71–77. A more accurate account is in Daniel Kirchner's notes from the *Daily Cal.*, 3:1, FSM Arch. Sherriffs counted the graduate students out, according to Eric Levine, *Daily Cal.*, Mar. 30, 1965. See also "Proposed SLATE Platform," fall 1964 (ditto), 1:34, FSM Arch.

17. The best coverage is in Frank J. Donner, *The Un-Americans* (N.Y., 1961), 1–3, 175–218. See also Conlin, 27–29; Heirich, 80–85; Horowitz, 16–17, 53, 66–91, 106–8, 130–43; Myerson, 50, 55, 60, 68–69; Roger Rapoport, *California Dreaming* (Berk., 1982), 64–65; HUAC, "Communist Target-Youth" (Wash., 1961), 5–10. The best press coverage is in *S.F. News-Call-Bulletin*, Jan. 23–30, 1961. See also *Berk. Gazette*, May 13, 1960, pp. 1, 2, 13; May 14, 1960, pp. 1, 2; May 16, 1960, p. 1; Mar. 3, 1961, pp. 1, 9; *Daily Cal.*, May 16, 1960, p. 1; Mar. 2, 1961, p. 1; *S.F. Chronicle*, May 13, 1960, pp. 1, 5, 26; May 14, 1960, pp. A, B, 1–3; May 15, 1960, pp. 1, 2, 4, 5; *S.F. Examiner*, May 14, 1960, pp. 1, 4. For an eyewitness see Wanda Collins to Kerr, May 15, 1960, 1302:5, UCPF. On Chessman see *Daily Cal.*, Feb. 18, 1960; May 30, 1960. On the suicide see Donner, 2, 176. On teachers, ibid., 2, 190–92, 194–95, 200; *Daily Cal.*, May 12, 1960.

18. Donner, 199, 201–3; Myerson, 69–71; Ralph Tyler in *Frontier*, June 1960, pp. 5–9. See also O'Brien, 117–60; James P. Walsh, *San Francisco's Hallinan* (Novato, Calif., 1982), 244–45; *Daily Cal.*, May 16, 1960; Mar. 2, 1961; editorial, *Oakland Tribune*, May 19, 1960; editorial, *S.F. Chronicle*, May 16, 1960; John F. Beery, "Student Demonstrations in San Francisco, May 12–14, 1960" (M.A. thesis, UCB, 1961). The number of Cal students arrested is in Alex C. Sherriffs to Herman T. Spieth, Oct. 5, 1960, 1302:11, UCPF. The size of the protest crowd is in Donner, 1. On Meisenbach see ibid., 203, 215; Irving Hall, "The Meisenbach Case," *The Californian*, June 1961, pp. 7–16; *Daily Cal.*, Apr. 18, 1961; May 4, 1961. On the film see Donner, 204–6, 216–18; Hoffman, 47–49.

19. On these issues see *Daily Cal.*, (staff resigns) Oct. 24, 1960; (Burns) Mar. 22, 1961; (SLATE banned) June 10, 1961; (Malcolm X, Pike) May 5, 8, 10, 16, 1961; (radio) Mar. 31, 1964 (quote); Sept 18, 1964; Feb. 23, 1965. On the radio station see also *S.F. Chronicle*, Feb. 19, 1965.

20. *Daily Cal.*, July 31, 1959; Aug. 28, 1964; Sept. 17, 1965, p. 1 (statistics); Sept. 21, 1965, p. 9 (quotes); *Berk. Gazette*, Aug. 14, 1965, p. 1; *N.Y. Times*, Nov. 3, 1968, p. 90; Phi Kappa Tau Fraternity at UCB, *Nu News*, Winter 1965; O'Brien, 214–16; Malcolm Burnstein et al., "People v. Savio and 571 Others" (1966), 411. On Greeks and the FSM see *Daily Cal.*, Oct. 15, 1964; Strong to Kerr, Oct. 21, 1964, 1293:13, UCPF.

21. Statistics on student housing, 1294:8, UCPF. Apartment living is noted in Burnstein, 397, 402; O'Brien, 218. Scholastic Aptitude Test scores in Burnstein, 400. The

comparison with the 1940s is in A. L. Ellington letter, *Berk. Gazette*, Apr. 5, 1965. On loneliness see Burnstein, 396. On alienation see James C. Whitney to Josephine Miles, Dec. 24, 1964, 6:26, Miles Papers. Dorm signs are in *Berk. Gazette*, Sept. 24, 1964, p. 13; editorial, *Daily Cal.*, Sept. 15, 1965, p. 8.

22. On jobs see Marie Angell et al., "Vocational Guidance and Employment Opportunities for Minority Group Members in Berkeley" (M.S.W. group project report, UCB, 1959), copy in Ruth A. Hart Papers. On housing see Thomas W. Casstevens, *Politics, Housing and Race Relations* (Berk., 1965). CORE is in Heirich, 85–87, 101; *Daily Cal.*, Apr. 22, 1964, p. 1; Apr. 23, 1964, pp. 1, 6. For a reaction see Don Mulford press release, Apr. 28, 1964, IGSL.

23. Widely different stories about Knowland appear in Bardach, 23; Conlin, 119; Lewis S. Feuer in *The New Leader*, Dec. 21, 1964, p. 5; *Daily Cal.*, Dec. 4, 1964; Kerr interview, 15, 18; Rossman, App. C, 1. Complaints include JRE letter, *Berk. Gazette*, Mar. 8, 1963, p. 11; *Daily Cal.*, Apr. 10, 1964, p. 3. On Sherriffs see Heirich, 75, 91–93, 95–96; *Calif. News Letter*, Oct. 5, 1964; *SLATE Supplement*, Sept. 15, 1964; Heller interview, 553; Kerr interview, 14–15, Sherriffs interview, 23–24, 27–29; Towle interview, 222–42, 291.21–291.22; Sherriffs to Vice President Oswald, Mar. 5, 1963, 1293:1, UCPF; Sherriffs to file, July 22, 1964; Sept. 4, 1964; Sherriffs to Thomas J. Cunningham, Sept. 18, 1964, all in 10:114, UCBCF; Joseph R. Mixer to Sherriffs, Aug. 3, 1964; Mixer memo, n.d.; Sherriffs to Kerr, Sept. 15, 1964; (Bradford Cleaveland,) "Education, Revolutions, and Citadels," all in 3:40, UCBCF. A description of the area by John F. Boler is in *Commonweal*, Feb. 5, 1965, p. 603. On sororities see Frances P. Gamble, "Effects of Campus Living Groups on Academic Values and Performance" (M.A. thesis, UCB, 1961). On discussion see Arleigh Williams to Katherine A. Towle, July 31, 1964; Towle statement, Oct. 9, 1964; Towle to John Jordan, Oct. 12, 1964, all in Towle Papers.

24. The new rules and their immediate consequences are in *Berk. Gazette*, Sept. 17, 1964, p. 1; Sept. 26, 1964, p. 1; *Daily Cal.*, Sept. 17–18, 21–23, 25, 29, 1964. On Towle see Heirich, 96–97, 105–6, 108–9; *N.Y. Times*, Mar. 14, 1965; *S.F. Chronicle*, Apr. 26, 1965; Heller interview, 541–42; Kerr interview, 14; Sherriffs interview, 26; Towle interview, iv, 150, 192–95, 198–200, 202–4, 291.24, and passim; obituary in *S.F. Chronicle*, Mar. 4, 1986; Towle memo, Sept. 17, 1964, 10:114. UCBCF; Towle to Strong, Oct. 12, 19, 21, 1964, Towle Papers. On legal ownership of the land see *S.F. Examiner*, Sept. 18, 1964; Heller interview, 542; Kerr interview, 94; Sherriffs interview, 21–22; Wellman interview, 156; Bolton to Kerr, Oct. 12, 1964 (2 memos), 1293:13, UCPF; Sherriffs to Kerr, Sept. 23, 1964, Towle Papers.

25. The meeting is in Kitty Malloy memo, Sept. 18, 1964; Sherriffs to Kerr, Sept. 20, 1964, both in 10:114, UCBCF. On Kerr's role see Draper in Harold Draper and Nathan Glazer in *New Politics*, 4 (1965), 26–27; Heirich, 109–10; Kerr interview, 15–17; Towle interview, 242, note; Regents Comm. on Educational Policy, Executive Session Minutes, Sept. 24, 1964. On bureaucracy see Constance interview, 211, 258, 269, 274; Ruth N. Donnelly, "The University's Role in Housing Services" (1970), interview; Lee A. Duffus, "The Administration of Residence Halls at the University of California at Berkeley" (M.B.A. report, UCB, 1960). On "All State" see *L.A. Times*, Apr. 19, 1965.

26. Bardach, 16; Heirich, 456, note 22, and passim. Quote is from Roger Sandall in *Landfall*, June 1965, p. 149. The FSM Archives are instructive. The FSM retained incoming correspondence, made copies of outgoing correspondence, kept copious phone logs, and recorded in detail discussions in FSM EC and FSM SC sessions.

27. On skirmishes see *Berk. Gazette*, Sept. 29, 1964, pp. 1, 2; *Daily Cal.*, Sept. 29–30, 1964; Sherriffs to file, Sept. 30, 1964; Kerr summary of meeting, Sept. 30, 1964, both in 3:40, UCBCF. On the mill-in see *Daily Cal.*, *Oakland Tribune*, *S.F. Chronicle*, and *S.F. Examiner*, Oct. 1, 1964; Kerr phone call to Strong, Oct. 1, 1964, 3:40, UCBCF; Gloria Copeland to file, Oct. 1, 1964, 1293:13, UCPF. On the eight see Arleigh Williams memo to Strong, Oct. 1, 1964, in UCB, Academic Senate, Ad Hoc Comm. on Student Conduct, "Materials" (1964). Chaired by Prof. Ira M. Heyman and commonly called the Heyman Comm. exhibits. On the sit-down see Heirich, 123–30, 143–49, 154–83; Rapoport, 82; *Berk. Gate*, Oct. 12, 1964, pp. 1, 6; *Berk. Gazette*, Oct. 2, 1964; *Daily Cal.*, Oct. 2, 5, 1964; Bolton to file, Oct. 2, 1964 (2 memos), all in 1293:13, UCPF; Sherriffs memo, Oct. 1, 1964; anon. memo, Oct. 2, 1964; Kitty Malloy memo, Oct. 2, 1964 (2 memos); Strong memo, Oct. 2, 1964, all in 3:40, UCBCF. On molesters see Bardach, 4.

28. In addition to the sources in note 27, on the sagging roof see Robert Hurwitt in *Express*, Sept. 28, 1984, p. 18. Car repairs are in Richard Rosenzweig, Mar. 14, 1967, photostat of check to UCB; William B. Boyd to Rosenzweig, July 31, 1967, both in 8:96, UCBCF. Savio's shoes are in Bardach, 4.

29. Biographical information from UCB, Public Information Office, 3:20, FSM Arch. The quote on Mississippi is from *S.F. Chronicle*, Oct. 3, 1964, p. 8. The best press biography is in *N.Y. Herald-Tribune*, Dec. 9, 1964. See also the Sunday magazine, *N.Y. Post*, Dec. 13, 1964; *N.Y. Times*, Dec. 9, 1964, p. 32; *L.A. Times*, Apr. 16, 1965, Pt. I, p. 3; May 22, 1965; *S.F. Chronicle*, Oct. 3, 1964, p. 8; Nov. 15, 1964; *Berk. Gazette*, Nov. 14, 1964; Dec. 9, 1964; Ronald Fraser, ed., *1968* (N.Y., 1988), 48–51, 92–93. An autobiography is in 3:20, FSM Arch. On Savio's name see *Berk. Gazette*, Apr. 1, 1965; May 19, 1965, p. 1; *S.F. Chronicle*, May 20, 1965, p. 5; Raymond Marcus et al., wire to Savio, Dec. 9, 1964, 2:13, FSM Arch. On Savio's marriage see *People's World*, June 5, 1965, p. 9. See also Conlin, 123–26; Feuer, *Conflict*, 443–44; Feuer in *New Leader*, Dec. 21, 1964, p. 9; T. Walter Herbert, Jr., in *Issue*, Spring 1965, p. 28; Seymour M. Lipset and Paul Seabury in *Reporter*, Jan. 28, 1965, p. 39; Heller interview, 547. For a retrospective see *Calif. Monthly*, Dec. 1984, pp. 18–20.

30. Quotes are from Sept. 30, 1964, in Heirich, 130; Oct. 1, 1964, ibid., 156; Mario Savio in *Free Student*, #1 (1965), 4; Mario Savio in *Humanity*, Dec. 1964, p. 4; Mario Savio et al., *The Free Speech Movement and the Negro Revolution* (Detroit, 1965), 16; Feuer in *New Leader*, Dec. 21, 1964, p. 9; Feuer, *Conflict*, 498, note. See also Heirich, 255, 375; *Daily Cal.*, Feb. 15, 1965; Savio, *Free Speech Movement*, 18; KPFK radio interview, Dec. 25, 1964, ibid., 19.

31. Heirich, 181–86; *Oakland Tribune*, Oct. 31, 1964; *S.F. Chronicle*, Oct. 3, 1964; *S.F. Examiner*, Oct. 4, 1964; Savio remarks, Oct. 2, 1964; Kitty Malloy memo of Strong phone call, Oct. 2, 1964, 8:20 a.m.; Bolton-Lohman phone calls, Oct. 2, 1964, 5:10 p.m. and 5:45 p.m.; Bolton-Woodward phone call, Oct. 2, 1964, 5:15 p.m., all in 1293:13, UCPF; Lincoln Constance memo, Oct. 2, 1964, 3:40, UCBCF; Savio memo of Kerr-Savio conversation, Oct. 2, 1964, 3:13, FSM Arch.; transcript of Savio's remarks, Oct. 2, 1964, approx. 7:30 p.m., 1293:13, UCPF.

32. Savio notebook, Oct. 4–11, 1964, pp. 2–10, 12, 29 (quotes at 2, 12, 10), 1:3, FSM Arch. On Aptheker see *L.A. Times*, May 2, 1965, Sec. A, p. 3; Mar. 24, 1982, Pt. I, pp. 3, 30, 31; Kenneth Lamott, *Anti-California* (Boston, 1971), 151–53; autobiography in 1:18, FSM Arch.; *Calif. Monthly*, Dec. 1984, pp. 18–20.

33. On FSM SC membership see 1:6, FSM Arch. Bettina Aptheker gave a slightly

different list at the sit-in trial. *Berk. Gazette*, May 12, 1965. The best biographical sketches are in *L.A. Times*, Mar. 24, 1982, Pt. I, pp. 3, 30, 31. See also *S.F. Chronicle*, Nov. 15, 1964; autobiographies in 1:18, FSM Arch.; Box 677, Brown Papers. (SG) *L.A. Times*, May 22, 1965; *S.F. Chronicle*, May 22, 1965, p. 3; (JW) Bardach, 12; Feuer, *Conflict*, 441–42, 447 (quote); Weinberg in Joan Morrison and Robert K. Morrison, *From Camelot to Kent State* (N.Y., 1987), 225–33; (AG) see the article by the "other" Art Goldberg in *S.F. Bay Guardian*, June 14, 1979, p. 10; (JG) speech, Mar. 6, 1963, in *Women for Peace Newsletter* file, Herstory Coll. (film); (Roysher) *L.A. Times*, Jan. 10, 1965; (Rossman) Michael Rossman's autobiography, *The Wedding within the War* (Garden City, N.Y., 1971); (DG) David L. Goines, *Posters* (Natick, Mass., 1985). An inaccurate understanding of FSM leadership is in FSM Organizational Chart, 1294:11, UCPF.

34. Red diaper babies are in *Despite Everything*, Jan. 1965, p. 5. On Garson see *Tocsin*, Nov. 6, 1962, p. 4. Kerr's remarks are noted in Robert Aronoff, "Public Opinion and the Free Speech Movement" (1970), 4; *Daily Cal.*, Nov. 30, 1964. Outrage is expressed ibid., Oct. 14, 1964; Michael Nagler in *Studies on the Left*, 5 #1 (1965), 56, Anthony E. Neville in *Johns Hopkins Magazine*, Oct. 1965, p. 20; Gilbert H. Robinson to Kerr, Nov. 30, 1964, 2:18, FSM Arch. See also Ron Moscowitz notes on coffee with John Leggett, ca. early 1965, Box 675, Brown Papers.

35. The shrewdest observer is Feuer, *Conflict*, 423–29. See also Lucille Birnbaum and Leonard D. Cain, Jr., in *Issue*, Spring 1965, pp. 23 24, 38; Michael P. Lerner in *Judaism*, 18 (1969), 473–78; Nathan Glazer, *Remembering the Answers* (N.Y., 1970), 222–44.

36. For examples of hostility see KNXT television editorial, Dec. 4, 1964, 2:17, FSM Arch.; and the unflattering photograph of Savio in *N.Y. Times*, Dec. 9, 1964, p. 32. Aronoff, "Public Opinion," passim; Bardach, 34–38; Colin Miller in *Frontier*, Apr. 1965, pp. 14–15; Edwin Lasman, "Berkeley 1964: The Movement, the Press, the Public" (1974), 1; Neville, 20–21; Michael Rossman, *New Age Blues*, (N.Y., 1979), 45; Ward Tabler in *Humanist*, Mar.-Apr. 1965, p. 50; Towle interview, 219; *N.Y. Times*, Mar. 14, 1965; *People's World*, Dec. 12, 1964, p. 1; Dec. 19, 1964, p. 1. Oct. 4 meeting in Savio notebook, Oct. 4–11, 1964, p. 10, 1:3 FSM Arch.

37. Anon. postcard to Savio, postmarked Dec. 12, 1964, 2:37; FSM Arch.; anon. to FSM, postmarked Feb. 13, 1965; John J. Barlow to FSM, postmarked Feb. 12, 1965; Rev. Glenn B. Ogden to Savio, Feb. 13, 1965, all in 2:38, FSM Arch.; anon. note, n.d., 2:37, FSM Arch.

38. The two key documents were issued by UCB, Academic Senate's Ad Hoc Comm. on Student Conduct, chaired by Prof. Ira M. Heyman. These are entitled "Materials" and "Proceedings" (both 1964). On distrust see Draper in Draper and Glazer, 27–28. For Strong's attitude see his interview, *Fresno Bee*, Oct. 19, 1964; Strong to Ronan E. Degnan, Oct. 14, 1964, 8:90, UCBCF. For arbitrary citations see *S.F. Chronicle*, Oct. 30, 1964; *S.F. News-Call-Bulletin*, Oct. 28, 1964. The administration position may be followed in Kerr statement (not issued), Oct. 8, 1964; Sue Johnson to Bolton, Oct. 8, 1964; Nathan Glazer and Lewis Feuer to Kerr, Oct. 15, 1964, all in 1293:13, UCPF; Degnan to Strong, Oct. 21, 1964, 8:90, UCBCF; Strong memo, Oct. 15, 1964, 3:40, UCBCF; Sherriffs to Strong, Oct. 29, 1964; Strong memo of phone call from Arleigh Williams, Oct. 29, 1964; Strong memo, Oct. 30, 1964; Kerr to Strong, Nov. 2, 1964 (2 memos), all in 3:41, UCBCF; Degnan to Williams, Oct. 6, 1964; Strong to Kerr, Nov. 17, 1964, both in 8:91, UCBCF; Regents Executive Session Minutes, Oct. 16, 1964; Transcript of Regents Informal Sessions, Nov. 19–20, 1964. On the alteration of

penalties see Heirich, 227, 232, 241, 249–50; Heyman to Strong, Oct. 22, 1964; reply, Oct. 26, 1964; Kerr to Regents, Oct. 26, 1964, all in 1293:13, UCPF; Akiko (Owen) memo, Oct. 23, 1964, 2:22 p.m.; Strong memo of phone call to Kerr, Oct. 23, 1964, 5:35 p.m., both in 8:90, UCBCF; Kerr to Strong, Nov. 2, 1964 (2 memos); Strong to file, Nov. 4, 1964; Strong statement (draft), Nov. 13, 1964; Heyman Comm. to Kerr, Nov. 16, 1964; Kerr notes, Nov. 20, 1964, all in 1293:14, UCPF; Kerr to Regents, memo, Nov. 20, 1964, in 3:13, FSM Arch.; Strong to Academic Senate, Nov. 24, 1964, FM.

39. Heirich, 224, 226–29, 241–42; *Daily Cal.*, Oct. 14, 1964; Kent Pursel letter to Regents in *Oakland Tribune*, Oct. 27, 1964; *S.F. Chronicle*, Nov. 11, 1964; FSM SC–Strong meeting memo, Oct. 11, 1964; Kerr list; Bolton to Kerr, Oct. 21, 1964; Kerr to Robert Brode, Oct. 26, 1964, all in 1293:13, UCPF; Kerr to Strong, Nov. 2, 1964; Frank Kidner to Kerr, Nov. 9, 1964 (2 memos), all in 1293:14, UCPF; Sherriffs memo, Oct. 12, 1964, 11:10 a.m.; Akiko (Owen) memo, Oct. 23, 1964, 3:10 p.m., both in 8:90, UCBCF; Strong call to Heyman, Nov. 9, 1964, 8:55 a.m.; statement by ten history faculty, Nov. 23, 1964, both in 8:91, UCBCF. The committee's dissolution is in Strong to Savio, Nov. 13, 1964, 1:21, FSM Arch.

40. FSM internal memo, ca. Oct. 15, 1964, 1:5, FSM Arch.; Sandor Fuchs in *SLATE Newsletter*, ca. Nov. 1964, p. 3, 2:52; FSM Arch.; Informal minutes, FSM EC meeting, Nov. 7, 1964, 1:1, FSM Arch.; Marston Schultz notes on FSM EC meeting, Nov. 11, 1964, 2:48, FSM Arch.; Bardach, 27–29; Heirich, 217–24; *Daily Cal.*, Oct. 16, 1964; Nov. 11, 18, 24, 30, 1964; *S.F. Chronicle*, Nov. 11, 1964; Paul Forman to Kerr, Oct. 10, 1964; Nov. 11, 1964, both in 2:18, FSM Arch.; Jo Freeman to ?, Nov. 18, 1964, 2:24, FSM Arch.; Strong to Kerr, Oct. 29, 1964; reply, Oct. 30, 1964, both in 1293:13, UCPF; Bolton record of phone call with Lipset, Nov. 11, 1964; Akiko (Owen) to Strong, Nov. 11, 1964, both in 1293:14, UCPF. On the quarter system see Kerr to Lipset (copy), Jan. 6, 1965; Thomas S. Kuhn to *N.Y. Times*, Dec. 31, 1964, both in 1293:6, UCPF.

41. Jo Freeman to ?, Nov. 18, 1964, 2:24, FSM Arch. See also Bolton to Kerr, Nov. 13, 1964, 1293:1, UCPF.

42. Reports and transcripts are sprinkled throughout UC files. E.g., FSM rally transcript, Oct. 6, 1964, 1294:10, UCPF; report on noon rally, Dec. 7, 1964; Dave Fulton report on FSM rally, Dec. 7, 1964, both in 1294:1, UCPF.

43. "Free Speech Songbook" (1964), 5, 6, 9, 12, 17. On sales see *FSM*, 22; *Daily Cal.*, Jan. 7, 1965. On funds see Dustin Miller to Gretchen (Kittredge), ca. Dec. 1964, 2:43, FSM Arch. Savio liked to sing. *Calif. Monthly*, Dec. 1984, p. 19. See also "FSM Song Sheet—Nov. 17" (mimeo), 1:25, FSM Arch.

44. On discipline see George S. Murphy to Dean Arleigh Williams, Nov. 5, 1964; Strong to Kerr, Nov. 9, 1964, both in 1293:14, UCPF. On Elberg see Frank Kidner to Kerr, Nov. 9, 1964, 1293:14, UCPF; Bolton to Elberg, Jan. 8, 1965, 1294:2, UCPF. On tables see *Daily Cal.* and *S.F. Chronicle*, Nov. 11, 1964; Peter Matteson letter, *Daily Cal.*, Nov. 19, 1964; Analysis by the Graduate Division of 274 Names, 3:19, FSM Arch.; 274 signers, petition, Nov. 10, 1964; Towle to students (draft submitted to and annotated by Kerr), Nov. 12, 1964; Towle to heads of eight student organizations, Nov. 18, 1964, all in 1293:14, UCPF. On the 65 cited students see Arleigh Williams memo, Nov. 9, 1964, 8:91, UCBCF; Alan W. Searcy memo, Nov. 11, 1964; Kitty Malloy memo, Nov. 9, 1964, both in 10:114, UCBCF. The 835 letters were noted in *Daily Cal.*, Nov. 30, 1964. On TAs not being cited see Robert Hurwitt in *Express*, Sept. 28, 1984, p. 18. The key document is Sherriffs memo, Nov. 8, 1964, 10:114,

UCBCF. On the march to the Regents meeting see Heirich, 250–56; anon. report on the FSM rally after the Regents meeting, Nov. 20, 1964, 1293:14, UCPF. "Merrimac" is in *Calif. Pelican*, Dec. 1964, p. 10.

45. Heirich, 265–66; *Berk. Gazette*, Apr. 3, 1965; *Daily Cal.*, Nov. 30; Dec. 2, 1964; Weissman quoted in *S.F. Chronicle*, Dec. 1, 1964; George S. Murphy to Arleigh Williams, Nov. 5, 1964; Strong to Kerr, Nov. 9, 1964; Thomas Cunningham to Strong, Nov. 25, 1964; Ron Anastasi to Kerr's office, phone call, Nov. 25, 1964, all in 1293:14, UCPF; Bolton (?) record of phone call with Martin Roysher and Steve Weissman, Dec. 1, 1964; Walter Herbert to Bolton, Dec. 1, 1964, both in 1294:1, UCPF; Strong memo, Nov. 10, 1964; Kerr phone call to Strong, Oct. 29, 1964; Strong memo, Nov. 22, 1964, all in 3:41, UCBCF; Landon call to Strong, Oct. 30, 1964; Strong to Heyman, Nov. 3, 1964; Alan W. Searcy memo, Nov. 4, 1964, 10 a.m.; Strong memo, Nov. 13, 1964; Lincoln Constance to Strong, Nov. 15, 1964; Kerr phone call to Strong, Nov. 17, 1964, 10 a.m.; Errol W. Mauchlan to Strong, Nov. 17, 1964; Adrian Kragen to Strong, Nov. 17, 1964; Williams to Strong, Nov. 18, 1964, all in 8:90, UCBCF; Kitty Malloy memo, Nov. 8, 1964; John Landon to Williams, Nov. 30, 1964; Cunningham to Strong, Dec. 4, 1964, all in 8:91, UCBCF; Transcript of Regents Informal Session, Nov. 19, 1964; Regents Minutes, Nov. 20, 1964; Strong, "Student Demonstrations and Student Discipline at Berkeley, Fall Semester, 1964" (first draft, Feb. 8, 1965), in "Education Issues," vol. 2, Appendix. For reaction see Carl Schorske to Strong, Nov. 30, 1964, 2:7, FSM Arch.; Henry F. May press conference, Dec. 4, 1964; Henry N. Smith et al., "Independent Faculty Student Legal Fund," Dec. 1964 (broadside); Samuel Silver broadside, Dec. 1964? (ditto), all in FMS.

46. On fellowship see Paul Byer in *HIS, Magazine of Inter-Varsity Christian Fellowship*, June 1965, pp. 1–2; Ginger Johnston, ibid., 16; *Daily Cal.*, Dec. 2, 1964. On faculty see *Grad. Student J.*, Spring 1965, pp. 13–34, 75–91; Geoffrey White in *Spartacist*, May-June 1965, p. 13; Dept. of Anthropology meeting resolves, Dec. 4, 1964, FM.

47. On organizing see Heirich, 270–72, *Berk. Gazette*, Dec. 2, 1964, pp. 1–2; *S.F. Chronicle*, Dec. 2, 1964; Sherriffs memo, Nov. 4, 1964; Strong memo, Nov. 10, 1964; Sherriffs memo, Dec. 1, 1964, 2 p.m.; Strong memo, Dec. 2, 1964, 11:50 a.m., all in 3:41, UCBCF. On the clergy see Elden E. Jacobson, "The Berkeley Crisis: A Case Study of Protestant Campus Ministers" (Ph.D. diss., Yale Univ., 1966); T. Walter Herbert, Jr., statement, Dec. 4, 1964, 2:7, FSM/CSHE; William F. Shepard to Kerr, Nov. 10, 1964 (3 memos); Herbert to Kerr, Nov. 12, 1964, all in Box 1293, UCPF; Strong memo, Nov. 22, 1964, 9:40 a.m., 3:41, UCBCF. On ASUC see Forrest Tregea phone call from several ASUC officers, Dec. 1, 1964, 3:41, UCBCF. On the planning meeting see Officer R. E. Hull, UCB Police Dept. report, Dec. 1, 1964, 1:1, UCBCF.

48. Savio's speech was taped by KPFA radio and issued as part of a record, "Is Freedom Academic?" The excerpt is quoted in Heirich, 271–72. On the religious atmosphere see Michael J. Lawrence letter, *Daily Cal.*, Dec. 7, 1964. On Baez see Ralph J. Gleason in *Ramparts*, Apr. 1965, p. 36.

49. The evidence for these two paragraphs is contradictory and must be considered as a whole. Heirich, 274–75; Rapoport, 82–84; *Berk. Gazette*, Dec. 4, 1964, extra, p. 1; *Daily Cal.*, Apr. 8, 1965; May 4, 1965; May 26, 1965, p. 20; *Oakland Tribune*, May 26, 1965, p. 2; June 18, 1965, p. 4; *S.F. Chronicle*, Apr. 3, 1965; *S.F. Examiner*, Dec. 3, 1964; May 4, 1965, p. 4; *Ramparts*, Oct. 1966, p. 24 (quote); *BCU Bulletin*, Nov. 1964, p. 2; *Despite Everything*, Jan. 1965, p. 4; Calif. Senate Fact-Finding Comm. on Un-American Activities, *Thirteenth Report* (Sacramento, 1965), 101; *Thirteenth Re-*

*port Supplement* (Sacramento, 1966), 9, 17–18, 28–29, 54–55, 66–70; FSU, "The Trial," July 19, 1965 (4pp. broadside; Kerr's annotated copy is in 1293:6, UCPF); Hale Champion, "Communication and Problem-Solving" (1981), interview, 64, 69; May L. B. Davis, "An Appointment Secretary Reminisces," in "The Governor's Office under Edmund G. Brown, Sr." (1981), interview, 30, 31, 33; Frederick G. Dutton, "Democratic Campaigns and Controversies, 1954–1966" (1981), interview, 146; Heller interview, 554; Richard Kline, "Governor Brown's Faithful Advisor," in "Governor's Office," interview, 25–26; Sherriffs interview, 37; Towle interview, 258, 291.18; Kerr statement, Dec. 3, 1964, FSM/H; Strong report to Forbes Comm. of Regents, Feb. 9, 1965, p. 10, 1294:2, UCPF. A less than candid version is in Edmund G. Brown, Sr., *Reagan and Reality* (N.Y., 1970), 141. Key documents are Strong memo, Dec. 2, 1964, 10:10 a.m.; Sherriffs memo, Dec. 2, 1964, 11 a.m., both in 4:42, UCBCF. See also Gov. Brown's phone logs, desk calendars, Box 68, Brown Papers; Fred Jordan memo, ca. Dec. 8, 1964, Box 675, Brown Papers. On Meese see *Berk. Gazette,* May 3, 1965; *Daily Cal.,* May 4, 1965, p. 1; *S.F. Examiner,* May 4, 1965, p. 4; *The Defender: Free Speech Trial Newsletter,* Apr. 18, 1965, pp. 3, 5, 6; Lou Cannon, *Ronnie and Jesse* (Garden City, N.Y., 1969), 301; *S.F. Bay Guardian,* Apr. 4, 1984, p. 9; "This World" section, *S.F. Sunday Examiner-Chronicle,* June 22, 1986, p. 7.

50. Heirich, 275–77; Bettina Aptheker in *FSM,* 16–18; Michael Rossman, "Breakthrough at Berkeley," *Center Magazine,* May 1968, p. 42; Marshall Windmiller in *Liberal Democrat on the Pacific Scene,* Jan. 1965, p. 11; *Berk. Gate,* Dec. 7, 1964, pp. 1–3, 6–7; Dec. 14, 1964, pp. 1–2; *Daily Cal.,* Dec. 4, 7, 9, 1964; *S.F. Chronicle,* Dec. 3, 1964; April 7, 1965; Barbara Goldberg, "Recollections of December 2nd," 5pp., 3:19, FSM Arch.

51. The best account on the police is Joel Pimsleur in *Columbia Daily Spectator,* Dec. 18, 1964 (policeman quoted; no pagination). See also *Berk. Gazette,* Dec. 28, 1964; Charles E. Moore, Jr., in *Police Chief,* Apr. 1965, p. 53; "Some Statements concerning Police Brutality . . . " (ditto); "Advice to Prisoners" (mimeo), both in 1:25, FSM Arch. On bail see Henry N. Smith and Richard Herr memo to faculty, Dec. 3, 1964 (ditto), FMS; *Berk. Gazette,* Dec. 4, 1964, extra, p. 1.

52. (85 percent) Analysis of Sproul Arrestees, 1294:1, UCPF; (nonactivists, nonradicals) Bardach, 32; Katherine L. Jako, *Dimensions of the Berkeley Undergraduate through the Sixties* (Berk., 1971), 39; (liberals) Ann M. Heiss, "Berkeley Doctoral Students Appraise Their Academic Programs" (Center for the Study of Higher Education, UCB, 1964), 12; (family background) Heiss, 7; R. T. Morris and R. J. Murphy, Dept. of Sociology, UCLA, "University of California Student Opinion Survey April 1965" (1965), no pagination; Robert H. Somers, "The Mainsprings of the Rebellion: A Survey of Berkeley Students in November, 1964" (1965), 32; William A. Watts and David Whittaker, "Free Speech Advocates at Berkeley," *Journal of Applied Behavioral Science,* 2 #1 (Jan.-Mar. 1966), 49; (political differences) Somers, 31; (religion) ibid., 34; Watts and Whittaker, 54; (grads) UCB, Academic Senate, *Education at Berkeley* (Berk., 1966), 49 (commonly called the Muscatine report); (college class) Somers, 5; (age) ibid., 30; (certain majors) Muscatine, 24; (Greeks) Somers, 29; (South Campus) Heirich, 210, 212, 350; (grades) Bardach, 32; (intellect) Paul Heist, "Intellect and Commitment: The Faces of Discontent" (Center for the Study of Higher Education, UCB, 1965), Table 3, p. 22a; (psychology) ibid., Table 2, opp. p. 19.

53. (split) Bardach, 15; Morris and Murphy, no pagination; Muscatine, 25; Somers, 5; Watts and Whittaker, 47; (55–38 percent) Edward E. Sampson, Jacob P. Siegel, and Alan N. Schoonmaker, "The FSM and the Berkeley Campus" (Western Psychological

Assn. meeting, June 1965), p. 12; (partisanship) ibid., 13; Somers, 31; (political change) Jako, 23; (religious change) ibid., 20; (disaffection) Watts and Whittaker, 54. See also Somers, 34; (foreign parentage) Morris and Murphy, no pagination.

54. On Strong see Heirich, 470, note 32; 290; Heller interview, 550; David W. Reed to John H. Reynolds, Dec. 6, 1964; Reynolds and others, statement, Dec. 9, 1964 (annotated); Kitty Malloy to file, Dec. 12, 1964; Strong memo, Dec. 20, 1964, all in 4:42, UCBCF; Malloy memo, Dec. 22, 1964, Box 45, Hardin B. Jones Papers, HI. On faculty see Mark Harris, *Twentyone Twice* (Boston, 1966), 125–26; *Berk. Gazette*, Dec. 5, 1964; Norman Jacobson to students, Dec. 3, 1964, 3:19, FSM Arch.

55. On the strike see Bardach, 15, 35; Feuer, *Conflict*, 451; Heirich, 278–79, 285–88, 350; *Berk. Gazette*, Dec. 4, 1964, extra, p. 1; *Despite Everything*, Jan. 1965, pp. 6–7; *Grad. Student J.*, Spring 1965, pp. 22, 25–26; political science TAs meeting, Dec. 2, 1964, leaflet, FSM/H; Sherriffs memo, Dec. 1, 1964, 4:50 p.m.; Akiko (Owen) memo, Dec. 3, 1964, 8:30 a.m.; Malloy memo, Dec. 5, 1964, all in 4:42, UCBCF. For an excellent first-person account see Robert Hurwitt in *Express*, Sept. 28, 1984, pp. 24–25. Faculty alarm is expressed in Henry F. May to the Dept. of History, Nov. 13, 1964, 2:8, FSM Arch. On TAs see *N.Y. Times*, Mar. 21, 1965, p. 83; Muscatine, 175, 177. On GCC see *Daily Cal.*, Dec. 2, 1964; *S.F. Chronicle*, Nov. 11, 1964; Starobin in *Grad. Student J.*, Spring 1965, pp. 17–26; GCC organizational meeting minutes, Dec. 7, 1964, 1:23, FSM Arch. This last source also covers the effect of the strike. See also Nicholas Zvegintsev to Arthur M. Ross, Feb. 27, 1965, 1:23, FSM Arch.

56. Bardach, 9; Harris, 133; Heirich, 291–97; *Berk. Gazette*, Dec. 7, 1964, 2nd extra; *N.Y. Times*, Dec. 8, 1964, p. 1; Ralph J. Gleason column, *S.F. Chronicle*, Dec. 9, 1964; Constance interview, 275–77; Heller interview, 551; Wellman interview, 154; Wilson interview, 224–25, 248; Dept. Chairmen's Proposal, Dec. 6, 1964 (ditto); Kerr address, Greek Theatre, Dec. 7, 1964, both in FSM/H; John H. Rowe to Kerr, Dec. 8, 1964, 2:7, FSM Arch.; Edward S. Rogers to Charles E. Smith, Dec. 12, 1964, 1294:1, UCPF.

57. Bardach, 30–31; Glazer, 21–22; Heirich, 300–15; *Daily Cal.*, Dec. 9–11, 1964; *S.F. Chronicle*, Dec. 10, 1964; Constance interview, 277; Heller interview, 561; McLaughlin interview, 78–79; Wellman interview, 155; Kerr statement, Dec. 8, 1964; Herbert McClosky statement, Dec. 8, 1964, both in FSM/H; David Pesonen to Savio, Dec. 8, 1964, 2:19, FSM Arch.; Kerr to Sidney Hook, Mar. 9, 1965, 1293:6, UCPF.

58. Heirich, 117, 319–21; Miller in *Frontier*, 17–18; *S.F. Chronicle*, Dec. 20, 1964, p. 16; Heller interview, 542, 544, 547–48, 555–56; Transcript of Meeting of Regents and Emergency Executive Comm. of the Berk. Division, Academic Senate, chaired by Prof. Arthur Ross, Dec. 17, 1964; Portion of Transcript of Regents Informal Session, Oct. 15, 1964; Transcript of Regents Informal Session, Nov. 19, 1964. See Gov. Brown phone logs, calendars, Box 68; Ron Moscowitz to Brown, Dec. 16, 1964, Box 724; Moscowitz to Brown, Dec. 31, 1964, Box 675, all in Brown Papers. Cunningham to Sherriffs, Sept. 21, 1964, in Sherriffs interview, 26a–26c; see also p. 43; Cunningham to Strong, Oct. 19, 1964, 1293:13, UCPF; Alan W. Searcy memo, Dec. 14, 1964; Malloy memo, Dec. 16, 1964, both in 4:42, UCBCF; Strong notes on Regents meeting, Dec. 18, 1964, 8:91, UCBCF; unidentified phone call, Dec. 15, 1964, phone logs, 1:13, FSM Arch.

59. Heirich, 321; *Berk. Gazette*, Jan. 7, 1965; Kerr in *L.A. Times*, Jan. 8, 1965; Adrian Kragen in Alumni Council tentative minutes, Jan. 16, 1965; Strong to Richard Erickson, Feb. 18, 1965, both in 3:4, FSM Arch.; Strong report to Forbes Comm. of

the Regents, Feb. 9, 1965, 1294:2, UCPF; *Oakland Tribune*, Mar. 12, 1965; *Berk. Gazette*, Mar. 12, 1965; *L.A. Times*, Mar. 13, 1965; *N.Y. Times*, Mar. 13, 1965; *S.F. Chronicle*, Mar. 13, 1965; "This World," Mar. 21, 1965, p. 3; *S.F. News-Call-Bulletin*, Mar. 12, 15, 1965; Ruth A. Hart, "Concern for the Individual: The Community YWCA and Other Berkeley Organizations" (1978), interview, 224; Constance interview, 278; Wellman interview, 156. For Strong's speech see *Berk. Gazette*, Sept. 11, 1965 (quote); *S.F. Chronicle*, Sept. 11, 1965, p. 2.

60. Heirich, 321–22, 381; *Berk. Gazette*, May 7, 1965, p. 1; *L.A. Times*, Apr. 19, 1965 (quotes); *S.F. Chronicle*, Jan. 4, 1965; Feb. 19, 1965; "This World," Mar. 21, 1965, p. 3; Elinor Langer in *Science*, Apr. 16, 1965, pp. 346–48; Constance interview, 281, 283–84; Heller interview, 558–60; McLaughlin interview, 63; Wellman interview, 132; Meyerson statement, Jan. 3, 1965, Towle Papers; Meyerson in Alumni Council tentative minutes, Jan. 16, 1965, 3:4, FSM Arch.; Meyerson statement to Regents, Mar. 13, 1965; Ron Moscowitz to Gov. Brown, July 6, 1965, both in Box 803, Brown Papers; Gov. Brown to Laurence J. Kennedy, Jr., Mar. 30, 1965, 10:108, UCBCF; Edwin A. Pauley to Edward W. Carter, June 22, 1965, Box 40, Jones Papers, HI.

61. In general see Heirich, 377–78, 381; Heller interview, 565–71. On the Meyer Comm. see Univ. of Calif. Regents, Special Comm. to Review Univ. Policies, *Report* (Berk., 1965). This was rebutted by William Kornhauser et al., "Campus Autonomy and the Regents: A Reply to the Meyer Report" (1965), 4pp.; William Kornhauser et al., "Critique of the Meyer Committee Regulations" (1965), 8pp. Theodore Meyer to Brown, Apr. 6, 1965; Ron Moscowitz to Tom Hickey, Apr. 12, 1965; Moscowitz to Winslow Christian, Apr. 27, 1965; Laurence J. Kennedy, Jr., to Regents, May 18, 1965, all in Box 803, Brown Papers. The text of the Byrne Report was leaked to the *L.A. Times*, May 12, 1965. *Daily Cal.*, Feb. 10, 11, 1965; May 14, 1965; *L.A. Times*, May 14, 1965, Pt. I, p. 3; *S.F. Chronicle*, May 22, 1965, p. 10; Philip L. Boyd to William E. Forbes, Apr. 26, 1965; Jerry Byrne to Brown, May 7, 1965; reply, May 10, 1965, all in Box 803, Brown Papers. On Kerr's decentralization see *Berk. Gazette*, June 18, 1965; *Daily Cal.*, May 14, 1965; *Oakland Tribune*, June 18, 1965, p. 1; *S.F. Chronicle*, May 22, 1965, p. 10; June 19, 1965, p. 1. On the appointment of Roger Heyns as chancellor see Chapter Three, note 45.

62. The key document is "The Van Loucks Deposition with a Key to the Numbers in the Whinnery Report" (mimeo), 4pp., FSM/H. Heirich, 356–61; *Berk. Gazette*, Mar. 6, 1965; May 21, 1965, p. 6; *Daily Cal.*, Mar. 4, 5, 11, 1965; *S.F. Chronicle*, Mar. 5, 1965; May 20, 1965; UCB Chancellor, Ad Hoc Comm. on Student Conduct, "Report and Recommendations" (1965), 11. (Commonly called the Whinnery report.) Towle interview, 255–57; "DW" memo, Mar. 4, 1965, 2:45 p.m., 4:58, UCBCF. On Klein see *Berk. Gazette*, Mar. 10, 1965; June 23, 1965; *SPIDER*, Mar. 15, 1965, p. 22; Whinnery report, 9–10.

63. Excerpts from rally, Mar. 3, 1965, in UCB Police Lt. M. F. Chandler report, Mar. 5, 1965, 4:58, UCBCF; Dean Johnson rally report to Kerr, Mar. 3, 1965; "Events in Connection with the Obscenity Issue," both in 1294:2, UCPF; *Daily Cal.*, Mar. 5, 1965; Michael Kogan and Paula Katz letter, ibid., Apr. 26, 1965; *L.A. Times*, Apr. 22, 1965, Pt. I, p. 11. FSM phone logs, Dec. 16, 1964, 1:13, FSM Arch. Goldberg elaborated in *Issue*, Spring 1965, p. 32; *SPIDER*, Mar. 3, 1965, p. 22. See also Heirich, 361.

64. Opposition was noted in *Daily Cal.*, Apr. 23, 1965; the 80 percent is from Morris and Murphy, no pagination. The analogy with Bruce was made by the attorney Alexander Hoffman in testimony before the Whinnery Comm. See Whinnery report,

6; John Cohen, ed., *The Essential Lenny Bruce* (N.Y., 1967). For the debate inside the FSM see Heirich, 362–63; David Lauer in *Berk. Gazette*, Mar. 10, 1965; FSM SC meeting, Mar. 9, 1965, 1:19, FSM Arch.; Neil Smelser to file, Mar. 12, 1965, 1:1; UCBCF. On Savio see Heirich, 375; *Berk. Gazette*, Mar. 11, 1965; Apr. 26, 1965; *Daily Cal.*, Apr. 28, 1965; *S.F. Chronicle*, Apr. 27, 1965.

65. Heirich, 363–67; Langer, 346–48; *Berk. Gazette*, Mar. 10, 11, 26, 1965; *N.Y. Times*, Mar. 11, 14, 1965; *S.F. Chronicle*, Mar. 10, 1965; Mar. 11, 1965, p. 13; Mar. 13, 14, 1965; *S.F. Examiner*, Mar. 15, 1965; *S.F. News-Call-Bulletin*, Mar. 15, 1965; *Tocsin*, Mar. 18, 1965, p. 1; *Fortune*, Oct. 1965, p. 142. Savio's quote is in Johnson rally report to Kerr, Mar. 11, 1965, 1294:2, UCPF. Heller interview, 586–87; author's conversation with Seymour M. Lipset; Constance interview, 283; Wellman interview, 132; Hugh Burns press conference, Mar. 11, 1965, 3:20, FSM Arch.; Don Mulford press releases, Mar. 12, 17, 1965, IGSL; Moscowitz to Brown, Mar. 2, 1965; Meyerson statement to Regents, Mar. 13, 1965; Arthur M. Ross to Brown, Mar. 13, 15, 1965; Kerr to Brown, Mar. 23, 1965, all in Box 803, Brown Papers; Hardin B. Jones memo, ca. 1965, Box 1, John H. Lawrence Papers, HI; Emergency Executive Comm. to Academic Senate, Mar. 10, 1965, FM; FSM SC, "Statement of the FSM SC and the GCC Executive Committee," Mar. 10, 1965 (broadside), FSM/H; "The Big Lie," Mar. 11, 1965 (broadside), UC/H; FSM phone logs, Mar. 10, 1965, 1:11 FSM Arch.

66. In general see Heirich, 358, 368 (Savio quoted at 371–72); "Free Speech in Jeopardy," Mar. 22, 1965 (2-sided broadside), UC/H. On *SPIDER* see *Berk. Gazette*, Mar. 19, 24, 26, 1965; Apr. 9, 1965, p. 9; Apr. 20, 1965; *Daily Cal.*, Mar. 19, 22–24, 1965; *S.F. Chronicle*, Mar. 19, 20, 23, 24, 1965; Apr. 1, 1965; *Esquire*, Sept. 1965, pp. 90–91. A biographical sketch of the *SPIDER* editor Steve DeCanio is in *Oklahoma City Times*, Mar. 26, 1965. See also Hunter S. Thompson in *The Nation*, Sept. 27, 1965, pp. 156–57. An early advertisement for *SPIDER* is in *SLATE Newsletter*, undated but prior to Mar. 1, 1965, 2:52, FSM Arch. Meyerson to faculty and students, Mar. 22, 31, 1965, both in FM; "Position on SPIDER and Obscenity," ca. Mar. 1965 (broadside); report on noon rally, Mar. 19, 1965 (broadside); William J. Bouwsma to Meyerson, Mar. 23, 1965; "Shame," Mar. 24, 1965 (broadside), all in FSM/H; Meyerson to Kerr, Mar. 19, 1965; Meyerson staff meeting memo, Mar. 24, 1965, both in 7:83, UCBCF; Dean Johnson rally reports to Kerr, Mar. 19, 24, 1965; Kerr to Regents, Mar. 22, 1965; Bolton to Kerr, Mar. 22, 1965, all in 1294:2, UCPF. For the play see (Richard Schmorleitz,) *For Unlawful Carnal Knowledge, a Play* (Berk.?, 1965?); *Daily Cal.*, Mar. 11, 1965; Johnson report to Kerr, Mar. 16, 1965, 1294:2, UCPF; Meyerson to Schmorleitz, Mar. 19, 1965, 2:2, FSM Arch.

67. Key documents are the Whinnery report and the transcript of its hearings entitled "Proceedings of the Ad Hoc Committee on Student Conduct," Apr. 15, 1965, 11:132, UCBCF. See also *Berk. Gazette*, Mar. 27, 1965; Apr. 10, 1965; Sept. 11, 1965, p. 2; Sept. 21, 1965, p. 1; *Daily Cal.*, Mar. 18, 1965; Aprl. 1, 7–9, 28, 1965; Sept. 15, 1965, p. 1; *S.F. Chronicle*, Mar. 16, 17, 1965; Apr. 3, 9, 20, 22, 1965; Dean Arleigh Williams to Faculty Comm. on Student Political Activity, Mar. 18, 1965, 2:5, FSM Arch.; Cunningham to Meyerson, Mar. 15, 1965; Thomas Parkinson to John R. Whinnery, Mar. 16, 1965; Kerr to Meyerson, Apr. 27, 1965, all in 4:58, UCBCF. For biographical sketches see "Due Process," brochure, 2:52, FSM Arch. For support of Whinnery see Scott Freber letter, *Daily Cal.*, Apr. 26, 1965. On hearing officers see Emergency Executive Comm. to Meyerson, Apr. 20, 1965, FM; *S.F. Chronicle*, Apr. 23, 1965; Sept. 11, 1965, p. 2. On Nicholas Zvegintzov see untitled broadside, May 1965? (mimeo), FMS. On rising litigiousness see Towle interview, 267; Thomas J.

Cunningham, "Legal Aspects of Campus Unrest" (1965), 11–14; Thomas J. Cunningham, "Some Comments on Campus Unrest and the Role of the University Attorney," speech, June 1968, in an Appendix to his "Southern California Campaign Chairman for Earl Warren, 1946" (1976), interview, esp. 4–13. The four students sued the Regents with ACLU help. *Berk. Gazette*, Aug. 31, 1965, p. 1; *Daily Cal.*, Oct. 8, 1965, pp. 1, 14; *S.F. Chronicle*, Sept. 1, 1965, p. 7. The suit failed. *Goldberg* v. *Regents* (1967), 248 Cal. App. 2nd 867; 57 Cal. Reptr. 463. Obscenity trial results are in *Berk. Gazette*, Apr. 20, 22, 1965; May 12, 1965; June 8, 1965; July 31, 1965; *Daily Cal.*, May 11, 1965; *L.A. Times*, June 9, 1965, Pt. I, p. B; *S.F. Chronicle*, Apr. 21, 1965 p. 2.

68. Burnstein brief; Brown's views are in *L.A. Herald-Express*, Dec. 3, 1964; UCLA *Daily Bruin*, Dec. 4, 1964; *Oakland Tribune*, Dec. 4, 1964. Rossman, *New Age*, 46–47; *Berk. Gazette*, June 3, 5, 1965; *The Defender: Free Speech Trial Newsletter*, Apr. 18, 1965, p. 4; FSU, "The Trial," July 19, 1965 (4pp. broadside), UC/H; Bolton to Kerr, Jan. 13, 1965; Neil Smelser to Meyerson, Jan. 19, 1965, both in 1294:2, UCPF; Kitty Malloy memo, Feb. 16, 1965; Meyerson memo, Feb. 16, 1965, both in 7:80, UCBCF.

69. On Burnstein see *The Defender*, Apr. 18, 1965, p. 3. On Treuhaft see Jessica Mitford, *A Fine Old Conflict* (N.Y., 1977). His arrest is in *Berk. Gazette*, Dec. 4, 1964. Meese's role is in *S.F. Bay Guardian*, Apr. 4, 1984, p. 9. On the political nature of the trial see FSU, "The Trial," July 19, 1965 (4pp. broadside), UC/H; Barbara Garson notes, 1:30, FSM Arch.; Savio in *Berk. Gazette*, July 30, 1965, p. 2. On the single jury trial see Burnstein brief, 3. The defense strategy is in Burnstein to "Defendant," ca. Jan. 1, 1965; Jan. 10, 20, 1965, all in 1294:11, UCPF. The letters are less interesting than the fact that they appeared in Kerr's files. The particular photocopying process suggests that these copies came from the prosecutor, who seems to have had a spy among the defendants. See also Smelser to Meyerson, Jan. 18, 1965, 7:80, UCBCF.

70. On the trial see *Berk. Gazette*, May 13, 14, 20, 25, 26, 1965; June 2, 11, 1965; *Daily Cal.*, Apr. 22, 1965; *L.A. Times*, May 26, 1965 Pt. I, p. 12; *S.F. Chronicle*, Apr. 3, 7, 1965; May 20, 1965, p. 5; *S.F. Examiner*, May 4, 1965, p. 4; *The Defender*, May 23, 30, 1965 (pamphlets), both in FSM/H. On Brown see Henry M. Elson to Edsel W. Haws, Apr. 28, 1965, 1294:3, UCPF. Kerr's chair is in *Berk. Gazette*, May 26, 1965; Goldberg's quote is in *L.A. Times*, May 26, 1965, Pt. I, p. 12. On Treuhaft see *Oakland Tribune*, Oct. 8, 1965, p. 18. Student records are in Davis, 13; *Daily Cal.*, Feb. 16, 1965; Kerr to Strong, Dec. 30, 1964, 1294:4, UCPF. The room denial is in *Despite Everything*, Jan 1965, p. 11; *S.F. Chronicle*, Dec. 14, 1964. On policy see Regents Comm. Meeting Executive Session Minutes, Jan. 22, 1965; Towle interview, 263–66. For faculty views see Terry J. Lunsford, "The 'Free Speech' Crisis at Berkeley, 1964–1965: Some Issues for Social and Legal Research" (Center for Research and Development in Higher Education, UCB, 1965), 10; "FSM Defense," Feb. 9, 1965 (broadside); "On Dec 2nd They Were in Sproul Hall . . . ," Feb. 11, 1965, both in UC/H; Anthropology Dept. meeting resolves, Dec. 4, 1964, FM. For an opposing view see Don Mulford press release, Jan 25, 1965, 4:2, Mulford Papers, HI. On Jackie Goldberg see *Berk. Gazette*, Aug. 4, 1965, p. 1; Kerr to Earl Cheit, Aug 17, 1965, 1293:6, UCPF.

71. The data are in Burnstein brief, 193, 287–326. Defendant reactions are in Barbara Garson notes on trial, 1:30, FSM Arch.; Jerry Goldstein, ASUC president, press conference, July 21, 1965, 3:19, FSM Arch.; defense counsels' statement, July 19, 1965; David Noble, "Affidavit," July 31, 1965, both in 2:8, FSM/CSHE. Savio is quoted

in *L.A. Times*, July 27, 1965, Pt. I, p. 3. Support for Crittenden is in Don Mulford press release, Aug. 9, 1965. The trial is best followed in the press. *Berk. Gazette*, Apr. 26, 1965; June 28–30, 1965; July 3, 1965; (Michael Duke) July 19, 1965; July 28, 29, 1965; Aug. 2, 3, 1965; Aug. 4, 1965, p. 1; Aug. 5, 1965, p. 1; Aug. 13, 1965, p. 1; Aug. 30, 1965, p. 9; *Daily Cal.*, May 11, 1965; *L.A. Times*, July 20, 1965, Pt. I, p. 3; July 21, 1965, Pt. I, p. 3; July 27, 1965, Pt. I, p. 3; July 30, 1965, Pt. I, p. 3; Aug. 5, 1965; Aug. 14, 1965, Pt. I, p. 5; *N.Y. Times*, Aug. 6, 1965, p. 28; *Oakland Tribune*, Oct. 2, 1965, p. 2; *S.F. Chronicle*, July 20, 22, 1965; Aug. 4, 1965, pp. 6, ($10 fine normal) 40; Aug. 5, 1965, p. 4; Aug. 6, 1965, p. 4. On the appeal see FSM Defense Fund, "Dear Professor," Aug. 10, 1965, 2:8, FSM/CSHE; *Daily Cal.*, June 22, 1967.

72. *S.F. Chronicle*, July 30, 1965, p. 2. Another version is in Dean Johnson rally report, July 29, 1965, 1294:3, UCPF. Hamilton is quoted in *Berk. Gazette*, July 29, 1965. For the attack on Parkinson see Josephine Miles to Kerr, Jan. 20, 1961, Miles Papers.

73. *Daily Cal.*, Dec. 9, 1964; Feb. 15, 1965; *N.Y. Times*, Mar. 29, 1965; anon. essay quoted at 3, 2:49, FSM Arch.; Meyerson quoted in Alumni Council tentative minutes, Jan. 16, 1965, p. 11. On counseling see Trombley, 24; *Daily Cal.*, Dec. 17, 1964; *S.F. Chronicle*, May 17, 1965, p. 1. See also James L. Jarrett, "College Students—The New Breed," *Saturday Review*, Mar. 20, 1965; U.S. National Student Assn. resolution condemning *in loco parentis*, 18th National Student Congress, 1965, 3:21, FSM Arch.

74. On Kaufman see Bob Kaufman, *Selected Writings* (L.A., 1980); Kitty Malloy memo of staff meeting, Apr. 23, 1965, 8:91, UCBCF. On CCC see GCC draft statement, Spring 1965, 1:24, FSM Arch. Intimidation is in *Daily Cal.*, Dec. 2, 1964. On AFT see Robert Richheimer to Henry F. May (draft), Jan. 6, 1965, 1:24, FSM Arch.; History TAs in Local 1570 requests, Jan. 1965; History TAs report, Jan. 6, 1965; Mike Shute, "Statement"; Hand, Starobin, and Miller, "Union Election" statement; membership by dept., Feb. 12, 1965; "Preliminary Report of the Special Comm. on Health Insurance to the Council of Delegates, Local 1570, AFT," all in 1:14, FSM/CSHE; Local 1570, AFT, Executive Comm., open letter, Spring 1965; Local 1570, AFT, *Newsletter*, Mar. 25, 1965; June 14, 1965, all in 1:24, FSM Arch. See also Edward P. Morgan News, ABC Radio transcript, June 24, 1965, 2:46, FSM Arch.

75. Heirich, 375–76; *Daily Cal.*, May 5, 1965; Heller interview, 557. On membership see *Berk. Gazette*, Apr. 29, 1965; May 20, 1965; Aug. 5, 1965, p. 1. On Brown's puzzlement see ibid., May 4, 1965; Sept. 7, 1965, p. 9. On Mulford's suspicions see his press release, May 17, 1965. The idea is in "FSM Newsletter," Nov. 17, 1964, p. 4; FSM, "We Want a University" (before Jan. 4, 1965), 10, both in UC/H; FSU, *Bulletin Number One* (Berk., ca. 1965); FSU, *Bulletin Number Two* (Berk., 1965); Margaret Klein phone call, Feb. 1, 1965, phone logs, 1:11, FSM Arch.; FSU, "Union Cards on the Table," May 4, 1965, 1294:9, UCPF; "Western Union Telegram," May 14, 1965 or later (mimeo), 1:29, FSM Arch.; (FSU dormant) Margaret Cheney to Kerr, June 28, 1965, 1293:6, UCPF; "FSU Orientation," fall 1965 (mimeo), 1:29, FSM Arch.; David C. Fulton rally report to Kerr, Apr. 28, 1965; Edward Carter wire to FSU, May 18, 1965, both in 1294:3, UCPF.

76. Brad Cleaveland quoted in *Daily Cal.*, Apr. 8, 1965; Brad Cleaveland, "The Greatest Need in the U.S.A." (ca. 1965), 2:52, FSM Arch.; Michael Rossman, *On Learning and Social Change* (N.Y., 1972), esp. 25–28, 71–72, 96–102; Eric Levine, "Berkeley Free Speech Controversy" (1965), 22; student quoted in "Some Organizing Ideas" (mimeo), 2, 1:1a, FSM Arch. *DuBois Clubs-Newsletter*, misdated Jan. 1, 1964,

handed out Feb. 5, 1965, 2:52, FSM Arch. Survey data are in Heiss, 39; Muscatine report, 11, 12; Somers, 7, 11. On the experimental college see Heirich, 396; Joseph Tussman, *Experiment at Berkeley* (N.Y., 1969), *Daily Cal.*, Apr. 8, 1965; N.Y. *Times*, Mar. 21, 1965, p. 8E. See also Martin Trow in *American Behavioral Scientist*, May-June 1968, pp. 43–48.

77. Rossman, *On Learning*, esp. 102–9. FUB originated in the Dec. 1964 strike. Robert Starobin in *Grad. Student J.*, Spring 1965, p. 22; David Fulton to Kerr, Feb. 17, 1965; Dean Johnson notes on rally, Jan. 4, 1965; Johnson report to Fulton, ca. Feb. 1, 1965, all in 1294:2, UCPF. FUB history can be traced in its catalogs, 1966–70. For the flavor see *Steps: Journal of the FUB*. A short history is in FUB, *Catalog*, Fall 1968, pp. 15–16.

78. Savio quotes are from *Issue*, Spring 1965, p. 28; N.Y. *Herald-Tribune*, Dec. 9, 1964. See Savio in *Humanity*, Dec. 1964, pp. 1, 4; Rossman, *New Age*, 61–66. See also Charles Denton column, *S.F. Examiner*, Dec. 3, 1964; Wendy-Jo Wondsell in *L.A. Times*, Apr. 18, 1965, Sec. A. p. 15; Mrs. J. Sentovich to Gov. Brown, n.d., 2:30, FSM Arch.; Jonathan Rodgers in "Barrington Bull," Dec. 1964 (mimeo), 3:19, FSM Arch.

79. On generations see Feuer, *Conflict*; Ralph J. Gleason column, *S.F. Chronicle*, Dec. 9, 1964, p. 49. See also *Issue*, Spring 1965, p. 38. This explanation is attacked by Robert Kaufman and Michael Folsom in *FSM*, 32. In general see Mark Gerzon, *The Whole World Is Watching* (N.Y., 1970; orig. 1969); Kenneth Keniston, *Young Radicals* (N.Y., 1968); Michael W. Miles, *The Radical Probe* (N.Y., 1973). On student revolt globally see Marjorie Hope, *Youth against the World* (Boston, 1970); Stephen Spender, *The Year of the Young Rebels* (N.Y., 1969; orig. 1968). On Berlin see German Subject Coll., HI. On the U.S.: (Harvard) Lawrence E. Eichel et al., *The Harvard Strike* (Boston, 1970); Steven Kelman, *Push Comes to Shove* (Boston, 1970); (UC, San Diego) William J. McGill, *The Year of the Monkey* (N.Y., 1982); (Columbia) Jerry L. Avorn, *Up against the Ivy Wall* (N.Y., 1969); James S. Kunen, *The Strawberry Statement* (N.Y., 1970; orig. 1969); Dotson Rader, *I Ain't Marchin' Anymore* (N.Y., 1969); The Cox Commission, *Crisis at Columbia* (N.Y., 1968); Spender, 1–35; (S.F. State) William Barlow and Peter Shapiro, *An End to Silence* (N.Y., 1971); Harris, *Twentyone*.

80. May, esp. 388–89; Miles interview, 103–5; Rossman in *Center Magazine*, May 1968, pp. 40–49. See also Rossman, *New Age*, 46; Harris, 134; N.Y.-*Times*, July 7, 1968, p. 42; Henry Nash Smith to Leo Marx, Dec. 22, 1964, 3:4, Smith Papers; Smith to John William Ward, Dec. 28, 1964, 5:10, Smith Papers.

# Chapter 2.

(epigraph) Black Panther Party, *Bulletin No. 1* (1968).

1. On porters see William B. Rumford in Walter Gordon, "Athlete, Officer in Law Enforcement and Administration . . . " (1979–80), interview, 1:175–76; Roy F. Nichols in *Berk. Gazette*, Oct. 18, 1963, p. 3. On Gibson see Allen Broussard's foreword, Lawrence P. Crouchett, *William Byron Rumford* (El Cerrito, Calif., 1984), xiii; Evilio Grillo in Harriet Nathan and Stanley Scott, eds., *Experiment and Change in Berkeley* (Berk., 1978), 1–7; Vivian O. Marsh, ibid., 29, 32; Frances M. Albrier, "Determined Advocate for Racial Equality" (1979), interview, 175, 193; Roger Kent, "Building the Democratic Party in California, 1954–1966" (1981), interview, 105; William B. Rumford, "Legislator for Fair Employment, Fair Housing, and Public Health" (1973), interview, 24. On Dellums see C. L. Dellums, "International President of the Brother-

hood of Sleeping Car Porters and Civil Rights Leader" (1973), interview, 8–9, 57.

2. Albrier interview, xiv, 61–62, 95–96; Rumford interview, xi, 2, 5, 7–8, 12, 15; Crouchett, *Rumford*. For other examples see Tarea H. Pittman, "NAACP Official and Civil Rights Worker" (1974), interview, 21–22; Gordon interview, 1:95, 2:vii, 45; Minnie Ruth in Gordon interview, 1:359; Redmond C. Staats, Jr., ibid., 1:388.

3. Albrier interview, 95–96, 252; A. Wayne Amerson, "Northern California and Its Challenge to a Negro in the Mid-1900s" (1974), interview, 19; Dellums interview, 70; Harry Kingman in Gordon interview, 1:152; William B. Rumford in Nathan and Scott, 18 (quote); Rumford interview, 19; Crouchett, *Rumford*, 60.

4. Albrier interview, 134, 139; Amerson interview, viii, 29, 36, 41. On the newcomers see *Bayviewer*, Feb. 1969, p. 6; John C. Leggett, *Race, Class, and Political Consciousness* (Cambridge, Mass., 1972), 37; Bernice H. May, "A Native Daughter's Leadership in Public Affairs" (1976), interview, 10; Rumford interview, 21–22; Al Sweetwyne in Gordon interview, 1:146. See also Pauli Murray, *Song in a Weary Throat* (N.Y., 1987), 258–60.

5. Claude B. Hutchison, "The College of Agriculture, University of California, 1922–1952" (1961), interview, 515–16; Albrier interview, 216–17.

6. Rumford in Nathan and Scott, 9, 12; Rumford interview, 28–31, 54; see 5:17, William B. Rumford Papers. In general see *Berk. Review*, Oct. 8, 1960, p. 5; Albrier interview, 176; Frederick G. Dutton, "Democratic Campaigns and Controversies, 1954–1966" (1981), interview, 60, 92; Ruth A. Hart, "Concern for the Individual: The Community YWCA and Other Berkeley Organizations" (1978), interview, 165–67; R. Kent interview, 101; May interview, 281.

7. Republican control is noted by T. J. Kent, Jr., in Arthur Harris et al., *Bernice Hubbard May* (Berk., 1971), 18, 22. On liberals see ibid., 13–17; T. J. Kent, Jr., in Nathan and Scott, 79–82, 85; Joseph P. Lyford, *The Berkeley Archipelago* (Chicago, 1982), 18; Hart interview, 154–61, 191, 279–81; Hutchison interview, 501.

8. Hutchison interview, 468; *Berk. Review*, Dec. 3, 1959, p. 7 (quote); Hart interview, 134; *Berk. Gazette*, Sept. 20, 1963, p. 1; Sept. 23, 1963, pp. 1 (quote), 2; Sept. 24, 1963, pp. 1, 2; Oct. 4, 1963, p. 16; Oct. 17, 1963, p. 1. On the blackamoor see ibid., May 25, 1965.

9. T. J. Kent, Jr., in Harris, *May*, 13–17; Nichols in Nathan and Scott, 20–21; Albrier interview, 198–99; May interview, 1–3, 9, 174–75, 250; Pittman interview, 127.

10. May interview, 7 (quote), 189–90, 202, 217. On the initiative see 1:19–20, Geoffrey White Papers, HI. On Harris see *Berk. Review*, July 13, 1961, pp. 4–5. On Nichols see *Berk. Gazette*, Oct. 11, 1963, p. 1; Oct. 25, 1963, p. 1; Oct. 1, 1964, p. 5; *Berk. Review*, Mar. 23, 1961, pp. 10–12; Hart interview, 149–53 (quote at 149).

11. CRF, "An Analysis of the Factors Concerning the Fair Housing Ordinance Vote and City Elections in Berkeley, California, April 2nd, 1963" (1963), 10, 12; CRF, "An Analysis of the Results of the Fair Housing Election in Berkeley, California Held April 2, 1963" (1963), 44; T. J. Kent, Jr., in Harris, *May*, 18–25; Lyford, *Berkeley*, 19; Kent in Nathan and Scott, 78; Hutchison interview, 480; May interview, 188, 228, 230.

12. On Sweeney see *Berk. Review*, Oct. 5, 1961, p. 7; Sweeney in Nathan and Scott, 254 (quote); May interview, 10; Sweeney campaign literature, 1961, IGSL. On the candidates see *Berk. Gazette*, Mar. 1, 1961, p. 1; Mar. 2, 1961, p. 15; Mar. 11, 1961, p. 7; Mar. 24, 1961, p. 1; Mar. 29, 1961, p. 1; Apr. 3, 1961, p. 1; Apr. 5, 1961, p. 1. The liberal program is in T. J. Kent, Jr., "A Program for Berkeley, 1961," in Nathan and Scott, unpub. Kent Appendix B, IGSL. See also Kent misc. campaign

materials, 1961, IGSL. Election analysis is in *Berk. Review*, Apr. 6, 1961, pp. 1, 5.

13. Berk., Mayor's Comm. on Children and Youth, "Report" (1959), esp. 2. On pathology see Council of Social Planning-Berk. Area, "Phase II—Multi-Problem Families" (1962). Berk., "The First Fifty Years of the Community Welfare Commission" (1959), esp. 37; Berk. City Council, "Berkeley's Workable Program for Urban Renewal" (1961).

14. Amerson interview, 29; Progressive Missionary Baptist Church, *Thirtieth Anniversary, 1935–1965* (Oakland, 1965), 2; Kent in Harris, *May*, 34; Dutton interview, 17. On Codornices see Berk., "First Fifty Years," 40–44; Rumford interview, 54–55; Rumford press release, Mar. 22, 1954, 9:2, Rumford Papers.

15. Lois Heyman, "The Estimation of Need for Low Cost Housing in Berkeley" (M.B.A. report, UCB, 1966), 39–41; homeowners in Walsh (Stuart) and Associates, *The Future of Downtown Berkeley* (S.F., 1962), 23; *BCU Bulletin*, Mar. 1966, p. 2; Berk., Office of Social Planning Coordinator, "A Profile of Population Changes and Mobility in Berkeley, California, 1950–1960" (1963), 4.

16. Berk. Law Students Democratic Club, Comm. on Discrimination in Housing, "Survey of East Bay Realtors" (1961); Berk., Community Welfare Commission, "Report of the Citizens' Committee to Study Discrimination in Housing in Berkeley" (1962), 23, 26, 28–33 (chaired by Henry Poppic, and commonly called the Poppic report); BUSD, "Co-Sponsored Workshop on Interracial Gains and Goals" (1961), 24–25; *Berk. Review*, Jan. 4, 1962, pp. 5, 9; May interview, 269. See also League for Decency in Real Estate, brochure, ca. 1962, 2:7, Rumford Papers; Western Regional CORE, *Newsletter*, Apr.?, 1963, p. 1; May 1, 1963, p. 1, both in 2:13 CORE/WRO; Western Regional CORE, "Statement on Discrimination in Housing in the State of California," Apr. 1963 (mimeo), 6:4, CORE/WRO.

17. Poppic report, 3, 19; David L. Cutter in Cutter Laboratories, "Cutter Laboratories, 1897–1972: A Dual Trust" (1975), interview, 2:250–51; May interview, 270–71. The best press coverage is by J. L. Pimsleur in "This World," *S.F. Chronicle*, Mar. 17, 1963, p. 4. See also *Berk. Gate*, July 12, 1966, p. 1.

18. Kent in Harris, *May*, 25–27; May interview, 210; *BCU Bulletin*, June 1965, p. 1; July 1965, p. 1; Jan. 1966, p. 1; Thomas W. Casstevens, *Politics, Housing and Race Relations* (Berk., 1965), 8. See also Catherine B. Wurster to Paul Ylvisaker, Mar. 8, 1963, 8:2, Wurster Papers.

19. Casstevens, 56–58; May interview, 273, 287.

20. CRF, "Factors," 16–17; Wallace J. S. Johnson, *Responsible Individualism* (N.Y., 1967), 30–31; May interview, 264, 267 (quote), 285.

21. In addition to Pimsleur's article see *S.F. News-Call-Bulletin*, Feb. 21, 1963, p. 25; *Berk. Gazette*, Mar. 5, 1963, p. 1; Mar. 7, 1963, pp. 1, 2; Mar. 8, 1963, p. 11; Mar. 19, 1963, p. 8; Mar. 20, 1963, p. 1; Mar. 21, 1963, pp. 1, 2; Mar. 25, 1963, p. 9; Mar. 26, 1963, pp. 1, 14; Mar. 27, 1963, pp. 1, 27; Mar. 29, 1963, p. 1; Apr. 1, 1963, pp. 1, 3; Apr. 4, 1963, p. 13; Comm. for Fair Housing, Appeal for Funds, Spring 1963, 2:13, Rumford Papers; Fred Stripp campaign literature, 1963, 5:2, Wurster Papers; Western Regional Office to Calif. CORE contacts, Mar. 6, 1963, 1:1, CORE/WRO; Amerson interview, 78; May interview, 265; Kent in Harris, *May*, 27; Wallace J. S. Johnson, *A Fresh Look at Patriotism* (Old Greenwich, Conn., 1976), 68, 71; Casstevens, 1–2, 60–62, 73, 77. See also CRF, "Factors."

22. *Berk. Gazette*, Apr. 3, 1963, pp. 1, 2, 4; CRF, "Fair Housing. A Post-Election Survey in Berkeley, California, April 2, 1963" (1963), 6, 8, 32–34, 37, 43–44; Cas-

stevens, 1, 63, 66, 81. For other analyses see Leggett, esp. 78–82; Leonard A. Marascuilo, "Attitudes toward De Facto Segregation in a Northern City" (ERIC research report, UCB, 1967), 44; anon. paper, "1963 Berkeley City Election Results," 2:9, Rumford Papers.

23. Albrier interview, 203; May interview, 190–91, 287; CRF, "Fair Housing," 31; Jim Dempsey column, Berk. Gazette, Apr. 1, 1963, p. 15; Oct. 1, 1963, p. 1.

24. On the legislative process see Amerson interview, 81; Donald L. Bradley, "Managing Democratic Campaigns, 1943–1966" (1982), interview, 174–75; Richard Kline, "Governor Brown's Faithful Advisor," in "The Governor's Office under Edmund G. Brown, Sr." (1981), interview, 18; May interview, 3; William Becker to Roy Reuther, Mar. 5, 1963; E. Anne Newton to William B. Rumford, both in 2:13, Rumford Papers. On the Rumford Act see Mark Harris, Twentyone Twice (Boston, 1966), 105, 139; William Becker, "Working for Civil Rights: with Unions, the Legislature, and Governor Pat Brown," in "The Governor's Office," interview, 35–36, 39; Pittman interview, 100, 124–25; Rumford interview, 112–13; Rumford column, Berk. Gazette, Mar. 12, 1963, p. 8; Rumford speech, Mar. 17, 1965, 8:5, Rumford Papers; Malcolm Burnstein, "Who Can Afford Civil Rights?" (1963), 5pp., 4:1, Rumford Papers. On reaction see Rumford in S.F. Examiner, Nov. 23, 1963, p. 6; supporting letters, Mar. 1963, 1:5, Rumford Papers; CORE to Rumford, June 22, 1963; Rumford press release, June 24, 1963, both in 1:3, Rumford Papers.

25. On Proposition 14 see Berk. Gazette, Feb. 25, 1964, p. 1; America, Jan. 28, 1967, pp. 142–44; Bradley interview, 157–58; Kline interview, 19, 21; Jesse Unruh memo, Oct. 15, 1964, 1:12, Rumford Papers; Connie Briscoe to Rumford, Oct. 15, 1964; reply, Nov. 10, 1964; Alfred C. Hexter to Rumford, Nov. 13, 1964; reply, Nov. 25, 1964; Richard W. Lundberg to Rumford, Nov. 9, 1964, all in 9:13, Rumford Papers; Catherine B. Wurster to Sadie, Nov. 3, 1964, 8:6, Wurster Papers. On the council see Berk. Council Resolution, Nov. 26, 1963, 1:5, Rumford Papers; Bruce L. Brown to A. J. Force, Nov. 27, 1963, 1:9, Rumford Papers; John D. Phillips to Rumford, May 17, 1963, 2:15, Rumford Papers. On conservatives leaving see David L. Cutter interview, 2:252. On Watts see Bradley interview, 186; Kline interview, 8; CORE press release, Nov. 1964, 2.15, CORE/WRO. On 1966 see Bradley interview, 191, 193, May interview, 3; Rumford interview, 98–107; Rumford to Amelia Fry, Mar. 28, 1974, 11:24, Rumford Papers.

26. BPD, "Zoning Density Study—Report No. 2" (1958). On apartments see L. Heyman, 43–45; Leland G. Neuberg, "Rents, Changes in Rents, and Rent Control in Berkeley" (Master of City Planning thesis, UCB, 1974), 51–54; Walsh, 30–31; Robert Stock letter, Berk. Gazette, Mar. 6, 1961, p. 9; Sept. 19, 1963, p. 3; Berk. Review, Mar. 10, 1960, pp. 1–2; May 12, 1960, p. 1; July 27, 1961, p. 2; Feb. 8, 1962, p. 12; Berk., "Berkeley's Model Neighborhood Proposal" (1967), Pt. II, Sec. B, p. 2. On rezoning see L. Heyman, 27; Kent in Harris, May, 28–30; Kent in Nathan and Scott, 92–93; Margaret S. Gordon, ibid., 279; May interview, 342–45. See also Panoramic Hill Assn. to residents, Feb. 8, 1962 (mimeo), in Pamphlet Boxes of Materials on Berkeley Real Estate.

27. L. Heyman. On West Berkeley see BPC, Berkeley Master Plan–1955 (Berk., 1955), 50, 52; Berk., West Berkeley Neighborhood (Berk., 1971); Johnson, Look, 104–6; Berk. Gazette, Sept. 11, 1963, p. 1. On Oceanview see Jerry S. Mandel, "A Residential Alternative to Special Industrial Zoning" (1965), esp. 1, 4–8 (quote at 4); Wallace Johnson in Nathan and Scott, 202–3; Lyford, 132–33.

28. On South Campus see BPC, Berkeley Master Plan Amended to October 1964

(Berk., 1964), new pp. 104a–b; Johnson, *Look*, 106–9; Johnson in Nathan and Scott, 203–5; May interview, 346–48. The housing authority is in Berk., "Model Neighborhood," Pt. III, Sec. B, p. 1. Rental units are noted by Gordon in Harris, *May*, 44. On Model Cities see Berk., "Model Neighborhood," Pt. I, Sec. A–H, pp. 1–3; Pt. II, Sec. B, pp. 2–4, Pt. III, Sec. A, p. 1; Sec. B, pp. 1–3; Sec. C, pp. 1–2. In general see Catherine B. Wurster to Wally (Johnson?), Aug. 15, 1962, 7:10, Wurster Papers; Wallace Johnson proposal, Feb. 15, 1964, 5:2, Wurster Papers.

29. BUSD, "Co-Sponsored Workshop" (1961), 5; Carol R. Sibley, *Never a Dull Moment* (Berk., 1972, 158); *Berk. Gazette*, Mar. 14, 1967, p. 9; Oct. 31, 1967, p. 9; L. Heyman, 25–27; Reginald Major, *A Panther Is a Black Cat* (N.Y., 1971), 18; Alan B. Wilson, "The Effect of Residential Segregation upon Educational Achievement and Aspirations" (Ph.D. diss. (Ed.), UCB, 1960), 67–69.

30. Berk., Board of Education, Comm. to Study Certain Interracial Problems, *Interracial Problems and Their Effect on Education in the Public Schools of Berkeley, California* (Berk., 1959), 29 (chaired by Redmond C. Staats, Jr., and commonly called the Staats report); Kathryne T. Favors, "A Study of the Intergroup Education Project of the BUSD" (Ed.D. diss., UCB, 1969), 38; Albrier interview, 110–13; Lyford, 187; Sibley, *Never,* 6.

31. Staats report, 10, 29; BUSD, "Co-Sponsored Workshop" (1961), 5, 14; Lyford, 187; Sibley, *Never*, 2, 5, 6; Favors, 37; *Berk. Review*, May 5, 1960, p. 6.

32. Wilson, 69, 72, 81–84; Berk., Board of Education, De Facto Segregation Study Comm., *Report* (Berk., 1963), 1–2, 9, 14, 20 (chaired by John S. Hadsell and commonly called the Hadsell report); Sibley, *Never,* 36.

33. Staats report, 11, 27. On tracks see Hadsell report, 12, 14, 69; Neil V. Sullivan with Evelyn S. Stewart, *Now Is the Time* (Bloomington, Ind., 1969), 129, 138; *Berk. Gazette*, Oct. 1, 1964, p. 1. On black problems see Hadsell report, 19–20.

34. Charles S. Benson and Peter B. Lund, *Neighborhood Distribution of Local Public Services* (Berk., 1969), 77; BUSD, "Co-Sponsored Workshop" (1961), 21; Ira M. Heyman, "Race and Education in Berkeley, California" (1966), 114–16; *Berk. Gazette*, Oct. 28, 1963, p. 3; Mar. 18, 1964, p. 4. On social clubs see Berk., Mayor's Comm. on Children and Youth, "Report" (1959), 13; Staats report, 21, 23–28; Hadsell report, 16, 78–79; AFT Local 1078, *The Classroom Teacher,* Nov. 17, 1959, p. 3; Dec. 5, 1960; *Berk. Gazette*, Oct. 30, 1963, p. 5; Mar. 2, 1964, p. 3; *Berk. Review*, Jan. 7, 1960, p. 2; Hart interview, ii, 139–45. See William Graebner, "Outlawing Teenage Populism: The Campaign against Secret Societies in the American High School, 1900–1960," *Journal of American History*, 74 (1987), 411–35.

35. BUSD, "Co-sponsored Workshop on Change in an Interracial Community" (1962), 16–17; Hadsell report, 78. On black parental dissatisfaction see Favors, 69–70. See the cogent testimony of Floyd R. Hann in Calif. Senate Fact-Finding Comm. on Education, *Hearing, Oakland, Oct. 18, 1962* (Sacramento, 1962), 26–30.

36. Staats report, passim. On the 1961 election see Spurgeon Avakian to Sen. Clair Engle, June 26, 1961, Box 1, Roger Kent Papers; Sibley campaign literature, 1961, IGSL. On the superintendent see Carol R. Sibley, "Building Community Trust: Berkeley School Integration and Other Civic Endeavors, 1943–1978" (1980), interview, 118, 172–74; Favors, 40.

37. BUSD, "Co-Sponsored Workshop" (1961); BUSD, "Co-Sponsored Workshop" (1962).

38. BUSD, "Co-Sponsored Workshop" (1961), 20–21, 24. On black problems see I. M. Heyman, 80–82; Sibley, *Never,* 69–72; Sibley interview, 116–19. On the middle

class see BUSD, *Desegregation of the Berkeley Public Schools* (Berk., 1964), 8; Robert D. Frelow, "A Comparative Study of Resource Allocation: Compensatory Education and School Desegregation" (Ph.D. diss. (Ed.), UCB, 1970), 13, 19, 93, 96, 104; Wilson, 12–19, 41, 57, 101–2. See also Staats report, 14; Hadsell report, 29–31.

39. BUSD, *Desegregation*, 13, 15, 19, 22; Hadsell report, esp. 30; Marascuilo, 170–72; Sibley, *Never*, 39, 42–44, 50; Sullivan, 41–44; Daniel Adelson, ed., *Man as the Measure: The Crossroads* (N.Y., 1972), 37–38. For a summary see I. M. Heyman.

40. Staats report, 9; AFT Local 1078, *The Classroom Teacher*, Nov. 1963, p. 1. On the Ramsey plan see BUSD, *Desegregation*, 3, 13; *Berk. Gazette*, Mar. 4, 1964, p. 1; editorial, Mar. 6, 1964, p. 12; Sibley, *Never*, 44–46.

41. Sibley, *Never*, 61–62, 94; Sullivan, 61–62, 65–66, 71–76; Cutter interview, 2:252; Sibley interview, 128, 181; I. M. Heyman, 93–94; Sally E. James, "School Desegregation in Berkeley, California" (1977), 9, 17–18.

42. Sibley interview, 174–77 (quote at 176), 196–98, 212, 239–40; Sibley, *Never*, 97–99; Sullivan, esp. xv. On educational parks see BUSD, *Integrated Quality Education* (Berk., 1968), 54–65.

43. I. M. Heyman, 47–58; Sibley, *Never*, 55–60; Sullivan, 32; *Berk. Gazette*, Oct. 7, 1964, p. 1; *BCU Bulletin*, Sept. 1964, p. 1; Oct. 1964, p. 3 (quote); Berk. Friends of Better Schools, analysis, Oct. 6, 1964, 5:2, Wurster Papers; Ruth W. Avakian to Roger Kent, Sept. 23, 1964; reply, Sept. 25, 1964, both in Box 1, Roger Kent Papers.

44. On conservatives leaving see Gordon in Harris, *May*, 42; Baird and Mary Ann Whaley letter, *Berk. Gazette*, Feb. 21, 1964, p. 12; *BCU Bulletin*, Nov. 1964, p. 3 (quote); Feb. 1965, p. 1; July 1965, p. 2. On the campaign see Sibley, *Never*, 47 48; *Berk. Gazette*, Sept. 24, 1964, p. 1; Sept. 30, 1964, p. 1; Oct. 2, 1964, pp. 1, 16; Oct. 5, 1964, p. 14; Sibley recall campaign literature, 1964, IGSL. On Sibley see Hart interview, 169; Sibley interview, 183–86, 190; *Berk. Gazette*, Sept. 1, 1964, pp. 1, 2. On other candidates see ibid., Sept. 2, 1964, p. 1; Sept. 8, 1964, pp. 1, 2; Sept. 11, 1964, pp. 1, 2; Sept. 15, 1964, pp. 1, 3; Sept. 21, 1964, pp. 1, 2; Sept. 22, 1964, pp. 1, 2.

45. BUSD, *Integration of the Berkeley Elementary Schools: A Report to the Superintendent* (Berk., 1967), Sibley, *Never*, 103–9.

46. Sullivan, 82–109, 145–46, 153–66; Sibley, *Never*, 75, 112–13; BUSD, Comm. on Instructional Program for Integration, *Report* (Berk., 1967); BUSD, *Integrated Quality Education*; Favors, 158 60; BUSD, "Co-Sponsored Workshop" (1961), 16 18; James, 7.

47. Sullivan, 50, 88–90 (first quote at 89; others at 90; last at 50).

48. Cutter interview, 2:252; James, 18, 20; *N.Y. Times*, Sept. 8, 1968, p. 61, *Black Panther*, Oct. 5, 1968, p. 13. Sullivan attributed success to the involvement of students. Adelson, 51. On Sullivan's departure see Sibley, *Never*, 117–18; Sibley interview, 253. The photographs are in Virginia T. Hadsell and Grethel C. Newcom, *Equal Start* (S.F., 1968).

49. Patrick J. Glynn, "Did Desegregation Work?" *Journal of Contemporary Studies*, Summer 1981, pp. 43–52; James, 18–20; Lyford, 192–93; Sibley interview, 243; Sullivan, 167. See also *Community High School Newsletter* (1969).

50. On Garfield see *Berk. Gazette*, Mar. 15, 1969, p. 2; *American School Board Journal*, Dec. 1965, pp. 5–6. On Berkeley High see *BCU Bulletin*, Oct. 1967, p. 1; Lyford, 168–69; Sibley, *Never*, 122–24, 128–35, 158; Sibley interview, 131a, 215, 227–29, 239, 243, 246–47, 257–58, 271; Sullivan, 127–28, 142, 181–86; *Berk. Gazette*, Oct. 1, 1966, p. 1; Sept. 21, 1968, p. 1; Sept. 24, 1968, p. 1; Oct. 2, 1968, p.

1; *Community High School Newsletter*, Mar. 5, Apr. 14, May 16, Sept. 30, 1969.

51. Sibley, *Never*, 119; Donald R. Hopkins in Nathan and Scott, 122. See the revealing remarks of Mrs. Tami Tanabe at the Human Relations and Welfare Commission, Special Meeting, minutes, June 11, 1964, p. 2, copy in Sibley recall campaign literature, 1964, IGSL. On enrollment see James, 2; Sibley, *Never*, 205.

52. Pittman interview, 37, 91; Dellums interview, 60; "Dear Fellow Member of BIC" (2-sided leaflet, n.d. but before 1960), 10:4, Rumford Papers.

53. On the Fair Employment Practices Commission see Albrier interview, 183; Becker interview, 34, 40–42; Pittman interview, 86–88, 95–97, 105, 111–12; *Berk. Gate*, May 8, 1968, p. 2. On statistics see Jan E. Dizard, "Patterns of Unemployment in Berkeley, California" (1968), 3; Lol D. Raasch, "Unemployment in Berkeley and the Programs Designed to Alleviate the Problem: A Current Analysis" (M.B.A. report, UCB, 1967), 24; Catherine B. Wurster to Don ?, Nov. 14, 1961, 7:7, Wurster Papers. On unions see League of Women Voters of Berk., *Minority Employment in Berkeley: A Survey of Employers* (Berk., 1969), 15; Marie Angell et al., "Vocational Guidance and Employment Opportunities for Minority Group Members in Berkeley" (M. S. W. group project report, UCB, 1959), 64, 89–91, copy in Ruth A. Hart Papers; Leggett, 55; Berk. Study Comm. on Equal Employment Opportunities, "Employment Opportunities for Members of Minority Groups in Berkeley" (1958), 3, 7, 13, typed carbon in 3:4, Rumford Papers; E. A. Cutter, Jr., in Cutter interviews, 2:50–51.

54. Angell, 56, 60–62, 68, 79, 84, 98 (quotes at 79, 60); Berk. Study Comm., "Employment," 3, 7, 9, 13, 16, 23; Margaret S. Gordon in Nathan and Scott, 273; Richard M. Betts and G. Michael Yovino-Young, "The Berkeley Downtown in Depth" (M.B.A. report, UCB, 1963), 47. See also League of Women Voters, *Minority Employment*, 1–2.

55. May interview, 214, 292 note, 294, 298–99; Margaret S. Gordon in Nathan and Scott, 273–74, 301–2; *Berk. Gazette*, Mar. 22, 1963, p. 1; Feb. 13, 1964, p. 1; Angell, 97; *The Berkeley Project* (Berk., 1966), 1.

56. On pressure see BUSD, "Co-Sponsored Workshop" (1961), 23; Rumford in Nathan and Scott, 10–11; *Berk. Review*, Aug. 11, 1960, pp. 1–2; "Dear Fellow Member of BIC," 10:4, Rumford Papers; Berk. Study Comm., "Employment," 10.

57. Sally Belfrage, *Freedom Summer* (N.Y., 1965), 206; Elizabeth Sutherland, ed., *Letters from Mississippi* (N.Y., 1966; orig. 1965), 184; Howard Zinn, *SNCC: The New Abolitionists* (Boston, 1965), 39; Lewis S. Feuer, *The Conflict of Generations* (N.Y., 1969), 441, 446; Bruce Payne in *The New Student Left*, ed. Mitchell Cohen and Dennis Hale, rev. ed. (Boston, 1967), 79–96; Katherine A. Towle, "Administration and Leadership" (1970), interview, 274; *Berk. Gate*, Oct. 22, 1963, p. 4. See also Clayborne Carson, *In Struggle* (Cambridge, Mass., 1981).

58. On CORE see William Barlow and Peter Shapiro, *An End to Silence* (N.Y., 1971), 43, 46; *Berk. Gazette*, Feb. 27, 1964, p. 1; Mrs. Joseph R. Cabral letter, ibid., Mar. 4, 1964, p. 20; Forrest E. Tregea to Alex C. Sherriffs et al., June 29, 1964; Arleigh Williams to Gretchen Kittredge, July 9, 1964; Williams to Katherine A. Towle, July 9, 1964, all in 1293:1, UCPF; David C. Fulton rally report, Jan. 11, 1965; Dean Johnson to Kerr, Mar. 19, 1965, both in 1294:2, UCPF. On demonstrations see *Berk. Gate*, 1 #7, ca. Jan. 1964, pp. 1, 3; *Berk. Gazette*, Mar. 16, 1964, p. 1; *Daily Cal.*, Mar. 16, 1964, p. 1; *Tocsin*, Apr. 21, 1964, p. 2; Barlow and Shapiro, 44; Michael Myerson, *These Are the Good Old Days* (N.Y., 1970), 111–13, 121. On downtown see (Genevieve Hughes?) to CORE, N.Y., N.Y., Dec.?, 1963, 1:1, CORE/WRO; Virginia

Burton, Berk. CORE, to Robert E. Hink, July 20, 1964, 1:4 CORE/WRO; Western Regional CORE, *Newsletter*, June 1, 1963, p. 2, 2:13, CORE/WRO. For a complete report see Lawrence T. Gurley, Berk. CORE, to Chet Duncan, Mar. 5, 1964, 1:2, CORE/WRO.

59. Mr. and Mrs. J. B. Neilands to CORE, Mar. 9, 1964, 1:2, CORE/WRO. On the Sheraton-Palace see *Berk. Gazette*, Mar. 7, 1964, p. 1; Mar. 9, 1964, pp. 1, 3; Mar. 16, 1964, p. 8; Mar. 18, 1964, p. 4; *Daily Cal.*, Mar. 2, 1964, p. 1; Mar. 6, 1964, pp. 1, 3, 12; Mar. 9, 1964, p. 1; Mar. 12, 1964, pp. 1, 8; Mar. 16, 1964, p. 1; *S.F. Chronicle*, Mar. 2, 1964, pp. 1, 6; Mar. 6, 1964, pp. 1, 13; Mar. 7, 1964, pp. 1, 6, 7; Mar. 8, 1964, pp. 1, 1A–1B; Mar. 9, 1964, pp. 1, 18; *Tocsin*, Mar. 18, 1964, pp. 1, 4; *Despite Everything*, Mar. 10, 1964; Barlow and Shapiro, 45; Myerson, 114–16, 118; DeCanio quoted in *The Nation*, Sept. 27, 1965, p. 156. Duncan quoted in Duncan to Leonard S. Blunt, May 25, 1964, 1:2, CORE/WRO. On Mulford see *Daily Cal.*, Apr. 22, 1964, p. 1; Apr. 23, 1964, pp. 1, 6; Mulford press release, Apr. 28, 1964, IGSL. Kerr's response is in *Daily Cal.*, May 6, 1964, p. 1. For a later demonstration see Berk. Campus CORE, "The CORE Restaurant Project," Apr. 21, 1965 (4pp., offset), 2:5, FSM/CSHE.

60. *Berk. Gate*, Feb. 24, 1964, pp. 1, 5–6, Supplement; *Berk. Gazette*, Feb. 26, 1964, pp. 1, 2; Feb. 27, 1964, pp. 1, 2; Feb. 28, 1964, pp. 1, 2; Mar. 2, 1964, p. 10; Mar. 3, 1964, p. 1; Mar. 5, 1964, p. 14; Mar. 6, 1964, p. 12; Mar. 11, 1964, p. 10; Mar. 18, 1964, p. 24; Mar. 19, 1964, p. 9; *BCU Bulletin*, Mar. 1964, p. 1; *Daily Cal.*, Feb. 18, 1964, p. 6; Feb. 19, 1964, p. 1; Feb. 21, 1964, p. 1; Feb. 24, 1964, p. 1; Feb. 25, 1964, pp. 1, 6; Feb. 26, 1964, p. 8; Feb. 27, 1964, p. 1; Feb. 28, 1964, pp. 1, 7; Mar. 2, 1964, pp. 1, 3; Mar. 4, 1964, p. 1; *S.F. Chronicle*, Feb. 26, 1964, p. 12; Feb. 27, 1964, pp. 1, 18; Feb. 29, 1964, p. 1; Evelyn L. Ritter to CORE, ca. Feb. 1964, 1:2, CORE/WRO; Howell Baum to CORE, Feb. 20, 1964, 1:8, CORE/WRO; Geoffrey White, "The Student Revolt at Berkeley," *Spartacist*, May-June 1965, p. 8. Compare Lucky's, 5:4 with Safeway, 5:7, CORE/WRO.

61. Dizard, opp. 11, opp. 55, 56, opp. 30. See also Assembly Legislative Reference Service, "High School Dropouts: California in the National Perspective" (1963), 4:15, Rumford Papers; *Oakland Tribune*, May 12, 1963, p. 40; Alpha Phi Alpha Fraternity, Inc., Gamma Phi Lambda Chapter, Berk., *Newsletter*, Sept. 7, 1963, 9:5, Rumford Papers; Betty Jo. Grimes to Robert W. Crown, Feb. 28, 1963, 5:31, Rumford Papers; *Berk. Gazette*, Sept 10, 1963, pp. 1, 2; Oct. 18, 1963, p. 3. On Workreation see Council of Social Planning-Berk. Area, "Community Action under 'Economic Opportunity Act of 1964' " (1965), 17; Berk. Workreation Council, Inc., "Annual Report, 1965–1966" (1966), in Pamphlet Boxes of Material on Berkeley Business and Commerce; Dan Dewey to Rumford, Apr. 7, 1961, 5:17, Rumford Papers. On the Youth Opportunity Center see Raasch, 34.

62. On the Neighborhood Youth Corps see Berk. City Manager, *Newsletter*, May 21, 1965; Sept. 22, 1965; Raasch, 63–66. On the Office of Equal Opportunities see BCM, *Newsletter*, May 21, 1965; Ed Montgomery speech, *Berk. Gate*, Mar. 8, 1966, pp. 8–9; editorial, p. 5; *Berk Barb*, Nov. 4, 1966, p. 3 (quote); May interview, 303; Raasch, 82–88. For a devastating and revealing discussion see David Wellman, "Putting-On the Poverty Program," *Steps*, #2 (ca. 1967), 51–66. An important conference on this topic was held in Berkeley in 1965. Margaret S. Gordon, ed., *Poverty in America* (S.F., 1965).

63. On Griffin see *Berk. Gate*, Mar. 30, 1964; Apr. 13, 1964; *Daily Cal.*, Mar. 18,

1964, pp. 1, 10; Mar. 20, 1964, p. 1; Mar. 31, 1964, p. 8; Apr. 2, 1964, p. 1; Apr. 6, 1964, pp. 1, 6; Apr. 16, 1964, p. 1; Apr. 22, 1964, pp. 1, 7; May 11, 1964, p. 1; Alex C. Sherriffs to Kerr, July 15, 1964, 1293:1, UCPF. On Malcolm X see George Breitman, *The Last Year of Malcolm X* (N.Y., 1967), esp. 146; Malcolm X, *Malcolm X Speaks*, ed. George Breitman (N.Y., 1966; orig. 1965), esp. 42, 111, 139; Major, 63; Gene Marine, *The Black Panthers* (N.Y., 1969), 18–22; *Black Politics*, Feb. 1968.

64. On Carmichael see Stokely Carmichael, *Stokely Speaks* (N.Y., 1971), esp. ix–xi, 17–43, 77–99, 145–64; Stokely Carmichael and Charles V. Hamilton, *Black Power* (N.Y., 1967); David L. Lewis, *King: A Biography*, 2nd ed. (Urbana, 1978), 324–26; Donald R. Hopkins in Nathan and Scott, 119. On Black Power see Robert L. Allen, *Dialectics of Black Power* (N.Y., 1968); Mary Jane Johnson in Favors, 270–71; Michael Lerner column, *Daily Cal.*, Oct. 6, 1966, p. 12; "The Challenge of Black Power" (2-sided leaflet, Oct. 1966), BPP, SPP. On the word "black" see Malcolm X's speech, Nov. 1963, in Malcolm X, 4. Carmichael's speeches are covered in *Berk. Barb*, Feb. 4, 1966, p. 2; Nov. 25, 1966, pp. 1, 3; *Daily Cal.*, Feb. 20, 1967, pp. 1, 3 (quote at 1). On the Greek Theatre speech see ibid., Oct. 7, 1966, p. 1; Oct. 11, 1966, p. 1; Oct. 24, 1966; Oct. 25, 1966, p. 1; Oct. 27, 1966, p. 1; Oct. 31, 1966, pp. 1, 16; *Berk. Gate*, Nov. 1, 1966, p. 1 (quote); *Berk. Barb*, Nov. 4, 1966, p. 3; *L.A. Herald-Examiner*, Oct. 30, 1966, p. 1; James Reston column, *N.Y. Times*, Oct. 23, 1966; Oct. 30, 1966; editorial, *Phila. Inquirer*, Nov. 2, 1966; *S.F. Chronicle*, Oct. 31, 1966, p. 12; *S.F. Sunday Examiner-Chronicle*, Oct. 30, 1966, Sec. I, pp. 1, 10; *New Left Notes*, Nov. 4, 1966, pp. 1, 8; James H. Rodger to Kerr, Oct. 30, 1966, 1293:6, UCPF; R. Johnsen to Kerr, Oct. 30, 1966, 1294:4, UCPF. The text of the speech is in Carmichael, *Speaks*, 45–60.

65. On 1965 see Gordon in Nathan and Scott, 276, 280; *Berk. Gazette*, Apr. 7, 1965, p. 1. In general see Donald R. Hopkins in Nathan and Scott, 105–35; *Berk. Barb*, Apr. 22, 1966, p. 3; *Daily Cal.*, Apr. 19, 1968, p. 5; press clipping, n.d., 8:9, Rumford Papers. On Miller see Hopkins, 109, 113, 117; *Berk. Citizen*, May 6, 1966, p. 13; obituary in *Express*, Mar. 8, 1985, pp. 3–4. On Green see Hopkins, 108–9, 113–14, 119, 122; *Berk. Citizen*, May 6, 1966, p. 13. On music see Radio Station KDIA, "Report," May 15, 1962, 5:13, CORE/WRO. On Dellums see Hopkins, 114, 116–18, 120; Gordon, 311; Albrier interview, 200, 272; *Berk. Citizen*, Mar. 3, 1967, p. 2; Marine, 118.

66. R. G. Davis, *The San Francisco Mime Troupe* (Palo Alto, 1975), 49–61 (quote at 56). Sgt. R. R. Ludden to Lt. M. F. Chandler, Oct. 1, 1965; E. F. Cheit to Roger Heyns, June 10, 1966, both in 4:59, UCBCF; Kerr to Heyns, June 23, 1966; Cheit memo, June 28, 1966, both in 8:97, UCBCF.

67. Carmichael, *Speaks*, 28; Hopkins in Nathan and Scott, 115. See *Black Politics*, Jan. 1968, preface, Apr.-May 1968, p. 5. This journal had ties both to the Black Panther party and to the Trotsky-oriented Socialist Workers party.

68. Sol Stern in *N.Y. Times Magazine*, Aug. 6, 1967, pp. 10ff; Stewart E. Albert in *Liberation*, July-Aug. 1968, p. 34; Berk., *Model Cities Program* (Berk., 1968), Pt. 3A, pp. 3–4; Tom Hayden, *Trial* (N.Y., 1970), 119; Gary T. Marx in *Berk. Gazette*, Nov. 2, 1966, p. 3. For a succinct statement see Newton's interview in Carl Oglesby, ed., *The New Left Reader* (N.Y., 1969), 231–38. For an insightful interpretation see Helen L. Stewart, "Buffering: The Leadership Style of Huey P. Newton, Co-Founder of the Black Panther Party" (Ph.D. diss., Brandeis Univ., 1980).

69. Bobby Seale, *A Lonely Rage* (N.Y., 1977), 25–41, 46–48, 71–72, 78, 81, 96,

101, 124; Bobby Seale, *Seize the Time* (N.Y., 1970), 6–11; Marine, 24; Joseph Conlin, *The Troubles* (N.Y., 1982), 153–56.

70. Huey P. Newton, *Revolutionary Suicide* (N.Y., 1973), 11–41, 45, 47, 49, 53, 59–65, 68–71, 92, 105–7; Seale, *Time*, 12, 15–16, 20, 25; Earl Anthony, *Picking Up the Gun* (N.Y., 1970), 26; Marine, 12–17, 31; Conlin, 150–53; Stewart, 54–55; *N.Y. Times*, May 21, 1967, p. 66.

71. Newton, 72–73, 109; Seale, *Time*, 26–34; Seale, *Rage*, 146, 149; Marine, 33–34; Major, 200–202; *Berk. Barb*, Apr. 1, 1966, p. 1.

72. Seale, *Time*, 35–36, 38, 41, 44 (quote), 59, 62, 65, 73; Newton, 115–16. The ten point platform is in Major, 285–88, and in Philip S. Foner, ed., *The Black Panthers Speak* (Phila., 1970), 246–48. See also Stewart, 97–99.

73. Robert L. Allen, *Black Awakening in Capitalist America* (Garden City, N.Y., 1969), 69; Conlin, 156; *Berk. Barb*, Feb. 17, 1967, p. 1; *Ramparts*, July 1966, pp. 51–54; "Support the Black Panther Party!" (leaflet, July 1966); "Support the Black Panther!" (leaflet, Oct. 1966), both in BPP, SPP; SNCC, "Has SNCC Changed?" (2-sided leaflet, ca. 1966), IGSL.

74. Anthony, 18 (quote), 34, 94–95; Conlin, 165; Major, 67, 73; Marine, 40–42; Harris, *Twentyone*, 119; Newton, 120; Seale, *Rage*, 158; Allen, *Black Awakening*, 69–70; Seale, *Time*, 148. On the capitol see ibid., 153, 156; Seale, *Rage*, 168, 171; Anthony, 18; Major, 77–79; Marine, 62–63.

75. Anthony, 38, 88–89; Hayden, *Trial*, 152; Major, 60; *Ebony*, Aug. 1969, pp. 106ff; Alprentice ("Bunchy") Carter, "The Genius of Huey Newton" (1969), in Foner, 27–28.

76. On crime see Ruth-Marion Baruch and Pirkle Jones, *The Vanguard* (Boston, 1970), 38; G. Louis Heath, ed., *Off the Pigs!* (Metuchen, N.J., 1976), 105; Conlin, 164; Major, 75, 117–18; Sheriff Frank Madigan testimony, U.S. House Comm. on Internal Security, *Black Panther Party Hearings*, 91st Cong., 2nd Sess. (Wash., 1970–71), Pt. 4, pp. 4917–18, House Library vol. 481–4. On the breakfast program see Heath, 85; Major, 85–86; Marine, 74; Black Panther Party, *Bulletin No. 9*, Jan. 6, 1969, p. 2. On Mao books see Seale, *Time*, 80–84; Marine, 40.

77. Allen, *Black Awakening*, 222–23; Anthony, 58; Newton, 133–35; Seale, *Time*, 132; Major, 66, 70, 143; Marine, 48–55, 180; Stewart, 68; *Tocsin*, Oct. 23, 1963, p. 1; Cleaver "Rap Sheet," Sept. 17, 1968, 1214:2, UCPF; *Sat. Eve. Post*, Nov. 16, 1968, pp. 30ff. See also Lee Lockwood, *Conversation with Eldridge Cleaver* (N.Y., 1970).

78. Cleaver introduction, Jerry Rubin, *Do It!* (N.Y., 1970), 10–11; Art Goldberg (the journalist) in *S.F. Bay Guardian*, June 14, 1979, p. 15.

79. Newton, 125, 165–66; Major, 139; Stewart, 176; Sacramento State *Hornet*, Oct. 4, 1968 (quote), copy in 1214:1, UCPF; *BCU Bulletin*, May 1969, p. 2 (quote); Madigan testimony, 4921. See the party's publications, and esp. those illustrated by Emory Douglas. E.g., "It's All the Same" (leaflet, n.d.), BPP, SPP; Black Panther Party, *Bulletin No. 7*, Nov. 1, 1968, p. 3.

80. Major, 240; Baruch and Jones, 34; Hayden, *Trial*, 117–18; María-José Ragué Arias, *California Trip* (Barcelona, 1971), 137; *Berk. Dispatch*, Apr. 10, 1968, pp. 1–2; Apr. 17, 1968, pp. 1, 3; Marine, 71. See the astute remarks in Tom Hayden, *Rebellion in Newark* (N.Y., 1967), 69–70. For evidence of illegal activities see U.S. Senate, Select Comm. to Study Governmental Operations with Respect to Intelligence Activities, *Supplementary Detailed Staff Reports of Intelligence Activities and Rights of Americans*, Book III (Wash., 1976), 185–224 (commonly called the Church report).

81. On the shootout see Major, 79, 179–81; Marine, 76–78; Newton, 171–76. On the trial see Charles Garry and Art Goldberg, *Streetfighter in the Courtroom* (N.Y., 1977). The birthday celebration is in Anthony, 83; Major, 96; Seale, *Time*, 212; *Berk. Barb*, Feb. 23, 1968, p. 3. The text of Carmichael's speech is in Carmichael, *Speaks*, 111–30. Newton's message from prison is in Foner, 47–49.

82. Anthony, 44–47, 127–28 (quote at 127); Newton, 182, 188–89, 192; Seale, *Time*, 203–7, 217, 274–79; Garry introduction, Edward M. Keating, *Free Huey!* (Berk., 1971), xvii–xviii; Marine, 79–105; *Berk. Gazette*, Sept. 7, 1968, p. 1; Sept. 9, 1968, p. 1; Sept. 10, 1968, p. 1; Sept. 28, 1968, p. 1. In general see Black Panther Party, Ministry of Information, *Bulletin Numbers 1 and 2* (1968), BPP, SPP.

83. On the raid see Seale, *Time*, 223–25; Major, 25, 204, 294–95; Marine, 130–31; *Berk. Barb*, Jan. 24, 1969, p. 9; Black Panther Party, *Bulletin No. 4* (1968), BPP, SPP. On the council see May interview, 317–19 (quotes at 319); Gordon in Nathan and Scott, 315–16; *Berk. Barb*, Mar. 1, 1968, p. 3; Mar. 8, 1968, p. 5; *Daily Cal.*, Feb. 26, 1968, p. 1; Feb. 28, 1968, p. 1. See also Thomas L. McLaren in Nathan and Scott, 253–54.

84. Seale, *Time*, 229, 231, 235; Lyford, 3 (quote), 168; Marine, 134, 140 (quote).

85. On the shootout see Major, 186–94; Marine, 136–42, 150, 154; Stewart, 74; *Berk. Barb*, Apr. 12, 1968, p. 1. On Cleaver's later admissions see *New West*, May 19, 1980, pp. 19–20. Subsequent events are in Anthony, 111–12 (quote at 112); Cleaver affidavit, Eldridge Cleaver, *Post-Prison Writings and Speeches*, ed. Robert Scheer (N.Y., 1969), 3–12; Major, 12, 98; Marine, 107–9.

86. Baruch and Jones, 35. On the Peace and Freedom party see Seale, *Time*, 207–9; Major, 89–95; Marine, 110–21; *Berk. Gazette*, Nov. 4, 1968, p. 1; *Daily Cal.*, Mar. 1, 1968, p. 15; May 23, 1968, p. 12; *Peace and Freedom News*, Mar. 4, 1968; Mar. 30, 1968, pp. 1, 5; July 8, 1968, pp. 1–2, 7; July 25, 1968, p. 3; Aug. 12, 1968, p. 2; Oct. 15, 1968, p. 4; Kenneth Lamott, *Anti-California* (Boston, 1971), 144–51. Campaign literature is in the Peace and Freedom party section, Cleaver 1968 Folder, SPP. On the coalition see Anthony, 48–49, 58, 65, 88; Hayden, *Trial*, 121–23; Stewart, 52–53; Hal Draper in *Independent Socialist*, June-July 1968, p. 6; *Berk. Barb*, Oct. 4, 1968, p. 8 (quote). On the election see Anthony, 97; Seale, *Time*, 210; *Berk. Gazette*, Nov. 7, 1968, p. 1; *Peace and Freedom News*, Nov. 29, 1968, p. 3.

87. On the Board of Educational Development see UCB, Academic Senate, *Education at Berkeley* (Berk., 1966), 113 (commonly called the Muscatine report); *Daily Cal.*, Oct. 2, 1968; Edward Sampson in Adelson, 138–40; numerous documents, 1:5–6, 2:18, 7:82, UCBCF. On the controversy see Major, 147–48; *Berk. Barb*, Sept. 20, 1968, p. 7; Oct. 4, 1968, p. 1; *Berk. Gate*, Oct. 8, 1968, p. 3; *Berk. Gazette*, Sept. 12, 1968, pp. 1, 2; Sept. 14, 1968, p. 1; Sept. 19, 1968, pp. 1, 11; Sept. 24, 1968, pp. 1, 2; Sept. 25, 1968, p. 1; Sept. 26, 1968, p. 1; Sept. 28, 1968, p. 1; Oct. 1, 1968, pp. 1, 2; Oct. 4, 1968, pp. 1, 2; Oct. 7, 1968, p. 2; Oct. 8, 1968, pp. 1, 2; Oct. 10, 1968, p. 1; Oct. 16, 1968, p. 1; Oct. 19, 1968, p. 1; editorial, *Oakland Tribune*, Sept. 26, 1968, p. 1; Kathleen Lorbeer letter, *L.A. Times*, Sept. 21, 1968, Pt. III, p. 4; *N.Y. Times*, Sept. 21, 1968, p. 14; Sept. 29, 1968, p. 84; Oct. 6, 1968, p. 35; Oct. 8, 1968, p. 75; Oct. 19, 1968, p. 35; *S.F. Chronicle*, Sept. 19, 1968, p. 5; Black Panther Party, *Bulletin No. 7*, Nov. 4, 1968, p. 4; *Mid-Peninsula Observer*, Sept. 23, 1968, p. 2; Roger W. Heyns, "Berkeley Chancellor, 1965–1971" (1987), interview, 49; documents in 2:18–20, 7:82, UCBCF; letters, 1214:1–2, UCPF. On the Regents see Elinor R. Heller, "A Volunteer Career in Politics, in Higher Education, and on Governing Boards" (1984), interview, 609–12; John R. Coyne, Jr., *The Kumquat Statement* (N.Y., 1970),

62, 65; *University Bulletin*, Sept. 27, 1968; Regents materials in 1:5, 2:18–20, UCBCF, and in 1214:2, UCPF. On Cleaver's speaking tour see William J. McGill, *The Year of the Monkey* (N.Y., 1982), 12–14, 26–27, 41–42; Seale, *Time*, 257–58; Cleaver speech, Sacramento State, transcript, Oct. 2, 1968; Cleaver KLAC radio interview, transcript, Sept. 13, 1968, both in 1214:2, UCPF. On the Sproul rally see Coyne, 68–69 (quote at 69); Mulford to Dorothy B. Chandler, Oct. 14, 1968; Glenn Campbell to President Charles Hitch, Oct. 10, 1968, both in 2:18, UCBCF. The duel challenge is in Coyne, 146, 148. See also Cleaver speech, American University, Washington, D.C., transcript, Oct. 18, 1968, 4:55, UCBCF.

88. On athletics see *Daily Cal.*, Jan. 24, 1968, p. 1; Feb. 1, 1968, p. 1; Feb. 21, 1968, p. 4; Apr. 1, 1968, p. 1; Apr. 2, 1968, p. 1; Apr. 12, 1968, p. 1; May 16, 1968, p. 1; May 17, 1968, p. 1. On Bob Presley see Herb Michelson, *Almost a Famous Person* (N.Y., 1980). Grapes are in *N.Y. Times*, Oct. 20, 1968, p. 58. For statistics see *Daily Cal.*, Oct. 3, 1967, pp. 9, 12–13; Nov. 22, 1967, pp. 1, 10.

89. On the Sproul sit-in see *Berk. Gate*, Oct. 29, 1968, pp. 1–3, 7; *Berk. Gazette*, Oct. 23, 1968, pp. 1, 2; *Daily Cal.*, Oct. 23, 1968, pp. 1, 8; arrest list, 1:5, UCBCF; Unruh wire to Heyns, Oct. 22, 1968; UCB statement, Oct. 22, 1968, both in 2:18, UCBCF. On the Moses sit-in see Coyne, 89–101; *Berk. Barb*, Oct. 25, 1968, pp. 3, 11 (banners), 13; Nov. 1, 1968, pp. 5, 6; Nov. 22, 1968, p. 11; Jan. 3, 1969, p. 7; Feb. 21, 1969, p. 11; *Berk. Gate*, Oct. 29, 1968, pp. 1, 8–10; *Berk. Gazette*, Oct. 24, 1968, pp. 1, 2; Oct. 25, 1968, p. 1; Oct. 26, 1968, pp. 1, 2; *Daily Cal.*, Oct. 24, 1968, p. 1; Oct. 25, 1968, pp. 1, 3; Oct. 31, 1968, p. 1; Nov. 11, 1968, p. 1; Jan. 3, 1969, pp. 3, 12; Jan. 6, 1969, pp. 1, 8; Feb. 13, 1969, p. 9; *N.Y. Times*, Oct. 24, 1968, p. 32; Oct. 25, 1968, p. 51; *S.F. Express Times*, Oct. 30, 1968, pp. 3, 6, 14; Dec. 18, 1968, p. 5; Independent Socialist Club, *IS*, Dec. 1969, pp. 17, 20; *Guardian*, Nov. 2, 1968, p. 3; *Liberation News Service*, Oct. 25, 1968, pp. 11–12; Nov. 1, 1968, pp. 3–7; *Mid-Peninsula Observer*, Oct. 28, 1968, pp. 3, 15; Kirkpatrick Sale, *SDS* (N.Y., 1973), 492–93; Heyns interview, 98–99; arrest list, 1:5, UCBCF; Heyns statement, Oct. 25, 1968, 1214:1, UCPF; materials in 2:18, UCBCF.

90. On San Francisco State see Barlow and Shapiro; *Berk. Barb*, Dec. 6, 1968, p. 4; Dec. 13, 1968, p. 3; Jan. 3, 1969, p. 5; Jan. 10, 1969, pp. 3–5; Jan. 31, 1969, p. 5; Major, 82–84. On San Diego, McGill, 55. On TWLF demands see *Berk. Barb*, Jan. 31, 1969, p. 4; 10:111, UCBCF. On TWLF see Coyne, 59; McGill, 90, 103; Asian American Political Alliance, AAPA, Nov.-Dec. 1968; Feb. 1969; *Bayviewer*, Feb. 1969, p. 11; *Berk. Gate*, Feb. 4, 1969, pp. 1–9; Feb. 25, 1969, pp. 1–6, 8–9; *Black Politics*, Jan.-Feb. 1969, pp. 12–13; *Daily Cal.*, Jan. 15, 1969, p. 1; Jan. 16, 1969, p. 1; Jan. 20, 1969, p. 1 (quote); Jan. 21, 1969, pp. 1, 5; Jan. 24, 1969, p. 21; Jan. 27, 1969, p. 1; Jan. 31, 1969; Feb. 3, 1969, pp. 2, 16; Feb. 6, 1969. On Nabors see *Berk. Barb*, Mar. 7, 1969, p. 4; Coyne, 59 (quote).

91. On Wheeler see Coyne, 115–16; *Berk. Barb*, Jan. 24, 1969, p. 3; *Daily Cal.*, Jan. 23, 1969, p. 1; Jan. 24, 1969, p. 20; *S.F. Express Times*, Jan. 28, 1969, p. 5; TWLF news conference, Jan. 23, 1969, 10:111, UCBCF. Chants are in *S.F. Express Times*, Jan. 28, 1969, p. 5. On blocking see Coyne, 112. On blackjacks see *Berk. Barb*, Feb. 7, 1969, pp. 4, 14–15; Feb. 14, 1969, p. 5. Local 1570, ibid., p. 3; *S.F. Express Times*, Feb. 18, 1969, p. 7; Local 1570, "A Message to Non-Striking Students" (leaflet), in Mitchell Goodman, ed., *The Movement toward a New America* (N.Y., 1970), 312–13. The library incident is in Coyne, 116. Press coverage was massive. See *N.Y. Times*, Feb. 6, 1969, p. 28; Feb. 9, 1969, p. 59; Mar. 1, 1969, p. 29; Mar. 15, 1969, p. 22. See also *S.F. Express Times*, Feb. 25, 1969, pp. 3, 10 (Glusman quote); *Berk. Barb*,

Feb. 21, 1969, pp. 5–6. The black man is quoted by Pat and Fred Cody in Nathan and Scott, 153. On Macias see *Berk. Barb*, Feb. 28, 1969, p. 5; Mar. 7, 1969, p. 4. The Guard, ibid., p. 3. On the strike's failure, ibid., Mar. 14, 1969, p. 7; *S.F. Express Times*, Mar. 11, 1969, p. 6. See also Timothy W. Armistead in *Issues in Criminology*, 4 (1969), 171–84; Ad Hoc Faculty Observers Comm. to Academic Senate, Mar. 4, 1969, 5:66, UCBCF; numerous documents, 10:111–12, UCBCF; Madigan testimony, 4912–25.

## Chapter 3.

(epigraph) *Grad. Student J.*, Spring 1965, p. 91, note 53.

1. In general see Maurice Isserman, *If I Had a Hammer* (N.Y., 1987); William L. O'Neill, *A Better World* (N.Y., 1982); and Joseph R. Starobin, *American Communism in Crisis, 1943–1957* (Cambridge, Mass., 1972). On specifics see Frank J. Donner, *The Un-Americans* (N.Y., 1961), esp. 61–70; Frank J. Donner, *The Age of Surveillance* (N.Y., 1980), 4, 7, 9, 13, 16, 94–95, 130–32. For the communist perspective see Peggy Dennis, *The Autobiography of an American Communist* (Westport, 1977), esp. 176, 203; Al Richmond, *A Long View from the Left* (N.Y., 1972); Nat Yanish, *Pursuit and Survival* (S.F., 1981); William M. Mandel letters, *Berk. Barb*, Nov. 29, 1968, p. 14; Dec. 20, 1968, p. 2. On the bipartisan nature of the attack see Roger Kent to Robert B. River, Nov. 2, 1961; leaflet, Oct. 28, 1961, both in Box 8, Roger Kent Papers; Don Mulford to Clark Kerr, May 7, 1963; reply, May 14, 1963, both in 1293:1, UCPF; Berk. School of Anti-Communism announcement, Feb. 1–5, 1965, 1294:9, UCPF; "We Refuse to Debate Marxists," Apr. 23, 1965, leaflet, 1294:11, UCPF; Adrian A. Kragen memo, Dec. 6, 1960; Henry Helson to Dean Lincoln Constance, Mar. 22, 1961; BUSD announcement, Sept. 1, 1961; Richard C. Placone to Harry Wellman, Sept. 29, 1961, all in 1302:1, UCPF; William Petersen to Kerr, Mar. 2, 1962, 1302:2, UCPF. See also Mrs. Evelyn L. Dutton to Kerr, Nov. 13, 1964, 1304:7, UCPF; S. L. Shride to the Regents, May 25, 1963, 1304:13, UCPF; V. L. Westberg to Kerr, May 27, 1966, 1304:15, UCPF.

2. On the thirties see Richmond, 343; Henry F. May, "The Student Movement: Some Impressions at Berkeley," *American Scholar*, 34 (1965), 388–89; Henry F. May, *Coming to Terms* (Berk., 1987), 185, 200–207; *Berk. Gate*, Jan. 4, 1965, p. 1; J. K. Galbraith, "Berkeley in the Age of Innocence," *Atlantic*, June 1969, p. 65; Thomas J. Kent, Jr., "Professor and Political Activist," in "Statewide and Regional Land-Use Planning in California, 1950–1980" (1983), interview, 2:15; Josephine Miles, "Poetry, Teaching, and Scholarship" (1980), interview, 320; Kerr commencement address, June 12, 1965, pp. 1–7, 3:3, FSM Arch. On the congenial environment see Nathan Glazer, *Remembering the Answers* (N.Y., 1970), 14–15; Fred Halstead, *Out Now!* (N.Y., 1978), 155. On moving to Berkeley see Lewis S. Feuer, *The Conflict of Generations* (N.Y., 1969), 439; Isserman, 22, 31, 56; Joseph P. Lyford, *The Berkeley Archipelago* (Chicago, 1982), 175; Dennis, 11, 258–88; Worden McDonald, *An Old Guy Who Feels Good* (Berk., 1978), 120, 122, 149, 153. The quote is from *BCU Bulletin*, Sept. 1965, p. 3. See also *Berk. Barb*, Feb. 18, 1966, p. 3. On Berkeley see American Security Council, *Washington Report*, Feb. 8, 1965, copy in 1294:2, UCPF; and the local anticommunist publication, *Tocsin*, 1961–66.

3. On the CIO see Richmond, 244, 293, 296. On *People's World*, ibid., 271, 273, 274, 294, 300, 364. On Richmond's arrest, ibid., 302, 351, 360. UCB policy is in *Berk. Gazette*, Mar. 20, 1961, p. 4. On Mandel see Feuer, *Conflict*, 440; *Berk. Barb*,

Oct. 15, 1965, p. 1; *Berk. Gazette,* May 14, 1960, p. 2; Apr. 12, 1969, p. 1; *Berk. Review,* Feb. 1, 1962, pp. 5, 9; *Tocsin,* Dec. 12, 1964, p. 1; Free Univ. of Berk., *Catalog,* Spring 1968, p. 9; Hardin B. Jones to Edwin Pauley, Apr. 8, 1969, 2:EP, Jones Papers, HI. On SLATE see Calif. Senate Fact-Finding Subcommittee on Un-American Activities, *Eleventh Report* (Sacramento, 1961), 23; *Daily Cal.,* Mar. 1, 1961; Mar. 22, 1961; June 10, 1961; *Tocsin,* June 20, 1964, p. 2; Michael Rossman et al., "Administrative Pressures and Student Political Activity at the University of California: A Preliminary Report" (1964), Appendix on HUAC, pp. 11–14. On Hallinan see Vincent Hallinan, *A Lion in Court* (N.Y., 1963); James P. Walsh, *San Francisco's Hallinan* (Novato, Calif., 1982). The teachers are in Donner, *Un-Americans,* 2, 190–95. On KPFA see *KPFA Program Folio,* Feb. 25, 1963, insert; U.S. Senate Comm. Hearings, *Pacifica Foundation Hearings,* 88th Cong., 1st Sess. (Wash., 1963), Pt. 1, Senate Library vol. 1581.

4. On members see Isserman, 28, 31; Richmond, 367. The Calif. style is noted in Isserman, 63, 67; Richmond, 382–86. On SDS see Kirkpatrick Sale, *SDS* (N.Y., 1973), 161, 168. On the DuBois Clubs see Dennis, 267–68; Paul Jacobs and Saul Landau, *The New Radicals* (N.Y., 1966), 48–51 (quote at 51); Michael Myerson, *These Are the Good Old Days* (N.Y.; 1970), 110–11, 124–26; Jack Newfield, *A Prophetic Minority* (N.Y., 1967; orig. 1966), 124–25, 129; James P. O'Brien, "The Development of a New Left in the United States, 1960–1965" (Ph.D. diss., Univ. of Wisconsin, 1971), 275–76. On the Sino-Soviet split, Dennis, 268. On Czechoslovakia see Richmond, 413, 429. In general see Dennis, 203, 260, 265, 267–68. See also Bob Kaufman, *Selected Writings* (L.A., 1980), esp. vi–vii, 243–65.

5. On Reynolds see *BCU Bulletin,* June 1967, p. 1; *Tocsin,* Aug. 21, 1962, pp. 1, 4; May 25, 1964, p. 3; Sept. 9, 1965, p. 3. On May see *Berk. Barb,* Oct. 1, 1965, p. 4; *Tocsin,* Jan. 15, 1964, p. 4. Seeger is noted in *Berk. Gate,* Oct. 3, 1967, pp. 10–11; *Daily Cal.,* Sept. 29, 1967, p. 9; Sept. 24, 1968, p. 15. Robeson is in Carol Sibley, *Never a Dull Moment* (Berk., 1972), 3. For the history of KPFA see *KPFA Program Folio,* 10th Anniversary Edition, Apr. 12, 1959; *Berk. Review,* Dec. 10, 1959, p. 7. Berkwood School, ibid., Dec. 24, 1959, p. 4; *Tocsin,* Oct. 23, 1963, p. 4.

6. Scheer is in *Berk. Barb,* Special Issue, Dec. 11, 1981; *Tocsin,* Oct. 7, 1965, p. 2. On Hayden's trip see Tom Hayden, *Reunion* (N.Y., 1988), 33–35; Hayden interview, *Rolling Stone,* Oct. 26, 1972, p. 38; James Miller, "*Democracy Is in the Streets*" (N.Y., 1987), 45–47; Rossman, "Administrative Pressures," Appendix on the *Daily Cal.,* pp. 8–9. Hayden's later time in Berkeley is noted in Hayden, *Reunion,* 327–38, 378, 420–26; Miller, 306–8, 318; Tom Hayden, *Rebellion and Repression* (N.Y., 1969), 11, 60; Tom Hayden, *Trial* (N.Y., 1970), 108–9. On Aptheker see *L.A. Times,* May 2, 1965, Sec. A, p. B; *Tocsin,* Oct. 23, 1962, pp. 1, 4. On UCB admission policy see Mrs. Peter J. Peterson to Kerr, Apr. 27, 1960; reply, both in 1302:8, UCPF. On Garson see Feuer, *Conflict,* 405; *Tocsin,* Nov. 6, 1962, p. 4. Camejo is in John R. Coyne, Jr., *The Kumquat Statement* (N.Y., 1970), 92; Halstead, 22–23, 490; *Berk. Barb,* Mar. 15, 1968, p. 8.

7. For a classic statement of the tension see William Mandel to Ron (Anastasi), Dec. 5, 1964, 1:19, FSM Arch. On the SDS see Miller, who reprints the Port Huron Statement as an appendix. Older, less satisfactory accounts include Irwin Unger, *The Movement* (N.Y., 1974); and Sale. Also useful are Todd Gitlin, *The Whole World Is Watching* (Berk., 1980), esp. 133–34; Isserman, esp. 208, 212; Stanley Aronowitz, "When the New Left Was New," in *The Sixties, without Apology,* ed. Sohnya Sayres et al. (Minneapolis, 1984), 11–43; *N.Y. Times Magazine,* Nov. 7, 1965, pp. 25ff. It is im-

portant to note that SDS was neither urban nor Jewish. See Isserman, 203, 207; Miller, 107.

8. The decline of ideology, noted by Daniel Bell and others in the fifties, contributed to growing alienation. See David Horowitz, *Student* (N.Y., 1962), 7–11. For a shrewd insight on ideology as a pacifier see Halstead, 132. The scornful quote is from Geoffrey White to Art Fox, Oct. 15, 1962, 1:5, White Papers, HI. By 1964 leftist youths were ready for action. See *Tocsin*, June 20, 1964, pp. 1, 4. Joe McDonald's "Who Am I" was written in 1965. See Ed Denson column, *Berk. Barb*, Dec. 29, 1967, p. 4. The lyrics reveal the pain of a disillusioned old leftist. Available on *The Life and Times of Country Joe and the Fish* (Vanguard VSD 27, 1971). Oglesby's quote is from the brilliant introduction to his edited *The New Left Reader* (N.Y., 1969), 15. The absence of ideology disturbed the local movement's theoreticians. For an analysis of Old Left v. New Left see Stewart Albert in *Berk. Barb*, Aug. 26, 1966, p. 5. See Marvin Garson, writing as "Silens Dewgood," ibid., July 14, 1967, p. 8, and the communist reply, July 28, 1967, p. 10. The fact that these varied views appeared in the same publication is itself a comment on the nature of Berkeley radicalism. See also Harold S. Jacobs, "The Personal and the Political: A Study of the Decline of the New Left" (Ph.D. diss. (Soc.), UCB, 1978), esp. 60, 62, 63, 72, 75, 82, 85, 95.

9. On Cuba see Calif. Senate Fact-Finding Comm. on Un-American Activities, *Thirteenth Report* (Sacramento, 1965), 79; R. G. Davis, *The San Francisco Mime Troupe* (Palo Alto, 1975), 95; Feuer, *Conflict*, 477. On the FPCC see *Tocsin*, Dec. 4, 1963, p. 3; Truth about Berk. Comm., *Berkeley* (Yorba Linda, Calif., 1966), 3. On Rubin as typical see Halstead, 156. For Rubin's biography see Jerry Rubin, *Growing (Up) at Thirty-Seven* (N.Y., 1976), 70–75; *Berk. Barb*, June 30, 1967, p. 1; *Berk. Gate*, Nov. 2, 1964, p. 2; *Tocsin*, Feb. 11, 1965, p. 1; Neil Smelser to Martin Meyerson, May 19, 1965, 12:133, UCBCF.

10. Coyne, 19; Miller, 173; Rubin in *Berk. Gazette*, Oct. 28, 1965, pp. 1, 8; Rubin in *Berk. Gate*, Mar. 8, 1966, p. 2; *Tocsin*, Oct. 21, 1965, p. 3. For a shrewd analysis see Stephan Weissman, "What the Students Want," *New Leader*, Jan. 4, 1965, pp. 11–15. For a cogent statement see Free Univ. of Berk., *Catalog*, Summer 1967, p. 4. The slogan is in Wini Breines, *Community and Organization in the New Left, 1962–1968* (N.Y., 1982), 18. Rubin quoted in Jerry Rubin, *Do It!* (N.Y., 1970), 235.

11. Early opposition to the war is noted in *Tocsin*, Oct. 23, 1963, p. 1; Nov. 13, 1963, p. 1; Feb. 25, 1965, p. 1; Mar. 4, 1965, p. 3. On the Michigan teach-in see Joseph Conlin, *The Troubles* (N.Y., 1982), 212; Halstead, 46–47; Miller, 229. On the innovative aspect see Michael Rossman, *New Age Blues* (N.Y., 1979), 102. Roger Heyns played a role in setting up the teach-in. On the Berkeley public meeting see *Daily Cal.*, Mar. 26, 1965, p. 3. The Washington march is in Halstead, 31–32, 36, 40; Miller, 227–33; Sale, 174.

12. BP Report, "Vietnam Day Committee" (1965), 1–2, IGSL; Halstead, 54–61, 66. On Smale see Calif. Senate Fact-Finding Comm. on Un-American Activities, *Thirteenth Report Supplement* (Sacramento, 1966), 79, 86–87, 110; *Oakland Tribune*, Oct. 29, 1965, p. 2; interview, *Dust*, Winter 1966, pp. 37–38, 1303:5, UCPF; *Tocsin*, Aug. 19, 1965, p. 4; biog. fact sheet, 2:6, Mulford Papers, HI. On planning see *Berk. Gazette*, May 1, 1965, p. 1; May 14, 1965, p. 1; *Daily Cal.*, May 3, 1965; May 14, 1965; May 20, 1965, p. 1; ASUC Minutes, May 4, 1965, 3:8, FSM Arch.; Neil Smelser to Martin Meyerson, May 11, 1965; Rubin and Smale to Meyerson, May 11, 1965, both in 10:117, UCBCF; Meyerson to all deans, May 14, 1965; Smelser to Meyerson, May 18, 1965; May 19, 1965, all in 12:133, UCBCF. On the speakers see VDC leaflet,

May 21, 1965, 1294:9, UCPF; VDC, "Vietnam Days," program; VDC, "Early Morning Activities," both leaflets in VDC 1965, SPP. On Mailer see *KPFA Program Folio*, June 28, 1965, p. 20. On Stone see *S.F. Chronicle*, May 22, 1965, pp. 1, 4. Transcripts of many radical speeches were published in *We Accuse* (Berk., 1965). A cleansed version of Mailer's is in Norman Mailer, *Cannibals and Christians* (N.Y., 1966), 68–82.

13. *Berk. Gazette*, May 18, 1965, p. 1; May 21, 1965, pp. 1–2; May 22, 1965, pp. 1–2; *L.A. Times*, May 22, 1965, Pt. I, pp. 1, 14; May 24, 1965, Pt. I, p. 3; *S.F. Chronicle*, May 22, 1965, pp. 1, 4; *People's World*, May 29, 1965, pp. 1, 2, 6. On the State Dept. see the *Daily Cal.*, May 20, 1965, p. 12. On Scalapino see his statement, May 20, 1965 (quote), 12:133, UCBCF; *Berk. Gazette*, May 20, 1965, p. 1; *Daily Cal.*, May 21, 1965, p. 1; contra, VDC, "VDC Answers Prof. Scalapino" (2-sided mimeo, May 1965), ICSL. On Burdick see *Berk. Gazette*, May 20, 1965, p. 7; *S.F. Chronicle*, May 20, 1965, p. 18. Burdick's untimely death is noted in *Berk. Gazette*, July 27, 1965. For reaction to the teach-in see Newell Hart letter, Logan, Utah, *Herald Journal*, May 27, 1965, 4:1, FSM Arch.; Leone Weaver memo of conversation with Ruediger Bilawski, May 21, 1965; Smelser memo, May 27, 1965; UCB grounds and buildings memo, May 28, 1965, all in 12:133, UCBCF. On the march to the draft board see BP Report, 2; Richard Krech letter, *Berk. Gazette*, May 26, 1965. On James Petras see *Tocsin*, Sept. 25, 1963, p. 1.

14. On "Operation Abolition" see *BCU Bulletin*, June 1965, p. 1. See also ibid., July 1965, p. 2; Sept. 1965, p. 4. Basson to Petersen, July 14, 1965 (quote), 40:misc., Hardin B. Jones Papers, HI. See also *Despite Everything*, July 1965; notes on VDC meeting, July 6, 1965, 60:VDC, Jones Papers. On publicity see Smale interview, *Dust*, Winter 1966, p. 48.

15. Miller, 243; Rubin, *Do It!*, 32–34; *Berk. Gazette*, July 28, 1965; Aug. 5, 1965, pp. 1, 7, 10; Aug. 6, 1965, pp. 1, 2; Aug. 7, 1965, pp. 1, 2; *S.F. Chronicle*, Aug. 4, 1965; Aug. 6, 1965, pp. 1, 7; Aug. 7, 1965, pp. 1, 8; Aug. 16, 1965, p. 8; *Tocsin*, Aug. 12, 1965, p. 4; VDC, "Telegram to President Johnson," Aug. 6, 1965, leaflet, 1294:9, UCPF.

16. BP Report, 2–3; Rubin, *Do It!*, 35–36; *Berk. Barb*, Aug. 13, 1965, pp. 1–2; *Berk. Gazette*, Aug. 12, 1965, pp. 1, 2, 8; *Daily Cal.*, Aug. 13, 1965, pp. 1, 4 (signs quoted); *S.F. Chronicle*, Aug. 12, 1965, p. 3; Aug. 13, 1965, pp. 1, 10; VDC, "Stop the Troop Train!" Aug. 12, 1965, leaflet; VDC, "Troop Train Picket No. 4," Aug. 12, 1965, leaflet, both in VDC 1965, SPP. On littering see *Berk. Gazette*, Aug. 23, 1965, pp. 1, 2; *Daily Cal.*, Aug. 27, 1965, p. 9; Sept. 17, 1965, p. 3; Oct. 11, 1965, p. 10.

17. Editorial, *Berk. Barb*, Aug. 13, 1965; Boris Raymond letter, ibid., Sept. 30, 1966, pp. 10–11; Special Issue, ibid., Dec. 11, 1981; Scherr interview, *Daily Cal.*, Mar. 8, 1966, pp. 9–10; *Sunday Ramparts*, Oct. 2, 1966, p. 5; *San Diego Union*, Mar. 5, 1969; Arthur Seeger, *The Berkeley Barb* (N.Y., 1983), 11–13, 35–37; Robert J. Glessing, *The Underground Press in America* (Bloomington, Ind., 1970), 20–21, 84, 89–90, 124; Lawrence Leamer, *The Paper Revolutionaries* (N.Y., 1972), 30, 32–33; Abe Peck, *Uncovering the Sixties* (N.Y., 1985), 30–31, 321.

18. On troops see Halstead, 86; VDC, "Stop the Troop Train!" Aug. 12, 1965, VDC 1965, SPP. Bort quoted in *Berk. Gazette*, Aug. 11, 1965, p. 1. Rubin quoted in Rubin, *Do It!*, 38. DeBonis quoted in *Daily Cal.*, Aug. 13, 1965, p. 7. *Berk. Barb*, Aug. 13, 1965, p. 2 (quote). On the council meeting see *Berk. Gazette*, Aug. 10, 1965, p. 1; Aug. 11, 1965, pp. 1, 2; *S.F. Chronicle*, Aug. 11, 1965, p. 7.

19. For public opinion polls see *Oakland Tribune*, Dec. 11, 1965, p. 8; *S.F. Chron-*

*icle*, Nov. 10, 1965. On the Landauer group see *Berk. Gate*, Sept. 29, 1965, pp. 3–4; *Berk. Gazette*, Sept. 11, 1965, pp. 1, 5; *Daily Cal.*, Aug. 20, 1965, p. 5; Sept. 15, 1965, pp. 1, 7; Sept. 17, 1965, p. 8; Sept. 21, 1965, p. 9; Sept. 24, 1965, p. 1; Landauer et al., "Dear Faculty Member," Sept. 9, 1965, leaflet with attached 4pp. "Open Letter," VDC 1965, SPP. For the VDC response see *Daily Cal.*, Sept. 16, 1965, p. 6; Sept. 20, 1965, pp. 3, 12; VDC, "Reply," Sept. 13, 1965, 8pp., VDC 1965, SPP. The reply provoked Landauer et al., "Dear Faculty Member," n.d., leaflet, VDC 1965, SPP. The anti-anti-VDC group is in *Daily Cal.*, Sept. 21, 1965, p. 8. On the Faculty Peace Comm. see *Oakland Tribune*, Oct. 8, 1965, p. 18; David Krech et al., "Dear Colleagues," Sept. 1965, 1294:9, UCPF; Dean Johnson to Earl Bolton, Oct. 7, 1965, 1294:4, UCPF. For the prowar group see *Berk. Gazette*, Aug. 18, 1965, p. 1; Sept. 15, 1965, pp. 1, 2; *Daily Cal.*, Sept. 21, 1965, p. 8; Sept. 24, 1965, p. 12; David W. Louisell et al., "Dear Faculty Member," Sept. 13, 1965, leaflet, VDC 1965, SPP. *Berk. Barb*, Sept. 24, 1965, p. 4 (quote).

20. BP Report, 3; Rubin, *Growing*, 77 (quotes); *Berk. Gazette*, Oct. 12, 1965, p. 1; Oct. 13, 1965, p. 1; Oct. 14, 1965, pp. 1, 3; Oct. 15, 1965, pp. 1, 2, 19; *Daily Cal.*, Sept. 28, 1965, p. 1; Oct. 1, 1965, p. 1; Oct. 12, 1965, p. 1; Oct. 13, 1965, p. 1; Oct. 14, 1965, p. 1; Oct. 15, 1965, pp. 3, 5, 12; *N.Y. Times*, Oct. 11, 1965, p. 7; *Oakland Tribune*, Oct. 15, 1965, pp. 1, 2; *S.F. Examiner*, Oct. 12, 1965, pp. 1, 12; Oct. 13, 1965, p. 10; VDC leaflets, VDC 1965, SPP; *VDC News*, July-Aug. 1965, 1294:9, UCPF.

21. BP Report, 4–5; Bernice H. May, "A Native Daughter's Leadership in Public Affairs" (1976), interview, 382–83; Michael Rossman, "Breakthrough at Berkeley," *Center Magazine*, May 1968, pp. 43–44; *Berk. Gazette*, Aug. 18, 1965, p. 16; VDC, "Please Give Us Your Name," Oct. 1965, leaflet, VDC 1965, SPP. On Houlihan see *Berk. Gazette*, May 3, 1966, p. 1; *Daily Cal.*, Jan. 5, 1967, p. 9.

22. *Berk. Gazette*, Oct. 14, 1965, p. 1 (Coakley quote); Oct. 18, 1965, pp. 1, 4; Oct. 21, 1965, p. 1; *Daily Cal.*, Oct. 8, 1965, p. 1; Oct. 11, 1965, p. 1; Oct. 20, 1965, p. 1; Oct. 21, 1965, p. 1; Frank Orme letter, Nov. 11, 1965, p. 13; *Oakland Tribune*, Oct. 2, 1965, p. 1; editorial, Oct. 15, 1965, pp. 1, 2; Dec. 1, 1965, p. 1; *N.Y. Times*, Oct. 15, 1965, p. 3; Mulford press release, Oct. 15, 1965, IGSL. Jim Alexander to Brown, Oct. 18, 1965; Oliver Johnson to Brown, Oct. 17, 1965, both in Box 804, Brown Papers; Coakley to Brown, Oct. 1, 1965, 1294:4, UCPF (on this copy, Kerr's annotation suggests an injunction); Kerr to Heyns, Oct. 2, 1965; Oct. 3, 1965; Thomas J. Cunningham to Heyns, Oct. 6, 1965; Coakley, Madigan, Addison Fording, and Edward Toothman to Heyns, Oct. 14, 1965; Dick Hafner to Earl Cheit, Oct. 15, 1965; Cheit to Milton Gordon, Oct. 25, 1965; reply, Oct. 30, 1965; Cunningham to Coakley, Oct. 30, 1965, all in 12:134, UCBCF. Scheer quoted in *Sunday Ramparts*, Jan. 1, 1967, p. 5. On Poole see Cohelan to Roger Kent, July 11, 1968; July 22, 1968, both in Box 7, Roger Kent Papers; *Berk. Barb*, Mar. 28, 1969, p. 6; *Oakland Tribune*, Dec. 1, 1965, p. 1; Dec. 2, 1965, p. 1.

23. On the teach-in see BP Report, 5; VDC, "Final Program-International Days of Protest," Oct. 15–16, 1965, 2-sided leaflet, VDC 1965, SPP; Alexander Grendon memo, Oct. 19, 1965, 4:AG, Hardin B. Jones Papers, HI. On the march see BP Report, 6–7; Halstead, 87; Rubin, *Do It!*, 40–42; Tom Wolfe, *The Electric Kool-Aid Acid Test*, 191–201; Wallace Johnson in Harriet Nathan and Stanley Scott, eds., *Experiment and Change in Berkeley* (Berk., 1978), 187–88; Ilona Hancock, ibid., 367; *Berk. Gazette*, Oct. 16, 1965, pp. 1, 2; *Daily Cal.*, Oct. 18, 1965, pp. 1–3, 8–9; *Oakland Tribune*, Oct. 15, 1965, pp. 1, 2; Oct. 16, 1965, pp. 1, A, B; *S.F. Chronicle*, Oct. 16, 1965, pp 1, 7;

Mulford to Kerr, Oct. 20, 1965; reply, Nov. 5, 1965, both in 12:135, UCBCF. Scherr is in Leamer, 32. The march drew wide attention. *L.A. Times*, Nov. 2, 1965, Pt. II, pp. 1–3; Nov. 3, 1965, Pt. II, p. 2; *N.Y. Times*, Oct. 16, 1965, pp. 1, 2; Paris *Herald Tribune*, Nov. 4, 1965, p. 10; *American Opinion*, Dec. 1965, pp. 14–17; Henry Nash Smith to Leo Marx, Oct. 22, 1965, 3:4, Smith Papers.

24. In addition to the sources in note 23 see Halstead, 285; Wolfe, 201; *Daily Cal.*, Oct. 18, 1965, p. 9 (quote); Nov. 27, 1967, p. 6.

25. BP Report, 7–9; Allen Ginsberg in *The Sixties*, ed. Lynda R. Obst (N.Y., 1977), 160; Halstead, 87–88; Rubin, *Do It!*, 43–44 (Ginsberg and the Angel quoted at 43); Johnson in Nathan and Scott, 185–86; *Berk. Gazette*, Oct. 18, 1965, pp. 1, 2; *Daily Cal.*, Oct. 18, 1965, p. 1; *Oakland Tribune*, Oct. 17, 1965, pp. 1, B; *S.F. Sunday Examiner-Chronicle*, Oct. 17, 1965, pp. 1, 1B; *N.Y. Times*, Oct. 17, 1965, p. 43.

26. BP Report, 9–12; Ginsberg in Obst, 160–61; Halstead, 88–89; Wallace J. S. Johnson, *Responsible Individualism* (N.Y., 1967), 98–105; Johnson in Nathan and Scott, 191–92; Rubin, *Do It!*, 44–46 (Ginsberg quote at 45); Mulford press release, Oct. 19, 1965; Mulford speech, Oct. 19, 1965, both in IGSL; *Berk. Gazette*, Oct. 19, 1965, p. 1; Oct. 21, 1965, p. 1; Oct. 26, 1965, pp. 1, 3; Oct. 27, 1965, pp. 1, 4; Oct. 28, 1965, p. 1; Nov. 19, 1965, p. 1; Nov. 20, 1965, p. 1; Nov. 22, 1965, pp. 1, 18; *Daily Cal.*, Oct. 19, 1965, p. 1; Nov. 3, 1965, p. 1; Nov. 11, 1965, p. 1; Nov. 15, 1965, p. 1; Nov. 18, 1965, p. 1; Nov. 22, 1965, p. 9; *L.A. Free Press*, Nov. 12, 1965, p. 1; Nov. 19, 1965, p. 1; *N.Y. Times*, Oct. 24, 1965, p. 74; Nov. 20, 1965, p. 6; Nov. 21, 1965, p. 32; *Oakland Tribune*, Nov. 16, 1965, p. 1 (editorial); Nov. 18, 1965, p. 1; Nov. 19, 1965, pp. 1, 6; Nov. 20, 1965, p. 1; Nov. 21, 1965, pp. 1, A; *S.F. Chronicle*, Nov. 20, 1965, p. 1; *S.F. Sunday Examiner-Chronicle*, Nov. 21, 1965, Sec. 1, pp. 1, B. See the excellent feature series in the *L.A. Times*, Nov. 2, 1965, Pt. II, pp. 1–3; Nov. 3, 1965, Pt. II, pp. 1, 2; Nov. 4, 1965, Sec. II, pp. 1, 8. VDC, "General Membership Meeting Tonite!" n.d., leaflet; "The Right to March," n.d., 2-sided mimeo; "Alternative," n.d., leaflet; VDC, "Protection of the November 20 March," Nov. 11, 1965, leaflet; VDC, "VDC Policy and Information on Arrests," Nov. 1965, leaflet; "Allen Ginsberg's Suggestions . . . ," Nov. 1965, 6pp.; VDC, "Why We March . . . ," Nov. 1965, leaflet, all in VDC 1965, SPP; Michael Rossman, "An Alternative Proposal for November 20," Oct. 28, 1965, 4pp., 2:5, FSM/CSHE. On the Angels see Ginsberg in Obst, 161–62; Rubin, *Do It!*, 46; Wolfe, 150–58.

27. For Cohelan's biography see Serge Lang, *The Scheer Campaign* (N.Y., 1967), 5–8, 11–12, 15, 18; *Berk. Review*, Nov. 12, 1959, p. 9; T. J. Kent, Jr., in Nathan and Scott, 82, 85; "The Record of Jeffery Cohelan," pp. 1–2, SC 2, SPP. As a Cold-War Democrat see Pat and Fred Cody in Nathan and Scott, 140; *Berk. Barb*, Sept. 10, 1965, p. 1; *Berk. Gazette*, Mar. 11, 1963, p. 2. On Simon's campaign see Lang, 11–12; *People's World*, Aug. 21, 1965, p. 10; Alex C. Sherriffs to Cohelan, Aug. 4, 1965, inclosing Hafner notes on VDC meeting, July 7, 1965; Cohelan reply, Aug. 9, 1965, all in 12:133, UCBCF; VDC, "Vietnam Oriental Peace Groups," June 17, 1965, leaflet, VDC 1965, SPP; Daniel Simon, open letter, Aug. 9, 1965, SC, SPP. On the August picketing of Cohelan's office see Calif. Senate Comm. on Un-American Activities, *Thirteenth Report Supplement* (1966), 131; *Berk. Barb*, Aug. 20, 1965, pp. 1, 2; *Berk. Gazette*, Aug. 18, 1965, p. 16; *Daily Cal.*, Aug. 20, 1965, p. 4; *S.F. Chronicle*, Aug. 22, 1965, p. 14; Cong. of Unrepresented People, leaflet, Aug. 21, 1965, 1294:9, UCPF. On the February sit-in see *Berk. Barb*, Feb. 4, 1966, p. 1; Apr. 22, 1966, p. 3; *Daily Cal.*, Feb. 2, 1966, p. 1; Feb. 3, 1966, p. 1; Feb. 4, 1966, p. 1; Feb. 8, 1966, p. 1; VDC, "What Is Cohelan Doing about the War?" Feb. 3, 1966, 1294:9, UCPF.

On his 1966 campaign see *Berk. Barb*, June 3, 1966, p. 7.

28. Halstead, 156, 158–60 (Stapleton quote at 159), 162–65; Lang, 17–18; Michael Rossman, *On Learning and Social Change* (N.Y., 1972), 26; MacDougal in *Despite Everything*, Apr. 1966, pp. 5–13; Brian Turner quoted in Feuer, *Conflict*, 474; *Berk. Barb*, Nov. 26, 1965, p. 3; Jan. 21, 1966, p. 1; Jan. 28, 1966, pp. 1–2; Feb. 18, 1966, pp. 3, 5; *N.Y. Times Magazine*, Jan. 30, 1966, pp 13, 27. See the shrewd remarks in Jacobs and Landau, 65–69.

29. On Scheer see Scheer's introduction to Davis, 9; Feuer, *Conflict*, 460–61; Horowitz, 154; Lang, 15; Ephraim Kahn et al., "Dear Friend" (1966), SC, SPP; *Contemporary Authors* (Detroit, 1982), 106:437–38. Additional information is in Maurice Zeitlin and Robert Scheer, *Cuba, Tragedy in Our Hemisphere* (N.Y., 1963), on the page facing the inside cover, and in the same place in the variant English edition: Robert Scheer and Maurice Zeitlin, *Cuba: An American Tragedy* (Harmondsworth, Eng., 1964).

30. An early Scheer article on Vietnam is in Paul Krassner's *The Realist*, Mar. 1964.

31. On the film see *Daily Cal.*, May 8, 1964, p. 1; May 14, 1964, pp. 1, 16; May 21, 1964, p. 3. For a complaint concerning a later film see James Platt to Martin Meyerson, Apr. 1, 1965, 12:133, UCBCF. On the pamphlet see Lang, 15. Robert Scheer, *How the United States Got Involved in Vietnam* (Santa Barbara, 1965), 80 pp. Published in July; 3rd printing, Dec. Copy in SC, SPP. Some of this material was published in *Ramparts*, Jan-Feb. 1965, pp. 23–28.

32. Halstead, 160–61; *Berk. Barb*, Mar. 11, 1966, pp. 2 (quote), 5; Feb. 18, 1966, p. 2 (quote). See also ibid., Jan. 14, 1966, pp. 1, 2. On the campaign see Lang; SC, SPP, esp. Scheer's "Statement of Candidacy"; feature story, *People's World*, May 14, 1966, p. 9; Charles Sellers statement, *Daily Cal.*, Mar. 21, 1966, pp. 7, 11; *N.Y. Times*, May 30, 1966, p. 38.

33. Lang, xii–xiii, 15, 19–20, 200 (speech quoted); *Berk. Barb*, Jan. 21, 1966, p. 2; Jan. 28, 1966, p. 2; *Oakland Tribune*, June 7, 1966, p. 25; Scheer for Congress, "Dear Friends," Jan. 29, 1966, leaflet, SC 2, SPP.

34. Lang, 19 (quote); Richmond, 433; Bloice interview in Lang, 48–50.

35. Lang, 15, 19, 21–22, 104, 183; *Berk. Barb*, Jan. 21, 1966, p. 1; *Berk. Review*, Oct. 27, 1960, p. 8; *Sun-Reporter*, May 28, 1966, p. 4; E. Bay Friends of SNCC, Executive Comm., "Comments on Scheer and Treuhaft," leaflet, SC, SPP.

36. Margaret S. Gordon in Arthur Harris et al., *Bernice Hubbard May* (Berk., 1971), 49; Lang, xiii, 40, 45, 53–55, 83, 90, 92–94, 96–97, 104; *Berk. Citizen*, May 20, 1966, p. 4; *Berk. Gazette*, Apr. 15, 1966, p. 1; Apr. 29, 1966, p. 6; May 5, 1966, p. 6; May 26, 1966, p. 6; May 30, 1966, p. 3; June 2, 1966, p. 6; *Berk. Barb*, Jan. 28, 1966, p. 3 (quote); *Daily Cal.*, Feb. 14, 1966, p. 1; Cohelan statement, Mar. 15, 1966, IGSL; "Cohelan and Coakley? Liberalism and Reaction?" n.d., leaflet, SC, SPP.

37. On the clubs see T. J. Kent, Jr., in Nathan and Scott, 98; Frederick G. Dutton, "Democratic Campaigns and Controversies, 1954–1966" (1981), interview, 166; *Berk. Barb*, Feb. 18, 1966, p. 3; May 13, 1966, p. 1; *Berk. Gazette*, Apr. 12, 1966, p. 3; *Daily Cal.*, Feb. 16, 1966, p. 7; Spurgeon Avakian to Roger Kent, Apr. 11, 1962; Nov. 5, 1963; to Gov. Brown, Sept. 4, 1963, all in Box 1, Roger Kent Papers; Jeffery Cohelan to Kent, Dec. 2, 1960; Oct. 3, 1968; replies, Dec. 7, 1960; Feb. 23, 1961, all in Box 7, Kent Papers. On Casady see Lang, 40; *Ramparts*, Oct. 1966, pp. 19–20; Roger Kent, "Building the Democratic Party in California, 1954–1966" (1981), interview, 256–57, 260; Richard Kline, "Governor Brown's Faithful Adviser," in "The Governor's Office under Edmund G. Brown, Sr." (1981), interview, 25; *Berk. Barb*, Feb. 25, 1966, p. 3; *Berk. Citizen*, Apr. 8, 1966, p. 3; *Daily Cal.*, Sept. 25, 1965, p. 1; Mar. 21,

1966, p. 9. On the campaign see Lang, 39; interviews with workers, ibid., 60–73; *Berk. Barb*, Jan. 21, 1966, p. 3; Apr. 8, 1966, p. 2; June 10, 1966, p. 1; *Berk. Citizen*, June 10, 1966, p. 3; May 20, 1966, p. 12; *Berk. Gazette*, Apr. 9, 1966, p. 2; May 4, 1966, p. 3; May 18, 1966, p. 9; *Daily Cal.*, May 16, 1966, p. 5.

38. Davis campaigned extensively for Scheer. See Davis, 37–38, 69–70, 77, 86 (quote), 124, 126, 203. Hayden, *Rebellion and Repression*, 41; *Berk. Barb*, Jan. 21, 1966, p. 3; Feb. 4, 1966, p. 2 (quote); Feb. 25, 1966, p. 2; *Daily Cal.*, Mar. 4, 1966, p. 3; Lang, 39 (quote). See also *Berk. Citizen*, June 10, 1966, p. 3. Scheer's brilliant speech to the CDC is in Lang, 41–43; Scheer interview, ibid., 113–17; Robert Scheer for Congress, "Draft Platform," 4pp., IGSL.

39. Lang, exp. xi–xii, 35, 40 (quote); *Berk. Barb*, June 3, 1966, pp. 1–2; *Daily Cal.*, Apr. 29, 1966, p. 3; *People's World*, May 7, 1966, p. 3. Scheer's ideals were similar to those of C. Wright Mills. One can see the same influences on Edward Keating at *Ramparts* and on Eugene McCarthy's presidential bid. See Miller, esp. 94.

40. Lang, 59, 109; *Berk. Barb*, June 10, 1966, pp. 1 (quote), 2; June 17, 1966, p. 3; *Berk. Citizen*, June 10, 1966, p. 4, Aug. 19, 1966, p. 2; *Berk. Gazette*, June 8, 1966, pp. 1–2. For a thorough analysis see Richard C. Howell, "A Contextual Perspective on Political Leadership" (M.A. thesis, S.F. State College, 1972), esp. 82–84. On the White House see Lewis Chester et al., *An American Melodrama* (N.Y., 1969), 64; Lang, xiv.

41. Rubin in *Obst*, 170–71 (quote at 170); Rubin, *Do It!*, 57–65; Rubin quoted in Halstead, 165; Rubin, *Growing*, 78 (last two quotes); *Berk. Barb*, Aug. 12, 1966, pp. 1, 5, 9; Aug. 19, 1966, p. 5; Aug. 26, 1966, p. 5; *Berk. Citizen*, Aug. 12, 1966, p. 2; *Oakland Tribune*, Aug. 18, 1966; *S.F. Chronicle*, Aug. 5, 1966.

42. On Smale's trip see *S.F. Examiner*, Aug. 5, 1966, p. 5; Aug. 6, 1966; *Berk. Barb*, Aug. 12, 1966, pp. 1, 9; *Berk. Gazette*, Aug. 26, 1966; *N.Y. Times*, Aug. 27, 1966, p. 1; *S.F. Chronicle*, Aug. 6, 1966; Smale press conference, Moscow, n.d., 2pp., 1303:5, UCPF. On the grant see Serge Lang to Thomas Sorenson, Sept. 12, 1966; Sept. 23, 1966; Sept. 29, 1966; Oct. 16, 1966; Smale to Lang, Sept. 28, 1966; Leon Henkin to Vice-Chancellor Robert E. Connick, Sept. 22, 23, 1966; Lang to Heyns, Oct. 4, 1966; Lang to Earl Cheit, Oct. 16, 1966; Wolfe memo to file, Nov. 15, 1966; Smale reply to *Science*, n.d.; American Mathematical Society, *Notices*, 778–86, all in 1303:5, UCPF. On the NSF grant see *Daily Cal.*, Oct. 2, 1967; Oct. 6, 1967, p. 18; *Oakland Tribune*, Sept. 15, 1967; Oct. 2, 1967; Henry Helson to Bill Arnold, Aug. 8, 1967; Harry R. Wellman to Inez Wenz, Dec. 13, 1967; *Lawrence Daily Journal-World*, clipping, all in 1303:6; UCPF; Rep. Richard Roudebush to Hardin B. Jones, Oct. 17, 1967, 40:misc., Jones Papers, HI. For later fallout see *S.F. Chronicle*, Oct. 22, 1968, p. 4.

43. Berkeley SDS did not participate in the Scheer campaign; for a defense of this self-destructive decision see Carolyn Craven et al., "Notes from the Underground" (1966), pp. 1–3, SC, SPP. See also Sale, 277. On the bombing see Donner, *Age*, 145, 435–40; *Berk. Gazette*, Apr. 9, 1966, pp. 1, 2; Apr. 11, 1966, p. 1, 3; Apr. 12, 1966, pp. 1, 2; *Oakland Tribune*, Apr. 9, 1966, pp. 1, A; Apr. 11, 1966, p. 16; *S.F. Chronicle*, Apr. 9, 1966, p. 1; *S.F. Sunday Examiner-Chronicle*, Apr. 10, 1966, p. B; *BCU Bulletin*, Mar. 1966, p. 3; *Sunday Ramparts*, Oct. 2, 1966, p. 5. The best coverage of the riot is in the *Oakland Tribune*, Apr. 13, 1966, pp. 1, 5; Apr. 14, 1966, pp. 1, 11 (Albert quote at 11). See also Halstead, 162–63; Wallace Johnson, "The Need to Know" (1968), 4, IGSL; *Berk. Barb*, Apr. 8, 1966, p. 1; Apr. 15, 1966, pp. 1, 3 (Garson quote at 3), 5; May 20, 1966, p. 10; *Berk. Citizen*, July 22, 1966, p. 2; *Berk. Gazette*, Apr.

11, 1966, p. 5; Apr. 13, 1966, pp. 1, 2 (chant and DeBonis quoted at 2); Apr. 15,
1966, p. 8; Apr. 21, 1966, p. 8; May 2, 1966, p. 1; *Daily Cal.*, Apr. 13, 1966, pp. 1-
3; Apr. 14, 1966, pp. 1, 16; Apr. 15, 1966, pp. 12-13; Marvin Garson columns, Apr.
19, 1966, p. 12; May 3, 1966, p. 12; *S.F. Chronicle*, Apr. 13, 1966, pp. 1, 14; Apr.
14, 1966, p. 2. For the effect upon Scheer see Lang, 217-18.

44. Halstead, 161; McLaren in Nathan and Scott, 237 (quotes); *Berk. Barb*, July 8,
1966, p. 3. For a trenchant essay see Buddy Stein and David Wellman, "The Scheer
Campaign," *Studies on the Left*, Jan.-Feb. 1967, pp. 62-77.

45. On the appointment see Elinor R. Heller, "A Volunteer Career in Politics, in
Higher Education, and on Governing Boards" (1984), interview, 593; Donald H.
McLaughlin, "Careers in Mining Geology and Management, University Governance
and Teaching" (1975), interview, 62-64, 81; Harry R. Wellman, "Teaching, Research,
and Administration: University of California, 1925-1968" (1976), interview, 161; *L.A.
Times*, Aug. 8, 1965, Sec. A, p. 2; *N.Y. Times*, July 27, 1965, pp. 1, 67; July 29,
1965, p. 24. On Heyns see Roger W. Heyns, "Berkeley Chancellor, 1965-1971" (1987),
interview, esp. iv-v; 1-2, 28-39, 43, 148-50; Kenneth Lamott, *Anti-California* (Boston, 1971), 111-17; Garff B. Wilson, "The Invisible Man" (1981), interview, 210, 213,
225-28; *S.F. News-Call-Bulletin*, July 27, 1965. On constraints see Heyns to President
Charles Hitch, Nov. 5, 1968, 2:18, UCBCF. On Cunningham see "RHC" memo to
Heyns, ca. Oct. 1967, 2:24, UCBCF. The Oakland establishment and conservatives
among the Regents may have deprived Heyns of his own counsel in order to use Cunningham to restrain the chancellor. For an example see Cunningham legal opinion,
Mar. 14, 1968; Cunningham ruling to Boyd, Apr. 3, 1968; Heyns report to Academic
Senate, Apr. 16, 1968, all in 3:28, UCBCF.

46. Heyns is quoted in Hardin B. Jones memo, p. 13, ca. 1965, 1:HBJ, John H.
Lawrence Papers, HI. O. Cort Majors to Richard E. Erickson, Feb. 10, 1966, 1294:4,
UCPF. On the Right see *Oakland Tribune*, Sept. 29, 1965, p. 1; *S.F. Chronicle*, Oct.
27, 1965, p. 1; Oct. 28, 1965, p. 42; Nov. 24, 1965; *BCU Bulletin*, Sept. 1966, p. 3;
Alexander Grendon, "Research with Hardin Jones at Donner Laboratory, 1957-1978"
(1985), interview, 45-52; Heller interview, 564; Heyns interview, 95-96; Albert G.
Pickerell to Adrian A. Kragen, Oct. 10, 1960, 1302:11, UCPF; Gerald Lee to Kerr,
Aug. 20, 1966, 1303:4, UCPF; Hardin B. Jones to Gov. Brown, Oct. 12, 1965, Box
802, Brown Papers; Jones to Heyns, Aug. 30, 1965, 2:Jones, Jones Papers, HI; Jones
notes, Feb. 1969 (quote); Jones to Pauley, n.d. (draft), ca. Jan. 1969 (quote), both in
2:Edwin Pauley, Jones Papers. See 3:R. E. Combs, Jones Papers; Alex Grendon to Gov.
Brown, 4:AG, Jones Papers. On the Left see Rubin, *Do It!*, 125, 147, 252; *Sacramento
Bee*, Sept. 25, 1966; *Spartacist*, May-June 1965, pp. 14-15; *Studies on the Left*, 5 #1
(1965), 65-67; David C. Fulton to Kerr, Sept. 2, 1965, 1294:4, UCPF; Jacob J. Finkelstein to Leon Henkin, May 24, 1966, 3:Academic Misconduct, Jones Papers. On
the phone harassment see Jones memo, pp. 14-15, ca. 1965, 1:HBJ, Lawrence Papers.

47. Heyns gave two important speeches. The one at the Greek Theatre is in *Berk.
Gazette*, Sept. 22, 1965, pp. 1, 10; *S.F. Chronicle*, Sept. 23, 1965, p. 9. On the one
to the S.F. Commonwealth Club, Nov. 12, 1965, see FM. On Aptheker see unidentified clipping, NEA (a CIA front), Oct. 6, 1966, 1304:8, UCPF; *Daily Cal.*, Nov. 9,
1965, pp. 1, 5; Nov. 24, 1965, p. 1; *N.Y. Times*, Nov. 11, 1965, p. 28; Nov. 25,
1965, p. 52; *N.Y. Times Magazine*, Jan. 30, 1966, pp. 28, 30, 32; *Oakland Tribune*,
Nov. 9, 1965, p. 1; Nov. 27, 1965, p. 1; *S.F. Chronicle*, Nov. 10, 1965, p. 8; Dec. 3,
1965. On Searle see Calif. Senate Fact-Finding Comm. on Un-American Activities,
*Thirteenth Report Supplement* (1966), 73; Feuer, *Conflict*, 462; Ed Montgomery speech,

*Berk. Gate*, Mar. 8, 1962, p. 8; *Daily Cal.*, Sept. 15, 1965, p. 1; Sept. 16, 1965, p. 1; Edward P. Morgan News, ABC Radio, transcript, June 24, 1965, 2:46, FSM Arch.; Alex Grendon notes, Dec. 9, 1965, 4:AG, Jones Papers; Jones memo, ca. 1965, pp. 11, 17–19, 1:HBJ, Lawrence Papers; Marvin Garson writing as "Silens Dewgood," *Berk. Barb*, July 14, 1967, p. 8; communist reply, July 28, 1967, p. 10; Melvin Calvin to Heyns, Feb. 19, 1968; John R. Searle, "The Three Stages of Student Revolt" (1968), both in 9:98, UCBCF. Searle published a different version in *N.Y. Times Magazine*, Dec. 29, 1968. On Searle's increasing conservatism see John R. Searle, *The Campus War* (N.Y., 1971). Jones to Thomas H. Carver, Feb. 10, 1969, 45:letters, Jones Papers; Fire and Police Association of Los Angeles, *Bulletin*, Oct. 16, 1969, p. 5, 1:12, Mulford Papers, HI.

48. Heyns statement for Regents, July 11, 1968 (not used); Irene Jerison and Eli A. Rubinstein, "Five under Protest" (Center for Advanced Study, Stanford, 1968), both in 9:98, UCBCF. On isolating activists see Richard P. Hafner, Jr., to Heyns, Dec. 13, 1967, 8:96, UCBCF; Melvin L. Perlman to Heyns, Dec. 4, 1966; Charles Kittel to Heyns, Dec. 1, 1966, both in 8:86, UCBCF. On Reagan's obtuseness see William J. McGill, *The Year of the Monkey* (N.Y., 1982), 82–83, 107, 158.

49. Heyns statement for Regents, July 11, 1968 (not used), 9:98, UCBCF. Calif. Assembly, *Report of the Select Committee on Campus Disturbances* (Sacramento, 1969), 21; *L.A. Times*, June 23, 1969. Two memos on statistics, 1964–69, are in 4:55, UCBCF. For an example see Heyns to Bettina Aptheker, Mar. 6, 1966; Mar. 10, 1966; Mar. 11, 1966; replies, Mar. 9, 1966; Mar. 10, 1966, all in 8:94, UCBCF.

50. *S.F. Chronicle*, Apr. 12, 1966, p. 3; Heyns to Jesse W. Tapp, June 6, 1966, 1303:2, UCPF. On the VDC's illegal rally see *Daily Cal.*, Feb. 7, 1966, p. 1; Mar. 8, 1966, p. 1; Mar. 16, 1966, pp. 1, 10; Mar. 31, 1966, p. 1; *New Left Notes*, Feb. 11, 1966, p. 1. On PROC see Halstead, 162, *Berk. Barb*, Aug. 12, 1966, p. 5; *Berk. Gate*, Mar. 22, 1966, pp. 1, 4; Mar. 29, 1966, pp. 3, 4; *Berk. Gazette*, Apr. 9, 1966, p. 2; *Daily Cal.*, Mar. 16, 1966, pp. 1, 10; Mar. 23, 1966, p. 1; Apr. 1, 1966, p. 1; Apr. 12, 1966, p. 14; Lois K. Thomas to Heyns, May 6, 1966; Damon F. Tempey to Heyns, May 6, 1966; Heyns to Marion Pastor, May 12, 1966; Heyns statement, May 12, 1966; Betty Neely memo, Oct. 18, 1966, all in 8:94, UCBCF. Quotes are from *Berk. Barb*, Apr. 8, 1966, p. 3.

51. On Charter Day see *Daily Cal.*, Mar. 10, 1966, p. 1; Mar. 28, 1966, pp. 1, 11; Marvin Garson column, Mar. 29, 1966, p. 12; *N.Y. Times*, Mar. 26, 1966, p. 2; *New Left Notes*, Apr. 1, 1966, p. 1. On the debate see Halstead, 142–43; *Daily Cal.*, Mar. 28, 1966, p. 3; Marvin Garson column, Mar. 29, 1966, p. 12; Serge Lang to *Newsweek*, Apr. 8, 1966 (unpub.), 1303:5, UCPF. The dance is noted in Calif. Senate Fact-Finding Comm. on Un-American Activities, *Thirteenth Report Supplement* (1966), 133; *Berk. Barb*, Mar. 25, 1966, p. 8; *Oakland Tribune*, Apr. 12, 1966, p. 11; *Sunday Ramparts*, Nov. 6, 1966, p. 1 (quote); Voice of Americanism broadcast transcript, n.d., 1293:9, UCPF; Coakley to Heyns, Apr. 7, 1966; reply, Apr. 18, 1966; Cheit memo of call to Bill Graham, May 4, 1966, all in 12:137, UCBCF; VDC Dance memo, 2:5 Mulford Papers; Heyns to Kent D. Pursel, Apr. 28, 1966, 40:misc., Jones Papers. On VDC tables see broadside, Apr. 11, 1966 (mimeo), FSM/H. On May events see *Berk. Barb*, May 20, 1966, pp. 1–2; May 27, 1966, p. 3; *Daily Cal.*, May 19, 1966, p. 3; VDC program leaflet, May 16, 1966, VDC 1966, SPP. On the ban see *Berk. Barb*, Aug. 19, 1966, p. 1; *Berk. Gazette*, Aug. 17, 1966, *Daily Cal.*, Aug. 24, 1966, p. 8; *N.Y. Times*, Aug. 15, 1966, p. 3; *S.F. Chronicle*, Oct. 8, 1966; Jim Sicheneder to Dean Jim Lemmon, Aug. 5, 1966; Lemmon to Peter Camejo, Aug. 12, 1966; Camejo

to Mrs. Jean Dobrzensky, Aug. 15, 1966, all in 12:136, UCBCF.

52. The proposed ban of microphones is covered in *Daily Cal.*, Sept. 30, 1966, p. 3; Nov. 7, 1966, p. 12; Nov. 9, 1966, p. 1; Nov. 10, 1966, p. 1; Searle, *Campus War*, 101. On the rally see *Daily Cal.*, Nov. 7, 1966, p. 1; *Sunday Ramparts*, Nov. 6, 1966, pp. 1, 4; "The Save the Steps Rally" (1966), transcript. On the campaign see Hale Champion, "Communication and Problem-Solving: A Journalist in State Government" (1981), interview, 58–60, 64, 67–69; Roger Kent interview, 280–81; Kline interview, 25–26; *Daily Cal.*, Nov. 3, 1966; *N.Y. Times*, May 14, 1966, p. 14; Sept. 10, 1966, p. 13; Sept. 16, 1966, p. 27; James Reston column, Oct. 23, 1966; editorial, Riverside *Daily Enterprise*, June 1, 1966. For Reagan's use of this issue see Lou Cannon, *Ronnie and Jesse* (Garden City, N.Y., 1969), 82–83; campaign files, Ronald Reagan Papers, HI. Savio's denial of readmission is in *Berk. Gazette*, Jan. 20, 1967; *Daily Cal.*, Nov. 9, 1966, p. 1; *N.Y. Times*, Nov. 9, 1966, p. 43. On the Regents see Heller interview, 585, 587, 589; *Berk. Citizen*, Nov. 18, 1966, p. 1; *Daily Cal.*, Nov. 16, 1966, p. 3; Bill Boyarsky, *The Rise of Ronald Reagan* (N.Y., 1968), 229, 236.

53. *Berk. Barb*, Dec. 2, 1966, pp. 1–3; Special Strike Issue, Dec. 5, 1966, p. 4; *Daily Cal.*, Dec. 1, 1966, pp. 1, 9; Searle, *Campus War*, 104. On Heyns's absence and Cheit as a hawk see *Sunday Ramparts*, Dec. 4, 1966, p. 3; Tom Collins column, *Daily Cal.*, Nov. 15, 1967, p. 18.

54. Sheldon S. Wolin and John H. Schaar, *The Berkeley Rebellion and Beyond* (N.Y., 1970), 53–57; *Berk. Barb*, Dec. 2, 1966, p. 1; Dec. 5, 1966, p. 3; *Daily Cal.*, Dec. 1, 1966, pp. 1, 9; London *IT*, Jan. 16, 1967, p. 4; *N.Y. Times*, Dec. 1, 1966, p. 29; *Science*, Dec. 9, 1966, pp. 1304–6; Michael S. Fuss statement, n.d., 8:88, UCBCF. On Albert see Free Univ. of Berk., *Catalog*, 1st Session 1966, p. 2; *S.F. Bay Guardian*, June 14, 1979, pp. 13–14; *S.F. Sunday Examiner-Chronicle*, Feb. 27, 1966, Sec. 1, p. 4; (Miller) *Berk. Barb*, Mar. 3, 1967, p. 1; Mar. 31, 1967, p. 13; *Berk. Gate*, Oct. 3, 1967, p. 10; (Smith) *S.F. Bay Guardian*, June 14, 1979, pp. 9–10; (Wald) Rubin, *Do It!*, 29 (quote); *San Diego Union*, Mar. 2, 1969; feature story, *Wall Street Journal*, May 15, 1967, p. 18. On the trial see Rubin, *Do It!*, 30–31; *Berk. Gate*, Oct. 3, 1967, p. 9; *Berk. Gazette*, Jan. 20, 1967, pp. 1, 7; Mar. 1, 1967; *Daily Cal.*, Mar. 1, 1967, p. 1; *Oakland Tribune*, Jan. 20, 21, 1967; "Justice Is Not Blind" (mimeo misdated Mar. 6, 1965, actually 1967), FSM/H.

55. For the chancellor's brilliant understanding of the situation see "ECL" rough notes of Heyns's comments to Regents, Dec. 7, 1966, 1293:6, UCPF. On the strike see Feuer, *Conflict*, 458; Rossman, "Breakthrough," 45–46; Rubin, *Do It!*, 30; *Berk. Barb*, Dec. 2, 1966, pp. 1, 3; Special Strike Issue, Dec. 5, 1966; *Daily Cal.*, Dec. 1, 1966, pp. 1, 12; Dec. 2, 1966, pp. 1, 2, 12; Dec. 6, 1966, pp. 1, 8; Jan. 30, 1967, p. 1; *L.A. Times*, Dec. 11, 1966, Sec. C, pp. 1, 7; *N.Y. Times*, Dec. 2, 1966, pp. 1, 28; Dec. 3, 1966, p. 33; Dec. 4, 1966, p. 85; Dec. 5, 1966, pp. 1, 55; Dec. 6, 1966, p. 29; Dec. 7, 1966, p. 36; Dec. 8, 1966, pp. 36, 46; *New Left Notes*, Dec. 2, 1966, pp. 1–2; "Keep Striking!!" Dec. 1966, leaflet; AFT Local 1570, "Where We Stand," Jan. 1967, leaflet, both in 2:14, FSM/CSHE; Kerr to Heyns, Dec. 2, 1966; Marjorie Woolman to Regents, Dec. 3, 1966; Kerr to chancellors, Dec. 3, 1966; "nancy" memo, Dec. 6, 1966; Regents Minutes, Dec. 6, 1966; Mulford to Theodore R. Meyer, Dec. 5, 1966; reply, Dec. 6, 1966; Kerr to Heyns, Dec. 9, 1966, all in 8:88, UCBCF. See survey data in William A. Watts et al., "Alienation and Activism in Today's College Age Youth," *Journal of Counseling Psychology*, 16 (1969), 1–7. For hostility to the strike see John S. Hadsell to Heyns, Dec. 3, 1966; Marshall Madison to Heyns, Dec. 7, 1966; Mrs. Robert McNamara to Heyns, n.d., all in 7:85, UCBCF; James B. Widess

to Heyns, Dec. 5, 1966 (quote); John Hewitt and Michael Thorn to Heyns, Dec. 4, 1966; Brinton H. Stone to Earl F. Cheit, Dec. 2, 1966; Daniel E. Koshland, Jr., to Cheit, Dec. 14, 1966; Ki-Shik Han to Heyns, Dec. 2, 1966; Peter Berger to Jan D. Blais, Jan. 18, 1967; Reinhard Bendix to Heyns, Dec. 15, 1966; Inge Bell to Heyns, n.d.; *University Bulletin*, Dec. 12, 1966, p. 81, all in 8:86, UCBCF; (deleted) to Hans Rosenhaupt, Jan. 9, 1967 (quote), 8:89, UCBCF.

56. On Kerr's dismissal see McGill, 62; Boyarsky, 232, 237–39, 241–46; Cannon, 233–34; Heller interview, 587–89, 600–601; McLaughlin interview, 68; G. Wilson interview, 205–6, 209; Wellman interview, 203–6. For an unbelievable account see John E. Canaday, "Alumni Officer and University Regent" (1975), interview, 162–63. *Berk. Barb*, Jan. 27, 1967, p. 1; *Berk. Citizen*, Nov. 18, 1966, p. 1; *Berk. Gate*, Jan. 24, 1967, pp. 6–10; editorial, *Berk. Gazette*, Jan. 23, 1967, p. 6; Jan. 24, 1967; *Daily Cal.*, Nov. 16, 1966, p. 3; Jan. 9, 1967, p. 1; Jan. 13, 1967, p. 1; Jan. 23, 1967, pp. 1, 2, 5, 12; Jan. 25, 1967, pp. 3, 11, 12; Jan. 31, 1967, p. 1; *N.Y. Times*, Jan. 15, 1967, Sec. 4, p. 13; Jan. 21, 1967, pp. 1, 28; Jan. 24, 1967, p. 46; Jan. 25, 1967, p. 33; Jan. 26, 1967, pp. 17, 44; *S.F. Chronicle*, Dec. 7, 1966; Jan. 21, 1967, pp. 1, 7–9; Jan. 23, 1967, pp. 1, 7; Jan. 24, 1967, pp. 1, 12, 36, 39; Jan. 25, 1967, pp. 1, 42; *S.F. Sunday Examiner-Chronicle*, Jan. 22, 1967, Sec. 1, pp. 1, 6–8; editorial, Sec. II, p. 2; *Sunday Ramparts*, Special Supplement, Jan. 29, 1967. Hardin B. Jones to Ed Pauley, Aug. 21, 1966; Jones to John Canaday, Aug. 29, 1966, both in 40:misc., Jones Papers; Lee E. Preston to Josephine Miles, May 2, 1967, 5.22, Miles Papers; Henry Nash Smith to Leo Marx, Nov. 15, 1966, Jan. 31, 1967, Feb. 20, 1967, all in 3:4, Smith Papers.

57. On militants see Halstead, 161, 207; the conjectured quote is in Miles interview, 104. On the CNP see the *Communiqué for New Politics*, July 25, 1966–Feb. 3, 1969, esp. Nov. 30, 1968, p. 3; and its successors, *Coalition News* and *Berk. Monitor*. See also Calif. Senate Fact-Finding Subcommittee on Un-American Activities, *Fourteenth Report* (Sacramento, 1967), 97–128, 136–54 (leaflet quoted at 114); *Berk. Barb*, July 8, 1966, p. 2; July 15, 1966, p. 2; July 22, 1966, p. 2; *Berk. Citizen*, July 8, 1966, p. 3; *Berk. Gate*, Jan. 3, 1967, p. 3; Feb. 1, 1967, pp. 3, 5; *Berk. Gazette*, June 9, 1966, p. 3; Mar. 31, 1967, pp. 1, 2; Oct. 3, 1967; *Daily Cal.*, June 21, 1966, p. 5; June 29, 1966, pp. 1, 16; Sept. 28, 1966, p. 9; "West Magazine," *L.A. Times*, May 5, 1968, pp. 29–35. On the national CNP see *Berk. Barb*, Sept. 8, 1967, pp. 3, 4; Sept. 15, 1967, p. 9. On the state CNP see ibid., Sept. 22, 1967, p. 5; Oct. 6, 1967, p. 9. On Hancock see Nathan and Scott, 368–71.

58. On the BDC see T. J. Kent, Jr., in Nathan and Scott, 98–99; Gordon in Harris, May, 49–50; *Berk. Barb*, Mar. 17, 1967, p. 2; *Berk. Citizen*, Feb. 10, 1967, p. 1. On the CNP candidates see Calif. Senate Fact-Finding Subcommittee on Un-American Activities, *Fourteenth Report* (1967), 121–24; (Avakian) Halstead, 466; *Berk. Barb*, Jan. 27, 1967, p. 4; Feb. 3, 1967, p. 4; Mar. 10, 1967, p. 3; *Berk. Citizen*, Feb. 3, 1967, p. 2; *Berk. Gazette*, Mar. 28, 1967, p. 1; *Daily Cal.*, Feb. 17, 1967, p. 3; *BCU Bulletin*, Sept. 1967, p. 3 (quote); Oct. 1967, p. 1; May 1969, p. 9. On his evolution as a Maoist see Bob Avakian, *Bullets* (Chicago, 1985); (Harawitz) *Berk. Barb*, June 2, 1967, p. 7; *Berk. Gazette*, Mar. 29, 1967, p. 1; *People's World*, Mar. 11, 1967, p. 3; *BCU Bulletin*, Jan. 1966, p. 3; *Tocsin*, Mar. 11, 1965, p. 4; Box 677, Brown Papers; (Neilands) *Berk. Barb*, Mar. 24, 1967, p. 2; *Berk. Citizen*, Apr. 1, 1966, p. 15; Mar. 3, 1967, p. 3; *Berk. Gazette*, Mar. 23, 1967, pp. 1, 3; Mar. 27, 1967, pp. 1, 3; *Daily Cal.*, Mar. 29, 1967, p. 1; Apr. 3, 1967, p. 12; Sept. 30, 1968, p. 3; Nov. 4, 1968, p. 1; biog. fact sheet, 2:3, Mulford Papers.

59. Gordon is quoted in Harris, *May*, 49. Rubin's vote is in Rubin, *Do It!*, 146. On the campaign see Gordon in Nathan and Scott, 311–12; May interview, 397–404; *Berk. Barb*, Mar. 31, 1967, pp. 3–11; *Berk. Gazette*, Jan. 13, 1967, Feb. 8, 1967, pp. 1–2; CNP candidates letter, Feb. 9, 1967; Feb. 16, 1967; Feb. 23, 1967; Mar. 9, 1967; editorial, Mar. 14, 1967; *Daily Cal.*, Jan. 20, 1967, p. 5; Feb. 17, 1967, p. 3; *People's World*, Mar. 18, 1967, p. 3; *Sunday Ramparts*, Mar. 29, 1967, pp. 1, 3; *BCU Bulletin*, Apr. 1967, p. 1; Bay Area Spartacist Comm., "Why You Should Vote Socialist," Mar. 1965 (2-sided mimeo), 2:5, FSM/CSHE. On the returns see Lyford, 22; *Berk. Gazette*, Apr. 6, 1967, p. 2.

60. Wallace J. S. Johnson, *A Fresh Look at Patriotism* (Old Greenwich, Conn. 1976), v–vii; Johnson, *Responsible*, 56–57, 107–21; Johnson in Nathan and Scott, 193–201; Gordon, ibid., 311; *Berk. Barb*, Jan. 13, 1967, p. 7; Mar. 3, 1967, p. 3; Mar. 31, 1967, p. 5; *Daily Cal.*, Mar. 30, 1967, p. 3; Apr. 4, 1967, p. 9; *BCU Bulletin*, Jan. 1967, p. 1; Feb. 1967, p. 2.

61. Rubin, *Do It!*, 47–51; Rubin, *Growing*, 79; Jerry Rubin, comp., Portfolio of Jerry Rubin for Mayor of Berkeley (1967), ca. 20 items. See esp. the brochure, "For Mayor of Berkeley Jerry Rubin: The Program," 4–6, 8, 13–15, 18–20, 22; Johnson, *Look*, 72–75 (quote at 73); Johnson in Nathan and Scott, 206–28; Calif. Senate Fact-Finding Subcommittee on Un-American Activities, *Fourteenth Report* (1967), 115–17; *Berk. Barb*, Feb. 10, 1967, pp. 1, 3; Feb. 17, 1967, pp. 1, 5; Mar. 3, 1967, p. 3; Mar. 10, 1967, pp. 1, 2; Mar. 31, 1967, pp. 2, 3; Apr. 7, 1967, pp. 1, 7; June 2, 1967, p. 10; *Berk. Citizen*, Mar. 3, 1967, pp. 1, 4; *Berk. Gazette*, Apr. 3, 1967, p. 7; *Daily Cal.*, Feb. 10, 1967, p. 2; Mar. 29, 1967, p. 12; Mar. 31, 1967, p. 16; *People's World*, Mar. 25, 1967, p. 3; *Sunday Ramparts*, Feb. 12, 1967, pp. 1–2; *S.F. Bay Guardian*, June 14, 1979, p. 13. For returns see *Berk. Gazette*, Apr. 6, 1967, p. 1.

62. Cohelan to Jones, May 10, 1967, 40:misc., Jones Papers; Avakian in *Berk. Gazette*, Apr. 6, 1967, p. 2. See Mulford, ibid., Sept. 14, 1966, p. 1.

63. On Greene see *Berk. Barb*, Jan. 28, 1966, p. 8; Sept. 23, 1966, p. 4; *Daily Cal.*, Feb. 2, 1966, p. 13; Feb. 8, 1968, p. 17; *Communiqué for New Politics*, June 19, 1967, p. 1; VDC, "Saturday May 21, 1966 Protest," leaflet, VDC 1965, SPP; Felix Greene, *Vietnam! Vietnam!* (Palo Alto, 1966). On Duncan see his speech, VDC rally, Nov. 20, 1965, 5pp., VDC 1965, SPP; *Berk. Citizen*, Dec. 16, 1966, p. 2; *Daily Cal.*, Feb. 24, 1966, p. 13; Apr. 29, 1966; p. 3; Oct. 10, 1967, p. 1; *Oakland Tribune*, Oct. 13, 1967, p. 2. On KQED see *Berk. Barb*, Feb. 9, 1968, p. 2. "Newsroom" began during a strike that shut down San Francisco's daily newspapers. Videotapes are available at S.F. State Univ. On KPFA see, e.g., *Berk. Barb*, Apr. 4, 1969, p. 9; Marshall Windmiller commentary in Lang, 193–97. Circulations are in *Berk. Barb*, Mar. 31, 1967, p. 12.

64. On the Mime Troupe's skit see Davis, 81–82. The script for "L'Amant Militaire" is at 173–93. See also *Berk. Barb*, May 19, 1967, pp. 1, 11; *Daily Cal.*, Apr. 18, 1968, p. 10; *Communiqué for New Politics*, June 19, 1967, p. 2. On McDonald see *Daily Cal.*, Mar. 9, 1966, p. 10; Nov. 7, 1966, p. 1; Sol Stern, "Altamont," in *Counterculture and Revolution*, ed. David Horowitz et al. (N.Y., 1972), 127. On Baez see *Berk. Barb*, Nov. 15, 1968, p. 25; *Daily Cal.*, June 21, 1968, p. 1. Barbara Garson, *MacBird* (N.Y., 1967); reviewed, *Daily Cal.*, Mar. 30, 1966, p. 14. See also *Berk. Barb*, Sept. 9, 1966, p. 3; *Oakland Tribune*, Feb. 23, 1967; Donner, *Age*, 254. On baloney see *Berk. Barb*, Aug. 11, 1967, pp. 3, 7 (quotes at 7).

65. See Scheer commentary, Jan.-Feb. 1965, pp. 23–28; his important interview with Prince Sihanouk, July 1965, pp. 25–31; his scathing review of the analytical in-

adequacies of David Halberstam's *The Making of a Quagmire*, pp. 63–64, in the same issue, which was mostly devoted to Vietnam; and his "The Winner's War," Dec. 1965, pp. 19–22. Cleaver's first reports were "Notes on a Native Son," June 1966, pp. 51–56, and "Letters from Prison," Aug. 1966, pp. 15–26. On Michigan State University see Warren Hinckle III et al., "MSU: The University on the Make," Apr. 1966, pp. 11–22. On the National Student Association see Sol Stern, "NSA and the CIA," Mar. 1967, pp. 29–39. For reaction on campus see *Daily Cal.*, Feb. 15, 1967, p. 1; Feb. 16, 1967, p. 1; Feb. 21, 1967, p. 1. Suspicions about the burglary are in *Sunday Ramparts*, Apr. 9, 1967, pp. 1, 6. Proof is in Donner, *Age*, 437. See Angus Mackenzie, "Sabotaging the Dissident Press," in Geoffrey Rips et al., *Unamerican Activities* (S.F., 1981), 160–61. On Oakland see "Metropoly," Feb. 1966, pp. 25–50. On Johnson's friends see David Welsh, "Building Lyndon Johnson," Dec. 1967, pp. 52–64. Finances were noted in *S.F. Bay Guardian*, Mar. 27, 1969, pp. 1–2.

66. On frustration see Gitlin, *World*, 159; Hayden, *Rebellion and Repression*, 30; Brian Turner column, *Daily Cal.*, Apr. 15, 1966, p. 12; Feb. 20, 1967, p. 5. On channeling see Donner, *Age*, 233; Hayden, *Rebellion and Repression*, 28–29; *Berk. Barb*, June 9, 1967, p. 3; *Daily Cal.*, Oct. 17, 1967, p. 11; *Steps*, #2 (ca. 1967), 67–69; "Channeling" memo, 12:136, UCBCF. On the arbitrary nature of draft boards see Derald Glidden letter, *Daily Cal.*, Feb. 21, 1966, p. 8; Lawrence M. Baskir and William A. Strauss, *Chance and Circumstance* (N.Y., 1978). Antidraft organizing is in Coyne, 57; *Berk. Gate*, Jan. 3, 1967, pp. 1–2; Jan. 24, 1967, pp. 1–2, 4. For examples of individual difficulties see Dennis, 274–75; *Berk. Barb*, Oct. 29, 1965, pp. 1, 4; Sept. 30, 1966, p. 4, Feb. 10, 1967, p. 3, Mar. 3, 1967, pp. 1, 9, Mar. 10, 1967, p. 3, Apr. 28, 1967, p. 3; May 19, 1967, p. 6; June 2, 1967, p. 3; June 23, 1967, p. 2; Aug. 11, 1967, p. 5; Aug. 18, 1967, p. 2; Sept. 1, 1967, p. 3; Dec. 12, 1967, p. 1; *Berk. Gate*, Jan. 24, 1967, pp. 2, 9; Mar. 7, 1967, pp. 1, 5, 10; *Daily Cal.*, Mar. 14, 1966, p. 6; May 8, 1968, p. 2; *S.F. Chronicle*, Mar. 23, 1965.

67. The law penalizing the burning of draft cards was noted in *S.F. Chronicle*, Oct. 28, 1965, p. 42. On the ceremony in San Francisco see *Daily Cal.*, Oct. 17, 1967, p. 3. On The Resistance see Michael Ferber and Staughton Lynd, *The Resistance* (Boston, 1971), esp. 1, 78–91, 127–28; Lynd in Mitchell Goodman, ed., *The Movement toward a New America* (N.Y., 1970), 492–93; Breines, 43–44, 52; "Weekly Magazine," *Daily Cal.*, Nov. 28, 1967, pp. 8–10; Steve Hamilton in *Despite Everything*, Oct. 1967, pp. 27–30; Thomas Farber, *Tales for the Son of My Unborn Child* (N.Y., 1971), 76–97; Dale M. Heckman, "World Views and Students Who Take Risk for Ethical Conviction" (Ph.D. diss., Graduate Theological Union, Berk., 1970), esp. 141–42 (quote at 142). See the eloquent letter excerpted at 52. On motives, ibid., 45–49, 79. *Berk. Barb*, Apr. 28, 1967, p. 3; June 16, 1967, p. 7; Oct. 6, 1967, p. 4; Oct. 13, 1967, p. 11; Nov. 15, 1968, p. 25; *Berk. Gazette*, Oct. 13, 1967, pp. 1, 2, 8; *Daily Cal.*, Oct. 12, 1967, p. 6; Loren Goldner column, Oct. 16, 1967, p.8; *S.F. Chronicle*, Oct. 13, 1967, pp. 1, 11; Oct. 14, 1967, p. 7; *S.F. Bay Guardian*, Apr. 5, 1968, pp. 1, 7; *People's World*, Oct. 28, 1967, p. 8; The Resistance, leaflets, Aug. 15, 1967; Oct. 16, 1967 (quote), both in 2:24, UCBCF; "The Resistance to America," Apr. 28, 1968, leaflet, 15:last folder, Jones Papers. See also Barrie Thorne, "Resisting the Draft: An Ethnography of the Draft Resistance Movement" (Ph.D. diss. (Soc.), Brandeis Univ., 1971). On Harris see his remarks in Goodman, 445–46; David Harris, *Goliath* (N.Y., 1970); and his more mature *Dreams Die Hard* (N.Y., 1982); Joan Baez, *And a Voice to Sing with* (N.Y., 1987), 147–54; *Daily Cal.*, Jan. 8, 1968, p. 2; Jan. 18, 1968, p. 3; *Oakland Tribune*, Oct. 17, 1967, p. 5; *S.F. Chronicle*, Oct. 17, 1967, pp. 1, 13; interview,

Portland *Willamette Bridge*, Aug. 2, 1968, p. 8.

    68. *Daily Cal.*, Feb. 25, 1966, p. 6; Nov. 7, 1966, pp. 1, 16; Nov. 18, 1966, pp. 1 (quote), 3; Jan. 26, 1967, p. 13 (quote); Feb. 8, 1967, pp. 1, 3; *Berk. Barb*, Feb. 25, 1966, pp. 1, 7; Nov. 25, 1966, p. 5: *Berk. Gate*, Feb. 1, 1967, pp. 1, 8; *Sunday Ramparts*, Nov. 6, 1966, pp. 1, 4; Ruth A. Hart, "Concern for the Individual: The Community YWCA and Other Berkeley Organizations" (1978), interview, 258. For more bitter libertarian remarks see Tom Collins columns, *Daily Cal.*, Nov. 10, 1966, p. 12; Nov. 23, 1966, p. 13; Feb. 15, 1967, p. 6; Oct. 11, 1967, p. 12; L. J. O'Neale column, Oct. 18, 1967, p. 17; Tom McGivern column, Oct. 10, 1968, p. 8; Thomas Jacobsen column, Apr. 15, 1968, p. 8; *S.F. Bay Guardian*, Apr. 5, 1968, p. 9. On rising libertarianism see Henry C. Finney in *Sociology of Education*, 47 (1974), 214–50. For a shrewd and insightful analysis of the origins of the New Right see M. Stanton Evans, *Revolt on the Campus* (Chicago, 1961).

    69. On plans see *Berk. Barb*, Aug. 11, 1967, p. 7; Aug. 18, 1967, p. 2; *Berk. Gazette*, Oct. 13, 1967, pp. 1, 2; *Daily Cal.*, Sept. 27, 1967, p. 9; Oct. 10, 1967, p. 1; Oct. 13, 1967, p. 8; *Oakland Tribune*, Oct. 13, 1967, pp. 1, 2; Oct. 15, 1967, pp. 1, B; Nov. 28, 1967; *S.F. Chronicle*, Oct. 13, 1967, p. 11; Oct. 14, 1967, p. 1; *New Left Notes*, Sept. 4, 1967, p. 2; *Steps*, #2 (ca 1967), 34–42; Ferber and Lynd, 140–42; Sale, 375–77; Campus Mobilization Comm., leaflet, Oct. 4, 1967, 2:4, UCBCF. On the symbolism of induction centers see Dotson Rader, *I Ain't Marchin' Anymore* (N.Y., 1969; orig. 1969), 98. On Monday's events see Baez, 111, 146–47; Coyne, 30–31, 36; Rossman, "Breakthrough," 47; *Berk. Barb*, Oct. 20, 1967, p. 3; *Berk. Gazette*, Oct. 17, 1967, pp. 1, 2; *Daily Cal.*, Oct. 17, 1967, pp. 1, 13, 16; *N.Y. Times*, Oct. 17, 1967, p. 3; *Oakland Tribune*, Oct. 16, 1967, pp. 1, 7, 17; *S.F. Chronicle*, Oct. 17, 1967, pp. 1, 12; Oct. 18, 1967, p. 10.

    70. In general see *S.F. Sunday Examiner-Chronicle*, Oct. 15, 1967, Sec. A, pp. 1, 10 (Heyns quote at 10); *S.F. Chronicle*, Oct. 16, 1967, pp. 1, 5; "RHC" to Heyns, n.d., 2:24, UCBCF. Bardacke quoted in Ronald Fraser, ed., *1968* (N.Y., 1988), 152. On the ballroom see Gene Saenger proposals, Oct. 12, 1967; Oct. 15, 1967; Martin Malia and Carl Landauer leaflet, Oct. 16, 1967; Jan D. Blais to Reese Erlich, Oct. 10, 1967; Blais chronology, Oct. 16, 1967; Eugene Saenger to Heyns, Oct. 17, 1967, all in 2:24, UCBCF. Angry reactions came from Denzel Carr to Heyns, Oct. 15, 1967, 2:24, UCBCF; Brinton H. Stone to Earl Cheit, Nov. 16, 1967 (quote), 2:25, UCBCF. On the supervisors see *Berk. Gazette*, Oct. 14, 1967, pp. 1, 2; *Daily Cal.*, Oct. 12, 1967, pp. 1, 5; Oct. 13, 1967, p. 1; Oct. 16, 1967, p. 1; *Oakland Tribune*, Oct. 17, 1967, p. 7; *S.F. Chronicle*, Oct. 17, 1967, pp. 1, 12; Heyns interview, 92; Robert E. Hannon to Heyns, Oct. 11, 1967; reply, Oct. 13, 1967; Heyns to Gov. Reagan, Oct. 16, 1967; Heyns notes, Alumni Council talk, Oct. 14, 1967; Heyns notes for talk to Regents, Oct. 16, 1967; John Canaday to Theodore R. Meyer, Oct. 12, 1967; R. S. Muller to Heyns, Oct. 12, 1967; Kenneth M. Stampp to Heyns, Oct. 14, 1967; Edward Sampson to Heyns, Oct. 16, 1967; Charles Sellers to Heyns, Oct. 17, 1967, all in 2:24, UCBCF.

    71. Peter S. Steiner "minute by minute account" to Heyns, Oct. 17, 1967 (quote), 2:24, UCBCF. *Berk. Gazette*, Oct. 17, 1967, pp. 1, 2; *Daily Cal.*, Oct. 17, 1967, pp. 1, 2, 15, 16; *Oakland Tribune*, Oct. 17, 1967, pp. 1, 5; *S.F. Chronicle*, Oct. 17, 1967, pp. 1, 12.

    72. On Tuesday's events see Rossman, "Breakthrough," 47; Marvin Garson column, *Berk. Barb*, Oct. 20, 1967, p. 2; *Berk. Gazette*, Oct. 18, 1967, pp. 1, 2; *Daily Cal.*, Oct. 18, 1967, pp. 1, 3; Oct. 19, 1967, p. 8; Oct. 20, 1967, p. 1; *N.Y. Times*, Oct.

18, 1967, pp. 1, 10; *Oakland Tribune*, Oct. 17, 1967, pp. 1, 4 (quote), 6 (quote); Oct. 20, 1967, p. 22; *S.F. Chronicle*, Oct. 18, 1967, pp. 1, 8–10; *People's World*, Oct. 21, 1967, pp. 1, 12; Austin *Rag*, Oct. 23, 1967, p. 2; *L.A. Free Press*, Oct. 20, 1967, pp. 7, 27. On police violence see esp. *Daily Cal.*, Oct. 20, 1967, p. 21; Oct. 23, 1967, p. 8; *S.F. Chronicle*, Oct. 19, 1967, pp. 1, 15; *S.F. Bay Guardian*, Oct. 31, 1967, pp. 1, 7. Incredibly, this aspect was denied in *Berk. Gazette*, Oct. 20, 1967, p. 10. On Wednesday see Rossman, "Breakthrough," 47–48; *Berk. Gazette*, Oct. 18, 1967, pp. 1, 2; Oct. 19, 1967, pp. 1, 2; *Berk. Barb*, Oct. 20, 1967, p. 4; *Daily Cal.*, Oct. 19, 1967, pp. 1, 2; *S.F. Chronicle*, Oct. 19, 1967, pp. 1, 16. On Thursday see Rossman, "Breakthrough," 48; *Berk. Gazette*, Oct. 19, 1967, pp. 1, 2.

73. On plans see *Berk. Gazette*, Oct. 20, 1967, pp. 1, 2; *Daily Cal.*, Oct. 19, 1967, pp. 1, 3. On events see *Berk. Gazette*, Oct. 21, 1967, pp. 1, 3; *Oakland Tribune*, Oct. 20, 1967, pp. 1, 5, 7; *S.F. Chronicle*, Oct. 21, 1967, pp. 1, 4; Fraser, 155–56 (Bardacke quote at 156); Halstead, 345–46; Peter Marin in Goodman, 9; Rossman, "Breakthrough," 48. Dotson Rader, *Blood Dues* (N.Y., 1973), 8–10, 120, 145. See also Norman Mailer, *Miami and the Siege of Chicago* (N.Y., 1968), 153. The arrest tally is in *Daily Cal.*, Oct. 25, 1967, p. 1.

74. Lummis is quoted in *Despite Everything*, July 1968, p. 20. For reaction see Reese Erlich letter, *Berk. Barb*, Oct. 27, 1967, p. 9; *Berk. Gazette*, Oct. 20, 1967, pp. 1, 2; George Malsbury letter, p. 10; Oct. 21, 1967; Peter Camejo column, *Daily Cal.*, Oct. 26, 1967, p. 20; *Oakland Tribune*, Oct. 21, 1967, pp. 1, 2; Oct. 22, 1967, pp. 1, B; editorial, *S.F. Chronicle*, Oct. 24, 1967, p. 34. On the discipline controversy see *Daily Cal.*, Oct. 25, 1967; Nov. 10, 1967, p. 1; Nov. 13, 1967, pp. 1, 2; Nov. 14, 1967, pp. 1, 12, 16; Nov. 15, 1967, pp. 8, 18, 20–21; Nov. 17, 1967, pp. 1, 16; Nov. 20, 1967, p. 12; Nov. 22, 1967; Martin (?) to Heyns, Oct. 18, 1967; Albert Lepawsky to Heyns, Oct. 18, 1967; Bob Cole phone message to Heyns, Oct. 19, 1967, 1:30 p.m.; Regents meeting resolutions, Oct. 20, 1967; Chancellor Franklin Murphy luncheon remarks to Regents, Oct. 20, 1967, all in 2:24, UCBCF; Heyns to Murphy, Nov. 3, 1967; Ralph Smith to Heyns, Nov. 13, 1967; Thomas Parkinson to Heyns, Nov. 17, 1967 (quote); Robert Toll et al. to Heyns, Nov. 15, 1967; Campus SDS leaflet, Nov. 16, 1967; Jay Michael to Heyns, Nov. 16, 1967; Heyns statement, Nov. 19, 1967; 28 graduate students in history, petition, all in 2:25, UCBCF.

75. On the suspensions see *Daily Cal.*, Nov. 29, 1967, pp. 1, 3 (quote), 8 (quote), 9; Bill C. Haigwood column, *Berk. Gazette*, Dec. 8, 1967; Austin *Rag*, Dec. 11, 1967, p. 13; Heyns statement, Nov. 28, 1967, 2:25; UCBCF; Academic Senate vote, Dec. 4, 1967; "Crisis Report," pamphlet, Dec. 1967, both in 2:26, UCBCF; Heyns to Michael Scriven, Feb. 5, 1968, 3:29, UCBCF. On the skylight incident see Mrs. Judith K. Kirmmse memo, Nov. 30, 1967 (quote); Jim Lemmon to Cheit, Nov. 30, 1967, both in 2:25, UCBCF. The mill-ins are in *Berk. Gazette*, Dec. 4, 1967, pp. 1, 14; *Daily Cal.*, Nov. 30, 1967, pp. 1, 2; Dec. 1, 1967, pp. 1, 20; Dec. 8, 1967, p. 1; *S.F. Chronicle*, Nov. 30, 1967, pp. 1, 20; Dec. 1, 1967, pp. 1, 16; Dec. 2, 1967, p. 2; *S.F. Sunday Examiner-Chronicle*, Dec. 3, 1967, Sec. A, p. 5; *Liberation News Service*, Dec. 11, 1967, pp. 1, 2. On later discipline see *Daily Cal.*, Jan. 3, 1968, p. 1; Jan. 4, 1968, p. 8; Jan. 5, 1968, p. 1; Feb. 20, 1968, p. 1.

76. *Berk. Barb*, Jan. 26, 1968, p. 3; *Daily Cal.*, Jan. 23, 1968, p. 1; Jan. 25, 1968, p. 1; *S.F. Chronicle*, Oct. 21, 1967, p. 5; *S.F. Sunday Examiner-Chronicle*, Oct. 22, 1967, Sec. A, p. 12; Robley C. Williams memo, Dec. 27, 1967, 8:96, UCBCF; (Cannon) *Berk. Barb*, May 26, 1967, p. 3; *San Diego Union*, Mar. 2, 1969; quoted in Goodman, 229; (Mandel) *BCU Bulletin*, Apr. 1969, pp. 1–2; *People's World*, May 11,

1968, p. 9; (Erlich) Gene Saenger proposal, Oct. 12, 1967, 2:24, UCBCF; *Berk. Barb*, July 21, 1967, p. 3; *Daily Cal.*, Nov. 7, 1967, p. 2; Nov. 11, 1968, p. 3; Nov. 13, 1968, p. 3; (Segal) *Berk. Barb*, Jan 26, 1968, p. 3; (Hamilton) *S.F. Chronicle*, Aug. 16, 1966; *Tocsin*, June 15, 1966; *San Diego Union*, Mar. 2, 1969; (Smith) *Berk. Barb*, July 21, 1967, p. 3; *Berk. Gazette*, Oct. 19, 1967, p. 1; *Oakland Tribune*, Apr. 13, 1966, p. 5; *S.F. Bay Guardian*, June 14, 1979, pp. 9–10 (quote at 10); (Bardacke) e.g., *S.F. Express Times*, Feb. 8, 1968; p. 6; Breines, 122; Davis, 95 (quote); *Berk. Gazette*, Mar. 28, 1968, p. 20; editorial, Apr. 8, 1968, *S.F. Bay Guardian*, June 14, 1979, p. 11.

77. The best coverage is in *Berk. Barb*, Feb. 9, 1968, p. 2; Mar. 8, 1968, p. 2; May 10, 1968, p. 4; Sept. 20, 1968, p. 5; Nov. 8, 1968, p. 2; Nov. 15, 1968, p. 9; Nov. 22, 1968, p. 2; Jan. 3, 1969, p. 7; Jan. 10, 1969, pp. 7, 11; Jan. 17, 1969, p. 3; Jan. 24, 1969, pp. 5, 11; Feb. 7, 1969, p. 7; Feb. 14, 1969, p. 13; Feb. 28, 1969, p. 11; Mar. 7, 1969, pp. 5, 21; Mar. 14, 1969, p. 13; Mar. 28, 1969, p. 6; Apr. 4, 1969, p. 9. See also *Berk. Gazette*, Jan. 27, 1968, pp. 1, 2; Jan. 30, 1968; Feb. 23, 1968; Mar. 27, 1969, pp. 1, 2; Mar. 28, 1969, p. 1; Mar. 29, 1969, p. 1; editorial, Apr. 2, 1969, p. 10; *Daily Cal.*, Feb. 26, 1968, pp. 1, 12; Oct. 8, 1968, p. 3; Jan. 13, 1969, p. 2; Jan. 14, 1969, p. 1; Jan. 24, 1969, p. 15; Feb. 4, 1969, p. 6; Feb. 11, 1969, p. 20; Mar. 4, 1969, p. 11; *S.F. Express Times*, Jan 7, 1969, p. 5; Jan. 14, 1969, p. 3; Jan. 21, 1969, pp. 4–5; Frank Bardacke in *The Realist*, Nov.-Dec. 1969 (in Goodman, 480–85); *People's World*, Feb. 8, 1969, p. 1; Apr. 5, 1969, p. 12.

78. *Berk. Gazette*, Apr. 3, 1968; Apr. 25, 1968, pp. 1, 2; *Daily Cal.*, Jan. 18, 1968, p. 11; Jan. 22, 1968, p. 8; Jan. 26, 1968; Feb. 19, 1968, p. 1; Feb. 20, 1968, p. 5; Mar. 1, 1968, pp. 1, 21; Mar. 29, 1968, p. 1; Apr. 23, 1968, p. 3; CDO meeting transcript, Jan. 18, 1968, 23:CDO 3, Jones Papers; cover memo; anon. memo, both in 3:28, UCBCF. See also Rader, *I Ain't*, 159.

79. *Daily Cal.*, Apr. 1, 1968, p. 1; Apr. 2, 1968, p. 1; Apr. 15, 1968, p. 1; Morris Hirsch letter, Apr. 17, 1968; Apr. 18, 1968, p. 1; Apr. 22, 1968, p. 1; Apr. 23, 1968, p. 12; Apr. 30, 1968, p. 1; May 7, 1968, pp. 1, 7; May 9, 1968, p. 17; May 10, 1968, p. 3; May 14, 1968, p. 5; May 17, 1968, pp. 1, 17; Heyns interview, 95; Arleigh Williams to William C. Boyd, Feb. 28, 1968; Boyd to Richard Strohman, Mar. 4, 1968; Boyd to Thomas J. Cunningham, Mar. 8, 1968; Cunningham opinion, Mar. 14, 1968; Frederick Crews to Heyns, Mar. 27, 1968; Boyd to CDO faculty leaders, Mar. 29, 1968; Hardin B. Jones to Boyd, Mar. 30, 1968; Leon Henkin to Heyns, Apr. 1, 1968; Cunningham ruling to Boyd, Apr. 3, 1968, Boyd to Charles Sellers, Apr. 10, 1968; Heyns report to Academic Senate, Apr. 16, 1968; Regents Executive Session Minutes, Apr. 19, 1968; Heyns memo on Regents meeting, Apr. 22, 1968; Jones to Heyns, Apr. 24, 1968; reply, Apr. 29, 1968; Jan D. Blais to Boyd, May 6, 1968; CDO leaflets, May 8, 1968; Gov. Reagan to Theodore R. Meyer, May 10, 1968 (quote); Boyd to Cunningham, May 10, 1968; Earl F. Cheit to file, May 13, 1968; Sellers to Heyns, May 15, 1968; Regents Executive Session Minutes, May 17, 1968; Robert E. Hannon to Regents, Apr. 18, 1968; Heyns memo re Hannon, n.d.; Cunningham memo to Heyns, May 13, 1968, all in 3:28, UCBCF; Jones to Heyns, Mar. 10, 1968 (quote); reply, Apr. 29, 1968; Boyd to Jones, Mar. 29, 1968, all in Box 9, Jones Papers; Jones to Heyns, June 14, 1968, 1:Jones, Lawrence Papers; Mulford to Mr. and Mrs. Ransom A. Pierce, May 8, 1968, 4:6, Mulford Papers; Jones to DeWitt A. Higgs, July 24, 1968, 4:DAH, Jones Papers. Jones forwarded considerable material to Gen. Lewis B. Hershey, the director of the Selective Service System. E.g., CDO rally, Martin Roysher remarks, transcript, May 15, 1968, 4:Hershey 1, Jones Papers; CDO rally transcript, Apr. 24, 1968, 4:Hershey 2, Jones Papers. See also Regents Executive Session Transcript, Mar. 15, 1968; Regents Executive Session Minutes, Mar. 15, 1968. It is instructive that Jones

had access to the transcripts while the chancellor had to reply on the less detailed minutes.

80. *Berk. Barb,* May 24, 1968, p. 11; *Daily Cal.,* May 17, 1968, p. 17; May 20, 1968, pp. 1, 5 (quote at 5); May 21, 1968, p. 12; May 27, 1968, pp. 7–10; *People's World,* May 25, 1968, p. 2. On the Wells case see *Berk. Barb,* May 10, 1968, p. 11; July 19, 1968, p. 7; Aug. 2, 1968, p. 5; *Daily Cal.,* Feb. 2, 1968, pp. 1, 12; Apr. 12, 1968, p. 2; Apr. 17, 1968, p. 3; May 6, 1968, p. 8; May 7, 1968, p. 1; June 21, 1968, p. 1; Aug. 2, 1968, pp. 1, 12.

81. (polls) *Daily Cal.,* Apr. 23, 1968, p. 3; May 9, 1968, p. 1; (national data) May 1, 1968, p. 2; May 6, 1968, p. 1; May 7, 1968, p. 1; (survey) Apr. 25, 1968, p. 9; (ASUC referendum) Nov. 9, 1967, p. 3. On the McCarthy campaign see Eugene J. McCarthy, *The Year of the People* (N.Y., 1969); Arthur Herzog, *McCarthy for President* (N.Y., 1969); Ben Stavis; *We Were the Campaign* (Boston, 1969). On the local campaign see Coyne, 51–52; Halstead, 371; *Berk. Barb,* Dec. 8, 1967, p. 4; *Daily Cal.,* Feb. 27, 1967, p. 3; Mar. 1, 1968, p. 5; Mar. 27, 1968, p. 1; Apr. 5, 1968; Apr. 19, 1968, p. 5; Apr. 26, 1968, p. 1. On the decision to run see Chester, 85. For an incisive description of McCarthy's supporters see Mailer, 91. McCarthy's local victory is noted in *Coalition News,* Mar. 12, 1969, p. 3.

82. The best source is William C. Hanley's memo, pp. 1–9 (Cornejo quote at 3), 9:99, UCBCF. See also Margaret S. Gordon in Harris, *May,* 56–57; Lyford, 28–36; Pat and Fred Cody in Nathan and Scott, 142–45; Gordon, ibid., 312–13; Joel Rubenzahl, ibid., 320–21; John R. Coyne, Jr., *Fall In and Cheer* (Garden City, N.Y., 1979), 19–20; John K. DeBonis, *Quotations from Chairman DeBonis* (Berk., 1971), Appendix, p. 23; Johnson, "Need to Know," 18pp.; *Daily Cal.,* July 1, 1968, p. 1; July 12, 1968, p. 8; July 16, 1968, p. 4; Oct. 17, 1968, pp. 6–7; *L'enrage,* July 2, 1968; *Peace and Freedom News,* July 8, 1968, pp. 1–3, 8; *Ramparts,* Aug. 24, 1968, pp. 22–27; *S.F. Express Times,* July 3, 1968, pp. 1, 9–11 (quotes at 9). There was wide coverage in the underground press. The best report is in the Austin *Rag,* July 11, 1968, pp. 1, 12–13. See also ibid., July 25, 1968, p. 3; *Liberation News Service,* July 5, 1968, pp. 2–10; July 10, 1968, pp. 13–17; Madison *Connections,* July 17, 1968, pp. 5–6; *Mid-peninsula Observer,* July 15, 1968, p. 5; San Diego *Teaspoon Door,* July 5, 1968, pp. 1, 3, 7; Seattle *Helix,* July 3, 1968, p. 3. Hardin B. Jones to DeWitt A. Higgs, July 1, 1968, Box 1, Jones Papers; Jones memo of rally, June 4, 1968, 15:last folder, Jones Papers; Marvin C. Buchanan to Don Mulford, July 2, 1968, 1:6, Mulford Papers; Henry Nash Smith to Tony Tanner, July 9, 1968, 5:3, Smith Papers. On Friday see *Berk. Barb,* June 28, 1968, p. 11; July 5, 1968, pp. 2–6, 9; *S.F. Chronicle,* June 29, 1968, pp. 1, 12; J. Flynn eyewitness statement, 12:June 1968, Jones Papers. On Saturday see *Oakland Tribune,* July 2, 1968, p. 5; *S.F. Sunday Examiner-Chronicle,* June 30, 1968, Sec. A, pp. 1, 23. On Sunday see *Berk. Gazette,* July 1, 1968, pp. 1–3, 8; *Oakland Tribune,* July 1, 1968, pp. 1, 8; *S.F. Chronicle,* July 1, 1968, pp. 1, 12, 32.

83. Margaret S. Gordon in Nathan and Scott, 313–15; and in Harris, May, 57–58; Police Conduct Complaint Center, "Complaints Regarding Police Actions against Citizens, June 28–July 2, 1968" (1968); letters, *Berk. Gazette,* July 8, 1968, p. 5; July 9, 1968, p. 7. On Monday see *Berk. Gazette,* July 2, 1968, pp. 1, 2; *Oakland Tribune,* July 1, 1968, pp. 1, 8; *S.F. Chronicle,* July 2, 1968, pp. 1 (quote), 8–9, 20. On Tuesday and Wednesday see *Berk. Gazette,* July 3, 1968, pp. 1–3; July 4, 1968, pp. 1, 2; July 6, 1968, pp. 1, 2; July 9, 1968, pp. 1, 2; *Oakland Tribune,* July 3, 1968, pp. 1, 2, 8; *S.F. Chronicle,* July 3, 1968, pp. 1, 11 (quote), 18.

84. *Berk. Barb,* July 12, 1968, p. 1; *Berk. Gazette,* July 5, 1968, pp. 1, 2; July 9, 1968, pp. 1, 2; *N.Y. Times,* July 7, 1968, p. 42; *Oakland Tribune,* July 5, 1968, pp.

1, 6; *S.F. Chronicle*, July 5, 1968, pp. 1, 28 (first quote at 1; second at 1, 28); *S.F. Express Times*, July 10, 1968, pp. 2, 5, 7.

85. On the curdled atmosphere see Free Univ. of Berk., *Catalog*, Spring 1967, p. 7 (quote); *Berk. Gate*, Oct. 8, 1968, p. 2; *Berk. Gazette*, July 8, 1968, pp. 1, 2; Sept. 11, 1968, p. 10; *Capitalism Stinks*, July 25, 1968, p. 1; *S.F. Express Times*, July 3, 1968, p. 2. For a shrewd political analysis see *Communiqué for New Politics*, Dec. 24, 1968, p. 1. On the late summer see Pat and Fred Cody in Nathan and Scott, 145: *N.Y. Times*, Sept. 4, 1968, p. 36; *S.F. Chronicle*, Sept. 11, 1968, pp. 1, 26; *Liberation News Service*, Sept 9, 1968, pp. 7–9; *Milwaukee Kaleidoscope*, Sept. 13, 1968, p. 9; Farber, 71, 74, 98; Hanley memo, pp. 16–17, 9:99, UCBCF; Jack Wilson to Don Mulford, Aug. 20, 1968, 1:6, Mulford Papers.

## Chapter 4.

(epigraph) Herman's Hermits quoted by Nicholas von Hoffman in *Wash. Post*, Oct. 27, 1967, p. A4.

1. On architecture see Tom Wolfe, *From Bauhaus to Our House* (N.Y., 1981). On art see Thomas Albright, *Art in the San Francisco Bay Area, 1945–1980* (Berk., 1985), esp. 14–79; Glenn A. Wessels, "Education of the Artist" (1967), interview; Theodore Roszak, *The Making of a Counter Culture* (1967), (Garden City, N.Y., 1969), 127–28. On science fiction see Lawrence Ferlinghetti and Nancy J. Peters, eds., *Literary San Francisco* (S.F., 1980), See also Michael Rossman, *On Learning and Social Change* (N.Y., 1972), 199–200, 346, 349. On the Berkeley Renaissance see Allen Ginsberg, *Allen Verbatim*, ed. Gordon Ball (N.Y., 1974), 150; Louis Simpson, *North of Jamaica* (N.Y., 1972), 225. See also Josephine Miles to James D. Hart, July 6, 1970, 1:23, Miles Papers. In general see Marty Jezer, *The Dark Ages* (Boston, 1982).

2. Kenneth Rexroth, *An Autobiographical Novel* (Santa Barbara, 1982; orig. 1964), 364–67. On Ferlinghetti see Roszak, 297. For a brilliant essay on the beats see Seymour Krim's introduction to Jack Kerouac, *Desolation Angels* (N.Y., 1966; orig. 1965), 1–20. See also Elias Wilentz, ed., *The Beat Scene* (N.Y., 1960), 8–15. On Kerouac in the Bay Area, in addition to Kerouac's *The Dharma Bums* (N.Y., 1959; orig. 1958), see *Desolation Angels*, 86, 142, 155–58, 193–95, 207, 357–71; Dennis McNally, *Desolate Angel* (N.Y., 1979), 197, 202–4, 207–8, 210; Ann Charters, *Kerouac* (N.Y., 1974; orig. 1973), 235–50. Ginsberg's cottage is in Roszak, 129–36. On homosexuality see Allen Ginsberg, *Gay Sunshine Interview with Allen Young* (Bolinas, Calif., 1973), 3. Kerouac denied his homosexuality in *Desolation Angels*, 240.

3. On the word "beat" see Oglesby's introduction to Carl Oglesby, ed., *The New Left Reader* (N.Y., 1969), 4; Stanley I. Glick, "The People's Park" (Ph.D. diss., State Univ. of New York at Stony Brook, 1984), 8. On psychology see Jack Newfield, *A Prophetic Minority* (N.Y., 1967; orig. 1966), 32. On Kerouac see Kerouac's *On the Road* (N.Y., 1957; orig. 1955); *Desolation Angels*, 260, 309; Ginsberg, *Verbatim*, 146, 152–53. For a negative reaction see Josephine Carson to Josephine Miles, n.d., 2:17, Miles Papers.

4. On Ginsberg see Ginsberg, *Verbatim*, 131–32, 134, 136, 233–34; Ginsberg, *Gay Sunshine Interview*, 4, 6; Kerouac, *Desolation Angels*, 260; Glick, 8–9. See Allen Ginsberg, *Howl and Other Poems* (S.F., 1956). On the influence of "Howl" see Michael McClure, *Scratching the Beat Surface* (S.F., 1982), 12–13, 23–24; McNally, 196–97, 202–4; Roszak, 24; Wilentz, 14–15; Josephine Miles, "Poetry, Teaching, and Scholarship" (1980), interview, 165; Peter ? interview in Mitchell Goodman, ed., *The Movement toward a New America* (N.Y., 1970), 13–14. On the prosecution see *Express*, July 22, 1983.

5. Ginsberg, *Verbatim*, esp. 5–6, 20–21, 25–29, 117–18; Kerouac, *Desolation Angels*, 261, 327–28; Roszak, 125–26, 128–29.

6. On young intellectuals see David Horowitz, *Student* (N.Y., 1962), esp. 7–10, 156–57; Diane Wakoski to Michael Rossman, Sept. 13, 1960; Oct. 19, 1960; Nov. 26, 1960; Dec. 8, 1960; Feb. 18, 1961; Aug. 18, 1961; Nov. 3, 1961; Jan. 13, 1962, Wakoski Papers; *Despite Everything*, Feb. 1963, p. 3; Roger Rapoport, *California Dreaming* (Berk., 1982), 62. See also Ed McClanahan, *Famous People I Have Known* (N.Y., 1986; orig. 1985), 30. On paperbacks see James Miller, *"Democracy Is in the Streets"* (N.Y., 1987), 86. The essayists are noted in Roszak, 24–25; Miller, 80–82; Lewis S. Feuer, *The Conflict of Generations* (N.Y., 1969), 406–7; Mark Gerzon, *The Whole World Is Watching* (N.Y., 1970; orig. 1969), 22; on philosophy see William J. McGill, *The Year of the Monkey* (N.Y., 1982), 224; Newfield, 87–88. On Heinlein see *Sunday Ramparts*, Jan. 1, 1967, p. 8. In general see Henry F. May, "The Student Movement: Some Impressions at Berkeley," *American Scholar*, 34 (1965), 388.

7. For an example of a war refugee see Leo Lowenthal, *An Unmastered Past*, ed. Martin Jay (Berk., 1987). In general see Lewis A. Coser, *Refugee Scholars in America* (New Haven, 1984); Martin Jay, *Permanent Exiles* (N.Y., 1985). On Kael see *Daily Cal.*, Apr. 30, 1968, p. 3. Her reviews, 1961–64, are in Pauline Kael, *I Lost It at the Movies* (Boston, 1965). Landberg is in *Berk. Barb*, Apr. 1, 1966, p. 1; Apr. 15, 1966, pp. 1, 10; *Berk. Gate*, Apr. 19, 1966, p. 1; *Daily Cal.*, Mar. 24, 1966, p. 1; Oct. 24, 1967, p. 2. See *YWCA Newsletter*, Jan. 1961; Jan. 1962 (quote); Apr. 1962.

8. Malvina Reynolds, "Little Boxes," *Broadside*, Feb. 1963. See *BCU Bulletin*, June 1967, p. 1.

9. On Left ties see Maurice Isserman, *If I Had a Hammer* (N.Y., 1987), 59, 215–16; R. Serge Denisoff, *Great Day Coming* (Urbana, 1971). On civil rights see Feuer, *Conflict*, 400; James P. O'Brien, "The Development of the New Left in the United States, 1960–1965" (Ph.D. diss., Univ. of Wisconsin, 1971), 216–18. Folk was strong in Berkeley. Ed Denson column, *Berk. Barb*, Apr. 8, 1966, p. 5. For a perceptive review see Ralph J. Gleason in *Ramparts*, Apr. 1965, pp. 36ff. On Ochs see the interview in Gregory Mcdonald, *The Education of Gregory Mcdonald* (N.Y., 1985), 181–82; on Peter, Paul, and Mary see *Daily Cal.*, Mar. 8, 1966, p. 14. Dylan is in Miller, 117; Jon Wiener, *Come Together* (N.Y., 1984), 218–20; *Daily Cal.*, Feb. 11, 1966, p. 14; Gleason in *Ramparts*, Mar. 1966, pp. 27–34; Frank Bardacke in Goodman, 378–81. Quite useful is the film, *Don't Look Back* (D. A. Pennebaker, 1967). On Baez see Joan Baez, *And a Voice to Sing with* (N.Y., 1987), esp. 24–25, 28–29, 40–44, 83–85, 91–95, 118–26. See also her interview in Mcdonald, 97–106; Joan Didion, *Slouching toward Bethlehem* (N.Y., 1968), 42–60; *Berk. Barb*, Apr. 14, 1967, p. 12; Sept. 22, 1967, p. 5; Oct. 20, 1967, p. 3; *Daily Cal.*, Oct. 25, 1968, p. 7; Jan 24, 1969, p. 6. For songs see the biweekly *Broadside*, 1962–

10. Krassner interview, *S.F. Focus*, Mar. 1986, pp. 40ff; Jack McDonough, *San Francisco Rock* (S.F., 1985), 84, Roszak, 24. On The Committee see *Berk. Barb*, Dec. 26, 1966, p. 3; *Berk. Gazette*, Mar. 28, 1963, p. 11; *Daily Cal.*, Feb. 18, 1966, p. 11; Feb. 21, 1966, p. 3; *Ramparts*, Dec. 1964, pp. 11ff; Charles Perry, *The Haight-Ashbury: A History* (N.Y., 1985; orig. 1984), 19. See also Michael Myerson, *These Are the Good Old Days* (N.Y., 1970).

11. John Cohen, ed., *The Essential Lenny Bruce* (N.Y., 1967), esp. 26–38, 84, 88, 100, 167, 175, 180. For a thorough description of Bruce's legal problems see *The Realist*, Mar. 1964. In March 1965 Bruce cancelled an appearance at Cal. See 2:13, UCBCF. Bruce was satirized in Joel Beck's cartoon booklet, "Lenny of Laredo." See *Berk. Barb*, Jan. 7, 1966, p. 3. On Bruce's continuing influence see ibid., Mar. 28, 1969, p. 10;

*Daily Cal.*, Feb. 23, 1968, p. 10; July 30, 1968, p. 5; Jerry Rubin, *Do It!* (N.Y., 1970), 135. Abbie Hoffman's *Woodstock Nation* (N.Y., 1969), was dedicated to Bruce.

12. In general see McGill, 241, note 27; María-José Ragué Arias, *California Trip* (Barcelona, 1971), 125; Lauretta F. Link to Gov. Edmund G. ("Pat") Brown, Sr., Oct. 15, 1964, Box 724, Brown Papers. On the 2400 block of Telegraph see *Berk. Barb*, July 1, 1966, pp. 2, 3; *Berk. Citizen*, Sept. 30, 1966, p. 1; Thomas Farber introduction, Nacio J. Brown, *Rag Theater* (Berk., 1975), 7–10. On The Forum see *L.A. Times*, Apr. 18, 1965; *Berk. Barb*, Jan. 21, 1966, p. 1; Jan. 28, 1966, pp. 1, 2; May 27, 1966, p. 1; Nov. 25, 1966, p. 5. On the Med see Bob Biderman, *Letters to Nanette* (S.F., 1982), 86–88. Creed's is in *Berk. Barb*, June 14, 1968, p. 9. Moe's is in *Berk. Review*, Sept. 14, 1961, p. 2; *Daily Cal.*, Apr. 10, 1968. On Cody's see Pat and Fred Cody in *Experiment and Change in Berkeley*, ed. Harriet Nathan and Stanley Scott (Berk., 1978), 138; *Berk. Review*, Mar. 30, 1961, p. 5; Berk. Poetry Conference, 1965, *Checklists of Separate. Publications of Poets* . . . (Berk., 1965); *Publisher's Weekly*, Jan, 17, 1966, pp. 126–28; Fred Cody to Josephine Miles, Jan. 12, 1972, 2:30, Miles Papers; Fred Cody obituaries in *Express*, July 22, 1983, pp. 3–4; *Grassroots*, July 27, 1983, pp. 1, 6.

13. On pride in Telegraph see *Berk. Barb*, Aug. 27, 1965, p. 2; *Daily Cal.*, Apr. 15, 1966, pp. 12–13; Motley Deakin to Josephine Miles, June 11, 1961; Lydia Deakin to Miles, June 14, 1961, both in 2:47, Miles Papers. (Kampf) *L.A. Times*, Apr. 18, 1965, Sec. A, pp. B, 15–16; (Kevin) *Esquire*, Sept. 1965, pp. 86–87 (quote at 87); (Druding) *Ladies Home Journal*, Oct. 1965, pp. 82, 84, 170. For other examples see *Berk. Gazette*, Mar. 31, 1961, p. 1; *Daily Cal.*, Mar. 13, 1964, pp. 1, 6; *S.F. Examiner*, Oct. 11, 1965, pp. 1, 18; Oct. 12, 1965, pp. 1, 12; Oct. 13, 1965, pp. 1, 10; Oct. 14, 1965, p. 6.

14. *Berk. Gate*, Apr. 13, 1964, pp. 2 (quote), 5; *Daily Cal.*, Nov. 1, 1962, p. 1; Feb. 27, 1964, p. 1; Mar. 20, 1964, pp. 1, 8; Mar. 31, 1964, pp 1, 12; Apr. 1, 1964, p. 3; Apr. 8, 1964, p. 8; Apr. 13, 1964, p. 6; *S.F. Express Times*, Jan. 24, 1968, p. 1. On the sit-down see Charles B. Artman statement, early 1965, 1:20, FSM Arch.; Feuer, *Conflict*, 447. On street people see David Lauer letter, *Berk. Gazette*, Mar. 10, 1965.

15. On the Beatles see *Daily Cal.*, Mar. 10, 1966, p. 8; Wiener, *Come Together*. Chart positions are in *The Rolling Stone Rock Almanac* (N.Y., 1983). Dylan's amplification is noted in Miller, *Democracy*, 254. On the break with reason see Ginsberg, *Verbatim*, 34, 172. On sex see *Sunday Ramparts*, Nov. 6, 1966, p. 6.

16. *Berk. Gate*, Feb. 24, 1964, p. 4; *Daily Cal.*, Feb. 20, 1964, p. 3; Dan Paik, "Womb with a View," in "Free Speech Songbook" (1964), 9; Tom O'Hargan in Mcdonald, 139; Joseph Conlin, *The Troubles* (N.Y., 1982), 227; Feuer, *Conflict*, 420, 457; Gerzon, 198, 200. The Co-op is in *S.F. Magazine*, May 1965, p. 29. For gonorrhea statistics see *Daily Cal.*, Oct. 7, 1965, p. 1. The overheard conversation is from *Berk. Barb*, Aug. 27, 1965, p. 2.

17. On dormitory rules and the move to apartments see *Daily Cal.*, Feb. 19, 1964, p. 3; Mar. 5, 1964, p. 9; Mar. 13, 1964, p. 12; Apr. 24, 1964, pp. 1, 5; May 12, 1964, p. 1; May 14, 1964, p. 13; Sept. 18, 1964; Nov. 8, 1965, p. 1; Apr. 12, 1966, p. 12; *S.F. Chronicle*, Nov. 15, 1964; anon. essay, 2:49, FSM Arch.; Tom Hayden's 1962 essay in "Order and Freedom on the Campus" (1965), 2–3; NSA Resolutions, 18th National Student Congress, 1965, 3:21, FSM Arch.; Lois Heyman, "The Estimation of Need for Low Cost Housing in Berkeley" (M.B.A. report, UCB, 1966), 34. (10 percent) Hubert Lindsey, *Bless Your Dirty Heart*, ed. Howard G. Earl (Plainfield, N.J., 1973), 52. Druding is quoted in *Ladies Homes Journal*, Oct. 1965, p. 84. Statistics are

in Donovan Bess, "Berkeley Sex Report," in *Whole Berkeley Catalogue of Politics and Other Activities* (Berk., 1970), 39–40. In general see Goodman, 41; May, "Student Movement," 394.

18. On contraceptives see *Berk. Gate*, Apr. 13, 1964, p. 3 (quote); Feb. 22, 1965, p. 2; *Berk. Gazette*, Mar. 20, 1964, p. 7; Mar. 27, 1964, p. 1; *Daily Cal.*, Oct. 18, 1965, p. 5; Nov. 30, 1966, p. 1; ASUC Senate Minutes, Feb. 16, 1965, 3:8, FSM Arch. On abortions see *Berk. Barb*, Oct. 14, 1966, p. 2; Dec. 6, 1968, p. 14; *Berk. Gate*, Nov. 29, 1966, pp. 1, 3.

19. On the Sexual Fredom League see *Berk. Barb*, Sept 10, 1965, p. 2; Feb. 4, 1966, p. 5; Feb. 18, 1966, pp. 1, 7; Feb. 25, 1966, pp. 1, 2; Apr. 15, 1966, p. 1; May 20, 1966, pp. 1, 6; June 3, 1966, p. 6; July 15, 1966, p. 2; Aug. 12, 1966, p. 8; Aug. 26, 1966, pp. 1, 6; Sept. 9, 1966, p. 3; Sept. 30, 1966, pp. 1, 11; Jan. 27, 1967, p. 3; Apr. 21, 1967, p. 1; Apr. 28, 1967, p. 10; June 23, 1967, p. 13; Apr. 26, 1968, p. 5; June 14, 1968, p. 3; Oct. 18, 1968, p. 5; Dec. 13, 1968, p. 5; *Berk. Citizen*, Aug. 26, 1966, p. 2; Sept. 16, 1966, pp. 1, 3; *Berk. Gazette*, Feb. 22, 1967; *Daily Cal.*, Aug. 20, 1965, p. 11; Aug. 27, 1965, pp. 1, 2; Sept. 23, 1965, pp. 1, 12; Feb. 8, 1966, p. 7; Feb. 15, 1966, p. 1; Mar. 8, 1966, p. 2; *Sunday Ramparts*, Oct. 2, 1966; *Time* to Raymond S. Moore, Apr. 15, 1966, 8:97, UCBCF. On Poland see Arthur Seeger, *The Berkeley Barb* (N.Y., 1983), 29, 55. On Poland's earlier civil rights activity see Poland to Rep. John F. Shelley, June 21, 1962, 1:1, CORE/WRO. See also Jefferson F. Poland and Sam Sloan eds., *Sex Marchers* (L.A., 1968); Jefferson F. Poland and Valerie Alison, *The Records of the San Francisco Sexual Freedom League* (London, 1971); Sexual Freedom League Papers, Bancroft Library. On the *Barb's* role see Seeger, 55, 136, 138, 140; Russell Kirk column, *Berk. Gazette*, Jan. 14, 1969; Mar. 26, 1969; Mar. 27, 1969; July 9, 1969; July 16, 1969; Mar. 19, 1970; *Daily Cal.*, Oct. 6, 1967, pp. 1, 24; Feb. 2, 1968, pp. 1, 16; *Oakland Tribune*, July 18, 1969; Apr. 23, 1970; *S.F. Chronicle*, June 28, 1969. On Scherr see Boris Raymond letter, *Berk. Barb*, Sept. 30, 1966, p. 10; *Berk. Gazette*, Mar. 26, 1969, pp. 1, 2; Mar. 27, 1969, p. 2; *Sunday Ramparts*, Oct. 2, 1966, p. 5. Sex ads are noted in *Berk. Barb*, May 26, 1967, p. 1; Joseph P. Lyford, *The Berkeley Archipélago* (Chicago, 1982), 122–23. The first ad was on Mar. 18, 1966, p. 7. The prostitute is in *Sunday Ramparts*, Nov. 6, 1966, p. 3. For a serious discussion see *Berk. Barb*, Nov. 25, 1966, p 1.

20. The Jacopettis are in Perry, 22–23, 85. On topless see *Berk. Gazette*, May 8, 1965, p. 1; Gene Anthony, *The Summer of Love* (Millbrae, Calif., 1980), 93. "The Beard" is noted in *Berk. Barb*, July 22, 1966, p. 6; Aug. 19, 1966, p. 3; Feb. 17, 1967, p. 5; Mar. 10, 1967, p. 5; Apr. 14, 1967, p. 8; *Daily Cal.*, Aug. 17, 1966, p. 12; Aug. 31, 1966, p. 1; *Sunday Ramparts*, Oct. 2, 1966, p. 4; May 14, 1967, p. 8; Anthony, 92. In general see Michael McClure, *The Beard* (N.Y., 1967; orig. 1965), esp. 6, 94–96. For details of the controversy see Boxes 1 and 2, McClure Papers. On changing legal standards see *Berk. Barb*, Oct. 1, 1965, p. 2; *Berk. Gazette*, Mar. 26, 1965.

21. In general see *Berk. Barb*, Jan. 10, 1969, pp. 12–13; Jan. 31, 1969, p. 9; *Communiqué for New Politics*, Dec. 24, 1968, p. 4; *Daily Cal.*, Jan. 28, 1969, p. 2; *S.F. Express Times*, Aug. 14, 1968, p. 6; Aug. 28, 1968, p. 7; David M. Kennedy, *Birth Control in America* (New Haven, 1970). On Women for Peace see the Berk. Chapter's *Newsletter*, ca. 1962–69, in the important Herstory Coll. (film). On the beginning of the movement see Bay Area Women's Liberation, *Off the Pedestal*, Aug. 15, 1969, p. 2, filed under *Tooth and Nail Journal*, Herstory Coll. On the role of The Resistance see unidentified speaker, CDO meeting transcript, Jan. 18, 1968, p. 16, 23:CDO 3, Hardin B. Jones Papers, HI. On Heick see Free Univ. of Berk., *Catalog*, Summer

1968, p. 3 (quote). SPAZM is in *Berk. Barb*, June 14, 1968, p. 3; Feb. 28, 1969, p. 13; Mar. 7, 1969, p. 2. See the SPAZM section, Herstory Coll. On Anne Weills Scheer see Sara Davidson, *Real Property* (Garden City, N.Y., 1980), 186. The vibrator incident is in *Berk. Barb*, Oct. 11, 1968, p. 5; reaction, Oct. 18, 1968, p. 11. Although this topic deserves much attention, it is more of the seventies than of the sixties.

22. *Berk. Barb*, Dec. 9, 1966, pp. 1, 8; Mar. 3, 1967, p. 7; Mar. 10, 1967, p. 6; Mar. 17, 1967, p. 11; Tuli Kupferberg columns, July 28, 1967, p. 8; Aug. 4, 1967, p. 8; Aug. 11, 1967, p. 8; Corso quoted in Abe Peck, *Uncovering the Sixties* (N.Y., 1985), 14; Ragué Arias, 123; Conlin, 76, 229, 232, 237; Perry, 5, 249–51; Lewis Yablonsky, *The Hippie Trip* (N.Y., 1969; orig. 1968), 28, 33, 145, 197, 341.

23. *Berk. Barb*, Jan. 7, 1966, p. 5; *Berk. Gazette*, June 2, 1966, p. 5; *Daily Cal.*, Feb. 17, 1964, p. 1; Mar. 5, 1964, pp. 1, 2; Apr. 15, 1966, p. 1; Conlin, 230–31; Perry, 6, 199, 256.

24. Perry, 251–53.

25. Charles B. Artman statement, n.d.; Maynard Morris to Clark Kerr, rally report, Mar. 2, 1965, both in 1294:2, UCPF; Artman statement, early 1965; Artman carbon of statement, n.d.; Artman statement, n.d.; Artman statement at sentencing, Aug. 4, 1965, all in 1:20, FSM Arch.; Artman open letter, Dec. 7, 1964, 3:19, FSM Arch.; *L.A. Times*, Apr. 18, 1965, Sec. A, pp. B, 15; *S.F. Chronicle*, Mar. 16, 1965; Aug. 5, 1965, p. 4 (quote).

26. Lindsey, 162–63; Roszak, 140; *Berk. Barb*, Aug. 20, 1965, p. 2 (2 quotes); *Daily Cal.*, Aug. 27, 1965, p. 4 (2 quotes); *Berk. Gazette*, Aug. 24, 1965, pp. 1–2.

27. On the teepee see *Berk. Barb*, Aug. 20, 1965, p. 2; *Berk. Gazette*, Aug. 24, 1965, pp. 1–2; Sept. 7, 1965, p. 9; Sept. 15, 1965, p. 1; *Daily Cal.*, Aug. 27, 1965, p. 4. "Little Eagle" is in *Berk. Barb*, May 20, 1966, p. 7; Artman letter, *Berk. Gazette*, June 9, 1966, p. 8; *Daily Cal.*, Apr. 26, 1966, p. 3; May 18, 1966, p. 14. His quiet life is in *Berk. Citizen*, Nov. 11, 1966, p. 2; Mar. 10, 1967, p. 5. The arrest is in *Berk. Gate*, Mar. 7, 1967, pp. 1, 10 (quote); Apr. 25, 1967, pp. 1, 2; *Daily Cal.*, Mar. 29, 1967, p. 1; Mar. 30, 1967, p. 8. Free Univ. of Berk., *Catalog*, Spring 1967, p. 3. On the Pentagon see Anthony, 23. For his later life see *Berk. Barb*, Aug. 18, 1967, p. 5; Apr. 5, 1968, p. 17; June 21, 1968, p. 4; *Daily Cal.*, Nov. 4, 1968, p. 1; Hardin B. Jones note, n.d., 58:Artman, Jones Papers.

28. On authority see Ginsberg, *Verbatim*, 34; Rossman, *On Learning*, 81–82; Marvin Garson column, *Berk. Barb*, Dec. 2, 1966, p. 6; Peter Marin in Goodman, 8–9. "When the Music's Over" was issued on The Doors, *Strange Days* (Elektra EKS 74014, 1967). Tom Hayden, *Rebellion and Repressioon* (N.Y., 1969), 185. On power see Ralph Gleason column, *Berk. Barb*, Oct. 25, 1968, p. 14. In general see Greil Marcus, *Mystery Train*, rev. ed. (N.Y., 1982; orig. 1975).

29. Marcus, 58; Ed Denson columns, *Berk. Barb*, July 22, 1966, p. 4; Oct. 21, 1966, p. 6; Paul Goodman, *New Reformation* (N.Y., 1971; orig. 1970). See also Brian Turner column, *Daily Cal.*, May 13, 1966, p. 12; McClanahan, 42; Charles A. Reich, *The Greening of America* (N.Y., 1971; orig. 1970), 260–65, 268–69.

30. McDonough, esp. 11–12, 15–17; Simon Frith in *The Sixties, without Apology*, ed. Sohnya Sayres et al. (Minneapolis, 1984), 65–66. On folk in Berkeley see Ed Denson columns, *Berk. Barb*, Apr. 8, 1966, p. 5; Mar. 3, 1967, p. 6; Sept. 15, 1967, p. 8. On the beat see Wolfe, *Acid Test*, 353.

31. McClanahan, 30–35; Wolfe, *Acid Test*, 36–41, 44; Perry, 256. In general see Martin A. Lee and Bruce Shlain, *Acid Dreams* (N.Y., 1985).

32. Wolfe, *Acid Test*, 49–56, 58, 60–63, 90, 93–95, 101. On Leary see *Berk. Barb*,

May 20, 1966, p. 5; Oct. 7, 1966, p. 6; Dec. 16, 1966, pp. 2, 8; *Realist*, Aug. 1964, pp. 1, 17–18; Perry, 12–15; Roszak, 165–66. The two-year estimate is in Wolfe, *Acid Test*, 8. In general see Timothy Leary, *Flashbacks* (L.A., 1983).

33. Rossman, *On Learning*, 179; Lee and Shlain, 129. See also Wolfe, *Acid Test*, 121; *SLATE Newsletter*, undated but ca. Nov. 1964, p. 2, 2:52, FSM Arch.; *American Opinion*, Dec. 1968, p. 6. On the campaign to make LSD illegal see *Berk. Barb*, Apr. 22, 1966, p. 6; *Berk. Gazette*, Apr. 20, 1966, p. 3; May 30, 1966, p. 1; *Sunday Ramparts*, Oct. 23, 1966, p. 6; Anthony, 33. On Owsley, ibid., 54; Robert S. Anson, *Gone Crazy and Back Again* (Garden City, N.Y., 1981), 71–76; McDonough, 16; Perry, 3–4, 7, 80, 284; Wolfe, *Acid Test*, 188–89; Yablonsky, 132.

34. Kesey quoted in Perry, 34. On the Acid Tests see *Berk. Barb*, Mar. 18, 1966, p. 2; *Daily Cal.*, Feb. 10, 1966, p. 12; Wolfe, *Acid Test*, 46, 189, 214–15, 218, 221–23; Anthony, 107; McDonough, 6. On the Grateful Dead see Garcia interview, *Rolling Stone*, Jan. 20, 1972, pp. 34–38; *Berk. Barb*, Apr. 21, 1967, p. 6; *Sunday Ramparts*, Dec. 4, 1966, p. 8. On Helms see Anson, 41, 44, 92–93; Lee and Shlain, 142. On Graham see R. G. Davis, *The San Francisco Mime Troupe* (Palo Alto, 1975), 69; Anthony, 52–53, 81; McDonough, 6–7, 37–41; Perry, 16–17, 31–33, 35.

35. McDonough, 7–8; Perry, 42. On the Trips Festival see Anthony, 107, 116, 119; McDonough, 8; Perry, 46–48, 50; Wolfe, *Acid Test*, 223–34. On concerts see *Berk. Barb*, Oct. 29, 1965, p. 2; Nov. 5, 1965, p. 4; Mar. 25, 1966, pp. 7, 8; Oct. 7, 1966, p. 4; Nov. 25, 1966, p. 9; May 5, 1967, p. 3; May 12, 1967, p. 6; *Daily Cal.*, Oct. 28, 1965, p. 5; Nov. 7, 1966, p. 1; McDonough, 8; Perry, 55, 61, 63; Rossman, *On Learning*, 84–85; Sol Stern in *Counterculture and Revolution*, ed. David Horowitz et al. (N.Y., 1972), 127.

36. Ed Denson column, *Berk. Barb*, Oct. 13, 1967, p. 6; McDonough, 8, 15, 17, 75. On the Grateful Dead see McDonough, 135–36; Jim Miller, ed., *The Rolling Stone Illustrated History of Rock & Roll, 1950–1980*, rev. ed. (N.Y., 1980; orig. 1976), 266–68. On the Jefferson Airplane see *Berk. Barb*, Aug. 26, 1966, p. 6; *Daily Cal.*, Oct. 29, 1965, p. 3; McDonough, 145; Miller, *History*, 272–74; Perry, 72, 187, 200, 225; Wiener, 4; Wolfe, *Acid Test*, 321. On Big Brother see *Berk. Barb*, Sept. 20, 1968, p. 11; McDonough, 151; Miller, *History*, 275–79; *Rolling Stone Rock Almanac*, 149.

37. McDonough, 166, 171, 192, 194, 209, 216–17; Miller, *History*, 265–71. On the Joy of Cooking see McDonough, 156. On McDonald, ibid., 164–65; Sol Stern in Horowitz, *Counterculture*, 127; Ed Denson column, *Berk. Barb*, June 10, 1966, p. 5; Oct. 7, 1966, p. 12; Oct. 6, 1967, p. 3; Perry, 26–27. Denson became McDonald's manager. On Sly see McDonough, 206; Miller, *History*, 315–19; Marcus, 75–111; *Rolling Stone Rock Almanac*, 155. On Santana see McDonough, 200; *Rolling Stone Rock Almanac*, 177–79. On Creedence see Miller, *History*, 324–26; *Rolling Stone Rock Almanac*, 163, 175–77.

38. On lights see Albright, 170–74; McDonough, 62. On posters see *Berk. Barb*, July 14, 1967, p. 6; *Daily Cal.*, Nov. 30, 1966, pp. 1, 8 (quotes); Albright, 170–72; Anthony, 95; Conlin, 229; McDonough, 55–62; Perry, 38, 64, 290; Wolfe, *Acid Test*, 229. Thompson and Weller are in Perry, 190.

39. *Berk. Barb*, July 28, 1967, p. 6; Mar. 22, 1968, p. 3; May 31, 1968, p. 21; Aug. 2, 1968, p. 8; Jan. 3, 1969, p. 4; *S.F. Express Times*, Feb. 15, 1968, p. 1; Mar. 21, 1968, p. 3; Mar. 28, 1968, p. 13; May 9, 1968, p. 3; May 16, 1968, p. 3; Rossman, *On Learning*, 79–81; McDonough, 95–97; Perry, 174, 237. For details see Susan Krieger, *Hip Capitalism* (Beverly Hills, 1979).

40. Gleason columns, *S.F. Chronicle*, Oct. 17, 1966, p. 49, and "Datebook," *S.F.*

*Sunday Examiner-Chronicle*, July 7, 1968, p. 23. See Wenner's "Mr. Jones" columns, *Daily Cal.*, Feb. 10, 1966, p. 12; Feb. 24, 1966, p. 12; Mar. 10, 1966, p. 8; Mar. 17, 1966, p. 8; Mar. 31, 1966, p. 8; Apr. 29, 1966, p. 12; May 19, 1966, pp. 12–13, and under his own name, Oct. 5, 1966, p. 12; Oct. 12, 1966, p. 12; Oct. 26, 1966, p. 12; Jan. 18, 1967, p. 12; Jan. 25, 1967, p. 12; Feb. 2, 1967, p. 12. On Wenner see McDonough, 101–2; *Daily Cal.*, Nov. 15, 1967, p. 6; Craig Pyes in Horowitz, *Counterculture*, 104–6, 108–9. For a not entirely satisfactory account see Anson. See also *Tocsin*, Jan. 13, 1966, p. 4. On the FBI see Todd Gitlin in *Unamerican Activities*, ed. Geoffrey Rips et al. (S.F., 1981), 28; Angus Mackenzie, ibid., 165–66.

41. *Berk. Barb*, Jan. 13, 1967, pp. 1, 3; Jan. 20, 1967, pp. 1, 4; *Berk. Citizen*, Jan. 6, 1967, p. 3; Michael Lerner column, *Daily Cal.*, Oct. 27, 1966, p. 12; Jan. 18, 1967, p. 12; Tom Collins column, Jan. 19, 1967, p. 8; *S.F. Sunday Examiner-Chronicle*, Jan. 22, 1967, Sec. I, p. 11; *Sunday Ramparts*, Jan. 29, 1967, p. 4; Feb. 12, 1967, pp. 1–2 (Rubin quoted at 2); London *IT*, Feb. 13, 1967, p. 2; Anthony, 155, 162–65 (Ginsberg quoted at 162, Leary at 165); McDonough, 10; Perry, 121–29; Ragué Arias, 124; Rubin, *Do It!*, 54–56; Jerry Rubin, *Growing (Up) at Thirty-Seven* (N.Y., 1976), 80; Roszak, 65.

42. On bananas see *Berk. Barb*, Mar. 3, 1967, p. 6; Mar. 10, 1967, p. 1; Apr. 7, 1967, p. 15; Perry, 151–52, 155. On buttons see *Berk. Gate*, Mar. 7, 1967, p. 6; June 27, 1967, p. 1; *Berk. Barb*, Mar. 10, 1967, p. 1; *Berk. Citizen*, Sept. 9, 1966, p. 6. On carts see *Berk. Gate*, July 12, 1967, p. 1; July 25, 1967, p. 6; Oct. 3, 1967, p. 9; *Berk. Barb*, Mar. 3, 1967, p. 11.

43. On Mahler see *KPFA Program Folio*, July-Aug. 1965; *Berk. Barb*, Nov. 25, 1966, p. 9; Carl E. Schorske, *Fin-de-Siècle Vienna* (N.Y., 1980), xxiv. On KPFA see *KPFA Program Folio*, Oct. 1966, centerfold; Jan. 1967, p. 2; Feb. 1967, p. 3; July 1968, cover; *S.F. Express Times*, Mar. 18, 1969, p. 10.

44. On Crumb see *Berk. Barb*, Nov. 22, 1968, p. 9 (quotes); *Daily Cal.*, Feb. 18, 1969, pp. 10–11, 14; *S.F. Express Times*, Nov. 13, 1968; Peck, 304. On the raid on Moe's see *Daily Cal.*, Nov. 15, 1968, p. 5; Nov. 18, 1968, p. 2. Big Brother and the Holding Company, *Cheap Thrills* (Columbia 9700, 1968); Free Univ. of Berk., *Catalog*, Fall 1969. See also *Yellow Dog*, 1968–69, largely drawn by Crumb. On the festival see *Berk. Gate*, June 27, 1967, p. 4. The Jabberwock is in *Berk. Barb,*, Jan. 20, 1967, p. 3; Feb. 3, 1967, p. 8; July 7, 1967, p. 9; July 14, 1967, p. 3; *Berk. Citizen*, Jan. 27, 1967, p. 1; *Berk. Gate*, July 25, 1967, p. 6; *Daily Cal.*, Mar. 9, 1966, p. 10. See the collection of Jabberwock programs, Bancroft Library.

45. (waterbed) Perry, 278; (taxis) *Berk. Barb*, Sept. 1, 1967, p. 2; Sept. 8, 1967, p. 3; (Co-op) Reich, 423; (Marcuse) Herbert Marcuse, *One Dimensional Man* (Boston, 1964); Codys in Nathan and Scott, 141; (Laing) Ronald D. Laing, *The Politics of Experience* (N.Y., 1967); (Castaneda) Carlos Castaneda, *The Teachings of Don Juan* (Berk., 1968); (transcendental meditation) Conlin, 240; Perry, 241; (cults) John R. Coyne, Jr., *The Kumquat Statement* (N.Y., 1970), 177; Perry, 187, 295. On drugs see *Berk. Gate*, Mar. 22, 1966, p. 2; Oct. 18, 1966, pp. 1–2; *Berk. Gazette*, Nov. 20, 1965, p. 6; May 31, 1966, pp. 1, 3; June 6, 1966, p. 3; *Daily Cal.*, Apr. 13, 1966, p. 6; *Oakland Tribune*, June 5, 1966, p. 8; Mar. 29, 1967; Feuer, *Conflict*, 419; Gerzon, 219, 232, 243, 249, 252; Michael P. Lerner in Horowitz, *Counterculture*, 181; Michael Rossman, *New Age Blues* (N.Y., 1979), 4 (quote); Rossman, *On Learning*, 109, 115, 121; Miles interview, 103, 106; Mrs. Marie Turner to Don Mulford, Feb. 2, 1968, 4:5, Mulford Papers, HI. The "feel right" quote is by Rev. T. Walter Herbert in *Issue*, Spring 1965, p. 28. The "fabric" quote is in Rossman, *On Learning*, 31. On religion see Rossman,

*New Age*, 66; Herbert in *Issue*, 28; Rev. John S. Hadsell letter, Jan. 18, 1965, ibid., 2. In general see *Berk. Gazette*, Mar. 19, 1967, pp. 1–2; *S.F. Sunday Examiner-Chronicle*, Mar. 24, 1968; Perry, 264–68, 278–79; Helen H. Nowlis, *Drugs on the College Campus* (Garden City, N.Y., 1969), 21–26.

46. ("bushy" quote) *Berk. Barb*, Mar. 4, 1966, p. 5; ("hair" quote) Rubin, *Do It!*, 96; ("hippies" quote) Tom Collins in *Daily Cal.*, Jan. 19, 1967, p. 8; ("grass" quote) Rubin, *Do It!*, 99; ("generation" quote) ibid., 213; ("emotion" quote) Rubin, *Growing*, 36. Rossman quoted in Hardin B. Jones to Theodore R. Meyer, Oct. 7, 1966, 10:misc., Jones Papers. On dogs see *Berk. Gate*, Nov. 1, 1966, p. 5; Nov. 19, 1969, p. 1; *Daily Cal.*, Aug. 31, 1966, p. 5; Mar. 1, 1968, p. 20; Coyne, 42–46; Neil V. Sullivan with Evelyn S. Stewart, *Now Is the Time* (Bloomington, Ind., 1969), 26. ("no precedent" quote) Rossman, *On Learning*, 33. In general see *Berk. Citizen*, Mar. 3, 1967, p. 7; editorial, *Daily Cal.*, Sept. 30, 1968, p. 12; Gerzon, 263; Michael P. Lerner in Horowitz, *Counterculture*, 180; Reich, 278–79.

47. *Sunday Ramparts*, Dec. 18, 1966, p. 5; Anthony, esp. 9, 11, 14, 16, 23; Lindsey, 180; Perry, esp. 19–20; Rossman, *On Learning*, 88–93; Yablonski, 199–223.

48. *Berk. Barb*, Mar. 24, 1967, p. 1; Apr. 6, 1967, pp. 1, 5; Apr. 28, 1967, p. 5; May 5, 1967, p. 10; May 12, 1967, p. 4; June 2, 1967, p. 1; June 9, 1967, p. 1; Sept. 29, 1967, p. 3; *L.A. Free Press*, June 20, 1969, pp. 3, 18; *Ramparts*, Mar. 1967, pp. 5–26; Anthony, 27, 175; Perry, 78, 171, 200, 212, 243–45, 283, 285, 287; Yablonski, 294–95. The most acute portrait of the Haight is in Didion, 84–128. See also Nicholas von Hoffman's series, *Wash. Post*, Oct. 15–29, 1967, and his *We Are the People Our Parents Warned Us against* (Chicago, 1968).

49. *Berk. Barb*, Oct. 21, 1966, p. 3; Anthony, 27, 33–34; Davis, 69–70, 206; Perry, 90–91, 96–97, 105, 129, 141, 196; Peter Cohon in Goodman, *Movement*, 25. For the autobiography of a Digger see Emmett Grogan, *Ringolevio* (Boston, 1972).

50. Perry, 212, 291; Yablonsky, 163. For a portrait of rural hippie life see Raymond Mungo, *Total Loss Farm* (Seattle, 1977; orig. 1970). On Canyon see *Berk. Monitor*, May 17, 1969, p. 7; John Van der Zee, *Canyon* (N.Y., 1971), esp. 10, 36–37, 57–58, 60, 77–81, 100.

51. Editorial, *Berk. Gazette*, June 22, 1967; *Daily Cal.*, July 15, 1967; *Denver Chinook*, Dec. 11, 1969, p. 10; McGill, 241, note 27; Ragué Arias, 125. On panhandling see Perry, 291. Statistics from BPD, *The People of Berkeley: Where They Are* (Berk., 1973), 2–4; BPD, *The People of Berkeley: Who They Are* (Berk., 1973), i–v; Wallace J. S. Johnson, *A Fresh Look at Patriotism* (Old Greenwich, Conn., 1976), 64–65.

52. *Berk. Barb*, Jan. 14, 1966, p. 1; May 20, 1966, p. 3; July 1, 1966, p. 3; Aug. 19, 1966, p. 3; *Berk. Citizen*, May 13, 1966, p. 1; June 17, 1966, p. 3; July 8, 1966, p. 4; *Berk. Gate*, June 21, 1966, p. 9; July 12, 1966, pp. 1–2; Nov. 1, 1966, p. 3; *Berk. Gazette*, May 25, 1966, pp. 1–2; June 1, 1966, pp. 1, 3; Helga Williamson letter, May 6, 1966, p. 10; *BCU Bulletin*, Dec. 1965, p. 3; *Sunday Ramparts*, Oct. 2, 1966, p. 5; Bernice H. May, "A Native Daughter's Leadership in Public Affairs" (1976), interview, 378; John Hewitt and Michael Thorn to Heyns, Dec. 4, 1966, 8:86, UCBCF.

53. *Berk. Barb*, July 1, 1966, p. 1; July 8, 1966, p. 3; Oct. 7, 1966, p. 9; Oct. 21, 1966, p. 3; *Berk. Citizen*, July 22, 1966, p. 1; Aug. 22, 1966, p. 1; *Berk. Gate*, July 5, 1966, pp. 1–2; Aug. 2, 1966, pp. 1, 10; Michael Rossman, "Breakthrough at Berkeley," *Center Magazine*, May 1968, pp. 46–47.

54. Rising tension is noted in *Berk. Citizen*, Nov. 4, 1966, p. 2; Pat and Fred Cody in Nathan and Scott, 141 (quote). On unemployment see Jan. E. Dizard, "Patterns of Unemployment in Berkeley and the Programs Designed to Alleviate the Problem: A

Current Analysis" (M.B.A. report, UCB, 1967), 8; Margaret S. Gordon in Nathan and Scott, 289. The block party is in *Berk. Barb*, Apr. 14, 1967, pp. 1, 4, 5; *Daily Cal.*, Apr. 10, 1967, p. 13. On June's events see *Berk. Barb*, June 30, 1967, p. 3; *Berk. Gate*, July 12, 1967, p. 10; *Daily Cal.*, June 27, 1967; editorial, *Berk. Gazette*, Nov. 2, 1967; Chief of Police William P. Beall to City Manager William Hanley, Feb. 3, 1967, 1:6, Don Mulford Papers, HI. Several novels convey the flavor of the area. See Sara Davidson, *Loose Change* (N.Y., 1977); "Michael Douglas" (pseud. for Michael Crichton and Douglas Crichton), *Dealing or the Berkeley-to-Boston Forty-Brick Lost-Bag Blues* (N.Y., 1971); and Anne Steinhardt, *How to Get Balled in Berkeley* (N.Y., 1976).

55. On Bothwell see Lyford, 117–18 (quote at 118). The six officers are in *Berk. Gazette*, Oct. 10, 1968, p. 1. See also Police Conduct Complaint Center, "Complaints Regarding Police Actions against Citizens, June 28–July 2, 1968" (1968), 7–8, plus unpaginated reports of incidents; PCCC, "Berkeley Report: Police Personnel Complaints and Redress Remedies" (1970), 7, 24. The Red Mountain Tribe is in Lyford, 120. On Miller see *Berk. Barb*, Sept. 13, 1968, p. 5; Jan. 17, 1969, p. 7; Apr. 25, 1969, p. 11; *Berk. Gazette*, Sept. 25, 1968, p. 1. In general see Milwaukee *Kaleidoscope*, Sept. 13, 1968, p. 9; editorial, *Berk. Gazette*, Jan. 30, 1968. On the local drug culture see James T. Carey, *The College Drug Scene* (Englewood Cliffs, N.J., 1968).

56. For the cover see *Berk. Barb*, July 12, 1968, p. 1. On communes see Berk. Free Church, "Free Church Collective Handbook" (1970), Free Church Collectives Section, pp. 1–2; Miller, *Democracy*, 318. Razavi is in *Berk. Barb*, Aug. 2, 1968, p. 3; *S.F. Express Times*, Dec. 4, 1968, p. 4; Pat and Fred Cody in Nathan and Scott, 147–48 (quote at 148). On the wedding see *Berk. Barb*, Aug. 30, 1968, p. 4 (quote). In general see ibid., Aug. 30, 1968, p. 9; Sept. 6, 1968, p. 5; Sept. 13, 1968, p. 2; *Berk. Gazette*, Oct. 1, 1968, p. 1; *Daily Cal.*, July 1, 1968; the Red Family, *To Stop a Police State* (Berk., 1971), 13–14. For a different interpretation see Lyford, 28.

57. The meetings are in Pat and Fred Cody in Nathan and Scott, 146–47; Thomas L. McLaren, ibid., 237. On BBC patrols see *Berk. Barb*, Aug. 30, 1968, p. 5; Sept. 27, 1968, p. 11; *Daily Cal.*, Sept. 30, 1968, p. 1. On crime see *Berk. Barb*, Aug. 2, 1968, p. 3; *Berk. Gate*, July 12, 1967, p. 6; *Berk. Gazette*, July 18, 1968, p. 1; *Daily Cal.*, Apr. 18, 1968, p. 1; *S.F. Sunday Examiner-Chronicle*, Sept. 8, 1968, Sec. A, p. 3; Berk. Police Dept., *Annual Report* (Berk., 1970), 55, 63; Feuer, *Conflict*, 456. Runaway statistics are in Red Family, 11. On Mulford see *Berk. Review*, Oct. 13, 1960, p. 5; Mulford press releases, Mar. 7, 1963; Feb. 5, 1964; Nov. 2, 1964; Aug. 9, 1965, IGSL. The murders are noted in *Berk. Gazette*, Oct. 8, 1968, p. 1. On the crime wave as a myth see *Berk. Barb*, July 15, 1966, p. 1; *Berk. Citizen*, Aug. 5, 1966, p. 3; *Berk. Gate*, June 21, 1966, pp. 7–9; Red Family, 10. On police driving normal people away see *Berk. Barb*, Sept. 20, 1968, p. 9; Mar. 7, 1969, pp. 12–13.

58. On the University's plans see Glick, 27–29; Gar Smith, "A People's Park Chronology" (n.d.), 1; Robert M. Underhill, "University of California Lands, Finances, and Investments" (1967), interview, 328. On the city's early plans see May interview, 346–48; Wallace Johnson in Nathan and Scott, 203–5. The 1964 meeting is in Johnson, *Look*, 106–9. On 1966 see *Berk. Barb*, Mar. 25, 1966, p. 4; Apr. 1, 1966, p. 1; Apr. 8, 1966, pp. 1 (quote), 2; July 8, 1966, p. 2; *Berk. Citizen*, June 10, 1966, p. 1; *Berk. Gazette*, Apr. 2, 1966, p. 2; Apr. 5, 1966, pp. 1, 2; *Daily Cal.*, July 6, 1966, p. 1; Margaret S. Gordon in Nathan and Scott, 297; Berk., Urban Renewal Agency, "South Campus Urban Renewal Plan" (1966). In general see De Mars & Reay, *Design Program*

*for the South Campus Urban Renewal Project* (Berk., 1964); Riches Research, Inc., *Economic Analysis, South Campus Area* (Palo Alto, 1964).

59. *BCU Bulletin*, Mar. 1967, pp. 3–4 (quotes at 3). The 85 percent figure is in Lindsey, 140. The rhyme is from RR column, *Berk. Barb*, Dec. 23, 1966, p. 7. See also *Berk. Barb*, Feb. 10, 1967, p. 3; May 5, 1967, pp. 3, 7; editorial, *Berk. Citizen*, Sept. 30, 1966, p. 4.

60. On policy see Harry R. Wellman, "Teaching, Research, and Administration: University of California, 1925–1968" (1976), interview, 161–62. Leggett quoted in *Berk. Gate*, May 24, 1966, p. 3. Bort in *Berk. Gazette*, May 3, 1966, p. 10. Mulford quote, ibid., Apr. 6, 1967, p. 1. On the purchase see *Berk. Barb*, June 30, 1967, p. 10; *Berk. Gate*, July 12, 1967, p. 5; *Daily Cal.*, June 27, 1967; *BCU Bulletin*, Aug. 1967, p. 1; Glick, 33; Smith, 1. On the raid see *Berk. Barb*, Oct. 6, 1967, pp. 3, 14.

61. On demolitions and evictions see *Daily Cal.*, Feb. 15, 1968, p. 3; Feb. 21, 1968, pp. 1, 20; Mar. 1, 1968, p. 5; Apr. 23, 1968, p. 12; Charles Sellers letter, May 16, 1969; Glick, 34. The Vietnam analogy is in London *IT*, June 13, 1969, p. 3. For reflections see Barbara Lucas letter, *Berk. Barb*, May 10, 1968, p. 2; *Berk. Gate*, Apr. 2, 1968, p. 8; *Coalition News*, Mar. 12, 1969, p. 3; *Daily Cal.*, Apr. 18, 1968, p. 7; Jim Chanin in Nathan and Scott, 323.

62. On the Dutch Provos see *Berk. Barb*, Sept. 30, 1966, p. 7; Nov. 4, 1966, p. 5. On food see ibid., Nov. 25, 1966, p. 3; June 2, 1967, p. 7; June 16, 1967, p. 5; June 23, 1967, p. 13; Aug. 25, 1967, p. 7; *Daily Cal.*, Jan. 12, 1967, p. 8. On rock see *Berk. Barb*, Apr. 12, 1968, p. 7; Oct. 4, 1968, p. 3; *The Berkeley Book* (Berk., 1967), 8. On the store see *Berk. Barb*, July 14, 1967, p. 4; July 21, 1967, p. 5; July 28, 1967, p. 7; *Berk. Gate*, Oct. 3, 1967, p. 9. The bus is in *Berk. Barb*, July 14, 1967, p. 4; Aug. 18, 1967, p. 2; *Berk. Gate*, Oct. 3, 1967, pp. 9–10; *Berk. Book*, 20; Perry, 218, 230. In general see *Berk. Barb*, Feb. 3, 1967, p. 3; Mar. 10, 1967, p. 1; Sept. 1, 1967, p. 15; *Berk. Citizen*, Dec. 23, 1966, p. 2; Dec. 30, 1966, p. 3.

63. The symbol and motto are on the cover of the Berk. Free Church (BFC), "Handbook." On the symbol see Michael Ferber and Staughton Lynd, *The Resistance* (Boston, 1971), 251–52. On York see *Berk. Barb*, July 28, 1967, p. 7; Mar. 8, 1968, p. 8; *Oakland Tribune*, Aug. 20, 1967; *BCU Bulletin*, July 1967, p. 5; Aug. 1967, p. 5 (quote); Apr. 1969, p. 4. On Brown see *Berk. Barb*, Mar. 10, 1967, p. 3; Feb. 16, 1968, p. 3. On the church see BFC, "Handbook," A Short History of the BFC Section, 1–2; *Christian Century*, 85 (1968), 464–68. See also *Berk. Barb*, Aug. 4, 1967, p. 3; Aug. 11, 1967, p. 8; Aug. 18, 1967, p. 5; Dec. 8, 1967, p. 6; June 14, 1968, pp. 9, 15; July 5, 1968, p. 3; July 12, 1968, p. 5; Sept. 6, 1968, p. 11; Nov. 8, 1968, p. 11; Jan. 17, 1969, p. 11; *Daily Cal.*, Aug. 9, 1968, p. 2; Pat and Fred Cody in Nathan and Scott, 142; Ragué Arias, 151–53. See the liberation prayerbook: John P. Brown and Richard L. York, comps., *The Covenant of Peace* (N.Y., 1971), esp. 8, 10, 12, 22–30.

64. *Berk. Barb*, Dec. 23, 1966, p. 6; July 14, 1967, p. 3; July 21, 1967, p. 3; *Berk. Citizen*, Aug. 12, 1966, p. 1; *Berk. Gate*, Feb. 14, 1967, p. 9 (student quote); Apr. 25, 1967, p. 2 (dirty heart anecdote); Oct. 8, 1968, p. 5; *Berk. Gazette*, Nov. 5, 1966, p. 2; *Daily Cal.*, Feb. 6, 1968, p. 2; Lindsey, 24, 151, 166, 194; *The Golden Bear*, May 6, 1969, p. 2.

65. On Zen see *Berk. Barb*, Nov. 15, 1968, p. 9; Steven M. Tipton, *Getting Saved from the Sixties* (Berk., 1982), 95–175. On the Hare Krishnas see *Berk. Barb*, Apr. 14, 1967, pp. 1, 5; June 21, 1968, p. 10; Mar. 7, 1969, p. 9; *Daily Cal.*, May 22, 1968,

p. 9; Coyne, 24–25; Thomas Farber, *Tales for the Son of My Unborn Child* (N.Y., 1971), 101; Lindsey, 171–74; Perry, 130; *Whole Berk. Catalogue*, 44. On the religious crisis, in addition to Tipton, see Stanley Hauerwas in *America in Change*, ed. Ronald Weber (Notre Dame, 1972), 71–90.

66. On solipsism see Lindsey, 55–56; McGill, 224; Marcus, 125, 193–94; Patrick Meyers, *K2* (N.Y., 1983; orig. 1980), 16; Yvor Winters, *In Defense of Reason*, 3rd ed. (Denver, 1947). On poetry see *Berk. Barb*, Dec. 15, 1967, p. 2; May 31, 1968, p. 8; *Daily Cal.*, Feb. 2, 1967, p. 6; Ralph Gleason column, *S.F. Chronicle*, July 9, 1965; *The Nation*, Nov. 8, 1965, pp. 338–40; *Poems Read in the Spirit of Peace and Gladness* (Berk., 1966); Miles interview, 103–4, 159–61, 180–81, 196; Josephine Miles to Prof. Peters, Apr. 6, 1964, 1:1, Miles Papers; Robin Blaser to Miles, Oct. 10, 1967, 1:32, Miles Papers; Rosalie (Moore) Brown to Miles, Apr. 17, 1959, 1:46; Miles Papers; Fred Cody to Miles, Jan. 12, 1972, 2:30, Miles Papers; Adrien Stoutenberg to Miles, Mar. 28, 1965, 6:7, Miles Papers; Celeste T. Wright to Miles, Mar. 26, 1965, 6:41, Miles Papers. On sculpture see Albright, esp. 135–63. Jones's conversation is in Hardin B. Jones to Lewis W. Feuer, Apr. 23, 1969, 9:Feuer, Jones Papers.

67. On the trouble in January see *Daily Cal.*, Jan. 29, 1969, p. 1; Feb. 3, 1969, p. 1; Frank Madigan to Marjorie Woolman, Jan. 31, 1969; Heyns to President Charles Hitch, Feb. 3, 1969; Pete Steffens, AFT 1474, to Heyns, Feb. 3, 1969, all in 10:112, UCBCF. On the highway patrol see *Berk. Barb*, Feb. 7, 1969, pp. 3, 4, 14, 15; Feb. 14, 1969, pp. 3, 15; Feb. 21, 1969, pp. 1, 5, 6; Feb. 28, 1969, p. 5; *Daily Cal.*, Feb. 6, 1969, p. 1; Feb. 14, 1969, p. 1; Feb. 19, 1969, p. 1; Feb. 21, 1969, p. 1; Feb. 24, 1969, p. 1; Heyns announcement, Feb. 5, 1969; R. L. Johnson to Heyns, Feb. 10, 1969; Feb. 19, 1969; R. P. Haydon memo, Feb. 21, 1969, all in 10:111, UCBCF. For complaints see Leslie A. Hausrath to Heyns, Feb. 5, 1969 (quote); Gregg G. Schiffner to Heyns, Feb. 10, 1969; Franklin M. Henry to Heyns, Feb. 23, 1969; Oscar Paris to Jewell Ross, Feb. 25, 1969; Donald M. Friedman to Heyns, Feb. 27, 1969; William J. Bouwsma to Heyns, Feb. 28, 1969, all in 10:112, UCBCF. On the Guard see *Berk. Barb*, Mar. 7, 1969, p. 3; *Daily Cal.*, Feb. 24, 1969, p. 1; May interview, 384; Gov. Ronald Reagan statement, Feb. 5, 1969, 1:11, Mulford Papers. For an appreciation of Madigan see his testimony in U.S. House Comm. on Internal Security, *Black Panther Party Hearings*, 91st Cong., 2nd Sess. (Wash., 1970–71), Pt. 4, pp. 4912–25, House Library vol. 481–4. In general see Sgt. George T. Martin to UCB Police Chief J. P. Halloran, Mar. 11, 1969, 9:101, UCBCF; Hitch to John E. Canaday, Mar. 18, 1969, 10:111, UCBCF; Heyns statement, Apr. 1, 1969; Ad Hoc Faculty Observers' Comm. to Academic Senate, Mar. 14, 1969, both in 10:112, UCBCF.

68. On the campaign see *Berk. Gazette*, Mar. 25, 1969, p. 10; Apr. 1, 1969, p. 1; Apr. 3, 1969, p. 1; *Daily Cal.*, Jan. 24, 1969, p. 6; Feb. 13, 1969, p. 8; *Communiqué for New Politics*, Feb. 3, 1969, p. 1; *Coalition News*, Feb. 24, 1969, p. 2; Mar. 12, 1969, pp. 1–3; Mar. 27, 1969, p. 2; Apr. 19, 1969, pp. 1, 4; *Berk. Monitor*, May 3, 1969, pp. 4, 6; Wallace Johnson in Nathan and Scott, 226; Donald R. Hopkins, ibid., 119–20; Thomas L. McLaren, ibid., 238. On Hancock see *Berk. Barb*, Dec. 20, 1968; Mar. 21, 1969, p. 4; *Coalition News*, Feb. 24, 1969, pp. 1, 2; *Berk. Monitor*, May 3, 1969, p. 4; *Women for Peace Newsletter*, Mar. 1969, p. 2, Herstory Coll. (film); Hancock in Nathan and Scott, 369–73. Miller slogan in *S.F. Express Times*, Mar. 25, 1969, p. 6.

69. For the first People's Park see *Berk. Barb*, Mar. 7, 1967, p. 3; May 10, 1968, pp. 4, 9; May 24, 1968, p. 11; Smith, 2. On the committee see Pat and Fred Cody in Nathan and Scott, 148–51; Smith, 3–4.

70. On Delacour see Glick, 35–37. *Good Times*, Apr. 2, 1969, p. 6. The *S.F. Express Times*, is reviewed in *Daily Cal.*, Feb. 22, 1968, p. 9. In general see Pat and Fred Cody in Nathan and Scott, 153; Lyford, 40–53; Calif., Governor, *The "People's Park"*: *A Report on a Confrontation at Berkeley, California Submitted to Governor Ronald Reagan* (Sacramento, 1969), 1–5. Although sometimes inaccurate, this report is important because it uses sources, such as official police reports, that are not otherwise available. It was written by Jerry C. Martin, a former *Oakland Tribune* reporter and member of Reagan's staff close to Meese. Jerry C. Martin, "Information and Policy Research for Ronald Reagan, 1969–1975" in "Appointments, Cabinet Management, and Policy Research for Governor Ronald Reagan, 1967–1974" (1983), interview, 7, 10–11, 32. For good summaries of the issue see *N.Y. Times Magazine*, June 29, 1969, pp. 5ff; *Guardian*, June 7, 1969, pp. 3, 8, 12; Abraham H. Miller in *Politics and Society*, 2 (1972), 433–58.

71. On the meeting see Calif., Gov., *Report*, 3–5; *Ramparts*, Aug. 1969, p. 48; Coyne, 153; Glick, 37–39; Smith, 5. For biographical sketches see *S.F. Examiner*, June 8, 1969. On ecology as an issue see Donald Appleyard, "Patterns of Environmental Conflict: The Escalation of Symbolism" (Working Paper No. 289, Institute of Urban & Regional Development, UCB, 1978), 2. On radicals see Hoffman, 57 (Albert quote); Johnson, *Look*, 77; McGill, 107.

72. On Hayden see Coyne, 170; Hayden, *Rebellion and Repression*, 16; Tom Hayden, *Reunion* (N.Y., 1988), 331–35, 420–23; Hoffman, 57; Michael P. Lerner in Horowitz, *Counterculture*, 187; Miller, *Democracy*, 307–8. See "Berkeley Liberation Program" (1969). Reprinted in Goodman, 512–13. On PL see Dotson Rader, *Blood Dues* (N.Y., 1973), 19. The communist position is noted by Carl Oglesby in Harold Jacobs, ed., *Weatherman* (n.p., 1970), 123. See also *Ramparts*, Aug. 1969, p. 46. On impressing hippies see Johnson, *Look*, 7; McGill, 53–54; Norman Mailer, *Miami and the Siege of Chicago* (N.Y., 1968), 140; Rossman, *New Age*, 108–9; Todd Gitlin in Goodman, 506–7.

73. *Berk. Barb*, Apr. 18, 1969, p. 2. See also Glick, 41–42; Seeger, 13–15; Smith, 5; *S.F. Bay Guardian*, June 14, 1979, p. 10.

74. Glick, 44; Smith, 5; *Berk. Barb*, Apr. 25, 1969, p. 5 (quote); John Simon in Goodman, 509.

75. *Berk. Barb*, Apr. 25, 1969, p. 1 (cover); *Daily Cal.*, Apr. 22, 1969; Glick, 52–53; Rubin, *Do It!*, 224–28; Seale quote in Univ. of Calif., Santa Cruz, *Merrill News*, May 16, 1969 (mimeo), 2, PPS. See Goodman, Introduction, vi–ix.

76. Frank Bardacke, "Who Owns the Park?" *Berk. Barb*, May 9, 1969, p. 2. Reprinted in Goodman, 505. *Ramparts*, Aug. 1969, p. 49; Glick, 47, 49; Coyne, 150–52; Reich, 396. Opponents understood Bardacke's claim. Calif., Gov., *Report*, 13. See the shrewd comments in Wini Breines, *Community and Organization in the New Left, 1962–1968* (N.Y., 1982), 54. See also "Defend the Park," Apr. 29, 1969, leaflet, 5:65, UCBCF.

77. Calif., Gov., *Report*, 8; Glick, 54–55, 59; Smith, 5; *Peninsula Observer*, May 26, 1969, pp. 13, 20; Roger W. Heyns, "Berkeley Chancellor, 1965–1971" (1987), interview, 82–83; quote from "The Trouble in Berkeley," n.d., leaflet, PPS.

78. In general see *BCU Bulletin*, May 1969, p. 1 (quote); June 1969, pp. 2, 6; "By Madmen," leaflet reproduced in *Berk. Barb*, May 9, 1969, p. 3 (quote); Margaret S. Gordon in Arthur Harris et al., *Bernice Hubbard May* (Berk., 1971), 60; McGill, 82–83, 158; Heyns answers to American Zoetrope, Apr. 6, 1970, 5:66, UCBCF; *S.F. Bay Guardian*, Apr. 4, 1984, p. 9. On Sherriffs see Heyns interview, 108; Hardin B. Jones

memo, ca. 1966, p. 12, 1:Jones, John H. Lawrence Papers, HI; Elinor R. Heller, "A Volunteer Career in Politics, in Higher Education, and on Government Boards" (1984), interview, 598, 600, 607, 618–19, 633, 636, 657; G. Paul Bishop, "A Portrait Photographer's View of the University of California, Berkeley, 1947 to 1981" (1983), interview, 126; McGill, 83, 250, note 24; *Berk. Gazette*, Dec. 20, 1967; *Daily Cal.*, Jan. 3, 1968, p. 2; Prof. Lepawsky call to Heyns, May 27, 1969, 5:65, UCBCF; Sherriffs to Martin Meyerson, July 1, 1965; Sherriffs to Hardin B. Jones, John Sparrow, and Alex Grendon, Aug. 1, 1968, both in 40:misc., Jones Papers. See Alex C. Sherriffs, *Facts and Mythologies about Youth and Society as We Enter the 70s* (Sacramento, 1970).

79. On conservatives see Coyne, 135, 153–54; Glick, 80; Smith, 7; Red Family, 16. On negotiations with the city see Margaret S. Gordon in Harris, *May*, 61; Heller interview, 631–32; Johnson, *Look*, 83–84. On negotiations with the Regents see McGill, 145–46, 159; May interview, 377–78.

80. On negotiations see *Berk. Gazette*, May 10, 1969; *S.F. Chronicle*, May 22, 1969, p. 2; Appleyard, 21; Glick, 57–58, 61–68, 74; Smith, 6–9. On Van der Ryn see *Berk. Barb*, May 16, 1969, p. 2; Sim Van der Ryn, "Building People's Park" in *The Troubled Campus*, ed. G. Kerry Smith (S.F., 1970), 54–71; Van der Ryn to Heyns, May 12, 1969, 5:65, UCBCF.

81. On Sunday see Glick, 74; Smith, "People's Park," 7. On the consecration see "Earth Rebirth," in Brown and York, 12. On York's attitude see York to Heyns, Jan. 8, 1970, 5:66, UCBCF. On Monday see Smith, "People's Park," 8. On Tuesday, ibid., 8–9; McGill, 160–62; Glick, 75–77; *Ramparts*, Aug. 1969, p. 52; Heyns statement, May 13, 1969, 5:64, UCBCF. On Wednesday see Glick, 81–82; Smith, "People's Park," 9–11. On the Regents meeting see Regents Comm. on Finance, Executive Session Minutes, May 15, 1969, 5:64, UCBCF. On the fence see N.Y. *Rat*, May 30, 1969, p. 6.

82. Glick, 90–91; Smith, "People's Park," 11–12 (leaflet quoted at 12); Denise Levertov in *Daily Cal.*, May 16, 1969.

83. Calif., Gov., *Report*, 15–16 (police reports quoted at 16); Glick, 91–92; Smith, "People's Park," 12A, 19; Coyne, 155–56; Johnson, *Look*, 81; *Berk. Barb*, May 16, 1969, p. 3; May 23, 1969, p. 6; *Berk. Gazette*, July 12, 1969, pp. 1–2; *Oakland Tribune*, July 11, 1969; *S.F. Chronicle*, June 5, 1969; June 7, 1969, p. 4; Jim Lemmon to Arleigh Williams, memo on May 15, 1969 rally, dated May 20, 1969, 5:64, UCBCF.

84. Calif., Gov., *Report*, 17–21, note 49; Glick, 91–95, 151; Smith, "People's Park," 12A–13 (*Gazette* quoted at 12A); James Yandell, *Neither Law nor Order* (Berk., 1971), 22–25; Coyne, 141, 156–58; Lyford, 185; letter, *Berk. Gazette*, May 29, 1969; *Daily Cal.*, May 16, 1969, pp. 1, 32; *L.A. Times*, May 16, 1969, pp. 1, 3; *N.Y. Times*, May 16, 1969, p. 1, 50; *People's World*, May 24, 1969, p. 1–2; *Ramparts*, Aug. 1969, pp. 42–43; Detroit *Fifth Estate*, May 29, 1969, pp. 3–4; *L.A. Free Press*, May 23, 1969, pp. 3, 10, 20, 23–24; June 6, 1969, p. 3; N.Y. *Rat*, May 30, 1969, p. 7. On the incident at the library see Coyne, 144; Glick, 128; *ALA Bulletin*, July-Aug. 1969, p. 898; Abraham H. Miller in *Politics and Society*, 2 (1972), 449; Henry Nash Smith statement to UCB Police Dept., June 9, 1969, 1:7, Smith Papers; UCB Police Chief W. P. Beall to Sheriff Frank Madigan, n.d., 5:64, UCBCF.

85. Lennon quoted in Wiener, 92–93. Another supporter was the urban theorist Jan Jacobs. See her telegram in Berk. Free Church, "Handbook," Collective Study Section, 1.

86. Glick, 97, 114, 116; Smith, "People's Park," 13–15; Yandell, 28; *S.F. Chronicle*, May 19, 1969, p. 26 (photo); *People's World*, May 24, 1969, p. 1; *Ramparts*, Aug.

1969, pp. 55, 56, 59.

87. In general see Glick, 98–99; *Berk. Barb*, May 23, 1969, pp. 5–6; *Daily Cal.*, May 16, 1969; *Ramparts*, Aug. 1969, p. 55; *L.A. Free Press*, May 23, 1969, pp. 3, 12. On orders see Calif., Gov., *Report*, 28; Yandell, 36–37; Heyns interview, 97; Martin interview, 11; *S.F. Bay Guardian*, Apr. 4, 1984, p. 9; "This World," *S.F. Sunday Examiner-Chronicle*, June 22, 1986, p. 8; *N.Y. Times*, May 25, 1969, Sec. IV, p. 13. On Blanchard see Glick, 100–101; Smith, "People's Park," 13; *Daily Cal.*, May 16, 1969. On Rector see Calif., Gov., *Report*, 24–25; Glick, 101–7; Smith, "People's Park," 13; Yandell, 31–32; Wallace Johnson in Nathan and Scott, 214; Johnson, *Look*, 81–82; McGill, 179; John R. Searle, *The Campus War* (N.Y., 1970), 75–77; *Berk. Barb*, May 23, 1969, pp. 2–4; *Oakland Tribune*, May 20, 1969; July 11, 1969, pp. 1, 7; *S.F. Chronicle*, May 20–22, 1969; *L.A. Free Press*, May 30, 1969, p. 1, N.Y. *Rat*, May 30, 1969, p. 7. The estimate for injuries is in *Ramparts*, Aug. 1969, p. 52.

88. Glick, 97, 124–26; Yandell, 35, 49–50; *Berk. Gazette*, May 19, 1969; *Oakland Tribune*, May 16, 1969, p. 6; May 23, 1969, pp. 1, 7; *S.F. Chronicle*, May 16, 1969, pp. 1, 6; May 20, 1969; *S.F. Bay Guardian*, July 10, 1969, pp. 2, 15; Detroit *Fifth Estate*, May 29, 1969, p. 3; Joel Rubenzahl in Lyford, 47; Lt. Col. Ben McCulloch to Don Mulford, "Dissident Activities" report, May 19, 1969, 1:5, Mulford Papers; Henry Nash Smith to Tony Tanner, May 29, 1969, 5:3, Smith Papers. On Tolman Hall see Jack London and three other professors to Heyns, May 21, 1969, 5:64, UCBCF. On bizarre incidents see Roy Radner to Heyns, May 20, 1969; Frederick Berry and others, report, May 26, 1969; Dean W. D. Knight to Vice-Chancellor John Raleigh, Dec. 5, 1969, all in 5:64, UCBCF; Paula B. Gill to Gov. Reagan, May 21, 1969; (?) D. Sterling to Reagan, May 21, 1969; David Bradwell to Don Mulford, May 19, 1969; Marc Trachtenberg to Mulford, June 15, 1969; Paul S. Thayer to Mulford, May 28, 1969; Mary S. Odegard to Reagan, May 19, 1969, all in 2:1, Mulford Papers.

89. Smith, "People's Park," 19–23; McGill, 167; *Berk. Barb*, May 23, 1969, p. 10; *Berk. Gazette*, May 19, 1969, p. 1; letters, May 22, 1969; *Daily Cal.*, May 20, 1969, pp. 1, 16; *Oakland Tribune*, May 16, 1969, p. 6; May 19, 1969; letters, *S.F. Chronicle*, May 22, 1969; *N.Y. Times*, May 17, 1969, p. 30; May 18, 1969, p. 74; May 20, 1969, p. 34; *Ann Arbor Argus*, May 24, 1969, pp. 1, 8; unsigned (Alex Grendon?) statement, May 16, 1969; Grendon statement, May 16, 1969, both in Box 12, Jones Papers. See also Joel Rubenzahl in Nathan and Scott, 328–32.

90. *Berk. Gazette*, May 22, 1969, p. 2; *Daily Cal.*, May 22, 1969; *Oakland Tribune*, May 21, 1969; *S.F. Chronicle*, May 21, 1969, pp. 1, 4–5, 28; editorial, May 22, 1969; May 23, 1969, p. 2; *N.Y. Times*, May 21, 1969, pp. 1, 30; Glick, 130–33, 138–39, 141–42; Smith, "People's Park," 26–28; Yandell, 52–55; Rossman, *On Learning*, 227 (quote). For one example of reaction see Graduate Theological Union Student Association Minutes, May 21, 1969, Graduate Theological Union Archives.

91. The crucial account is Findley's. *S.F. Chronicle*, May 24, 1969, pp. 1, 12. See also Scheer in *Ramparts*, Aug. 1969, pp. 50–51; Jesse P. Ritter, Jr., in *Getting Busted*, ed. Ross Firestone (N.Y., 1970), 79–84; *Berk. Barb*, May 23, 1969, p. 7; May 30, 1969, p. 4; *Daily Cal.*, May 26, 1969; July 3, 1969; *Oakland Tribune*, May 23, 1969; May 27, 1969; *S.F. Chronicle*, May 23, 1969, pp. 1, 26; letters, May 28, 1969; *Guardian*, June 7, 1969, p. 3; *People's World*, May 31, 1969, pp. 1–2; Thomas L. McLaren in Nathan and Scott, 239–40; Glick, 148–49, 153–54; Smith, "People's Park," 34, 36.

92. On the UCB community see Academic Senate resolution, May 23, 1969; Heyns address to Academic Senate, May 23, 1969; Heyns to Regents Grounds and Building Comm., June 18–19, 1969, all in 5:64, UCBCF. On the council see Glick, 161–62;

Yandell, 73–74; May interview, 390. For DeBonis's attitude see John K. DeBonis, *Quotations from Chairman DeBonis* (Berk., 1971), 1, 2. On anger see Glick, 135–46; Smith, "People's Park," 36–39; Yandell, 36, 46, 70; *Berk. Gazette,* May 26, 1969; *Berk. Monitor,* May 31, 1969, p. 1; *Daily Cal.,* May 26, 1969; editorial, *S.F. Chronicle,* May 27, 1969; May 28, 1969; *N.Y. Times,* May 24, 1969, p. 23; May 25, 1969, p. 69; May 26, 1969, p. 37; Cleveland *Big US,* June 23, 1969, p. 4; *L.A. Free Press,* May 30, 1969, p. 27; Ruth A. Hart, "Concern for the Individual: The Community YWCA and Other Berkeley Organizations" (1978), interview, 257–61; Sol Stern in Horowitz, *Counterculture,* 116; Donald P. Smith to Don Mulford, May 29, 1969; David O. Weber wire to Mulford, June 18, 1969, both in 2:1, Mulford Papers. The issue led to a student strike at the Univ. of Calif., Santa Cruz. See *The Strike Daily,* May 22, 23, 26, 1969 (mimeo), PPS. This collection contains material about both UCB and Santa Cruz.

93. On plans see Glick, 159–60; Smith, "People's Park," 51; *Berk. Gazette,* May 28, 1969, p. 3; *Oakland Tribune,* May 28, 1969, p. 6; *S.F. Chronicle,* May 28, 1969; *N.Y. Times,* May 30, 1969, p. 12; *Outcry!,* May 1969; Carol R. Sibley, "Building Community Trust: Berkeley School Integration and Other Civic Endeavors" (1980), interview, 273–76; Univ. of Calif., Santa Cruz, *The Strike Daily,* May 27, 1969, 1 a.m. (mimeo); "Join the Struggle," n.d., leaflet, both in PPS. On the Codys see Pat and Fred Cody in Nathan and Scott, 154–57; Thomas L. McLaren, ibid., 242; Hart interview, 266; Lyford, 50–51. The sorority sign is in Kenneth Lamott, *Anti-California* (Boston, 1971), 169. On the march see Glick, 174–75; Yandell, 75; Pat and Fred Cody in Nathan and Scott, 156; *S.F. Chronicle,* May 31, 1969; June 12, 1969, p. 41; *N.Y. Times,* May 31, 1969, p. 24; *Despite Everything,* June 1969, pp. 1–8, 11 (quote at 1); Cleveland *Big US,* June 23, 1969, p. 5; Detroit *Fifth Estate,* June 12, 1969, pp. 3, 17; Vancouver *Georgia Straight,* June 11, 1969, p. 4; *BCU Bulletin,* June 1969, p. 1; Davis, 212.

94. *N.Y. Times,* June 14, 1969, p. 13; June 20, 1969, p. 21; June 21, 1969, p. 25; Edmund C. ("Pat") Brown, Sr., *Reagan and Reality* (N.Y., 1970), 147; McGill, 196–98, 210 (quotes at 197–210); Heller interview, 627–30; May interview, 377–78; Johnson, *Look,* 83–85; Wallace Johnson in Nathan and Scott, 218–21.

95. *Berk. Gate,* Nov. 19, 1969, p. 1; Don Mulford column, *Berk. Gazette,* June 2, 1969; June 5, 1969, p. 3; *S.F. Chronicle,* June 3, 1969; Yandell, 79, 83; Coyne, 141–43; Hancock in Nathan and Scott, 375; Thomas L. McLaren, ibid., 244; Alameda County Grand Jury, "Report on the People's Park Disorders" (1969). On the ASUC election see *S.F. Chronicle,* May 23, 1969; Coyne, 141; Glick, 129, 154.

96. Appleyard, 23–24; Glick, 183–86, 197–200, 204–5; Yandell, 12 (quote); Rader, 160–61; Pat and Fred Cody in Nathan and Scott, 176; Heller interview, 635; Berk., City of Berk.-UCB Community Affairs Comm.: Housing Task Force, *Housing: The City and the University* (Berk., 1975), Appendix.

## Epilogue

(epigraph) "Turtle Blues" is from Big Brother and the Holding Company, *Cheap Thrills* (Columbia 9700, 1968).

1. The atmosphere during the Cambodian invasion was electric. For two accounts see Michael Rossman, *The Wedding within the War* (Garden City, N.Y., 1971), 5–25; Karen J. Fowler, "Letters from Home," in *In the Field of Fire,* ed. Jeanne V. B. Dann and Jack Dann (N.Y., 1987), 71–89. Wenner is quoted in *S.F. Sunday Examiner-*

*Chronicle*, Feb. 27, 1966, Sec. 1, p. 4.

2. Restaurateur quoted in John R. Coyne, Jr., *The Kumquat Statement* (N.Y., 1970), 63.

3. *Berk. Review*, Feb. 8, 1962, p. 6; *Daily Cal.*, Mar. 26, 1962; (Geoffrey E. Berne) Jan. 9, 1968, p. 9; *FSM, the Free Speech Movement at Berkeley* (S.F., 1965), 37–38; María-José Ragué Arias, *California Trip* (Barcelona, 1971), 34.

4. Kupferberg in *Berk. Barb*, July 28, 1967, p. 8. Missile crisis quote in Mitchell Goodman, ed., *The Movement toward a New America* (N.Y., 1970), 41. Rossman in Goodman, 18. For allusions see Charles Aronson column, *Berk. Barb*, Aug. 27, 1965, p. 3; (Bill Glozer) Oct. 22, 1965, p. 3; Nathan Adler in *Berk. Gazette*, June 6, 1966, p. 3; John Chang column, *Daily Cal.*, Aug. 6, 1968, p. 4; *BCU Bulletin*, Oct. 1967, p. 8; Colin Miller in *Frontier*, Apr. 1965, p. 20; T. Walter Herbert, Jr., in *Issue*, Spring 1965, p. 28; Brother Antoninus in *Ramparts*, Sept. 1962, p. 56; Ralph Gleason, ibid., Mar. 1966, p. 30; YMCA, *Y's Bear*, Mar. 15, 1962 (mimeo), in Pamphlet Boxes of Materials on Charities, Clubs, Banks, YMCA of Berkeley, Box 3; "On Student Rights and Academic Freedom," Dec. 1967 (pamphlet), 2:26, UCBCF; Bettina Aptheker, *Big Business and the American University* (N.Y., 1966), 34; Todd Gitlin, *The Sixties* (N.Y., 1987), 317; Nathan Glazer, *Remembering the Answers* (N.Y., 1970), 241; David Horowitz, *Student* (N.Y., 1962), 7–9; Dotson Rader, *Blood Dues* (N.Y., 1973), 10; The Red Family, *To Stop a Police State* (Berk., 1971), 6.

5. James H. Corley, "Serving the University in Sacramento" (1969), interview, 75.

# Selected Sources

Unless otherwise indicated, unpublished sources are in the Bancroft Library, University of California, Berkeley. Other locations have been identified by the following abbreviations:

BLL   Boalt Law Library
EDL   Environmental Design Library
EL    Education Library
GDL   Government Documents Library
IGSL  Institute of Governmental Studies Library
SSL   Social Science Library

## Manuscripts, Pamphlets, Leaflets, and Ephemera

*Bancroft Library*
The most significant collection is the Social Protest Project containing more than 60,000 leaflets, etc., gathered on the University of California campus since the early sixties. Note: this collection has recently been reorganized.

Edmund G. ("Pat") Brown, Sr., Papers
Collection of Underground Comics
Faculty Memoranda . . . , 1964–65. Supplement. Bound vol.
Faculty Memoranda, Reports, Handbills, etc., 1964–65. Bound vol.
Free Speech Movement Archives and Papers, 1964–65
Free Speech Movement, Center for the Study of Higher Education Collection
Free Speech Movement, 1964–65, Scrapbook of Clippings from *Daily Californian*
Free Speech Movement, 1964–65, handout supplement. Bound vol.
Ruth A. Hart Papers
Jabberwock programs, 1967
Paul Jacobs, My Senate Campaign Book
Roger Kent Papers
Michael McClure Papers
Josephine Miles Papers
Pamphlet Boxes of Materials on Berkeley
Pamphlet Boxes of Materials on Berkeley Business and Commerce
Pamphlet Boxes of Materials on Berkeley Politics
Pamphlet Boxes of Materials on Berkeley Real Estate
Pamphlet Boxes of Materials on Charities, Clubs, Banks, YMCA of Berkeley

People's Park Strike of May 1969 Collection. Loose items.
Jerry Rubin, comp., Portfolio of Jerry Rubin for Mayor of Berkeley, 1967
William Byron Rumford Papers
Sexual Freedom League Papers
Henry Nash Smith Papers
Katherine A. Towle, Collection of Clippings
Katherine A. Towle Papers
University of California, President's Files
University of California, Berkeley Chancellor's Files, Control 893: Student Revolts.
    Note: boxes and folders have recently been renumbered.
University of California, Free Speech Movement, 1964–65, handbills. Bound vol.
Diane Wakoski Papers
Catherine Bauer Wurster Papers
*Institute of Governmental Studies Library*
Jeffery Cohelan newsletters, etc., 1961–66
T. J. Kent, Jr., miscellaneous campaign materials, 1961
John J. Miller newsletter, 1972
Don Mulford miscellaneous campaign materials, 1960
Don Mulford press releases, 1963–70
Peace and Freedom Party campaign letters, 1968
Carol Sibley miscellaneous campaign materials, 1961, 1964 recall
Wilmont Sweeney miscellaneous campaign materials, 1961
*Environmental Design Library, Rare Book Room*
People's Park, Berkeley, newspaper clippings, 1969
*Graduate Theological Union, Berkeley*
Graduate Theological Union Student Association Records, 1968–71
*Women's History Research Center, Berkeley*
Herstory Collection (film)
*Hoover Institution Archives, Stanford University*
German Subject Collection
Hardin B. Jones Papers
John H. Lawrence Papers
Don Mulford Papers
Ronald Reagan Papers
Geoffrey White Papers
*Stanford University Archives*
Frederick E. Terman Papers
*California Historical Society*
Anne Draper Papers
*State Historical Society of Wisconsin*
Congress of Racial Equality, Western Regional Office Papers (film)

## Interviews

Unless otherwise indicated, interviews were conducted by the Regional Oral History Office at the University of California, Berkeley; transcripts are in the Bancroft Library.

Frances M. Albrier
A. Wayne Amerson
William Becker
G. Paul Bishop
Donald L. Bradley
Hugh M. Burns
John E. Canaday
(UCLA Oral History Program)
Hale Champion
Lincoln Constance
James H. Corley
Thomas J. Cunningham
Cutter Laboratories
May L. B. Davis
C. L. Dellums
Ruth N. Donnelly
Frederick G. Dutton

John Gofman
Walter Gordon
Alexander Grendon
Ruth A. Hart
Roger W. Heyns
Elinor R. Heller
Claude B. Hutchison
Roger Kent
Thomas J. Kent, Jr.
Clark Kerr
Richard Kline
Donald H. McLaughlin
Jerry C. Martin
Bernice Hubbard May
Josephine Miles
Joseph R. Mixer
Tarea H. Pittman

Joseph A. Rattigan
Agnes R. Robb
Albert S. Rodda
William Byron Rumford
Keith Sexton
Alex C. Sherriffs
Carol R. Sibley
Stuart K. Spencer
Ida A. Sproul
George R. Stewart
Katherine A. Towle
Robert M. Underhill
Caspar W. Weinberger
Harry R. Wellman
Glenn A. Wessels
Garff B. Wilson

## Government Documents

Berkeley, "The First Fifty Years of the Community Welfare Commission" (Berk., 1959).

Berkeley, Citizens Advisory Committee, *Construction Needs in the Public Schools of Berkeley, California* (Berk., 1960); EL.

Berkeley City Council, "Berkeley's Workable Program for Urban Renewal" (Berk., 1961); EDL.

Berkeley, City of Berkeley—University of California Community Affairs Committee: Housing Task Force, *Housing, The City and the University* (Berk., 1975); EDL.

Berkeley Planning Commission, *Berkeley Master Plan—1955* (Berk., 1955).

————, *Berkeley Master Plan Amended to October 1964* (Berk., 1964).

Berkeley Planning Department, *Berkeley Facts* (Berk., 1964)

————, *Berkeley Facts* (Berk., 1971); EDL.

————, *The People of Berkeley: Where They Are* (Berk., 1973); EDL.

————. *The People of Berkeley: Who They Are? Demographic Profile* (Berk., 1973); EDL.

Berkeley Police Department, *Annual Reports*, 1961–68, 1970; BLL.

————, *A Guide for Parents and Youth* (Berk., ca. 1962).

————, "Vietnam Day Committee" (Berk., 1965); IGSL.

Berkeley Unified School District, Committee on Instructional Program for Integration, *Report* (Berk., 1967); EL.

————, "Co-Sponsored Workshop on Change in an Interracial Community" (Berk., 1962).

————, "Co-Sponsored Workshop on Interracial Gains and Goals" (Berk., 1961).

————, *Integration of the Berkeley Elementary Schools: A Report to the Superintendent* (Berk., 1967); EL.

Berk., Urban Renewal Agency, "South Campus Urban Renewal Plan" (Berk., 1966); EDL.

California, Governor, *The 'People's Park': A Report on a Confrontation at Berkeley, California Submitted to Governor Ronald Reagan* (Sacramento, 1969).

California, Legislature, Senate Fact-Finding Committee on Education, *Hearing, Oakland, Oct. 18, 1962* (Sacramento, 1962); GDL.

California, Legislature, Senate Fact-Finding Committee on Un-American Activities, *Thirteenth Report* (Sacramento, 1965); GDL.

———, *Thirteenth Report Supplement* (Sacramento, 1966); GDL.

———, *Fourteenth Report* (Sacramento, 1967); IGSL.

Council of Social Planning-Berkeley Area, "Community Action under 'Economic Opportunity Act of 1964' " (Berk., 1965).

———, "Phase II-Multi-Problem Families" (Berk., 1962).

———, "Report of Committee to Study Pre-School Education Needs and Resources in the City of Berkeley" (Berk., 1965).

U.S. Congress, House Committee on Internal Security, *Black Panther Party Hearings*, 91st Cong., 2nd Sess. (Wash., 1970–71); House Library vols. 481–84.

U.S. Congress, Senate Committee Hearings, *Pacifica Foundation Hearings before the Subcommittee to Investigate the Administration of the Internal Security Act and the Other Internal Security Laws of the Committee on the Judiciary*, 88th Cong., 1st Sess., Part 1 (Wash., 1963); Senate Library vol. 1581.

## Special Reports

Hadsell report. Berkeley, Board of Education, De Facto Desegregation Study Committee, *Report* (Berk., 1963); EL.

Heyman Committee exhibits. University of California, Berkeley, Academic Senate, Ad Hoc Committee on Student Conduct, "Materials" (Berk., 1964); BLL.

Heyman Committee hearings. University of California, Berkeley, Academic Senate, Ad Hoc Committee on Student Conduct, "Proceedings" (Berk., 1964); BLL.

Meyer report. University of California, Regents, Special Committee to Review University Policies, *Report* (Berk., 1965).

Muscatine report. University of California, Berkeley, Academic Senate, *Education at Berkeley* (Berk., 1966); BLL.

Poppic report. Berkeley, Community Welfare Commission, "Report of the Citizens' Committee to Study Discrimination in Housing in Berkeley" (Berk., 1962).

Staats report. Berkeley, Board of Education, Committee to Study Certain Interracial Problems, *Interracial Problems and Their Effect on Education in the Public Schools of Berkeley, California* (Berk., 1959).

Wennerberg report. Berkeley Unified School District, *Desegregation of the Berkeley Public Schools* (Berk., 1964); EL.

Whinnery report. University of California, Berkeley, Chancellor, Ad Hoc Committee on Student Conduct, "Report and Recommendations" (Berk., 1965).

## Newspapers and Periodicals

The most important newspapers were the conservative *Berkeley Daily Gazette*, the student-edited *Daily Californian*, and from 1965 on Max Scherr's radical, countercultural *Berkeley Barb*. This latter weekly, as well as starred (*) items below, was filmed for the Underground Newspaper Collection. During the sixties the Bay Area's daily newspapers were mediocre, and better coverage was often provided by Wallace Turner in the *New York Times* and William Trombley in the *Los Angeles Times*.

*BCU Bulletin*, 1963–75; an archconservative monthly.

*Berkeley Citizen*, 1966–67; a liberal pro-Cohelan weekly, tied to the Berkeley Co-op.

*Berkeley Gate*, 1963–71; a beat-tinged mimeographed publication that appeared sporadically and offered excellent coverage of the South Campus community, published and edited by Bob Weinzeimer.

*Berkeley Review*, 1959–62; a liberal weekly.

Black Panther Party, *Bulletin*, 1968–69; a militant black organ that appeared from time to time.

*Communiqué for New Politics*, 1966–69—*Coalition News*, February-April 1969—*Berkeley Monitor*, 1969–72; a white radical publication that appeared irregularly, edited by Ilona Hancock in 1968.

\* *Despite Everything*, 1963–69; a scholarly New Left quarterly.

Free University of Berkeley, *Catalog*, 1966–71; a radical-countercultural quarterly guide to course offerings.

*KPFA Program Folio*, 1959–69; a monthly guide to Berkeley's leftist, noncommercial radio station.

*Oakland Tribune*, 1965–69; a conservative, anti-Berkeley daily, published by William F. Knowland.

*Peace and Freedom News*, 1968–69; a biracial, radical publication issued irregularly.

*People's World*, 1960–69; a communist weekly, edited by Al Richmond.

*The Post*; a conservative black newspaper, published by Tom Berkley.

*Ramparts*, 1962–69; a Catholic, later New Left monthly, published by Edward M. Keating, 1962–67, and edited by Warren Hinckle III, 1964–69, and Robert Scheer, 1966–69.

*Root and Branch*, 1962–63; the first New Left quarterly (two issues), edited by Robert Scheer.

*San Francisco Bay Guardian*, 1966–69; a muckraking, New Left weekly.

*San Francisco Chronicle*, 1960–69; the most reliable, moderate daily. The columnist Ralph Gleason and the editor Scott Newhall lived in Berkeley.

*San Francisco Examiner*, 1960, 1965; a conservative, Hearst-owned daily.

\* *San Francisco Express Times*, 1968–69; a serious, New Left weekly, edited by Marvin Garson.

*SPIDER*, 1965; a politically radical, somewhat beat student mimeographed periodical involved in the Filthy Speech Movement.

*Steps*, 1966–ca. 1967; a radical quarterly (two issues), published for the Free University.

*Sun-Reporter*; the Bay Area's leading black newspaper, published in San Francisco by Dr. Carleton B. Goodlett.

*Sunday Ramparts*, 1966–67; a radical biweekly offshoot of *Ramparts* magazine. A complete file is on film at the University of Washington.

*Tocsin*, 1961–66; a HUAC-oriented, anticommunist weekly.

*Urban West*, 1957–70; a slick, middle-class black monthly.

\* *Yellow Dog*, 1968–69; an underground comic book issued irregularly, largely drawn by Robert Crumb.

## Books and Articles about Berkeley

Bob Biderman, *Letters to Nanette* (S.F., 1982); a novel.

James T. Carey, *The College Drug Scene* (Englewood Cliffs, N.J., 1968); a sociological study of Telegraph Avenue.

Thomas W. Casstevens, *Politics, Housing and Race Relations* (Berk., 1965).

Eldridge Cleaver, *Post-Prison Writings and Speeches* (N.Y., 1969).

John R. Coyne, Jr., *The Kumquat Statement* (N.Y., 1970); a conservative critique.

Lawrence P. Crouchett, *William Byron Rumford* (El Cerrito, Calif., 1984).

Sara Davidson, *Loose Change* (N.Y., 1977); a novel.

Angela Dellaporta and Joann Steck, eds., *The Daily Californian's Best of Berkeley* (Berk., 1980).

"Michael Douglas" (pseud. for Michael Crichton and Douglas Crichton), *Dealing or the Berkeley-to-Boston Forty-Brick Lost-Bag Blues* (N.Y., 1971); a novel.

Harold Draper, *Berkeley: The New Student Revolt* (N.Y., 1965).

"An FSM Miscellany," *Graduate Student Journal*, Spring 1965, pp. 13–34, 75–91.

Thomas Farber, *Tales for the Son of My Unborn Child* (N.Y., 1971).

Lewis S. Feuer, "Rebellion at Berkeley," *The New Leader*, Dec. 21, 1964, pp. 3–12. See replies by Paul Jacobs and Stephan Weissman, Jan. 4, 1965; by Clark Kerr, Jan. 18, 1965; and Feuer's rebuttals, Jan. 4 and 18, 1965.

Art Goldberg (the journalist), "Whatever Happened to the Class of '69?" *S.F. Bay Guardian*, June 14, 1979, pp. 9–16.

Arthur Harris et al., *Bernice Hubbard May* (Berk., 1971).

Max A. Heirich, *The Spiral of Conflict: Berkeley 1964* (N.Y., 1971).

David Horowitz, *Student* (N.Y., 1962); the first New Left volume.

Wallace J. S. Johnson, *A Fresh Look at Patriotism* (Old Greenwich, Conn., 1976).

———, *Responsible Individualism* (N.Y., 1967).

———, *The Uncommon Man in American Business* (N.Y., 1966).

Clark Kerr, *The Uses of the University* (Cambridge, Mass., 1963).

Serge Lang, *The Scheer Campaign* (N.Y., 1967).

Elinor Langer, "Crisis at Berkeley," *Science*, Apr. 9 and 16, 1965, pp. 198–202, 346–49. See letters, June 4, 1965, pp. 1273–78.

"Letter from Berkeley," *Despite Everything*, Special Issue, Jan. 1965.

Hubert Lindsey, *Bless Your Dirty Heart*, ed. Howard G. Earl (Plainfield, N.J., 1973).

Seymour M. Lipset and Sheldon S. Wolin, eds., *The Berkeley Student Revolt* (Garden City, N.Y., 1965).

David Lodge, *Changing Places* (N.Y., 1979; orig. 1975); a novel.

Joseph P. Lyford, *The Berkeley Archipelago* (Chicago, 1982); on the 1970s.

Henry F. May, "Living with Crisis," *American Scholar*, 38 (1969), 588–605.

Abraham H. Miller, "People's Park: Dimensions of a Campus Confrontation," *Politics and Society*, 2 (1972), 433–58.

Michael V. Miller and Susan Gilmore, eds., *Revolution at Berkeley* (N.Y., 1965).

Michael Myerson, *These Are the Good Old Days* (N.Y., 1970); a radical memoir.

Harriet Nathan and Stanley Scott, eds., *Experiment and Change in Berkeley* (Berk., 1978); the best account on city government. Unpublished appendices, IGSL.

Huey P. Newton, *Revolutionary Suicide* (N.Y., 1973).

Charles M. Otten, *University Authority and the Student* (Berk., 1970).

George A. Pettitt, *Berkeley: The Town and Gown of It* (Berk., 1973).

María-José Ragué Arias, *California Trip* (Barcelona, 1971); a Spaniard's travel account.

Michael Rossman, "Breakthrough at Berkeley," *Center Magazine*, May 1968, pp. 40–49.

———, *New Age Blues* (N.Y., 1979).

———, *On Learning and Social Change* (N.Y., 1972).

———, "Twenty Years Later," *Express*, Sept. 28, 1984, pp. 1ff.

———, *The Wedding within the War* (Garden City, N.Y., 1971).

Theodore Roszak, *The Making of a Counter Culture* (Garden City, N.Y., 1969).

Jerry Rubin, *Do It!* (N.Y., 1970).

———, *Growing (Up) at Thirty-Seven* (N.Y., 1976).

Bobby Seale, *A Lonely Rage* (N.Y., 1977).

———, *Seize the Time* (N.Y., 1970).

John R. Searle, *The Campus War* (N.Y., 1971).

Arthur Seeger, *The Berkeley Barb* (N.Y., 1983).

Carol Sibley, *Never a Dull Moment* (Berk., 1972).

Anne Steinhardt, *How to Get Balled in Berkeley* (N.Y., 1976); a novel.

Neil V. Sullivan with Evelyn S. Stewart, *Now is the Time* (Bloomington, Ind., 1969).

Joseph Tussman, *Experiment at Berkeley* (N.Y., 1969); on the University's Experimental College.

Robert H. K. Walter, *Stacy Tower* (N.Y., 1963); a novel.

Steven Warshaw, *The Trouble in Berkeley* (Berk., 1965); FSM photographs.

William A. Watts and David Whittaker, "Free Speech Advocates at Berkeley," *Journal of Applied Behavioral Science*, 2 (1966), 41–62.

*We Accuse* (Berk., 1965); the Vietnam Day teach-in transcript.

Sheldon S. Wolin and John H. Schaar, *The Berkeley Rebellion and Beyond* (N.Y., 1970).

## Unpublished Dissertations, Theses, and Papers

Eugene Bardach, ed., "The Berkeley Free Speech Controversy" (Berk., 1964).

John F. Beery, "Student Demonstrations in San Francisco, May 12–14, 1960" (M.A. thesis, Univ. of Calif., Berk., 1961); Main Library.

Berkeley Free Church, "Free Church Collective Handbook" (Berk., 1970).

"Berkeley Liberation Program" (Berk., 1969).

Malcolm Burnstein et al., "People v. Savio and 571 Others: Appellants' Opening Brief" (Berk., 1966).

California Research Foundation, "An Analysis of the Factors Concerning the Fair Housing Ordinance Vote and City Elections in Berkeley, California, April 2nd, 1963" (L.A., 1963).

———, "An Analysis of the Results of the Fair Housing Election in Berkeley, California Held April 2, 1963" (L.A., 1963).

———, "Fair Housing. A Post Election Survey in Berkeley, California, April 2, 1963" (L.A., 1963); EDL.

Jan E. Dizard, "Patterns of Unemployment in Berkeley, California" (Berk., 1968).

Kathryne T. Favors, "A Study of the Intergroup Education Project of the Berkeley Unified School District" (Ed.D. diss., Univ. of Calif., Berk., 1969); EL.

"Free Speech Songbook" (Berk., 1964).

Stanley I. Glick, "The People's Park" (Ph.D. diss., State Univ. of N.Y. at Stony Brook, 1984); Main Library.

Ann M. Heiss, "Berkeley Doctoral Students Appraise Their Academic Programs" (Center for the Study of Higher Education, Univ. of Calif., Berk., 1964); EL.

Ira M. Heyman, "Race and Education in Berkeley, California" (Berk., 1966).

Lois Heyman, "The Estimation of Need for Low Cost Housing in Berkeley" (M.B.A. report, Univ. of Calif., Berk., 1966); SSL.

Richard C. Howell, "A Contextual Perspective on Political Leadership" (M.A. thesis, S. F. State College, 1972); IGSL.

Terry Lunsford, "The 'Free Speech' Crisis at Berkeley, 1964–1965: Some Issues for Social and Legal Research" (Center for Research and Development in Higher Education, Univ. of Calif., Berk., 1965).

Jerry S. Mandel, "A Residential Alternative to Special Industrial Zoning" (Berk., 1965); EDL.

Leonard A. Marascuilo, "Attitudes toward De Facto Segregation in a Northern City" (research report, Univ. of Calif., Berk., 1964–65, issued as ERIC ED003825, 1967).

William L. Nicholls, II, "Public Reactions to the Student Protest Movement on the Berkeley Campus . . . " (Survey Research Center, Univ. of Calif., Berk., 1966).

"Order and Freedom on the Campus" (Center for the Study of Higher Education, Univ. of Calif., Berk., 1965).

William Petersen, "Faculty Rebellion at Berkeley" (Berk.?, 1965).

Police Conduct Complaint Center, "Berkeley Report: Police Personnel Complaints and Redress Remedies" (Berk., 1970).

———, "Complaints Regarding Police Actions against Citizens, June 28–July 2, 1968" (Berk., 1968).

Lol D. Raasch, "Unemployment in Berkeley and the Programs Designed to Alleviate the Problem: A Current Analysis" (M.B.A. report, Univ. of Calif., Berk., 1967); SSL.

Michael Rossman et al., "Administrative Pressures and Student Political Activity at the University of California: A Preliminary Report" (Berk., 1964).

"The Save the Steps Rally" (Berk., 1966).

Gar Smith, "A People's Park Chronology" (Berk., n.d.); IGSL.

Robert H. Somers, "The Mainsprings of the Rebellion: A Survey of Berkeley Students in November, 1964" (Berk., 1965).

# Glossary

AFL    American Federation of Labor; the organization of conservative craft unions that merged with the CIO to form the AFL-CIO in 1956.

ASUC    Associated Students of the University of California; the student government at Cal.

BBC    Better Berkeley Committee; an organization of merchants and street people that patrolled Telegraph Avenue.

BCU    Berkeley Citizens United; the city's largest archconservative political organization.

BDC    Berkeley Democratic Caucus; a citywide organization that coordinated local left-liberal California Democratic clubs and endorsed candidates.

CDC    California Democratic Council; a statewide organization that coordinated the left-liberal California Democratic clubs.

CDO    Campus Draft Opposition; a Cal student organization that collected pledges of draft refusal.

CIO    Congress of Industrial Organizations; the organization of militant unions that merged into the AFL-CIO in 1956.

CNP    Community for New Politics; a grassroots radical political movement.

CORE    Congress of Racial Equality; an activist civil rights organization that was strong in the Bay Area.

FSM    Free Speech Movement; an ad hoc activist student movement to gain political rights on the University of California campus.

FSU    Free Student Union (successor to the FSM); a broad student organization modeled on a labor union.

GCC    Graduate Coordinating Council; an organization of activist graduate students at Cal. The administration had barred graduate students from the ASUC.

HUAC    House Un-American Activities Committee; the U.S. Congress's main anti-communist investigatory committee. (Pronounced Hew-ack.)

LSD    Lysergic Acid Diethylamide; a hallucinogenic drug.

NAACP    National Association for the Advancement of Colored People; a large, mainstream civil rights organization.

PL    Progressive Labor; a radical, activist Maoist organization. Some members had been expelled from the Communist party for preferring China to the Soviet Union.

PROC    Peace/Rights Organizing Committee; a campus antiwar and civil rights organization. (Rhymes with rock.)

SCLC    Southern Christian Leadership Conference; a church-based, southern civil rights organization led by the Reverend Martin Luther King, Jr.

263

SDS   Students for a Democratic Society; a radical, activist student organization that was relatively weak in Berkeley.

SLATE   Not an acronym; a reform-minded, activist campus political party that did not exclude communists.

SNCC   Student Non-Violent Coordinating Committee; a black-led southern civil rights organization. (Pronounced Snick.)

TWLF   Third World Liberation Front; a militant, activist coalition of blacks, Chicanos, and Asians at Cal and San Francisco State College.

VDC   Vietnam Day Committee; a radical, activist antiwar group.

# Index

abortions, 131

acid. *See* Lysergic Acid Diethylamide (LSD)

activists: early, 17–19; strategy, 20–21; FSM, 23–24, 26–27, 30–34, 36; filthy speech, 38–41; civil rights, 73; sit-ins (1968), 84; Steppenwolf, 94; VDC, 98–99, 105; draft, 116–18; June 1968, 121–23

ad hoc committees: civil rights, 72, 76; Left cooperation, 90; draft, 116

Adler, Nathan, 253

Afro-American Student Association, 75

Alameda Co.: injunction, 116, 118; deputy sheriffs, 117, 122, 154; sheriffs shoot, 160–62

Albert, Stewart, 46, 80, 103, 105, 108–9, 112, 113, 119, 156–57, 166, 216, 222

Albrier, Frances, 51, 61

Alexander, Jim, 224

Algeria, 77, 85

Ali, Muhammad, 121

Allen, Steve, 128

American Civil Liberties Union (ACLU), 89, 132, 206

American Federation of Labor (AFL), 70

American Federation of Labor-Congress of Industrial Organizations (AFL-CIO), 98, 101

American Federation of Teachers, Local 1570, 44–45, 85, 109

American Indians, 85, 135, 157

Americans for Democratic Action (ADA), 99

Amerika, 143

anarchists, 109, 122, 144, 152, 156–57

Anastasi, Ron, 24, 201, 221

anticommunists, 15, 26, 53, 70, 87, 90, 92–93, 98, 101

antiwar movement, 91–92, 95, 102, 108, 111, 113, 135, 145, 152, 161; draft, 114–21; Cambodia, 167–70

apartments, 17, 56, 60

Aptheker, Bettina, 23–24, 45, 89, 106–7, 113, 132, 229

architecture, 124

Armistead, Timothy W., 220

Armor, David, 15

Arnold, Bill, 227

Aronowitz, Stanley, 221

Aronson, Charles, 253

arrests: HUAC, 16, Weinberg, 21; FSM sit-in, 32–33; filthy speech, 39; Sheraton-Palace, 73; Griffin, 74; Seale, 78, 82; Moses Hall, 84; conspiracy, 84, 119; troop trains, 93; VDC, 97, 105; Cohelan's office, 98; PROC, 108; navy table, 109; topless, 132; "The Beard," 132; Telegraph, 145–47, 150; People's Park, 164

art, 24, 124, 140, 142, 144, 153 54

Artman, Charlie Brown, 134–35, 148, 240

Asians, 55–56, 67, 69, 85, 127

Associated Students of the University of California (ASUC), 15, 31, 35, 109, 131, 160, 165–66; Senate, 91–92, 119

Avakian, Robert, 82–83, 111–13

Avakian, Ruth W., 213

Avakian, Spurgeon, 64, 66, 82, 212, 226

Axelrod, Beverly, 80

Baez, Joan, 31, 113, 116, 121, 127

banana hoax, 141

Bardacke, Frank, 116–19, 156–57, 166, 236, 239

Barlow, John J., 199

Basson, James, 93

Baum, Howell, 215

Bay Area Rapid Transit (BART), 111–112

Beach, Scott, 142

Beall, William P., 246, 250

"Beard, The," 132

Beatles, 130, 140, 154, 170

beats, 26, 99, 124–25, 128–30, 133–34

Beck, Joel, 239

Becker, William, 211

Bee, Carlos, 195

Be-In, 141

Bell, Daniel, 222

Bell, Inge, 231

Belli, Melvin, 109

Beloof, Robert, 194

Bendix, Reinhard, 231

Bergel, Peter, 164

Berger, Peter, 231

Berkeley: climate, 3–4; geography, 3–5; name, 4; early history, 4–7

Berkeley, George, 4

*Berkeley Barb*, 25, 89, 95–96, 98, 101, 103,

265

*Berkeley Barb* (*continued*)
112–13, 132, 142, 148, 150, 156–57, 166; founded, 94
Berkeley Citizens United (BCU), 56–57, 66–67, 88, 92, 111, 152; *BCU Bulletin*, 66, 150, 158
Berkeley Coalition, 154
*Berkeley Daily Gazette*, 5, 51, 56–57, 101, 113, 154, 160
Berkeley Democratic Caucus, 52, 75, 111–12, 154
Berkeley Free Church, 152, 159
*Berkeley Gate*, 131, 142
Berkeley High School, 57, 61–63, 69, 77, 82, 117
Berkeley Liberation Program, 156
Berkeley Realty Board, 92
Berkeley Renaissance, 124
Berkwood School, 89, 119
Berman, Jerry, 193
Berne, Geoffrey E., 252
Berry, Frederick, 251
Better Berkeley Committee (BBC), 147–48
Big Brother and the Holding Company, 139, 142
Bilawski, Ruediger, 223
Bingham, Stephen, 61
Birnbaum, Lucille, 199
Black House, 69
Black Muslims, 17, 74, 80
black nationalists, 78
Black Panthers, 6, 42, 48, 76–85, 88, 157, 168, 187
"Black Power," 75–76, 116
Black Student Union, 69
blackamoor, 52
blacks, 5–6, 18, 127, 133, 187; migration, 49–50; liberal politics, 51–54; housing, 54–61; education, 61–70; employment, 61, 63, 70–74; militants, 75–76, 78; radical politics, 81–82, 85–86, 92, 95–98, 100–101, 103, 113
Blair, Walter, 195
Blais, Jan D., 231, 234, 236
Blake, Larry, 122
Blanchard, Alan, 162
Blaser, Robin, 248
Bloice, Carl, 100, 113
Bloom, Jack, 84
Blue Cue Pool Parlor, 129, 147
Blunt, Leonard S., 215
Bohemian Grove, 10
bohemians, 124–25, 128–35, 137
Bolton, Earl, 197–201, 205–6, 224
books: titles, 39–40, 80, 89, 125, 137–38; bookstores, 14, 99, 125–26, 128–29
Bort, Joseph, 94, 150
Bothwell, Darryl, 147
Bouwsma, William J., 205, 248
Boy Scouts, 68

Boyd, Philip L., 204
Boyd, William B., 198, 236
Bradwell, David, 251
Brand, Stewart, 138
Bravo, Mark, 21
Bridges, Harry, 101
Briscoe, Connie, 211
Brode, Robert, 200
Brother Antoninus, 253
Broussard, Allen, 208
Brown, Benson, 24
Brown, Bruce L., 211
Brown, Edmund G. ("Jerry"), Jr., 21, 126
Brown, Edmund G. ("Pat"), Sr., 58, 60, 70, 75, 96, 108–9, 204–5, 208, 224, 226, 228, 240; FSM, 32, 38, 40, 42–43
Brown, John Pairman ("Jock"), 152
Brown, Rosalie (Moore), 248
Brown, W. T. ("Zack"), 53, 122, 154–55
Bruce, Lenny, 39, 128, 130
Buchanan, Marvin C., 237
Burbank Junior High School, 52, 65–66, 69
Burdick, Eugene, 92
Burns, Hugh, 16, 58, 205
Burnstein, Dan, 142
Burnstein, Malcolm, 42, 119, 132
Burton, Virginia, 214
buttons, 142
Byer, Paul, 201
Byrne, Jerome C., 38, 204

Cabral, Mrs. Joseph R., 214
Caen, Herb, 133, 143
Caffe Mediterraneum (Cafe Med), 103, 129, 147, 157
Cain, Leonard D., Jr., 199
Cal Conservatives for Political Action, 115
California College of Arts and Crafts, 169–70
California Democratic Council (CDC), 51–52, 102, 111
California Highway Patrol, 96, 122, 154
Calvin, Melvin, 229
Cambodia, 167–70
Camejo, Peter, 84, 89, 112, 118–19, 121–22, 229, 235
Campbell, Glenn, 219
Campus Draft Opposition, 120–21
Camus, Albert, 126
Canaday, John E., 11, 231, 234, 248
Cannon, Terry, 119
Canyon, 135, 144–45
Capper, Charles, 91
Carmichael, Stokely, 74–76, 81–82, 121, 187
Carr, Denzel, 234
Carson, Josephine, 238
Carter, Alprentice, 217
Carter, Edward W., 11, 17, 32, 40, 204, 207
Carver, Thomas H., 229
Casady, Si, 102
Castaneda, Carlos, 142–43

Castro, Fidel, 9, 90, 99
Catholics, 21–22, 33–34, 58, 114
censorship, 99–100, 104, 113, 117, 125–26, 132, 141–42
Center for the Study of Democratic Institutions, 100, 121
Central Intelligence Agency (CIA), 114
Chandler, Dorothy B., 11, 219
Chandler, M. F., 204, 216
Chang, John, 253
Chanin, Jim, 247
Chaplin, Charlie, 32
Charter Day (1962), 8; (1966) 108
Chavez, Cesar, 84
Cheit, Earl, 206, 216, 224, 227, 230, 234–36
Cheney, Margaret, 207
Cherkoss, Steve, 103, 105
Chessman, Caryl, 15, 94
Chez Panisse, 166
Chicanos, 69, 84–85, 101, 127, 140
Christian, Winslow, 204
city council, 60, 82, 94, 101, 122; how elected, 52. See also elections
city government: jobs, 71; job programs, 71, 74; VDC march, 96; South Campus, 147, 150; People's Park, 158–59
City Lights Bookstore, 99, 125
Civic Center Park, 82, 97, 152
civil liberties, 95, 100, 104
civil rights movement, 8, 18, 27, 71–75, 114, 127; songs, 28, FSM, 34, 46; dress, 133
class. See middle class; social class
Clavir, Judy, 80
Cleaveland, Brad, 45–46
Cleaver, Eldridge, 80–85, 110
Coakley, J. Frank, 96–97, 101, 106, 116, 119, 154, 224, 229
Coalition News, 154
Codornices Village, 5–6, 54–55, 60, 76–77
Cody, Fred, 129, 147, 164, 219, 225, 237–38, 240, 245–48, 252
Cody's bookstore, 121, 129, 148
coffeehouses, 14, 129, 142
Coffin, William Sloane, 121
Cohelan, Jeffery, 52, 71, 75, 98, 113, 165, 168, 224–26; challenged, 100–105
Cohon, Peter, 245
Cold War, 9, 99
Cole, Bob, 235
collectives, 189
College of California, 4
Collins, Tom, 230, 234, 244–45
Collins, Wanda, 196
Columbia Records, 141
Columbia University, 84
comedians. See entertainers
Comix, 142
comm/co, 144
Committee, The, 92, 128
Committee of 200, 36

communes, 89, 148, 189
communists, 23, 42, 44–45, 70, 87–90, 106, 108, 187–88; bookstore, 14; Scheer, 99–101; folk music, 127; comedy, 128; People's Park, 156
Community for New Politics (CNP), 110–12, 154
Community High School, 69
Congress of Industrial Organizations (CIO), 70, 88
Congress of Racial Equality (CORE), 18, 42, 56, 72–73, 129–30
Connick, Robert E., 227
conservatives, 6, 51, 55, 57, 60, 85; FSM, 24, 33; filthy speech, 39; BCU, 56–57; race, 66–67, 73; war, 94, 105–6, 112, 115–16, 119–20; hippies, 145, 148, 150, 165
Constance, Lincoln, 195, 198, 201, 220
contraceptives, 131
Co-op, 5–6, 53, 130, 142
Copeland, Gloria, 198
Corley, James, 171
Corso, Gregory, 133
counterculture, 46, 122–23, 142, 170–71, 189
Country Joe and the Fish. See McDonald, Joe
Craven, Carolyn, 227
Credence Clearwater Revival, 136, 140
Creed's bookstore, 126, 129
Crews, Frederick, 236
crimes, 148; Black Panthers, 79–80; Oakland scandal, 96; VDC bombing, 105; Ramparts burglary, 114; statistics, 149, 174
Crittenden, Rupert, 42–44
Crocker, George N., 12
Cross, Laurance, 6
cross burned, 57
Crown, Robert W., 215
Crumb, Robert, 142
Cuba, 90, 99
Cuban Missile Crisis, 8–9, 169
culture. See architecture; art; entertainers; literature; music; poetry
Cunningham, Thomas J., 37, 106, 120, 197, 201, 203, 205, 224, 236
Cutter, David L., 210–11
Cutter, E. A., Jr., 214

Daily Californian, 16–18, 118, 129–30, 141, 143
Daily People's World, 88
Davis, Loyal, 11
Davis, Ronnie G., 76, 99, 102–3, 119
Deakin, Lydia, 240
Deane, Dorothy, 195
DeBonis, John, 60, 94, 105, 155, 164
DeCanio, Steve, 73, 205
Degnan, Ronan E., 199
Delacour, Michael, 99, 155–57, 159, 166
Dellinger, David, 92

Dellums, C. L., 48
Dellums, Ronald V., 48, 75, 81–82, 111–13, 122–23, 155, 165–66
democrats, 33–34, 58, 78, 100–104; clubs, 51–52, 101–2, 111
demonstrations. *See* protests
Denson, Ed, 136, 239, 242–43
Denton, Charles, 208
*Despite Everything*, 126
Diebenkorn, Richard, 124
Diggers, 144
discrimination, 48–49, 52; housing, 54–61; education, 61–70; employment, 70–74
Dobbs, Harold, 72
Dobrzensky, Jean, 229
dogs, 143, 152, 166
Donahue, Tom, 140
Doors, The, 136
Douglas, Emory, 217
Dow Chemical Co., 114
Downs Memorial Methodist Church, 52
draft, 103, 114–21; Carmichael, 75; cards burned, 92, 115
Draper, Harold, 197, 218
dress: Black Panthers, 78–79; communists, 101; Rubin, 103; beats, 133; hippies, 133–34; Hare Krishnas, 153
Druding, Susan, 129, 131
drugs. *See* banana hoax; Lysergic Acid Diethylamide (LSD); marijuana; peyote
DuBois clubs, 45, 88, 99, 105
Duke, Michael, 43
Dulles, John Foster, 9
Duncan, Chet, 73, 215
Duncan, Donald, 113
Dutton, Evelyn L., 220
Dylan, Bob, 31, 127, 130, 138, 188

East Bay Municipal Utility District, 144
Eckels, Rick, 164
Eclair bakery, 129
ecology, 156, 165
education: discrimination, 18, 61–70; reform, 45–46, 53; statistics, 61–62, 173
Eichmann, Adolph, 22
Eisnehower, Dwight David, 9, 46
Elberg, Sanford, 29
El Cerrito, Calif., 55
elections (1959), 52–53; (1961) 53–54; (1963) 57–58; (1964 recall) 66–67; (1965) 75; (1966) 100–104; (1967) 110–12; (1968) 121; (1969) 154–55; statistics, 18, 83, 103–4, 121, 166, 176–80
Elks Club, 51
Ellington, A. L., 197
Elson, Henry M., 206
Emeryville, Calif., 93
employment, 71, 74; race, 61, 63, 70–74, 77; statistics, 70–71, 73–74, 147, 175, 181
Engle, Clair, 212

entertainers: S.F. Mime Troupe, 76, 92, 123, 165; Gregory, 92; The Committee, 92, 128; Steppenwolf, 94; Telegraph, 122–23; Bruce, 128
Erickson, Richard E., 203, 228
Erlich, Reese, 117–19, 234–35

faculty. *See* University of California, Berkeley, faculty
Faculty Peace Committee, 95
Fair Employment Practices Commission, 70
Fair Play for Cuba Committee, 90
Fairmont Hotel, 113–14
Family Dog, 138
Fanon, Frantz, 77
Federal Bureau of Investigation (FBI), 26, 88, 105, 113, 141
Fein, Lester, 115
Ferlinghetti, Lawrence, 125–26, 132
Feuer, Lewis, 197–99, 248
Fields, W. C., 80
films, 32, 99–100, 127, 132, 140, 162; titles, 16, 92, 154, 160, 196, 239
Filthy Speech Movement, 38–41, 130
Findley, Tim, 164
Finkelstein, Jacob J., 228
Finney, Henry C., 234
Flynn, J., 237
folk music, 89, 92, 113, 121, 127, 130, 136, 142, 188. *See also* music
Folsom, Michael, 195, 208
food: pig symbolism, 80–81; "Chicken Scalapino," 92; foreign, 95, 127, 142; Telegraph, 129; street vendors, 142; coffeehouses, 14, 129, 142; free, 152, 157; gourmet, 166, 171
Football Festival, 95
Forbes, William E., 38, 204
Force, A. J., 211
Fording, Addison, 224
Forman, Paul, 200
Forum, The, 78, 129, 131, 147–48
Foster, Richard, 164–65
Fowler, Karen J., 252
Fox, Art, 222
France, 46–47, 121
Franklin, Benjamin, 102
fraternities, 6, 15–17, 21, 34, 63. *See also* sororities
Freber, Scott, 205
Free Speech Movement (FSM), 10, 17–18, 22–26, 28–29, 35–36, 39, 45–47, 72–73, 83–84, 87, 91, 106, 117, 130, 134, 138, 170, 188; songs, 28–29; sit-in, 30–34; statistics, 33–34, 182–83; trial, 41–44; Steering Committee, 23–25, 40, 43, 138; Executive Committee, 23, 28
Free Store, 152
Free Student Union, 45
Free University of Berkeley, 46, 123, 132–33, 135, 142

freedom, 104, 126, 142, 144
Freeman, Jo, 200
Freud, Sigmund, 10, 128, 130, 142
Friedman, Donald M., 248
Frith, Simon, 242
Fry, Amelia, 211
Fuchs, Sandor, 21, 23, 200
Fulbright, J. William, 101
Fulton, David C., 200, 207–8, 214, 228
Fuss, Michael S., 230

Garbarino, Joseph, 195
Garcia, Jerry, 138
Gardner, Elizabeth, 21
Garfield Junior High School, 65–66
Garry, Charles, 42, 82, 119
Garson, Barbara, 24, 90, 113–14, 206
Garson, Marvin, 45, 89, 105, 155, 222, 229, 234, 242
Genasci, Sharon, 196
gender roles. See women
generations, 133–34, 136
Germany, 46–47
Gibson, D. G., 48, 51–52, 75
Gill, Paula B., 251
Ginsberg, Allen, 43–44, 97–98, 125–26, 137–38, 141
Gitlin, Todd, 244, 249
Glaser, Leonard, 129–30, 134
Glazer, Nathan, 196, 199
Gleason, Ralph J., 25, 138, 141, 193, 201, 203, 208, 239, 242, 248, 253
Glidden, David, 233
Glozer, Bill, 253
Glusman, Paul, 84–85, 156
Goetz, Bill, 196
Goines, David, 21, 24, 46, 147
Goldberg, Art (of FSM), 19, 21, 24, 30, 38–42, 130, 156
Goldberg, Art (the journalist), 199
Goldberg, Arthur (ambassador), 108
Goldberg, Barbara, 202
Goldberg, Jackie, 23–24, 30, 43
Goldberg, Suzanne, 24
Goldstein, Jerry, 206
Coldwater, Barry, 18, 34
Gontar, Jonathan, 142
Good Times, 155
Goodlett, Carleton, 101
Goodman, Paul, 126, 136
Gordon, Margaret S., 75, 111, 122, 211–14, 216, 218, 226, 231–32, 237, 245–46, 249–50
Gordon, Milton, 224
Gorilla Band, 123, 165
Graduate Coordinating Council (GCC), 35, 44
Graham, Bill, 138–39, 229
grape boycott, 84
Grateful Dead, 138, 141, 145

Greek Theatre: FSM, 35–36; Carmichael, 75; Charter Day (1966), 108; Vietnam Commencement, 120
Green, Otho, 75
Greene, Felix, 113
Gregory, Dick, 92
Grendon, Alexander, 106, 224, 228–29, 250–51
Griffin, Donald Q., 74, 76
Grillo, Evilio, 208
Grimes, Betty Jo., 215
Grodin, Joseph, 154
Guevara, Che, 80
Gullahorn, Barbara, 98
Gumbo, Judy, 80
Gurley, Lawrence T., 215

Hadsell, John S., 64–65, 230, 244
Hafner, Richard P., Jr., 224–25, 229
Haight-Ashbury, 141, 143–44
Haigwood, Bill C., 235
hair, 133–34, 143
Halberstam, David, 232
Hallinan, Conn ("Ringo"), 85
Hallinan, Vincent, 88
Halloran, J. P., 248
Halstead, Fred, 121
Hamilton, Steve, 44, 103, 108–9, 115, 117, 119
Han, Ki-Shik, 231
Hancock, Ilona, 111, 154–55, 159, 166, 224, 248, 252
Hanley, William C., 237, 246
Hann, Floyd R., 212
Hannon, Robert E., 234, 236
Harawitz, Howard, 111–12
Hare Krishnas, 97, 153, 161
Harris, Arthur, 53–54, 58
Harris, David, 115–16
Hart, James D., 238
Hart, Newell, 223
Hart, Ruth, 115
Hatch, Donald, 21
Hauerwas, Stanley, 247
Hausrath, Leslie A., 248
Haws, Edsel W., 206
Hayden, Sterling, 121
Hayden, Tom, 84, 89, 136, 156
Haydon, R. P., 248
Healey, Dorothy, 88
Hearst, Catherine, 11
Heick, Helen, 132–33
Heinlein, Robert, 126
helicopters: tear gas, 163–64
Heller, Lenny, 115
Hell's Angels, 97–98
Helms, Chet, 138
Helson, Henry, 220, 227
Hendrix, Jimi, 136
Henkin, Leon, 227–28, 236

Henry, Franklin M., 248
Herbert, T. Walter, Jr., 143, 198, 201, 244
Herman's Hermits, 124
Herr, Richard, 202
Hershey, Lewis B., 236
Hewitt, John, 230, 245
Hexter, Alfred C., 211
Heyman, Ira Michael, 26, 30, 198, 200–201
Heyns, Roger, 105–10; sit-ins, 84; draft, 116, 118, 120, 123; People's Park, 158–59, 165–66
Hickey, Tom, 204
Higgs, DeWitt A., 236–37
Hill, Lewis, 192
hills, 6, 51, 55, 57, 103
Hinckle, Warren, III, 114
Hink, Robert E., 214
Hink's, 71–72
hippies, 82, 123, 133–35, 140–48, 152–53, 156, 169–71, 189
Hiroshima, 169
Hirsch, Morris, 236
hispanic. See Chicanos
Hitch, Charles, 110, 165, 219, 228, 248
Hoffman, Abbie, 156
Hoffman, Alexander, 204
Hofmann, Hans, 10
Holocaust, 46, 169
Holy Hubert. See Lindsey, Hubert
Hook, Sidney, 203
Hoover, J. Edgar, 113
Hopkins, Donald R., 213, 216, 248
Hoppe, Art, 25
Horowitz, David, 126
Houlihan, John C., 96, 114
House Un-American Activities Committee (HUAC), 15, 88–90, 92, 94, 103, 136, 188
housing, 53–61; vote, 18; statistics, 55–56, 61; zoning, 60
"Howl," 125–26
Hughes, Genevieve, 214
Hull, R. E., 201
humor. See entertainers
Humphrey, Cliff, 155
Huntley, Fred, 112
Hurwitt, Robert, 198, 203
Hutchins, Mona, 24
Hutchins, Robert M., 121
Hutchison, Claude, 52–53
Hutton, Bobby, 83

immigrants, 34
in loco parentis, 44, 171
Independent Socialist Club. See Trotskyists
International Longshoremen's and Warehousemen's Union, 101

Jabberwock, 142
Jacobs, Jane, 250
Jacobsen, Tom, 115, 234

Jacobson, Norman, 203
Jacopetti, Ben, 132
Japan, 46–47
Japanese-American Citizens' League, 56
jazz, 133
Jefferson, Thomas, 100
Jefferson Airplane, 138–39, 141
Jennings, Dick, 195
Jensen, Lowell, 41
Jews, 15, 25, 32–34, 38–39, 58, 115, 126, 169, 221
jobs. See employment
John Birch Society, 112
Johnsen, R., 216
Johnson, Dean, 204–5, 207–8, 214, 224
Johnson, Lyndon, 83, 92, 100, 102–3, 113–14, 120
Johnson, Mary Jane, 216
Johnson, Oliver, 224
Johnson. R. L., 248
Johnson, Sue, 199
Johnson, Wallace, 57–58, 60, 111–12, 155, 165, 211–12, 224–25, 232, 246, 248, 251–52
Johnston, Ginger, 201
Jones, Frankie, 52–53
Jones, Hardin B., 106, 113, 120, 154, 195, 205, 221, 227–29, 231, 236–37, 242, 245, 249–50
Joplin, Janis, 136, 139, 167
Jordan, Fred, 202
Jordan, John, 197
Joy of Cooking, 139
Junior Chamber of Commerce, 52
junior high schools, 65–66, 69

Kael, Pauline, 127
Kahn, Ephraim, 226
Kaiser shipyards, 5
Kampf, Richard, 29, 129
Katz, Eli, 13–14, 27, 117
Katz, Paula, 204
Kaufman, Robert, 44, 195, 208
Keating, Edward M., 114, 227
Kennedy, John F., 8–9, 44, 46, 53, 99, 113, 168
Kennedy, Laurence J., Jr., 204
Kennedy, Robert, 101, 113–14, 120–21
Kent, Roger, 194, 213, 220, 224, 226
Kent, T. J., Jr., 12–13, 52–53, 192, 209–11, 225–26, 231
Kent State University, 169–70
Kerouac, Jack, 89, 125–26, 137
Kerr, Clark, 6, 8, 17, 38, 40, 44, 96, 105–6; described, 9–14; FSM, 19–20, 23–32, 35–37, 42–43; dismissed, 107, 109–10
Kerr, Kay, 7, 37
Kesey, Ken, 96, 98, 137–38
Kevin, 129
Khrushchev, Nikita, 9

Kidner, Frank, 200
Kierkegaard, Sören, 126
King, Martin Luther, Jr., 41, 66, 74–75, 82, 86, 116
Kingman, Harry, 209
Kirchner, Daniel, 196
Kirk, Russell, 241
Kirmmse, Judith K., 235
Kittel, Charles, 229
Kittredge, Gretchen, 24, 200, 214
Klein, Margaret, 207
Klein, Michael, 39
Knight, W. D., 251
Knowland, William F., 18, 72, 96, 106, 116, 154
Kogan, Michael, 204
Koshland, Daniel E., Jr., 230
KPFA radio, 6, 25, 88–89, 92, 113, 127, 142, 161–62
KQED television, 113, 138
Kragen, Adrian, 201, 203, 220
Krassner, Paul, 92, 128, 239
Krech, David, 224
Krech, Richard, 223
Kuhn, Thomas S., 200
Kupferberg, Tuli, 169, 242

labor unions, 28, 44–45, 49, 51, 58, 70–71, 77, 98
Laing, R. D., 142
Landauer, Carl, 95, 234
Landberg, Edward, 127
Landon, John, 201
Lang, Serge, 227, 229
Langer, Elinor, 204
language, 187–89
Lauer, David, 205, 240
Lawrence, Ernest O., 10–11, 13
Lawrence, Michael J., 201
Lawrence Radiation Laboratory, 10, 168
League of Women Voters, 51
Leary, Timothy, 137–38, 141
Lee, Gerald, 228
leftists, 14, 24–25, 90–91, 111. See also radicals
Leggett, John, 150, 199
Lehrer, Tom, 128
Lemmon, Jim, 229, 235, 250
Lennon, John, 161, 170
Lepawsky, Albert, 235, 250
Lerner, Michael P., 114, 199, 216, 244–45, 249
Levertov, Denise, 250
Levine, Eric, 196
liberals, 6, 8–9, 41, 44, 165, 170; race, 51–54, 56–57, 67, 73, 75, 86; leftists, 91, 94, 98–100, 111, 122
Liberated Women of Berkeley, 159
libertarians, 24, 39, 115, 126, 144, 156–57, 170

Lindsey, Hubert, 152–53
Link, Lauretta F., 240
Lipset, Seymour Martin, 198, 200, 205
literature, 124, 126, 140
Loading Zone, 147, 152
Local 1570. See American Federation of Teachers, Local 1570
London, Jack, 251
London, Oscar, 130
Longshoremen's Hall, 138
Lorbeer, Kathleen, 218
Los Angeles Times, 25
Louisell, David W., 224
Lowenthal, Leo, 10
Lowndes Co., Ala., 78
Lucas, Barbara, 247
Lucky's groceries, 18, 73, 78, 129–30
Ludden, R. R., 216
Ludwig the dog, 152
Lummis, Doug, 118
Lundberg, Richard W., 211
Lynd, Staughton, 233
Lysergic Acid Diethylamide (LSD), 135, 137–41, 143

"MacBird," 24, 113
McCarthy, Eugene, 120–21, 227
McCarthy, Joseph R., 16–17, 25
McClain, Erica, 81
McClaren, Thomas, 105
McClosky, Herbert, 203
McClure, Michael, 132
McCulloch, Ben, 251
Macdonald, Dwight, 126
MacDonald, Jeanette, 3
McDonald, Joe, 90, 97, 113, 136, 139–40, 142, 145, 152, 171
MacDougal, Philip, 126, 165, 226
McGill, William J., 165
McGivern, Tom, 234
machine symbol, 31
Macias, Ysidro, 85
Mackenzie, Angus, 244
MacKenzie, Scott, 144
McLaren, Thomas L., 154–55, 218, 228, 246, 248, 251–52
McLaughlin, Don, 195
McNamara, Mrs. Robert, 230
Mad, 128
MAD River, 152
Madigan, Frank, 154, 164, 217, 220, 224, 250
Madison, Marshall, 230
Mahler, Gustav, 142
Mailer, Norman, 92
Majors, O. Cort, 228
Malia, Martin, 234
Malloy, Kitty, 195, 197–98, 200–201, 203, 207
Malsbury, George, 235

Mandel, Bob, 119
Mandel, William, 88–89, 119, 220–21
mantras, 97, 138, 153
Mao Tse-tung, 80, 139
Maoists. *See* Progressive Labor (PL)
marches: VDC, 95–98; Memorial Day, 164–65
Marcus, Greil, 136
Marcus, Raymond, 198
Marcuse, Herbert, 142
marijuana, 32, 80, 108, 119, 123, 125, 129–30, 134–35, 138, 141, 143–44, 147–48, 189
Marin, Peter, 235, 242
Marsh, Vivian O., 208
Marston, Otis, 56
Martin, George T., 248
Martin, Jerry C., 249
Marx, Gary T., 216
Marx, Karl, 10, 100
Marx, Leo, 193, 208, 225, 231
Marxism, 76–77, 80, 123, 142
Matteson, Peter, 200
Mauchlan, Errol W., 201
May, Bernice Hubbard, 7, 51, 53–54, 58, 82, 89, 94, 111–12, 122, 155
May, Henry F., 47, 161, 168, 194, 201, 203, 207
May, Kenneth O., 89
May, Samuel, 89
May 2nd Movement, 119
Maybeck, Bernard, 5
Meade, Ken, 165
Meany, George, 98, 101
Meese, Edwin, III, 32, 41–43, 84, 158, 162, 166, 249
Meisenbach, Robert, 16
Mel's drive-ins, 72
Memorial Day, 164–65
Memorial Stadium, 8
Mendocino Co., 144
Merritt College, 76–78
Merry Pranksters, 96, 137
Mexican American Political Action, 101
Mexicans. *See* Chicanos
Meyer, Theodore R., 38, 204, 230, 234, 236, 245
Meyers, H., 194
Meyerson, Martin, 37–38, 40–41, 44, 91, 195
Michael, Jay, 235
*Michigan Daily*, 89
Michigan State University, 114
middle class, 126–27, 130–34, 144
Miles, Josephine, 47, 197, 207, 231, 238, 240, 248
militants. *See* activists
military training, compulsory, 13, 15
Miller, Abraham H., 249–50
Miller, Bill, 99, 109, 148, 155–56

Miller, Colin, 199, 203, 253
Miller, Dustin, 24, 200
Miller, John J., 75
Miller, Mike, 90
Miller, Stanley, 140
Miller, Steve, 139, 142
mill-ins, 118
Mills, C. Wright, 126, 227
minstrel shows, 76
Mississippi, 19–20, 22
Mitford, Jessica, 42
Mixer, Joseph R., 197
Moby Grape, 139
Moe's bookstore, 126, 129
Montgomery, Ed, 228
Montgomery Ward, 72
Moore, Raymond S., 241
Morgan, Julia, 5
Morris, Maynard, 242
Morrison, Jim, 136
Moscoso, Victor, 140
Moscowitz, Moe, 129
Moscowitz, Ron, 199, 203–5
Moses, Bob, 92
Moses Hall, 84
Mouse, 140
*Movement, The*, 119
movies. *See* films
Moyers, Bill, 103
Mulford, Don, 79, 96, 106, 116, 119, 148, 150, 154, 165, 196–97, 205–7, 215, 219–20, 224–25, 230, 232, 236–38, 244, 246, 251–52
Muller, R. S., 234
multiversity, 9–10
Murphy, Franklin, 235
Murphy, George, 59, 96
Murphy, George S., 200–201
Murra, Laura Shaw, 133
music, 28–29, 75–76, 92, 120–21, 123, 133. *See also* folk music; rock music; songs
Myerson, Alan, 128
Myerson, Mike, 128

Nabors, Jim, 85
Nagler, Michael, 199
Nakamura, 150
National Association for the Advancement of Colored People (NAACP), 52–53, 63, 75
National Guard, 85, 96, 154, 162–63
National Student Association, 114
Native Americans. *See* American Indians
navy table protest, 109, 119
Neely, Betty, 229
Negroes. *See* blacks
Neighborhood Youth Corps, 74–75, 150
Neilands, J. B., 73, 111–12, 116–17
Nelken, Michael, 194
Neville, Anthony E., 199
New Left. *See* radicals

*New York Times*, 25
Newhall, Scott, 117
newspapers: statistics, 113, 175
Newton, E. Anne, 211
Newton, Huey P., 77–81, 83
Neylan, John F., 11
Nichols, Roy F., 52–53, 58, 63, 66, 86, 208–9
Nicole's boutique, 128
Nixon, Richard, 121, 167
Nobel laureates, 10
Noble, David, 206
North Beach, 124–25, 128, 132, 136, 143
North Oakland, 76, 78

Oakland, 70, 72–73, 114, 169–70; blacks, 48, 77, 79, 81, 83; Army Base, 93, 95; VDC, 95–98; Induction Center protests, 116–19
"Oakland Seven," 119
*Oakland Tribune*, 18, 37, 72, 117
oath controversy, 11, 13, 88
Oberhaus, Patricia, 149
obscenity, 38–41, 84, 92, 130, 132
Oceanview, 4–5, 60–61
Ochs, Phil, 121, 127
Odegard, Mary S., 251
Office of Equal Opportunities, 74
Ogden, Glenn B., 199
Oglesby, Carl, 90, 125, 249
O'Hargan, Tom, 240
O'Neale, L. J., 234
Ono, Yoko, 161
Open Theater, 132
Oppenheimer, J. Robert, 88
Orme, Frank, 224
Oswald, Vice President, 197
Owen, Akiko, 200, 203
Owsley. *See* Stanley, Augustus Owsley, III

Pacific Gas and Electric, 73
Pacific Union Club, 11
pacifists, 92, 116
Paik, Dan, 29, 240
Parents Association for Neighborhood Schools (PANS), 66–67
Paris, Oscar, 248
Parkinson, Thomas, 43–44, 117–18, 205
participatory democracy, 90
Pastor, Marion, 229
Pauley, Edwin A., 11, 204, 221, 228, 231
Payne, Bruce, 193, 214
Peace and Freedom, 83, 110
Peace Corps, 8
Peace/Rights Organizing Committee (PROC), 107–8, 119
Pennebaker, D. A., 239
People's Park: conceived, 155–56; developed, 157–59; riots, 159–64; occupied, 162–65; aftermath, 165–66
*People's World*, 88–90, 100

Pepe's, 147
Peralta, José Domingo, 4
Perlman, Melvin L., 229
Perry Lane, 137
Persian Fuckers, 148
Pesonen, David, 203
Peter, Paul, and Mary, 127
Peters, Prof., 248
Petersen, William, 93, 220
Peterson, Mrs. Peter J., 221
Petras, James, 223
peyote, 135
pharmacy, 48–49
Phillips, John D., 71, 211
philosophy: hippies, 134, 144; Provos, 152; relativism, 153–54; users' rights, 157
physics. *See* science
Pickerell, Albert G., 228
Pierce, Ransom A., 236
"pigs," 80–81, 147, 152
Pike, James, 17
Pimsleur, Joel, 202, 210
Pitzer, Kenneth S., 195
Placone, Richard C., 220
Platt, James, 226
plays: "MacBird," 113; "The Beard," 132
poetry, 124–26, 153
Poland, Jefferson, 131–32
police, 16, 114, 122–23, 153, 158; Panthers, 78–81, 83; Oakland, 82–83, 97, 117–18; TWLF, 85; VDC, 93, 97, 105; hippies, 145–48; People's Park, 160–62. *See also* arrests; surveillance
police car: sit-down, 21, 23, 130
politics: ideology, ix; on campus, 14, 23, 27, 37; statistics, 34; and science, 104; clubs, 101–2, 111; generations, 115
Poole, Cecil, 96, 115
Poppic, Henry, 56
population, 5; statistics, 50, 146, 173
Port Chicago protests, 145
Port Huron Statement, 90
posters, 140, 144
Powell, Charles, 131
Presley, Elvis, 130
Preston, Lee E., 231
Price, Borden, 154–55
*Program Folio*, 142
Progressive Labor (PL), 108–9, 119, 156
Proposition 14, 59–60
prostitution, 132
Protestants, 25, 33–34, 39, 52, 58
protests: Chessman, 15; HUAC, 16; civil rights, 71–73; troop trains, 93–94; Cohelan's office, 98; Telegraph, 105; navy table, 109; Robert Kennedy, 113–14; Oakland Induction Center, 116–19; June 1968, 121–23; Port Chicago, 145; People's Park, 159–64
Provos, 152

psychology, 44, 137, 142
Pullman Co. porters, 48, 74
Pursel, Kent, 200, 229
Pyes, Craig, 244

Quakers, 116, 165
Quicksilver Messenger Service, 139

race relations, 18, 52, 64, 68–69, 74–76, 84–
    86, 168, 173
Rader, Dotson, 118
radicals, 25, 43, 61, 90–91, 94, 106–7, 109–
    14, 138, 141, 148, 187–88; strategy, 30–31,
    105, 107, 112–13, 164; Black Panthers, 76,
    80–82, 84–85; VDC, 92, 98–99; Scheer,
    100–104; draft, 114–21; June 1968, 121–
    23; People's Park, 156, 165–66, 170
radio: licenses, 17, 97; rock, 75, 140–41. See
    also KPFA radio
Radner, Roy, 251
Raleigh, John, 251
rallies: FSM, 28–29, 31; filthy speech, 38–39;
    Carmichael, 75; Cleaver, 84; Save-the-
    Steps, 108–9; draft, 116–18; Vietnam Com-
    mencement, 120–21; banana hoax, 141;
    People's Park, 160, 163
Ramparts, 80, 82–83, 114, 133, 140–41, 164
Ramsey, Marjorie, 65
Randolph, A. Philip, 48
Raymond, Boris, 223, 241
Razavi, Haj, 148
Reagan, Ronald, 11, 43, 84, 108–11, 120,
    131, 234, 248, 251; Kerr, 110; People's
    Park, 156, 158, 162, 164–66, 169
real estate interests, 5, 55–56, 59–60, 92
Realist, The, 92, 128
Rector, James, 162, 166
Red Mountain Tribe, 147–48
Redwing, 139
Reed, David W., 195, 203
Reinecke, Ed, 165
religion, 58, 115, 135–36, 143, 153–54, 165;
    FSM, 31, 33–34; statistics, 34; Zen, 92,
    125–26, 153; Berkeley Free Church, 152;
    Hare Krishnas, 153
republicans, 18, 34, 58, 72, 97, 112
Reserve Officers' Training Corps (ROTC), 13
Resistance, The, 115–16, 132, 152
Reston, James, 216, 230
Reuther, Roy, 211
Rexroth, Kenneth, 125
Reynolds, John H., 195, 203
Reynolds, Malvina, 29, 89, 127
Richheimer, Robert, 207
Richmond, Al, 88
Richmond, Calif., 5, 49, 55, 72
rightists, 43, 96, 106, 115
Ritter, Evelyn L., 215
Ritter, Jesse P., Jr., 251

River, Robert B., 220
Robeson, Paul, 89
"Robin Hood's Park Commissioner," 156
Robinson, Gilbert H., 199
rock music, 123, 130, 133, 135–37, 140–41;
    LSD, 137–41; concerts, 138–40, 145, 152.
    See also music
Rockefeller, Nelson, 121
Rodger, James H., 216
Rodgers, Jonathan, 208
Rogers, Edward S., 203
Rolling Stone, 141
Root and Branch, 99
Rosenhaupt, Hans, 231
Rosenthal, Dan, 115
Rosenzweig, Richard, 198
Ross, Arthur M., 37, 203, 205
Ross, Jewell, 248
Rossman, Michael, 24, 45–47, 105, 126,
    137–38, 143, 147, 163, 169, 208, 253
Roth, Randolph A., 192
Roudebush, Richard, 104
Rowe, John H., 203
Roysher, Martin, 24, 91, 201, 236
Rubenzahl, Joel, 237, 251
Rubin, Jerry, 80, 89–91, 100, 103, 109, 111–
    14, 119, 130, 135, 141, 143–44, 153, 222;
    VDC, 91, 93–99
Rumford, William Byron, 48–49, 51–52, 58,
    70, 75, 79, 210–11
Rumford Act, 58–60
Ruth, Minnie, 209
Ryder, Worth, 124

Saenger, Eugene, 234–35
Sahl, Mort, 128
Saint Augustine Episcopal Church, 82
Sampson, Edward, 117, 218, 234
Sanazaro, Paul, 64
Sandall, Roger, 197
San Francisco, 72–73, 80, 105, 113–14;
    HUAC, 16; hippies, 138–39, 141, 143–44.
    See also North Beach
San Francisco Bay, 6–7
San Francisco Chronicle, 25, 101, 117, 138,
    141, 161, 164
San Francisco Examiner, 16
San Francisco Express Times, 119, 155
San Francisco Mime Troupe, 76, 92, 99, 103,
    113, 123, 138–39, 165
San Francisco State College, 37, 85
San Francisco Tactical Squad, 160–61
Sanger, Margaret, 132
San Quentin Prison, 15
Santa Rita, 33, 164
Santana, 140
Sartre, Jean Paul, 126
Sather Gate, 14
Sather Gate Book Shop, 128

Savio, Mario, 40–41, 83, 89, 108–9; described, 21–23; FSM, 19, 21–26, 29–31, 36, 43–44, 46
Scalapino, Robert A., 36, 92
Scheer, Anne Weills, 89, 101, 133
Scheer, Robert, 78, 83, 90, 108, 114, 121, 126, 133, 164–65, 188; VDC, 92, 96–98, 105; campaign, 99–104
Scherr, Max, 89, 94, 96, 132
Schiffner, Gregg G., 248
Schlessinger, Wendy, 156
Schmorleitz, Richard, 205
schools. See education
Schorske, Carl, 142, 201
Schultz, Marston, 200
Schurmann, Franz, 108, 121
science, 8, 104; nuclear, 10, 13, 46
science fiction, 126
scientology, 143
Scriven, Michael, 235
Seaborg, Glenn, 13
Seabury, Paul, 198
Seale, Bobby, 6, 76–80, 82–83, 157
Searcy, Alan W., 200–201, 203
Searle, John, 106–7
Seeger, Pete, 89
Segal, Jeff, 119
Selective Service System. See draft
Sellers, Charles, 120, 226, 234, 236, 247
Sentovich, Mrs. J., 208
sex, 22–23, 32, 46, 125, 130–33, 142–43; statistics, 131
Sexual Freedom League, 77, 132
Shaffer, Ralph E., 194
Shelley, John F., 241
Shepard, William F., 201
Sheraton-Palace Hotel, 18, 73
Shere, Charles, 142
Sherriffs, Alex C., 18–20, 32, 158, 196
shop-ins, 73, 129–30
Shride, S. L., 220
Shute, Mike, 207
Sibley, Carol, 64, 66–67, 212–14
Sicheneder, Jim, 229
Siegel, Dan, 121, 160, 165
Silver, Samuel, 201
Simon, Daniel, 98
Simon, John, 249
sit-downs: police car, 21, 23, 30; VDC march, 97
sit-ins: Sheraton-Palace, 18, 73; FSM, 30–34; Moses Hall, 84; Cohelan's office, 98; navy table, 109
SLATE, 15–16, 88, 90, 128, 188
Slick, Grace, 139
Sly and the Family Stone, 140
Smale, Stephen, 90–91, 94, 97, 103–5, 222
Smelser, Neil, 205–6, 222–23
Smith, Charles E., 203
Smith, Donald P., 252

Smith, Henry Nash, 193–95, 201–2, 208, 225, 231, 237, 250–51
Smith, Michael, 105, 108–9, 117, 119
Smith, Ralph, 235
Snyder, Gary, 125–26, 141, 153
social class, 39, 58–59, 64
Socialist Workers party. See Trotskyists
songs, 32, 43–44; titles, 3, 29, 32, 76, 84, 90, 93, 97, 121, 123–24, 127, 136, 139–40, 142, 144, 167, 201, 242. See also music
Sopwith Camel, 139
Sorenson, Thomas, 227
sororities, 6, 21, 63, 73, 165; statistics, 17. See also fraternities
Soul on Ice, 80
Soul Students Advisory Council (SSAC), 77–78
South Campus, 34, 61, 94; urban renewal, 145–54; People's Park, 155–64
Southern Christian Leadership Conference (SCLC), 74–75
Southwest Berkeley, 48, 58, 60–61
Sparrow, John, 250
SPAZM, 133
Spenger's, 6
SPIDER, 40
Spieth, Herman T., 196
Spock, Benjamin, 92, 121
sports, 84, 119
Sproul, Robert Gordon, 6, 10–12, 14, 32
Sproul Hall, 14, 21, 28; sit-ins, 30–34, 84
Sproul Plaza, 14, 28; rallies, 75, 84–85, 108–9, 115–17, 120–21, 141, 160
Staats, Redmond C., Jr., 63, 209
Stampp, Kenneth M., 234
Stanford University, 115, 137
Staniford, Edward, 192
Stanley, Augustus Owsley, III, 138–39
Stapleton, Sydney, 24, 98
Stapleton, Mrs. Sydney, 21
Starobin, Robert, 203, 208
statistics, 121, 131, 148–49, UCB, 6, 12, 17, 33–34, 84; elections, 18, 83, 103–4, 166; population, 50, 146; housing, 55–56, 61; education, 61–62; employment, 70–71, 73–74, 147; tables, 173–85
Steffens, Pete, 248
Steiner, Peter S., 234
Steppenwolf bistro, 94, 152
Sterling, (?) D., 251
Stern, Sol, 216, 232–33, 243, 252
Stevenson, Adlai, 8, 14, 51
Stewart, Sylvester, 140
Stiles Hall, 14
Still, Clyfford, 124
Stock, Robert, 211
Stone, Brinton H., 116, 230
Stone, I. F., 92
Stop the Draft Week, 116–19
Store, The, 148

Stoutenberg, Adrien, 248
Strawberry Creek, 14
street people, 129–30. *See also* hippies
street theater, 123
strikes. *See* UCB-students
Stripp, Fred, 57, 117, 210
Strohman, Richard, 236
Strong, Edward W., 13, 19–20, 26, 30, 33, 35, 37, 42
Student Non-Violent Coordinating Committee (SNCC), 24, 72, 74–76, 92, 119, 187
Student Union, 14, 74, 116, 163
students. *See* UCB-students
Students for a Democratic Society (SDS), 75, 88, 90–91, 113, 115–16, 118–19, 188
Sullivan, Neil V., 66–69
*Sun-Reporter*, 101
surveillance, 28, 31, 93, 106, 113–14, 141, 165, 206
Sweeney, Dennis, 115
Sweeney, Wilmont, 53–54, 58, 75, 82, 122, 154–55, 209
Sweetwyne, Al, 209
Swingle, John, 154–55

Tabler, Ward, 199
Tanabe, Tami, 214
Tanner, Tony, 237, 251
taxes: statistics, 174
teachers: HUAC, 16, 88
teach-ins, 91–92, 95, 116
teaching assistants (TAs), 29, 35, 44–45, 85, 109
tear gas, 160, 162–64; first, 122
Telegraph Avenue, 7, 14–15, 19, 77–78, 94, 126–30, 145–47, 149–50, 152–53; protests, 9, 73, 95–98, 105, 121–23, 147, 162
television, 25, 93; KQED, 113, 138
Tempey, Damon F., 229
Thayer, Paul S., 251
Theta Xi, 17
Third World, 77, 86, 90, 115
Third World Liberation Front (TWLF), 85, 154
Thomas, Lois K., 229
Thomas, Norman, 92
Thompson, Hunter S., 205
Thompson, John, 140
Thomson, John, 38
Thoreau, Henry David, 31
Thorn, Michael, 230, 245
Thorne, Richard, 77, 131–32
Tilden Park, 6
*Time*, 121
*Toscin*, 188
Toll, Robert, 235
Toothman, Edward, 224
Tower of Power, 139
Towle, Katherine A., 19, 25
Trachtenberg, Marc, 251

transcendental meditation, 143
Tregea, Forrest E., 201, 214
Treuhaft, Robert, 42
trials: Meisenbach, 16; FSM sit-in, 41–44; obscenity, 41; Newton, 81–82; conspiracy, 84, 119; navy table, 109; Glaser, 130; Siegel, 165
Trips Festivals, 138–39, 141
Trombley, William, 194
troop-train protests, 93–94
Trotsky, Leon, 89
Trotskyists, 89–90, 98–99, 111, 119, 187–88; Independent Socialist Club, 98, 116; Socialist Workers party, 89–90, 112, 121; Young Socialist Alliance, 24, 90, 92, 98, 118, 121
Trow, Martin, 208
Turner, Brian, 21, 24, 30, 99, 131, 233, 242
Turner, Marie, 244
Tussman, Joseph, 45
Tyler, Ralph, 106

unions. *See* labor unions
U.S. Senate, 88
U.S. State Dept., 92, 99–100
University of California-Master Plan, 12
UC-Regents, 8, 10–11, 15, 17, 40, 84, 106, 109–10; FSM, 19, 26, 30, 37–38; war, 96, 118, 120; People's Park, 158–59, 165–66
University of California, Berkeley, 10–12, 22, 34, 37–38, 52, 74, 88, 95, 106, 168–69; early, 4; faculty, 10, 12, 27–29, 31, 35–37, 104, 126; oath, 11, 13, 88; bureaucracy, 11, 15, 18, 20, 23, 28–29, 42–43, 108; rules, 18–19, 27, 107–8; race, 56, 83–85; People's Park, 150–52, 154–56, 158–59, 161
UCB-Academic Senate, 118
UCB-Board of Educational Development, 83–84
UCB-Experimental College, 45
UCB-students, 6, 34, 44, 73, 75, 129, 131, 139, 149; disciplined, 21, 23, 26–27, 30, 39, 41, 84, 107, 118; strikes, 31, 35, 44, 85, 109–10; values, 44, 46–47, 89, 102, 107, 110, 165–68; statistics, 6, 131, 181–85; dress, 133–34
University of California, Santa Barbara, 17
University of Michigan, 91
Unruh, Jesse, 58, 211, 219
Up-Right, Inc., 111
Urban League, 75
urban renewal, 60–61, 149–50

Van der Ryn, Sim, 159
Van Loucks deposition, 204
Vietnam Commencement, 120–21
Vietnam Day Committee (VDC), 99, 105, 108–9, 132, 138, 189; teach-in, 91–92; troop trains, 93–94; Oakland march, 95–98; bombed, 105

Vietnam War, 25–26, 44, 73, 75, 91, 108, 113–14, 123, 188–89; support, 92–93, 95, 98; Scheer, 99–102; draft, 114–21; statistics, 121; Cambodia, 167–70
Von Hoffman, Nicholas, 238, 245

Wachter, Douglas, 16
Wakoski, Diane, 126
Wald, Karen Lieberman, 109
Wallace, Henry, 188
Walls, David, 193
Ward, John William, 208
Warren, Earl, 10, 11
waterbeds, 142
Waters, Alice, 166
Watts, Alan, 92, 126, 132
Watts riot (Los Angeles), 60, 96, 102
"We Shall Overcome," 32, 93, 136
Weasel, 77–78
Weaver, Leone, 223
Weber, David O., 252
Weinberg, Jack, 21, 23–24, 27, 31, 45, 72, 80, 97–98
Weinzeimer, Bob, 142
Weissman, Stephan, 24, 30–31, 97–99, 201
Weller, Tom, 140
Wellman, Harry R., 220, 227
Wells, John, 120
Welsh, David, 233
Wenner, Jann, 141, 167
Wennerberg, C. H., 64, 66
Wenz, Inez, 227
Wessels, Glen, 124
West Berkeley, 60–61, 75
West Oakland, 95, 101
Westberg, V. L., 220
Whaley, Baird, 213
Wheeler Auditorium fire, 85
Whelan's Cigar Store, 128
Whinnery, John R., 205
White, Geoffrey, 193, 201, 222
Whitney, James C., 197
Widener, Warren, 154–55

Widess, James B., 110
Wildavsky, Aaron, 92
Willard Junior High School, 65, 69
Williams, Arleigh, 197–201, 205, 214, 236, 250
Williams, Robley C., 235
Williams, Helga, 245
Williamson, Paul H., 155
Wilson, J. Stitt, 5
Wilson, Jack, 238
Wilson, S. Clay, 142
Wilson, Wes, 140
Windmiller, Marshall, 202
Winters, Yvor, 153
Wohlforth, Tim, 193
women, 24, 109, 132–33, 139–40, 159
Women for Peace, 24, 132, 155
Women's City Club, 51
Wondsell, Wendy-Jo, 208
Woolman, Marjorie, 230, 248
Workreation, 74
World War II, 5, 10, 49, 61, 70
Wright, Celeste T., 248
Wurster, Catherine B., 195, 210–12, 214

X, Laura, 133
X, Malcolm, 8, 16, 74–75, 80, 86, 187

Ylvisaker, Paul, 195, 210
YMCA, 14
York, Richard L., 152, 159
Young Democrats, 28
Young Republicans, 24, 33
Young Socialist Alliance. See Trotskyists, Young Socialist Alliance
youths, 38, 46–47, 74, 115; black, 63, 76, 78–79; sex, 130–33; runaways, 147–48, 152; statistics, 148
YWCA, 52, 76, 127

Zeitlin, Maurice, 99
Zen, 92, 125–26, 153
Zvegintzov, Nicholas, 203, 205